A Reference for Technical Writers at All Levels

Technical Writing

DIANE MARTINEZ

TANYA PETERSON

CARRIE WELLS

CARRIE HANNIGAN

CAROLYN STEVENSON

KAPLAN

PUBLISHING

New York

© 2008 by Diane Martinez, Carrie Wells, Carrie Hannigan, Tanya Peterson, and Carolyn Stevenson

Published by Kaplan Publishing, a division of Kaplan, Inc.
1 Liberty Plaza, 24th Floor
New York, NY 10006

Printed in the United States of America

August 2008
10   9   8   7   6   5   4   3   2

ISBN-13: 978-1-4277-9721-6

Kaplan Publishing books are available at special quantity discounts to use for sales promotions, employee premiums, or educational purposes. Please email our Special Sales Department to order or for more information at *kaplanpublishing@kaplan.com,* or write to Kaplan Publishing, 1 Liberty Plaza, 24th Floor, New York, NY 10006.

TABLE OF CONTENTS

PREFACE

Technical Writing was written for students, practicing technical writers, and instructors. The unique, two-part feature of this book serves several purposes and meets the needs of readers across the spectrum, from students or beginning writers learning about technical communication for the first time to experienced technical writers working on the job, as well as instructors in secondary and post-secondary environments.

Beginning Students and Writers

Part I was developed especially for the novice technical writer. One thing we, as technical communication instructors, noticed when choosing textbooks for introductory technical communication courses was that the content in many textbooks was usually more advanced than what students in such a course could readily learn about, practice in class, and apply to their writing assignments. So, with that in mind, whether you are a student new to technical communication or a beginning writer, part I covers basic definitions, foundational concepts about how to apply the writing process to technical writing assignments, shorter forms of writing that technical communicators encounter, general research practices and research information geared for academic environments, and essential concepts about page design, document revision, and delivering oral presentations.

While part I was written with the depth and breadth of content that we considered manageable for one semester or term of an introductory technical writing course, that does not mean that instructors will not ask you to read sections in part II. There are writing assignments in some introductory courses, as well as some that beginning writers may encounter, that require in-depth knowledge of one or more of the topics contained in part II, such as writing a feasibility or progress report. There are so many topics in technical communication that take a great deal of space to fully explain. When students who are new to this type of writing are inundated with chapter upon chapter of detailed information, the chances of them having the time in class to practice and then effectively apply what they learn is lessened. The idea behind the two-part feature of this book was to provide you with enough information in part I to give you a solid understanding of what technical communication is and effective uses for it, as well as present working definitions of those topics covered extensively in part II. You also may find the appendixes on grammar and citation helpful.

Advanced Students and Practicing Technical Writers

Part II was written with more experienced writers in mind. But just as we tell students who are new to technical communication that they may use some sections of part II, advanced students and practicing technical writers also may need to refresh their memories or understanding about the basics of certain topics that are covered in part I. One of the benefits of this book is that you only need this one book, not several that are written specifically for beginning students, advanced students, or for those working as technical writers. This book offers comprehensive information on learning about and practicing technical communication. It is the unique organization of the book that makes it user-friendly for such a wide audience.

Part II is written so that information is conveyed as it might be experienced in the workplace. Collaboration, or teamwork, is usually introduced in beginning technical communication courses, but it is demanded in most professional settings, which is why chapter 9 was placed in part II. Longer forms of technical communication, such as technical reports, user guides, and instructions, require in-depth explanation regarding audience analysis, content, format, and design, and entire courses or workplace projects may be dedicated to only one of these documents because there is so much to consider and work through. As noted in part I, technical communicators will encounter forms of writing commonly deemed as business or professional writing on the job, so some of those forms that are often delegated to technical writers, such as policy and procedure manuals, are covered in this section as well. Entire courses, conferences, and workshops are dedicated to proposal and grant writing, and so we, too, gave that subject a chapter all its own.

Other complex forms of writing that working technical communicators will encounter are training courses and materials, as well as writing and designing digital information, both also covered in this part of the book. Research, in part II, moves from the classroom or academic setting to the office, and covers topics such as copyright and conducting interviews with subject matter experts. Page and document design are taken to a whole new level with a chapter that covers complex information about text and visual representation.

The review process in the workplace is quite different from the peer reviews conducted in most classrooms, so this was reserved for part II as well. Other advanced knowledge necessary in the field of technical communication pertains to testing and usability issues. An emphasis on business presentations is covered extensively in part II as well. Another unique feature of this book is that we cover technical communication as it is experienced in other professions—the genres and unique characteristics of technical writing in medical, science, legal, business, and information technology fields. Additionally, we provide a chapter on how to prepare for jobs in technical communication, as well as a separate chapter on professional development in the field. Appendix A covers grammar basics, because this is always a great desk resource to have, and Appendix B covers citation information for the three main style guides: American Psychological Association (APA), Chicago Manual of Style, and Modern Language Association (MLA). Integrated in each chapter is information and discussion about ethical considerations and issues related to global audiences, including technological advances in the field.

Instructors and Directors of Technical Communication Programs

This book is a money-saving resource for students and instructors. In fact, this lone book can be used for an entire technical communication program that offers an introductory course in addition to the usual advanced classes on proposal and grant writing, writing and designing technical instructions and user guides, and writing for electronic environments, as well as page and document design. As mentioned previously, the two-part feature of this book contains fundamental and advanced material so that students have all that they need in one place. This is also a great feature for instructors because the information is common across many courses, and yet there are enough chapters that accommodate many different courses.

Note to Reader: Based on the standards defined by the communications industry, technical communication and technical writing are not necessarily interchangeable, as you will see throughout this book.

ACKNOWLEDGMENTS

Writing this book has been an exciting personal and professional endeavor for each of us. We would like to thank Dianne Fowler and Sara Sander for their encouragement and support when we were first putting this project together. It was inspiring to hear their confidence in our ability to put out a worthwhile book on this subject.

We also would like to thank our students who constantly inspire and motivate us to look at how we can best present material to them in an equally inspiring and motivating fashion.

Thank you also to our editors at Kaplan Publishing for their support and assistance through every step in the process of putting this book together.

We also would like to extend our thanks individually.

Diane Martinez thanks Megan Hendrix, you are a constant source of inspiration to me; Carol Brown for your belief in me; and Martin Martinez for your patience and understanding.

Tanya Peterson thanks her husband for his constant encouragement and support. She would also like to thank her family for always believing in her. Finally, she would like to thank Diane Martinez for making this idea a reality. You are an amazing woman and a constant inspiration to me. Thank you all!

Carrie Wells thanks her co-authors for an amazing experience, her family for teaching her to appreciate her education and look closely at all opportunities, and her good friends Michael O'Connor and Sally-Anne Moringello for nurturing her love of writing and editing and for unfaltering encouragement on this project. She would especially like to thank and apologize to her children, Alex, Dan, and Zac Hollibaugh for some heightened stress levels, postponed plans, and crazy nights. Lastly, she is grateful to her students who strive to learn and teach her every day, and one in particular, Lavynder Davis, for her misplaced admiration and encouragement.

Carrie Hannigan thanks her family, especially her parents, for their unconditional support and understanding, Mary Rosenquist for her heartfelt encouragement, and Andrew Thew for continually motivating me to just sit down and write what I know.

Carolyn Stevenson thanks Valerie Janesick for her continued guidance and mentoring as well as Kayla Stevenson for her continued patience.

PART I

INTRODUCTION TO TECHNICAL COMMUNICATION

CHAPTER 1

Defining Technical Communication

Technical communication is a distinct, focused form of written or verbal interaction. Technical writing, a common form of technical communication, is highly specialized and requires a specific level of expertise. Good technical communication is accurate, clear, and concise. In many situations, failure to meet these criteria could result in serious, life-altering consequences. Equally important is the technical communicator's understanding of audience, purpose, and context, which will be discussed in greater detail in chapter 2.

WHAT IS TECHNICAL COMMUNICATION?

Technical communication is written or verbal interaction designed to convey information of a complex nature to a specific audience. Although technical writing is one of the most common methods of technical communication, presentations and interviews also fall under the umbrella of technical communication. Technical writing, as its name implies, is informative writing, which involves technical, scientific, and engineering-based topics. Technical communicators write and edit user manuals, research and write grants and proposals, deliver presentations, and create a host of other intricate documents. Technical communicators are employed in a variety of professions including all of the sciences, medicine, and web-based fields.

Technical writing is, by definition, distinct from business writing or pro-fessional writing. However, the reality is that technical communicators often are asked to compose documents that are more closely aligned with those found in business or professional writing. There is a great deal of overlap between these three areas of communication. While this book will define each area individually, it is important to note that a good technical communicator will be prepared to understand each area thoroughly. For example, a technical communicator may be asked to compose a business letter or memo proposal, but these are not true "technical" documents. Because of such scenarios, this text also will cover the formats most commonly used in all three areas.

Business Writing

As previously stated, technical writing is writing that delivers highly spe-cialized industrial information. Business writing, on the other hand, deals with the type of writing and style of documents used by corporations, small businesses, and organizations. It is designed primarily with the goal of per-suasion in mind. A business writer is conveying information, but with the additional purpose of persuading the reader to agree with the author by the end of the document.

Consider the business proposal. It follows a very specific format and is designed to persuade the audience (usually another business or organization) to accept a bid to complete a work project. While technical and business writing do share some similarities, they are distinct forms of writing that require specific levels of expertise. Business writing also involves relation-ships: representative to client, supervisor to employee, employee to employee, or department to department. Technical writing is more universal in nature.

Professional Writing

Professional writing refers to written communication commonly utilized in the workplace, which includes documents such as résumés, cover letters, per-sonal statements, emails, and memos. Like business writing, much of profes-sional writing is designed to be persuasive. For example, a résumé and cover letter work together to convince the hiring manager that the candidate is right for the job. But professional writing also conveys essential information. An interoffice memo delivers a message to the selected recipients. Again, there is some overlap between technical, business, and professional writing, but they are still distinct styles of writing that should be treated differently.

EFFECTIVE TECHNICAL COMMUNICATION

To convey information effectively, technical communication must be accurate, clear, and concise. If the audience cannot understand or use the information presented, the writer has failed in his or her purpose.

Accuracy

Technical communication conveys information that is crucial to the success of real-world tasks. It has a very specific use to the reader. It results in decisions being made or machinery being constructed. Because of that, technical documents must be highly accurate. For example, think about a technical document as simple as instructions on how to assemble a free-standing shelving unit. If the directions failed to include a key step that affected the stability of the unit, it could fall over and injure someone. How much more serious would the consequences be if the instruction set belonged to a piece of large machinery or something as complicated as a space shuttle? Inaccurate technical documents can result in very real physical, financial, or environmental repercussions.

Consider the case of NASA's Genesis space mission that concluded with the space probe's return to Earth in 2004. The probe was designed with parachutes that would open and allow the probe to float softly down to Earth's surface. Unfortunately, the design documentation did not clearly specify which way the parachute sensors were to be installed; they were consequently attached upside down. As a result, the sensors did not properly convey the message, the parachutes did not open, and the probe crashed to Earth. All of the data it had collected could have been lost. Fortunately, most of the data was salvaged from the remains (Mishap Investigation Board 2006). Clearly, accuracy is a crucial component in technical communication.

Clarity

Equally important to technical communication is clarity. If a document such as an instruction set or a report does not contain clear information, the reader cannot comprehend the writer's intent or complete the necessary task. To continue with the example of the shelving unit, if the instruction set used vague terminology that confused the reader, the reader might end up connecting two pieces incorrectly. Once again, this could cause the unit to be unstable and inflict harm on someone should it fall over. Clear writing will prevent confusion and give the audience direction on completion of the task.

Conciseness

Finally, technical communication must be concise. Technical writing is characterized by direct language that gets right to the point. It avoids flowery descriptions that can obscure the meaning. Remember, technical writing is goal-oriented; its goal is to convey information. The reader should not have to sift through extraneous material to get the essential information needed. The various types of technical documents all have a specific format that allows the reader to quickly locate the information that is most important. All technical communication should include everything the reader or listener needs in an organized, no frills fashion. That does not mean that technical writing is ugly by any means. Its beauty is in its simplicity, in the clean and usable way that it conveys such sophisticated content.

REFERENCE

Mishap Investigation Board. 2006. "Genesis Mishap Investigation Board Report Volume I," Mishap Investigation Board. 10 October 2007, *www.nasa.gov/ mission_pages/genesis/main/index.html.*

CHAPTER 2

Purpose, Audience Analysis, and Context

To be an effective technical communicator, the writer must consider the *purpose* of the document, the intended *audience,* and the *context* in which the writer is writing or presenting. Failing to take these three things into account will directly affect the effectiveness of a technical document. If the audience cannot use, apply, or understand the information presented, then the author has failed to meet his or her objective.

PURPOSE, AUDIENCE, AND CONTEXT

Because technical communication has such specific goals and requirements, the technical communicator must have a plan for success. One of the first considerations must be the purpose. What is the ultimate goal of the communication? Knowing the purpose determines what format or style the author needs to use. An equal consideration is the audience. Knowing the audience is key to any successful technical communication. If the audience is known, the writer can tailor the communication to meet the needs of that audience. Finally, the technical communicator must consider context. Context largely determines how the reader or listener will receive and interpret the message. Thinking about context will help the writer determine what format is appropriate and how the subject should be approached. Failing to consider context may result in the message being rejected, particularly if the goal is to persuade.

Purpose

The first consideration of any technical communicator should be the purpose of the document or presentation. Technical communication is generally designed to be practical and useful. It may function simply to inform the audience about a policy or procedure, or it may be designed to motivate the reader or listener to take action. The writer must know the end goal of the communication in order to deliver the message effectively. For example, if a technical writer is creating a user guide that will be consulted when questions arise, the document should be designed to fulfill that purpose in the most effective way possible. It should have a detailed table of contents and clear headings, and it most likely will include very thorough definitions and explanations because it is an exhaustive work.

Purpose determines format. As will be discussed in chapter 3, each type of document used in technical and business writing follows a specific format. Additionally, these formats may have a preordained purpose. For example, the complaint letter is not used to deliver good news. It is explicitly designed to deliver a very specific type of information. So, if the purpose of the document being created is known, the writer can choose the appropriate format to showcase the information.

For instance, if a client has requested the creation of a document that includes the company's mission statement, rules, regulations, and employee performance guidelines, an email will not suffice. It would be too informal and far too brief to adequately convey all of that information. Because the document's ultimate purpose is to inform the audience rather than persuade them of a particular course of action, a proposal also would not be an appropriate format to use. Instead, a policy and procedure manual would be the best fit. This means that the technical writer should have a working knowledge of all general formats as well as what they are generally designed to do. This method will allow the writer to analyze the purpose of the document and choose the most appropriate format.

These specific formats also let the audience know what kind of information they can expect to receive. For instance, a progress report adheres to a specific design and gives the audience a hint as to the type of information it will contain. The writer should strive to meet the audience's expectations. If they are expecting a user guide, presenting them with a recommendation report is going to cause a number of problems. So, a writer should always consider what the audience is expecting and choose the format that best meets those expectations while honoring the purpose of the document.

Purpose also determines the type of information that is included in the document or presentation. While the origin of the telephone may be very interesting, it is not necessary information in a user guide for a cellular phone. Knowing the purpose allows the writer to choose what pertinent information to include. Composing a brief statement of purpose at the outset of a project will keep this objective at the forefront of the writer's mind. It does not have to be long or complex to be effective. The following is a good example:

> **Example Purpose Statement:** This report presents the findings of the investigation into the Reading Railroad train collision that occurred on January 24, 2005, along with recommendations for preventing future accidents.

Audience Analysis

When a project begins, a technical communicator also must consider the audience. Who are the intended readers? What are their individual needs? What will the audience members be doing with the information from the presentation or document? Additionally, the writer must consider the knowledge level of the audience. What does the audience already know and what is still needed in order to use the information? The answers to these questions allow the writer to tailor the content, format, and delivery to meet the specific needs of the reader or listener.

Define the Audience. As a technical communicator, it is difficult to prepare an effective document if the audience is not clearly defined. A good communicator must know who the audience is. Will the document be read by engineers or computer experts? Is the audience technically savvy or composed of laypeople? Knowing the audience will allow the writer to address them appropriately. A writer uses very different language when addressing a technical expert as opposed to addressing an audience that has limited technical knowledge. For instance, if a technical communicator was asked to write a report on the environmental impact of a new housing development on the local ecosystem, the writer would need to ascertain whether the intended audience is familiar with biological terminology. If they are not, the writer may need to define complex terms or include more specific examples to make sure the audience fully understands the information presented in the report. Who the audience is directly affects how the writer treats the subject. Taking the time to define the audience allows for clearer, effective technical documents and presentations.

The Technical Audience. When addressing a knowledgeable audience who is very familiar with the subject matter being discussed, definitions are largely unnecessary unless terms new to the industry are being addressed. An audience of experts may be annoyed by lengthy definitions or descriptions of processes or procedures that are commonplace in the industry. An effective technical communicator will not alienate or annoy the audience by wasting their time with extraneous or tedious information. Understanding the knowledge level of the audience ensures that the appropriate information is included in the document or presentation.

The Non-technical Audience. Occasionally, a technical communicator will have to address an audience that is not familiar with the subject at hand. In cases like these, the writer will need to take time to define and explain issues and concepts that are not common knowledge. For a non-technical audience, there is seldom such a thing as too much explanation of technical material. Examples that reference the audience's existing schema or knowledge can be very effective, as are definitions that break technical terms down into easily digestible parts.

Addressing Mixed Audiences. While it would be terribly convenient if the audience was composed of people who shared the same level of knowledge, it seldom works out that way. Generally speaking, a technical communicator will be creating documents or presentations that will be viewed by an audience with varying levels of expertise. Because of that, it is important that a technical communicator researches all potential audiences before commencing writing. Once the writer has determined who the majority audience is and whether there are any significant minority audiences that need to be considered, a decision can be made regarding if or how much of an accommodation should be made.

Audience Needs. A technical communicator also will take time to consider the specific needs of the audience. What is this information going to be used for? What does the audience need to do with it? For example, if the target audience needs to build something with the information included in a technical document, the writer will need to choose the best format in which to deliver the necessary information. An effective technical communicator is not going to use a memo to deliver a complex set of instructions to an engineer. Additionally, if the audience needs to be able to access specific pieces of information at a moment's notice, the writer wants to make sure to use clear, descriptive headings so sections are clearly identifiable.

The audience's needs also play a part when choosing the proper format for a document. For example, an idea for solving a problem can be presented in either a memo proposal or a standard proposal. Both are acceptable formats given the purpose of the document. However, understanding the audience can determine which format is the most appropriate given this particular case. If the target audience is extremely busy and receives a number of proposals each week, a memo proposal may be the best way to initiate contact because it will provide a concise explanation of the problem and solution. The busy reader may be more inclined to review a brief document that addresses the key points rather than sift through a much longer document. A longer proposal can be constructed at a later date if requested or required.

International Audiences. In today's global economy, a technical communicator should remember that he or she does not write for a single culture or ethnic group. Addressing an audience of mixed origin can add another dimension to audience analysis. There are several factors that must be considered when addressing an international audience. One primary concern is language. While some technical terms are universal, such as those involving computers, others are not. That means it may be necessary to include definitions of commonly used terms, even if the audience is knowledgeable in the field. Avoiding slang or clichés is also important when addressing a global audience. That type of language is not taught in the second language classroom, so it is unlikely that an international audience would be familiar with it. Additionally, rhetorical strategies differ greatly between cultures. While in some countries it is critical that writing move in a linear fashion toward a final point, in other countries, a circular writing style is preferred. Taking time to research these types of details will allow a technical communicator to meet the specific needs of an international audience.

Audience Analysis Checklist

To fully analyze the audience, a checklist or worksheet can be used. An example audience analysis checklist can be found in figure 2.1. A detailed discussion of each question and how it can be addressed in a document is included also.

Who is the primary audience? The primary audience is the target readers, the most important group of readers the writer hopes to reach. When writing a business proposal, the primary audience may be the investors. When writing a user guide, the primary audience is the consumers who will be using the product and thus need the document. Knowing the primary audience allows the writer to answer the other questions on the checklist.

Is there a secondary audience? If so, who? The secondary audience is a group of readers who may come in contact with the document, but they may not truly need the document. They simply may be coming in contact with it by way of reference. For example, a set of instructions may be developed for the customer service department that uses multiple computer monitors, while the sales department also may read the instructions to get a sense as to how the use of multiple monitors will work in their department. Identifying this latter group is still important, even though they are not the primary audience. The writer should still consider their needs when composing the instructions. Again, identifying this group allows the writer to more fully answer the remaining questions on the list.

FIGURE 2.1 *Audience Analysis Checklist*

- ☐ Who is the primary audience?
- ☐ Is there a secondary audience? If so, who?
- ☐ Was this document solicited?
- ☐ What will the target audience do with the document (e.g., make a decision, perform a task)?
- ☐ What does the target audience know about the topic being discussed?
- ☐ What further information will the audience need from the document in order to use it for the intended purpose?
- ☐ What expectations will the audience have for this document?
- ☐ What does the intended audience value? What will they seek out?
- ☐ What biases may the audience have toward the subject being addressed?
- ☐ What objections, if any, is the audience likely to raise?
- ☐ Are there any cultural considerations that may affect how the audience views the document?
- ☐ What external factors will influence how the audience receives the information?

Was this document solicited? Whether a given document was requested can influence how the audience receives the message. Unsolicited documents, such as proposals, may be met with skepticism and even annoyance or surprise. As a result, the writer must address the audience in a respectful way that makes good use of their time and addresses their concerns right from the outset. While one might argue that this should always happen with any type of document, it is even more vital when the document has not been requested. Additionally, an unsolicited document may need to persuade the audience that it is even worth reading. For example, if a writer is proposing an unsolicited solution to a problem, the writer should start by establishing that there is indeed a problem.

What will the target audience do with the document (e.g., make a decision, perform a task)? Knowing what the audience needs to accomplish with a document or the information it contains affects how the writer approaches the document. This question essentially establishes the purpose of the document, and the purpose guides the creation of the document.

In the event that a text has multiple audiences, the writer should consider the needs of each group and strive to meet those needs in the document. For example, the primary audience may need to make a decision based on the information presented in a feasibility report; consequently, the writer should make sure that the appropriate details and any outside research used are provided in the document. However, a secondary audience may only be seeking information to remain current on the decision-making process. They themselves are not making the decision, but merely following its progress. For this type of audience, a concise review of the entire report would be sufficient, so the writer should include an abstract or introduction that provides the appropriate amount of detail.

What does the target audience know about the topic being discussed? To properly address the audience's needs, the writer must understand the knowledge level of the audience. What do they already know about the subject being discussed? If the target audience comprises individuals the writer personally knows and has had previous interaction with, the audience's familiarity with the topic can be relatively easy to ascertain. This realization can prove more difficult with a distant or unfamiliar audience. In that case, the writer needs to do research to better understand the target audience. If the document will be read and used by the leaders of a company or organization, the writer should research the group and the individuals whenever possible.

Knowing the educational backgrounds of the readers most likely to see the document can help the writer gauge the audience's knowledge base. Additionally, knowing what role individual members of the audience play is valuable. For example, is the target audience composed of managers who have more of a theoretical knowledge of the subject, or is it made up of technicians who have a more practical understanding of the subject? The managers likely will need examples and perhaps even a few definitions, while the technicians will not. Finally, learning about past projects that audience members worked on can give the writer an idea of what type of technical jargon they already may be familiar with. In some instances, it even may be possible for the writer to meet with one or more representatives from the target audience. In that case, the writer should find out as much as possible about the audience—what they know, what they want, and what they need.

Failing to understand the knowledge base of the target audience could result in the writer alienating or insulting the readers. For example, a proposal given to a group of expert decision makers that is filled with elementary-level definitions may result in the rejection of the proposal simply because the audience perceives it as a waste of their time and an insult to their intelligence. Taking time to fully analyze the audience can help the writer avoid these kinds of problems.

What further information will the audience need from the document in order to use it for the intended purpose? Equally important as understanding what the audience already knows is understanding what they still need to learn about the subject. Again, researching the target audience will help the writer determine what background information, definitions, and supporting information to include. For example, a subject matter expert will not need a definition unless a term is completely new. However, experts will want plenty of details and evidence when applicable. Experts also will be looking for citations of any outside sources consulted. A lay audience, on the other hand, will need definitions of all technical terms. They also may benefit from additional charts and graphics to visually help explain difficult concepts.

What expectations will the audience have for this document? The writer should strive to meet as many of the audience's expectations as possible. Fully understanding how the audience will use the document can help the writer achieve this goal. However, it is also important to flesh out any additional expectations the audience has regarding the document. For example, what format is the audience expecting to see? If a CEO is expecting to receive a revised policy and procedure manual but is handed a memo with a few updated procedures instead, problems are likely to follow. Or, if a board of directors is expecting to receive a recommendation report that they can discuss and vote on but is instead presented with nothing but a collection of research and information, delays will ensue. Talking to the client and clarifying the expectations of a project will help a writer avoid misunderstandings like these.

What does the intended audience value? What will they seek out? Once again, to accurately answer these questions, a writer will need to do some research on the audience. A company or organization's website can be a good place to begin. What is its mission statement? What impression does it try to convey to outsiders with its site? For instance, does it seem like a very formal organization, or does it try to appear more relaxed and grassroots? What core values are implied by the information presented?

Understanding the culture of a company or organization can help the writer understand what is important to the audience, and therefore, what they will want to see in a document or presentation. For example, if a company is very concerned with the environmental impact of its products, a technical writer would be wise to discuss any negative environmental effects a proposal might have before submitting for their intended audience. Knowing what is important to the audience can help the writer reach them more effectively.

What biases may the audience have toward the subject being addressed? No audience is without its biases. However, the writer must ascertain if the audience holds any particular biases that may interfere with the delivery or reception of the message. Again, doing some additional research on the audience can help the writer identify and potentially overcome any biases. For example, finding out whether the company or organization has had any previous experience with the subject matter can be quite useful. One option is to speak to other technical communicators who may have previously worked with a given group. Also, tracking down interviews with company leaders or administrators can offer valuable insight into the audience's potential leanings.

Once the audience's biases are known, the writer can design a plan for overcoming or addressing them in the document. Sometimes, this can be as simple as acknowledging the bias and asking the readers to put that aside in favor of finding a workable solution for the good of the company. Other times, it may actually involve providing additional information to assuage any concerns. For example, when writing a grant proposal seeking funding for a project, keep in mind whether there are other parties involved who are at the opposite end of the political spectrum as the organization from which additional funding is being sought. These differences may need to be addressed so the funder understands that any contrary affiliations will not fundamentally affect the project.

What objections, if any, is the audience likely to raise? If the document is persuasive in nature, such as in the case of a proposal, the writer should anticipate and strive to address any potential objections the audience may have. Also, the writer should consider objections readers may have toward learning a new process if the document is a set of instructions being sent to veteran employees. Addressing a concern before the audience has time to fully articulate the objection can go a long way toward winning them over. It shows an understanding of them as audience members and demonstrates the time and effort the writer put forth when composing the document.

Are there any cultural considerations that may affect how the audience views the document? As discussed earlier in this chapter, addressing a global audience creates new obstacles for a technical writer. Differences in rhetorical strategies, language, and social rules can wreak havoc on how an international audience receives a document. Consulting an expert on the culture that makes up the primary audience can help the writer navigate this difficult territory. There are also many books available that can help a writer learn more about the cultural practices of a variety of audiences, such as the following:

- *Global Business Negotiations: A Practical Guide* by Claude Cellich and Subhash Jain

- *Doing Business in Asia: A Complete Guide* by Sanjyot P. Dunung

- *Do's and Don'ts Around the World: A Country Guide to Cultural and Social Taboos and Etiquette* by Gladson I. Nwanna

What external factors will influence how the audience receives the information? Finally, it is important for the writer to consider whether there are any outside forces or situations that will affect how the audience receives or interprets the message. For example, if a company is in the midst of a financial crisis, a proposal that seeks further funding for a project may not be well received. Taking time to research the background of an organization or audience will allow the writer either to frame the message in a positive manner or revise the plan for the document.

Context

Finally, the context in which the technical communicator is writing or presenting must be considered. The technical communicator does not compose in a vacuum. The circumstances surrounding the creation of a document or presentation directly affect how the audience receives and interprets the message. Failing to consider context can result in the message not being understood. A perfect example of this type of exchange often occurs with international audiences. When a technical writer fails to consider the cultural context of a document, it may result in an international reader misinterpreting the message or expecting something that is not delivered. Thinking about context allows the technical communicator to anticipate obstacles to the message.

Consider this example: A writer composes a proposal to suggest the implementation of a merit-based pay raise for all mid-level employees; however, she fails to research the financial situation of the company. If she had, she would have found that the company recently announced that it is on the verge of bankruptcy, and that layoffs are a strong possibility. How will that single fact affect how the proposal is viewed by those reviewing it? Context is always a factor that must be considered.

CHAPTER 3

Forms of Technical Writing

R eaders expect to see writing in certain formats where they easily can find information they need to know. Whether it is a simple email or a complex set of instructions, readers respond more actively to writing that conforms to well-known, common formats. As mentioned in chapter 1, technical, business, and professional writing overlap when it comes to writing responsibilities on the job. Given this inevitability of workplace writing, shorter forms that can be classified as technical, business, and professional writing are covered in this chapter. Longer, more complex forms also are defined in this chapter to provide beginning writers with an overview of what these longer forms entail; additionally, these complex documents are covered comprehensively in chapter 10.

EMAIL

Email often is considered an informal, conversational type of communication; however, when using email in the workplace, every email should be treated as a formal piece of written communication that is representative of the company. With the ability to forward on emails to anyone, a writer should never assume any privacy or exclusive audience.

It is not unusual for any professional to receive 100 or more emails every day. Given the volume of emails that have to be sorted through and read, an email composed with a busy reader in mind increases the chances it will be read and acted on accordingly. While it may seem elementary to go over the standard conventions and etiquette of email, because it is probably one of the most common forms of written communication today, a quick glance at one's in-box clearly demonstrates how these important conventions are easily overlooked or ignored.

Effective Composition of an Email

The following guidelines are written with busy readers in mind, and they offer general guidance in terms of professionalism and courtesy. There is more to composing an effective email than making sure that all components are filled in; there are also important considerations about who to send the email to and how to word everything from the subject line to the concluding paragraph in the body of the message.

To Line. Email, like any written communication, has a specific audience. The To line is reserved for the primary audience of the email, those who are directly affected or need the information contained in the message. Do not add persons or groups to an email unless it is certain they need the information. Guessing is not appropriate because it clutters people's in-boxes and only increases the amount of information they have to sift through every day. Make calls, if necessary, before sending out an email to be sure the people in the To line are the ones who need the information. Sending email to people who do not need the information creates unnecessary email traffic if someone responds who should not respond, or if someone creates a fuss over receiving the email unnecessarily.

Carbon Copy (cc) Line. The cc line is reserved for secondary audiences, those who are not directly addressed or affected but who still have some stake in knowing the information contained in the email. The cc line is sometimes considered hierarchical, so it is worth the time to know the primary and secondary audiences for certain.

Blind Carbon Copy (bcc) Line. The bcc line is reserved for those recipients to whom the sender wants to know the email reached, but does not want the other recipients to know. No one except for the sender and the person in the bcc line knows this person is included on the email. Some email programs may override the default setting of not sending a reply to the bcc person, which further encourages caution when using the "reply all" feature.

Subject Line. The subject line is often the most overlooked or dismissed part of email. A subject line establishes priority in an in-box. As a reader scans over the list of numerous emails every day, the subject line often determines what will be read now versus later, or maybe never at all.

When determining what to include in the subject line, the best rule of thumb is to be specific; tell the reader exactly what the email contains. The following are some example subject lines:

- *Poor choice of words:* To do list
  Better choice of words: Action items for CEO visit

- *Poor choice of words:* New process
  Better choice of words: New hiring process—immediate implementation

- *Poor choice of words:* Request for information
  Better choice of words: Request for software development update

Body. American audiences have certain expectations for body material in most correspondence, including email. The first is that they like to know the bottom line up front. The second is that they also expect pertinent details to follow, explaining the initial bottom line statement. The bottom line can do the following:

- **State what is expected as a result of the email.**
  Example: In preparation for CEO Ron Black's visit tomorrow, the following action items must be completed by the close of business today.

- **Tell what information the email contains and how it should be used.**
  Example: The following new hire process is to be implemented for all new hires beginning today, September 13, 2007.

- **Ask for specific information.**
  Example: Please send me the software development progress report for the dates April 15, 2007, to August 31, 2007.

International audiences are not always familiar with the up-front, bottom line approach of American correspondence. When writing for an international audience, a writer should research the *rhetorical strategy* (the general format of correspondence or documentation) and follow those conventions instead. The main goal of every piece of writing is to reach its intended audience, which means communicating in the format and language familiar to the audience instead of using the format and languge the writer is accustomed to.

There are further considerations a writer needs to keep in mind, whether writing to an American or international audience. Many times, the To recipients on an email can be hidden. When that happens, a reader may not know if an email is intended for him or her specifically or whether the email was distributed en masse. In either case, senders should always communicate the purpose of the email in the first sentence, such as: "Attached is the new expense report, which will be used for all expenses starting today." To simply send out an email with hidden To recipients and say "Use this report from now on," is not clear. Explain the purpose of the email up front and follow up with relevant details in subsequent body paragraphs.

The body paragraphs of an email should be formatted clearly, just as it would be if written in hard copy. The email should begin with an introduction that briefly states the purpose of the correspondence. Following the introduction are subsequent body paragraphs that offer relevant details about the directive given in the introduction. It is important to keep in mind that online communications are often skimmed, so while details are essential, be conscious of the length of the email, as longer emails generally tend not to be read thoroughly. To conclude, provide readers with point of contact information and, if possible, an alternative form of communication, such as a telephone number.

Attachments. Attachments should be referred to in the introduction. Generally, the attachment is supplemental to the email; however, if the attachment is the document that is to be used, then the email body should be brief and relied on only as an introduction to the attachment, as in the following example:

> Attached is the new hiring process document, which contains the new hiring form and directions for using this form. This process is to be implemented for all new hires beginning September 21, 2007. Please print or save this document for future use and reference.

Many in-boxes have limits on the size of files that can be submitted or received via email. As a rule of thumb, do not send attachments over five megabytes. If the recipient is traveling and using an Internet provider that is not on broadband, large attachments can slow up the process of opening an in-box, not to mention the time it can take to open the attachment itself.

When multiple files have to be sent as attachments, it might be better to break up the delivery into several emails or use compressed or zipped folders. If compressed folders are used, check if recipients have the ability to open them. If a series of emails is used to distribute multiple attachments, include in the subject line the total number of emails the recipient will be receiving, such as: New hiring process documentation, 1 of 3 total emails.

Replying. When replying only to the sender of an email, restrict information in the reply to only that which pertains to the subject of the email. Do not bring up a whole new subject just because that person is someone who might know the information. For instance, a common mistake is shown in the following example:

> **Subject:** Action Items for CEO Visit
>
> Joe,
>
> I completed the report for tomorrow's meeting with the CEO. The final copy can be found at Wilma/CEO Visit/SW Dev Team. The title of the report is Software Development Plan of Action for

2008. Let me know if you have questions or have any problems with the file.

Oh, by the way, do you know when the new hiring process takes effect? Do you also know where that new process document is stored on the server? I've got someone coming in on Friday and I want to be sure I process her correctly.

Thanks, Stan

In this example, a couple of problems could arise. First, Joe may respond to Stan's off-subject request, and if Stan happens to delete this email because he forgot he asked for the hiring process information in it, he may have to email Joe again asking for the same information. Likewise, Stan may remember he asked for this information and received a response from Joe, but forgot what email it was in. Either way, more email is often generated from trying to piggyback an off-subject question in a response email. It is better to simply begin a whole new email with an appropriate subject line for easy sorting and reading on both ends.

Reply All. Out of respect, and to minimize unnecessary email, restrict use of the "reply all" button for only when the response contains essential, additional, or explanatory information to the original email that is vital for all recipients to know. To use this feature when simply saying "thank you," "will do," or "sounds good," creates unnecessary email traffic on a server and clogs in-boxes with emails that have no value. Even when welcoming a new hire, forward a response to only the new hire and not the entire list.

INTEROFFICE MEMO

Interoffice memo refers to those memos that are distributed solely within a company and not to outside customers, clients, or partners. The memo form of communication most often is used to relay company policy or other important company-related information. Because interoffice means everyone who receives the memo works for the company, there may be a less formal tone for interoffice memos than for other business correspondence, such as business letters. This selective audience also means writers may make assumptions about the information they put into the memo; however, those assumptions may cause problems for some employees. For instance, even in a closed office setting where everyone who works for the company is in the same building, assuming everyone is familiar with their surroundings, company policies that may be referred to, and even the names of personnel can cause problems for new hires or those who possibly travel often and may be out of the office more than they are in the building. For those employees who are out of the office regularly or for new hires, providing names of personnel in memos can be a great help, because they may not know their coworkers' names and position titles as well as those who are in the office daily. While a writer does not want to treat readers as elementary students, it is still important to clarify information and provide personal contacts in an interoffice memo, as in the following example:

> **Subject:** Parking permits required as of September 3, 2007
>
> Parking permits are required for all GlobalComm employees beginning September 3, 2007. Permits can be picked up at the reception desk in the Human Resources (HR) office, Room 314. If you require special parking considerations, please call the receptionist, Joe Riley (x 7654), before going to HR, and he will fill out the appropriate paperwork and call you when your special permit has been approved and received.

In this example, the writer states the purpose of the memo up front so employees know they need to act on something by a certain date. It also gives directions for how to obtain the parking permits; but, what may seem like obvious information, such as where the human resources office is located or the name of the receptionist and his phone number, is still included, which makes the correspondence helpful to those who may not be as familiar with the human resources department as others may be, and yet the information flows and is not patronizing.

Effective Composition of an Interoffice Memo

The interoffice memo can be written in hard copy or adjusted for email distribution. Either way it is prepared, once again, there are certain expectations for those who receive this type of correspondence. To help meet these standards, the following guidelines explain the general conventions of writing an interoffice memo.

Date Line. In hard copy, this is the date the memo is actually distributed. If the memo is composed at the end of one day, but not circulated until the next, the date on the memo should be the circulation date. In email, the electronic system will automatically stamp the date and time the email was sent, so this line is generally not part of the actual email memo.

Dates and international audiences

Even with interoffice memos, a writer still may be dealing with international audiences. The American convention of mm/dd/yy (09/21/07) is not as common in other countries or within other cultures. To avoid confusion, it is best to spell out dates, such as September 21, 2007, or 21 September 2007.

To Line. In hard copy, this line can be general, such as "All floor managers," "All night shift employees (11:00 PM to 7:00 AM)," or "All full-time faculty." As with email, it is still important to determine the primary audience for the memo. The reason the To line in hard copy can be more general is because copies are made and distributed physically; therefore, specific names are generally not needed on the actual memo itself when referring to a group of people. If the memo is being distributed to others outside of the group, or to individuals not part of a group, then it is appropriate to use individual names. Generally, include an individual's title in the To line when that person is not well-known by the writer. In email, the same rules for the To line apply as stated in the previous email section in this chapter.

From Line. The From line can give a person's name, title, and department or division. A direct point of contact, however, should be established as to whom is actually responsible for the content of the memo. If a department is being used, then a clear delineation of the manager in that department should be included, such as "From: Human Resources, Ron Bloom, Director."

In email, the From line automatically will show whose email account is being used to send the email, but this does not always mean it is the person responsible for the content. In this case, it is courteous, especially for new employees, to have a point of contact included in the closing paragraph of the email body. For instance:

> If you have any questions about this new hiring process, please contact Ron Bloom in the Human Resources Department at 719-555-1212 or at *rbloom@ventures.com.*

Subject Line. The subject line determines priority, even in hard copy. A descriptive but brief explanation of what the memo addresses is the best way to determine the wording of a subject line, such as in the following examples:

> New expense report procedure to be implemented by September 21, 2007
>
> Mandatory training courses to be completed by December 15, 2007
>
> End of the semester checklist and sign-off sheet

The more descriptive the subject line, the more likely the memo will be read and acted on. If a subject line is vague or too general, as in "Expense Report Procedures," the memo may be dismissed. Readers who are already familiar with reporting their expenses may mistake the memo to be a summary of the process for those unfamiliar with the expense procedure. What the writer wants from readers should be part of the subject line, as in "New expense reporting procedures to be implemented by September 21, 2007."

Body. The body of a memo has an expected format and structure. Readers expect to see an introduction, body, and conclusion. American readers like to know the purpose of any type of correspondence or document from the very beginning; however, this format may need to be altered if the memo includes international employees, especially those working in a foreign country. For American readers, the first paragraph states the purpose of the memo, which can be to inform, request information, or delegate tasks. Stating the memo's intent in the first sentence tells readers right away what is expected as a result of reading the memo, as shown in the following examples:

> The end of the semester checklist given below must be completed and signed by all instructors before checking out for summer break on May 15.

> The following list of courses is mandatory for all employees and must be completed by December 15, 2007.

Stating the purpose up front gives the rest of the memo context for readers because they now know what the background or details relate to. Details or further explanation should follow the introduction. This should be restricted to only background or details that are relevant to the purpose of sending out the memo in the first place. An interoffice memo generally runs no longer than one page. A memo that runs a full page or longer most likely will be skimmed or not read in its entirety.

It is courteous to end a memo with contact information in case readers have questions or need further information. This is also a good place to reiterate due dates, especially if the memo is particularly long or if the due dates are quickly approaching. An example of an interoffice memo is shown in figure 3.1.

BUSINESS LETTERS

Business letters focus on relationships. They are formal correspondence that facilitates communication within a company or between a company and outside customers, partners, potential clients, or other stakeholders.

FIGURE 3.1 *Interoffice Memo*

A: This is the date of distribution.

B: General distribution is noted; however, each faculty member will be given the memo in hard copy.

C: This is the specific person who is responsible for the content of the memo.

D: The subject line indicates that the procedures given are new and the date they are to be implemented.

E: For easy reading, the Date, To, From, Subject, and first line of the body of a memo are double-spaced. The body of a memo is generally single spaced with a double space between paragraphs.

F: This clearly states what faculty are to do as a result of this memo and the date they are to use the information.

G: This gives only brief but relevant details about the new procedures.

H: Subheadings help separate the two procedures clearly.

I: The last paragraph provides readers with a point of contact and a phone number.

(A) Date: August 15, 2007

(B) To: English faculty

(C) From: Bill Durham, Department Chair

(D) Subject: New add/drop procedures to be implemented beginning August 20, 2007

(F) All English faculty members are to use the new add/drop procedures below beginning August 20, 2007.

(G) The following procedures were approved by the dean's office in July 2007, and were developed in order to place the responsibility of adding and dropping a class with the student and not with instructors or the department secretary. Whether adding or dropping a class, instructors should advise all students to meet deadlines as not doing so will result in the credit hours being their financial responsibility.

(H) Add Procedure

Students who wish to add a class that already has a full roster must receive written permission from the instructor. Students should obtain an add slip from the English department secretary, Cecelia Barton, Room 221. Instructors have the choice to sign this slip or not. Once signed, the student should take the slip to the registrar's office to be enrolled officially in the class. The deadline for students to add a class is September 10, 2007.

Generally, adding another student to an already full class should be reserved for English majors, or they should at least get first priority, especially seniors.

Drop Procedure

Students who wish to drop a class that they are already registered for must report to the registrar's office to drop the class. The deadline for dropping a class is September 10, 2007. Instructors are no longer required to sign drop slips. In fact, drop slips no longer exist and any student who approaches an instructor with a drop slip is using a slip from a previous semester that is no longer valid. If students do not meet the drop deadline, they still will be enrolled in the class whether or not they attend, and they will be charged for it as well.

(I) If you have any questions about these procedures, please contact Bill (x 2331). Please note the deadlines and advise students accordingly.

Business letters serve multiple purposes; thus, they will differ slightly in format and style. For instance, business letters may be written to do any of the following:

- Market to a particular group of people to draw in business

- Relay information, such as human resources sending out insurance information to company employees

- Address customer relations, which can include response letters to a request for information or adjustment letters replying to a complaint

While there is a general format for most business letters, there always will be some modification needed when considering audience and purpose.

Before composing business letters, a writer should acknowledge that any correspondence is representative of the writer's company. If a letter contains mistakes, misspellings, or inaccurate information, this can be seen by the reader as a reflection of the type of service to be expected. Furthermore, tone and formality also are direct indicators of the desired relationship.

This section discusses ways to write effective business letters that meet the expectations of an intended audience and purpose to produce a desired outcome. Specifically, audience, purpose, tone, formality, and format are addressed, and several examples are provided to illustrate effective letter writing.

Types of Letters

There is not one standard format known as the "business letter." Business letters serve several purposes and are addressed to various audiences, which means the format is often determined by the purpose and audience. This section covers three common types of business letters: cover letters, complaint letters, and adjustment letters. First, general definitions are provided to show the difference between these three types of letters. Next, audience and purpose, tone and formality, and general format are discussed, followed by details and examples that illustrate effective cover, complaint, and adjustment letter writing. The three types of business letters can be defined as the following:

1. **Cover letter.** There are several types of cover letters, such as a cover letter sent with a résumé; letters that introduce longer documents, such as proposals or marketing plans; or letters that accompany a product or service. Cover letters are generally short and introductory in nature because they often are paired with another document or product.

2. **Complaint letter.** These letters are generated by anyone who is dissatisfied with a particular business arrangement, which can include individuals or companies. Complaint letters may be about the poor technical support service provided to a customer or because of a product that was damaged when received by a consumer. Companies write complaint letters to other companies, such as when suppliers do not send the right type or number of products or if the merchandise received is of poor quality. No matter the situation, the desired outcome is generally that the customer wants compensation, such as a replacement or reimbursement.

3. **Adjustment letter.** This is a reply to a complaint letter and can go one of two ways: The letter either will give the customer what the customer asked for or it will not. There are certain ways to write good news and bad news letters, while still maintaining a positive rapport and hopefully the business of a customer.

Audience and Purpose

As with any documentation, effective business letters address a particular audience and purpose first. Form business letters do not take audience or purpose into consideration; thus, they usually are ineffective in building lasting positive relationships. Instead, form letters often make readers feel put off or as if they are an inconvenience and no one has time to deal with them individually. When possible, do not use standard form letters because they are not the best means to impress the intended readers. If form letters are necessary, audience analysis is still required.

The first place to start any type of letter writing is to get to know the person or group of people the letter will be addressed to so that correspondence can be personalized. Personalizing a letter begins with specific names. Letters that address a person using the person's name, for example, Ms. Gonzales, versus a generic opening, such as Dear Customer, are much more effective in grabbing a reader's attention.

If a letter is part of a mass mailing, then that audience should be broken down into smaller, more manageable groups, such as by region, gender, and profession. By doing so, letters can be revised according to each of the smaller groups of people, thus making them more personal and on target with the intended population. If the letter is an adjustment letter in response to a complaint by a customer, a form letter will most likely only anger the customer further. Getting to know the person by researching the account and even calling him or her will go a long way in customer relations, which can then be solidified in writing. Having this kind of background and rapport with a customer will make the letter writing easier because the audience is a real person as opposed to an unknown "complainer." These small gestures to get to know the customer will reveal necessary background information, which in turn helps to clarify the purpose of subsequent correspondence.

Clearly defining the purpose of the letter is the next step in addressing the intended audience in an appropriate manner. Is the letter intended to sell a product or service to a particular group of people, or is it a response or adjustment letter intended to reclaim a customer's patronage by handling the customer's complaint? One way to make letter writing easier and effective is to do a prewriting exercise. Write out the name of the person the letter is being addressed to, what is known about this person, the account, the history with the company, and the exact purpose of the letter. Having this kind of information readily available keeps letter writing targeted, while constantly reminding the writer of the audience and outcomes of the letter. For instance, the prewriting may look something like this:

Audience: Alice Hoffman, customer in Iowa City, Iowa

Background: Alice has been ordering coffee from us steadily for over five years. Her usual monthly bill totals $20 or more. She orders generally the same coffee (decaf), adding a flavored (decaf) coffee about three times per year. She claims the decaf coffee she has been receiving must be mislabeled because she has started having reactions to the coffee whereas she has never experienced this previously. She wants reimbursement for the past three months when this began and wants to quit the coffee club. Has anyone else complained about this? Ask other customer representatives.

Goal: Send Alice a reimbursement check; regain Alice's trust in the company and have her continue as a customer.

This type of prewriting exercise may seem tedious at first, but it will save time when writing the actual letter by not having to track down this pertinent information while composing. Beyond the convenience, this exercise also can help the writer assess the desired tone the letter should take.

Tone and Formality

The tone of a letter immediately and directly affects how readers feel about a business relationship and whether or not that relationship will continue in a positive light or become a negative experience. Tone is achieved through a writer's *diction*. Diction refers to specific words a writer uses; for example, note the difference between "This letter is meant to deal with your complaint" and "I am writing to address the unsatisfactory service you received." In the first instance, a tone of inconvenience and little or no concern is implied with the words and phrases "meant to deal with" and "complaint." No one wants to be "dealt" with when "complaining." Conversely, in the second sentence, a tone of sincere concern is conveyed with the phrase "I am writing," meaning the letter writer is taking this on personally. Also, the phrase "address the unsatisfactory service you received" tells the reader that the writer agrees that the service was not satisfactory. Thus, a positive experience will result from the second example because the tone conveyed via its diction is one of sincerity and willingness to make things right.

Business letters are formal correspondence even when the parties know each other well. Written communication is a way of formalizing verbal contracts or other conversations; thus, business letters become written records of business relationships. The formality of a letter begins with how a person is addressed. In most cases, the two parties will not have a personal relationship outside the boundaries of work; therefore, recipients should be addressed using titles such as Mr., Ms., Dr., or other appropriate titles, such as Reverend or Your Honor. If, however, the two parties have known each other for an extended amount of time or they have a relationship outside of work, then it may be appropriate to address the person on a first-name basis. First names also may be used if the recipient has told the writer to address him or her that way. With that in mind, care should be taken for international readers and their preferences for being addressed. As a general rule, always make recipients feel at ease by addressing them using either a formal title or the way in which they prefer to be addressed.

Letters should begin by using the standard "Dear Dr. Goldstein:" The use of "Dear" is standard and should not be dismissed. Additionally, notice that a colon follows the last name to imply a formal business relationship, whereas a comma after the salutation implies a less formal and personal relationship.

Using Ms.

All women should be addressed using Ms. No distinction should be made about whether the woman is married or has been married by using Mrs. or Miss. Because Mr. is a generic title for men and carries no marital distinction with it, Ms. offers the same respect for women and should be used as a standard. The only exception would be if a woman specifically tells a writer to address her using Miss or Mrs., in which case she is making the distinction herself.

Other conventions of formality include using business language versus conversational or slang words, such as the difference between writing "The location of the new office is in an ideal setting" and "The new place has an awesome view." Once again, formality is determined by diction, and in the case of business letters, it is in a company's best interest to use formal diction, which is consistent with other business standards. Format, which will be discussed next, is also a formal convention and should be adhered to in order to represent a company in the best and most professional light.

Format

Businesspeople expect business documentation to conform to certain standard formats. Correspondence or documentation that steps outside of these common forms may be considered suspicious or amateur, neither of which is conducive to strong business relationships. With well-known formats, readers know exactly where to find information they want and need. Not all readers have time to read every piece of documentation all the way through; therefore, it is important that the following formats are used so that readers are comfortable and know exactly what they have in their hands.

Letterhead. All correspondence that comes from a company should appear on a company's printed stationery or letterhead. Letterhead should include the company's name, logo (if applicable), address, phone, website, and email address. Complete contact information is important so that readers have several convenient options for reaching the company and the letter writer. An example letterhead's contact information is shown in figure 3.2.

While business letter composition will vary depending on audience and purpose, as shown in later parts of this chapter, the general structure follows these five broad guidelines:

1. **Introduction.** The introductory paragraph tells the reader right away what the letter is about, what is wanted, or what is needed. Most American audiences prefer the bottom line up front; this is relayed in the introductory paragraph. If a conversation preceded the letter, then that conversation should be referenced in the opening paragraph as well.

FIGURE 3.2 *Letterhead Contact Information*

FRONT RANGE DESIGN AND PRINTING

1234 University Avenue, Denver, CO 80936, 303-555-5555
www.frdesignandprinting.com, frdesignandprinting@xpress.com

---

2. **Body paragraphs.** Typically, there are only one or two body paragraphs that provide readers with background information or details pertaining to the order of business in the letter. These paragraphs are generally short and concise, providing only necessary information and no extraneous details. This goes back to the idea that people in the workplace are usually busy and do not have time to wade through details other than what directly relates to the immediate order of business.

3. **Closing paragraph.** Every business letter should conclude with a closing paragraph that restates the purpose of the letter and provides the sender's contact information.

4. **Complimentary close.** The letter should end with a complimentary close, such as Sincerely, Best, Regards, or Respectfully, followed by a comma.

5. **Signature block.** After the complimentary close, space down four lines and then type the name of the sender. The four-space block above the name is for a signature.

Block Style. Block style refers to how the information is set up and typed on the company's letterhead. In block style, aside from a company's contact information on the letterhead, everything is justified on the left side of the page, which leaves a clean line along the left margin on the page. The right side is not justified, will vary in length, and is referred to as a "ragged right." An example of a block style letter is shown in figure 3.3. Furthermore, there are other aspects of a letter that require formatting. In addition to page setup, format also includes expected paragraph structure and other letter elements discussed below and also illustrated in figure 3.3.

Modified Block Style. Modified block style is when the date and signature line are indented and paragraphs are also indented five spaces with no space in between, as shown in figure 3.4.

Both block and modified block style are commonly used in business, so either one is acceptable. If letterhead is not available or the letter comes

FIGURE 3.3 *Block Style Business Letter*

A: Two lines after the letterhead, type in the date the letter is actually mailed.

B: Two lines after the date, include the formal name and address for the customer.

C: Two lines after the address, the salutation addresses the customer formally with "Dear" and a formal title followed by a colon.

D: Two lines after the salutation, begin the opening paragraph by immediately telling the reader what the letter is about.

E: Paragraphs are not indented; rather a space appears between paragraphs for readability.

F: The next two paragraphs provide necessary background and details for the reader.

G: Notice that all of the text is left justified, and the right side of the letter is not justified, also referred to as a "ragged right."

H: End the letter appropriately, which in this case is to thank the customer for their business and provide contact information.

I: The complimentary close should be a common and respectful closing. This is followed by the signature block (four line spaces and then the sender's name typewritten).

FRONT RANGE DESIGN AND PRINTING

1234 University Avenue, Denver, CO 80936, 303-555-5555
www.frdesignandprinting.com, frdesignandprinting@xpress.com

(A) September 27, 2007

(B) Dr. Roberta Perez
Front Range Technical Institute
2266 Technical Institute Way
Falcon, CO 80831

(C) Dear Dr. Perez:

(D) Thank you for choosing Front Range Design and Printing to create and print the marketing brochures for Front Range Technical Institute. Per our phone call yesterday, we are ready to begin the initial stages of the design process and welcome any level of involvement you choose.

(E) Your designer is Patricia Beltran, who will contact you this week to set up an appointment to gather information on your preferences for brochure size, paper, colors, logo permissions, and standardized design of all pieces. She **(F)** also will ask for contact information for each department that will need a brochure. Patricia works directly with the writer for your project, Alex Trujillo, who will be working with the contact person in each department to gather information for the text of the brochures.

(G) Once a preliminary design has been created and a draft of the text is written, we will provide you with mock-ups for approval. There are approximately four stages of approval in the design process and two approvals needed when the brochures go to print. We will notify you one week in advance of each approval needed. Patricia also will provide you with a timeline for completion after your initial meeting with her.

(H) We look forward to this opportunity to serve Front Range Technical Institute, and like all of our customers, we will provide you with our best professional and personalized service at all times. If at any time you have questions or concerns, please contact me at 303-555-5555 or at annbrand@xpress.com.

(I) Sincerely,

Ann Brand

Ann Brand, President

FIGURE 3.4 *Modified Block Style Business Letter*

FRONT RANGE DESIGN AND PRINTING

1234 University Avenue, Denver, CO 80936, 303-555-5555
www.frdesignandprinting.com, frdesignandprinting@xpress.com

September 27, 2007

Dr. Roberta Perez
Front Range Technical Institute
2266 Technical Institute Way
Falcon, CO 80831

Dear Dr. Perez:

Thank you for choosing Front Range Design and Printing to create and print the marketing brochures for Front Range Technical Institute. Per our phone call yesterday, we are ready to begin the design process and welcome any level of involvement you choose.

Your designer is Patricia Beltran, who will contact you this week to set up an appointment to gather information on brochure size, paper, colors, logo permissions, and standardized design of all pieces. She also will ask for contact information for each department that will need a brochure. Patricia works directly with the writer for your project, Alex Trujillo, who will be working with the contact person in each department to gather information for the text of the brochures.

Once a preliminary design has been created and a draft of the text is written, we will provide you with mock-ups for approval. There are approximately four stages of approval in the design process and two approvals needed when the brochures go to print. We will notify you one week in advance of each approval needed. Patricia also will provide you with a timeline for completion after your initial meeting with her.

We look forward to serving Front Range Technical Institute, and like all of our customers, we will provide you with our best professional and personalized service at all times. If at any time you have questions or concerns, please contact me at 303-555-5555 or at annbrand@xpress.com.

Sincerely,

Ann Brand

Ann Brand, President

from an individual not part of a business, then an address block may be used in place of the letterhead. (See figure 3.6 for an example letter using an address block.)

Business letters serve several purposes; thus, the paragraph structure will differ slightly from one type of letter to the next. Below are three different types of business letters (cover, complaint, and adjustment) and a discussion of the specific paragraph structure for each.

Cover Letters

A cover letter is a short correspondence that tells readers what they have before them, such as a proposal, a product, or a brochure for products or services. Cover letters accompany these items so that there is no confusion about what is being received and why the individual has received it. Cover letters for résumés are discussed in chapter 20.

Cover letters have a general format that is easy to apply to several situations. As with all business letters, either a letterhead or address block should appear at the top of the page so that a reader knows who the accompanying document or product is from. An example is shown in figure 3.5. Cover letters should include the following three elements:

1. **Opening paragraph.** This tells readers exactly what accompanies the letter and why they received it.

2. **Body paragraphs.** These can be used either to pitch sales for the product or service or to provide readers with more details about the document or product they have received.

3. **Closing paragraph.** This tells readers what the sender wants them to do with the document or product and includes contact information.

Complaint Letters

Many times, complaints are given in person, over the phone, or emailed in the heat of the moment, which are all-around bad practices. Complaints need to be thought through and worded carefully so that the writer will receive exactly what he or she wants in response to the complaint.

FIGURE 3.5 *Cover Letter*

OPEN RANGE LANDSCAPING

1234 River Road, Missoula, MT 99876, 406-555-5555
www.openrangelandscaping.com

September 27, 2007

Kevin Holmes
4545 Prairie Lane
Missoula, MT 99876

Dear Mr. Holmes:

(A) Welcome to the neighborhood and congratulations on the purchase of your new home! We know you're busy moving into your new home, and we'd like to ease your mind about the landscaping around your house. Enclosed is a brochure for Open Range Landscaping that details our extensive services.

(B) Open Range Landscaping specializes in residential landscaping needs. We have landscape architects available who can draw up plans to be as simple or as elaborate as you choose. Our prices are the most competitive in the community, and we offer a 100 percent satisfaction guarantee! Our aim is to provide you with the most beautiful scenery around your home at the most affordable prices.

(C) Please take a look through our brochure and call us today for a free consultation.

We can be reached at 406-555-5555, or you can email us at openrange@powerhouse.com. You can also visit our website at *www.openrangelandscaping.com.* We look forward to helping you make your house your dream home!

Sincerely,

Tom G. Roots

Tom G. Roots
President, Open Range Landscaping

A: The introduction tells the reader why he has received the letter—he just bought a new home and probably needs new landscaping.

B: This paragraph provides some main points the writer wants to stress to the potential customer.

C: This paragraph tells the reader what to do with the information he has received. This paragraph also provides contact information.

A complaint letter has an expected format, just like all business letters. When the conventions for a complaint letter are not followed, the end result may be an ignored or "misplaced" letter; thus, there is no resolution to the problem, because no one wants to wade through a poorly written letter that is full of emotion and not enough facts. The best way to ensure a complaint is heard and desired compensation received is to follow some simple guidelines. Most importantly, compose the letter after the initial anger or emotion about the situation has settled.

The following is a general structure for a complaint letter, which is illustrated in figure 3.6:

1. **Introduction.** In the opening paragraph of a complaint letter, give the bottom line—say what is desired and briefly state why.

2. **Body paragraph(s).** These should provide the background information and pertinent details that led up to the decision about the desired compensation or action as stated in the opening paragraph. Background information can include relevant dates, associated costs, shipping details, history of phone conversations, or a concise narrative of what happened.

3. **Conclusion.** This paragraph restates the desired outcome of the letter and provides the sender's contact information.

A complaint letter should be short—usually no more than one-page long—and contain only relevant and important details that directly relate to the decision about the desired compensation or action as stated in the opening sentences. Anything longer may not be read in its entirety or result in confusion and erroneous compensation.

While it is understandable that the context for a complaint letter is that a customer is displeased or angry, the language of a complaint letter should be professional and formal, and the tone should convey a sense of dissatisfaction, not anger or sarcasm. To word a letter using anger, sarcasm, or slang, may result in immediate rejection of compensation or the customer simply being ignored. It is important to keep in mind that there is a person at the other end receiving the letter and determining what action should be taken.

FIGURE 3.6 *Complaint Letter*

(A) Alice Hoffman
3245 Westwood Lane
Iowa City, IO 05445

September 3, 2007

Coffee Cups
(B) Attention: Mr. Daniels, Director of Customer Service
P.O. Box 32209
San Francisco, CA 80998

Dear Mr. Daniels:

(C) I would like to cancel my membership with Coffee Cups. I believe the decaffeinated coffee that has been sent to me for the past three months is mislabeled and is really regular coffee. Furthermore, I would like to be reimbursed $65.85 for the past three months of my membership when I first started receiving the mislabeled coffee.

(D) In June, I received my usual order of Breakfast Blend decaf coffee, which includes three half- pound packages. Immediately upon opening the first half pound from the June shipment, I noticed that I was jittery upon finishing my first cup of coffee. I checked the labels of the other two boxes, which were clearly labeled decaffeinated. The next morning, I fixed another pot of coffee from the first box and noticed the same thing. The following two mornings, I fixed a pot of coffee from each of the other two boxes only to experience jitters with each one.

I decided that the boxes must have been mislabeled and went to the store to buy some decaf while waiting for next month's shipment. When July's shipment came in, I went through the same routine as the previous month because I once again experienced the jitters. Please note that I did not experience this reaction with the store-bought decaf. On July 7, I called Customer Service and was told I would be shipped a new order immediately. That replacement order arrived about the same time my August order arrived, and I went through six days of trying each box only to have the same reaction each time.

(E) I no longer trust that any future coffee I receive from this club is truly decaf and I don't want to take any more chances. You may send my reimbursement for the $65.85 ($21.95 each month) at my address shown above, and please cancel my subscription to Coffee Cups. This is very sad to me, because I really enjoyed the quality of your coffee the whole time I've been a member.

Sincerely,

Alice Hoffman
Alice Hoffman

A: When a letter is from an individual, an address block such as this one is acceptable.

B: This shows she did some research and called to find out who to address this to. She is a serious customer.

C: The introduction clearly states the problem and the desired outcome.

D: The two body paragraphs tell what happened and a history of the problem.

E: The desired outcome is restated and puts the reimbursement in clear numbers.

A company is not necessarily being addressed, but a person who works for that company certainly is.

Adjustment Letters

An adjustment letter is a response to a complaint letter. There are two types of adjustment letters: those with good news and those with bad news. A good news letter is when the message of the letter gives the complainant exactly, or comparatively close to, what he or she wants. A bad news letter is when there is some discrepancy and the compensation requested in the complaint letter is not going to be given for one reason or another; thus, the writer has to break the bad news to the reader.

As with other types of business letters, the same standard conventions apply. Even if the complaint letter did not follow the standards as previously outlined and instead ended up being rude, sarcastic, and maybe even confusing, the adjustment letter still should be professional. As mentioned earlier, whenever a business letter leaves the office, that piece of correspondence is representative of the company; therefore, no personal bias, no matter the situation, should creep into the business letter.

The letter from Alice Hoffman in figure 3.6 is easy to respond to because she was courteous, clear, and provided most of the background information needed to make a decision on whether to give her the compensation she requested. A good news letter, such as the one in response to Alice's letter, may look like the one in figure 3.7.

There are times, however, when a company has to give bad news. This can involve denying an employee a raise or telling a customer there will be no compensation for a complaint. Bad news is never easy to relay, nor is it easy to receive. Therefore, writers must organize bad news letters in a certain way. The purpose is not to conceal the bad news, but to prepare the reader to receive the bad news, to break the news gently but clearly, and to immediately follow up with further explanation or evidence.

To break bad news, writers have to set up the reader to receive the news by providing the relevant factual details that led up to the decision. Bad news should not be stated in the opening paragraph. Instead, place the bad news in the body of the letter, and not at the beginning or end of a paragraph, but in the middle.

FIGURE 3.7 *Adjustment Letter*

Coffee Cups

9987 Espresso Way, P.O. Box 32209, San Francisco, CA 80998
415-555-5555, *www.coffeecups.com*

September 10, 2007

Alice Hoffman
3245 Westwood Lane
Iowa City, IO 05445
304-445-5555

Dear Ms. Hoffman:

A I was distressed to read about the discomfort you experienced these past three months with the coffee you ordered from Coffee Cups as mentioned in your letter dated September 3, 2007.

B This is of great concern to us and I have launched a full investigation into the labeling of our coffees all the way from the processing plants to our shipping warehouse. Enclosed is a check for $65.85 for the past three months. We also would like to keep you as a customer.

C When one customer experiences adverse effects due to our coffees, we take that information seriously, and consequently, we have delegated personnel to monitor the decaffeination and labeling processes carefully so that there are no mistakes.

D I personally have taken an interest in your case and have spoken with the president regarding this incident. We want to keep you as a customer and have included two packages of your regular Breakfast Blend decaffeinated coffees for you to try. If you once again experience the same problems as before, I ask that you please call me personally. We will then, in turn, gladly honor your request to end your subscription with our company. If you do not have the same reaction, I also welcome a phone call from you and will be happy to reinstate your regular monthly order.

E If at any time you experience dissatisfaction with our coffees, you are welcome to call me personally and I will do what I can to resolve the issue. I can be reached at 415-555-5555, extension 345. We sincerely apologize for the inconvenience you experienced these past three months, and if you will please try the coffees included in this package, we hope to keep you as a customer so that you can once again enjoy the quality coffees our company provides.

Sincerely,

Jeff Daniels

Jeff Daniels, Director of Customer Service

A: Begins the letter with acknowledgment of the customer's complaint on a personal level. Also mentions her letter.

B: States what action will be taken—and what the company wants.

C: Actions the company has taken as a result of her letter. This is a goodwill message that tells the reader her complaint is valid and taken seriously.

D: The company has gone over and above the compensation she requested and gave her a way to continue in the coffee club without feeling like she's giving in. She also has a personal contact now.

E: This paragraph restates the personal contact she has access to and also restates their goal, which is to keep her as a customer.

In bad news letters, the introduction acknowledges the reader's request, as shown in the example below:

Dear Ms. Smith:

We appreciate your submission of the article titled "Growing your own salsa garden" for consideration in our Spring issue of *Gardens Gone Wild.*

The body paragraph (or paragraphs) first explains background information relevant to the case. Then the decision is stated, and the bad news is delivered in a professional manner. This is immediately followed up by an explanation for the decision. It is important to use clear language to state the bad news; do not sugar-coat or dodge the bad news by being evasive. *Euphemisms*—words or phrases that cushion the blow of blunt words or phrases—may be used, but only if it is certain that the intended audience knows what those euphemisms mean. Conversely, writers do not want to appear heartless or cold and state the decision without any sense of feeling or emotion. The following is an example of how bad news may be worded in the body paragraph so that the reader can process the decision:

We receive many freelance submissions each month, and our publication would not be of the same quality without writers like you submitting their pieces. Our magazine is staffed with writers who write about 90 percent of the magazine content. Therefore, we have to make sure that the 10 percent freelance content we choose is on target with our readership. The article you submitted entails a garden that has more structure to it than our readership indicates they want in their gardens; therefore, we cannot use your article. If you would like to rewrite the story so that it has more of a wild garden motif to it, then we will gladly consider that story for inclusion in the magazine.

Conclusion paragraphs always end with a wish for goodwill, as shown in the example below:

> Thank you for considering *Gardens Gone Wild* for your freelance submissions. Please feel free to submit future pieces or rewrite the above-mentioned article and resubmit. We wish you well in your endeavors as a freelance writer.

While the reader did not get what she wanted—publication of her article in the magazine—the reply is not harsh; it clearly tells the reader that the article will not be used. It even goes so far as to extend goodwill by asking the reader to rewrite and resubmit the article in question. If structured and worded correctly, bad news letters can be just as understandable and satisfying as good news letters.

Writing for International Audiences

In most cases, American business letters prefer to have the bottom line up front. That is, readers like to know what the subject or decision is right away. Conversely, other cultures, such as Japanese and Chinese cultures, do not follow these same conventions. Before sending a business letter to an international audience, it is important to study that culture and research their expected rhetorical strategies (the structure of documents) for business correspondence. For instance, in Japanese cultures, business letters may begin with a compliment or wish for well-being. Body paragraphs provide ample detail that lead up to the bottom line being spelled out in the end of the letter.

Additionally, words have different meanings in different cultures. When writing in English to an international audience, do not use slang, euphemisms, or idioms. *Idioms* are words and phrases that have cultural meaning, but the meaning of such phrases cannot be derived from the words themselves, such as: "She's flyin' high today." In America, that phrase means she is feeling good, but a non-native speaker may not know what is implied by "flyin' high." In addition, some words that are considered harmless in English carry different meanings in other cultures, such as the word "no," which is considered rude in some Middle Eastern countries. Only research into the specific culture will reveal these important details when writing a business letter.

TECHNICAL DEFINITIONS AND DESCRIPTIONS

A writer cannot shy away from using technical terms when they are appropriate, and yet a writer cannot assume that the reader will know what the term means from personal knowledge or the context of the sentence. It is then the writer's responsibility to provide a clear definition of technical terms in the document. Short definitions can appear in a glossary, footnote, or in the context of the sentence. It also might be necessary to provide a longer definition, which is referred to as an *extended definition*. These definitions need to be broken out of the paragraph of text to appear as separate paragraphs or sidebars so as to not break up the flow of the text. An example is shown below:

Extended Definition Example

LINUX is an operating system originally released in 1991 by Linus Torvalds, a student attending University of Helsinki in Finland. Although LINUX is not traditionally as popular as Microsoft Windows or even Apple MAC OS X, it has a strong following amongst those who are computer savvy, and it is increasingly reaching beyond that niche into government, business, and computer systems. Its popularity is due to the fact that it is freely distributed, unlike its expensive counterparts. Beyond being freely distributed, it is also open source, which allows users to modify and expand the operating system to meet their needs. Essentially, LINUX has two parts: 1) the kernel, which serves as the interface between a computer's hardware and other system software; and 2) a graphical interface, allowing for easier usage, or other application programs. The graphical interface is not a requirement, though, as many computer programmers prefer to rely on the command line to execute actions. Truly, the strength behind LINUX is its ability to flex to the requirements of users and organizations.

Likewise, even a writer who is conscientious of not being overly technical in a document must still rely on technical descriptions at some point. A description will employ similar writing techniques as when writing definitions; yet the difference is that a description should include further details, such as the functionality of the object being defined or other relevant details. For example, defining a *ballast* on a boat may take only a few sentences, whereas providing a technical description for a *ballast tank* on a boat may take several pages to fully capture the functionality and dynamics of the object. Ideally, the writing for either a technical definition or description is still concise, logical, and accurate, no matter the depth or length.

Audience Analysis

Analyze readers to meet their needs; not all terms may need to be defined. Terminology that may be commonly used in a particular field may not be common to the average user. If the average user is not the target reader, then there is not a need to define technical terms extensively, if at all. Whereas, if the target reader is familiar with the term, but there are various interpretations, then it should be defined as it applies to the context of the document. Identifying the needs of the target reader will save time when the writing process actually begins because the writing will focus on precisely what the reader needs in order to understand the term in the context of the overall document.

Research

The reader is relying on the writer to provide accurate information in every definition and description; additional understanding is then gleaned from this information as the reader gets further into the document. Thus, the term needs to be well researched, with sources cited as needed. If the research is relying on interviews, then it is important to confirm that the interviewee is defining and describing the term accurately for the context of the document. This confirmation can be achieved by conducting several interviews with different experts, contacting the original interviewee for a follow-up interview, or finding previously published material on the topic. Regardless of the approach, the ultimate goal is an accurate and clear definition for the reader.

Writing Process

Consider these suggestions when writing *definitions:*

- Do not use a technical term to define another technical term. The reader should not have to constantly cross-reference words to understand one term.

- Do not repeat the term (or a variation of the term) when defining it. Instead, rely on accurate synonyms.

- Include information only relevant to the context in which the term is used, even if the word has different definitions in different situations.

- Create an analogy that has a clear connection to the topic and term being defined. The analogy should be based on a concept that the reader is already familiar with.

- Use genus and differentia to define the term. Genus is the "family" or class that the term belongs to (i.e., what larger realm the term falls into). Differentia is how the term varies from other terms in the same genus. Here is an example of a term defined in this manner:

    A British Thermal Unit (BTU) is a unit of measurement (*genus*) used in the United States for the heat output value for heating and cooling systems (*differentia*).

Consider these suggestions when writing *descriptions:*

- Analyze the term from the perspective of someone not familiar with it by using common journalism questions: who, what, where, when, how, and why. This will prompt examination from every angle in order to accurately reflect details about the term, beyond just the physical description.

- Provide historical insight about the term, as long as it will help the reader find greater understanding, without overwhelming the reader with too much information.

- Think beyond the place and time of the writing of the description so that the reader can see if the object will evolve or change going forward. It is important to note what factors might influence this change.

- Use transitions to keep the description organized and logical.

- Keep the scope of the definition in clear relation to what the reader will find of value when reviewing the rest of the document. Although there might be interesting information relevant to the term, it may not be directly related to the document and the reader's need for understanding.

As noted above, both definitions and descriptions should focus on the details relevant to providing a better understanding to the intended reader in relation to the context of the document in which the term appears. Providing this information is a reliable means to keep the reader focused on the text, rather than putting the document down and seeking answers someplace else.

MEMO PROPOSAL

To write a memo proposal, a writer must be aware of two types of documents: the memo and the proposal. Memos were discussed in detail earlier in this chapter, and full-length proposals are discussed in chapter 11; however, the format for a full-length proposal does not need to be known in order to prepare a memo proposal. It is important, though, to know what a proposal is and what purpose it serves.

Proposals are documents that offer solutions to problems. A problem is usually identified and distributed to the larger community through a *request for proposal* (RFP). The RFP *solicits* proposals. The purpose of an RFP is to identify and explain a problem that needs a solution. There are whole organizations that make it their business to offer RFPs to various communities. For example, the National Science Foundation (NSF) works with different government agencies to identify problems and publish official RFPs. The government agencies work through the NSF to offer money to other organizations, such as universities or small businesses, that can build or implement solutions to the problems. In short, RFPs advertise or solicit problems. Organizations, businesses, or individuals who think they have an answer to the problem offer their solution by submitting a proposal. Proposals also can be *unsolicited,* meaning that while no one formally asks for a solution, an organization or individual identifies a problem and offers a solution at the same time. This most often is seen in the workplace where an employee will discover a better way to conduct business and sets out to present an idea to management. One way to do that is through the memo proposal.

Memo proposals are concise, abbreviated versions of a proposed idea. The reasons a memo proposal would be chosen over a formal proposal are usually time and expectations. As mentioned previously, businesspeople are often overscheduled as it is; reading long, detailed documents is not something they have time for unless they are expecting them. When an idea is first discussed, oftentimes it will go through several phases before becoming part of a full-length proposal. Sometimes it starts out as a memo that brings management's attention to the problem and a possible solution.

A memo proposal is usually one page in length and straightforward about identifying a problem and proposing a solution. One page is not enough to explain an entire idea in detail, but it is plenty of room to grab the audience's attention, make a decision to move forward, and request a full-length researched proposal, or alternatively, to pass on the idea. Because there is only one page in which to convince the reader, the information in a memo proposal has to be accurate and concise while also providing enough information to give a full picture of the proposed idea.

Memo Proposal Format

The following are guidelines for preparing a memo proposal, one section and paragraph at a time.

Date, To, and From Lines. Use the Date, To, and From lines as was shown in the memo format in figure 3.1 Interoffice Memo and as in this example:

> **Date:** October 13, 2007
>
> **To:** Bill King, Marketing Director; Alice Monroe, Operations Manager; and Craig Whitmore, Finance Director
>
> **From:** Daryl Smith, Customer Service Representative

Because a memo proposal is usually the beginnings of an idea, the audience should be narrowed down to only those who can actually make a decision about whether to move forward with the idea. Bringing in too many people early on can work against someone proposing an idea because there is more chance for others to object, even those who do not have decision-making authority.

Subject Line. The subject line is brief but descriptive about the idea in the memo proposal. The example below shows a poorly written subject line along with a better, revised one:

> *Poor subject line:* My idea to increase the amount of recycling in the office

> *Better subject line:* Recycling program to increase company profits

Introduction. The opening paragraph states directly what the problem is and how it will be solved. This section can be one to three sentences, depending on the subject, as shown in the following example:

> Implementing a company-wide recycling program at Environ can increase its annual profits through name recognition. Because Environ is an environmental engineering firm, it makes sense that the company engages in a recycling program that demonstrates to the community and potential customers its commitment to the environment. A high-profile recycling program will prove beneficial to the company, the community, and the global environment.

Body Paragraphs. The body paragraph (or paragraphs) should explain why the problem is a problem, specifically for the audience being addressed. Research may be used in a memo proposal, but it is usually brief, such as simply providing statistics, and not as extensive as would be expected in a full-length proposal. The body also describes the need for a solution and why it is in the company's best interest to implement the proposed solution, such as in the following example:

> Preserving the environment on a local and global scale is paramount to the public, and businesses that show their commitment to this cause can increase profits while actively participating in a

worthwhile community service. This has been shown to be effective for even the most environmentally harmful companies, such as mining, gas, and oil companies.

Continue by explaining the solution, once again in terms of what is important to the audience:

Such a program can be as simple as providing recycling bins next to all trash containers in the building. Furthermore, an Environ grassroots service that collects the recycling in the entire building and delivers it to the nearest recycling plant will go a long way toward name recognition and community service in the local area. While this additional service impacts the operating budget, the goodwill and advertisement Environ receives for providing this service will outweigh the expenses. It is estimated that within one year the additional revenues received from the name recognition of this service will outweigh all of the costs associated with the program.

Conclusion. Close by reiterating the main idea and telling the reader what is expected as a result of the proposal, as in this example:

Environ is concerned about the environment and that is part of its business. To those customers who are familiar with environmental engineering, this commitment is obvious; but for the public, the work within the company is obscure. By actively participating in a local recycling program with Environ's name attached to it, the public suddenly becomes aware of not only the company, but of its services, which will increase business and profits.

With your permission, I would like to take the lead on this project to present a fully researched proposal to other management personnel and to the board of directors about a company-wide and company-sponsored recycling program. Thank you for your consideration.

As the example passages show, there are no comprehensive details about a budget, or even operations for such a program, but the idea is planted and the writer tells the readers exactly what is expected as a result of this memo proposal. The readers have enough information to, at the very least, meet with the employee to ask questions and decide whether to proceed.

ABSTRACTS

Abstracts are short passages that provide an overview of long, multifaceted documents such as research articles, full-length proposals, and technical reports. Abstracts are used to give readers a synopsis of article or report content, which means they serve different functions for different audiences. The first is for an intended audience who may or may not be familiar with the document content. If readers were expecting the document, then the abstract serves as a refresher or confirmation of what is supposed to be covered in the paper. If, however, readers are not expecting the document, such as a manager who finds an unsolicited proposal on his or her desk one morning and asks, "What is this?" there are two sources this type of reader would turn to to answer that question: a cover letter and the document abstract. The other audience type that uses abstracts is readers who are searching for information. In this case, abstracts provide a valuable service in that readers can determine an article's or report's relevance to their own work by reading the abstract instead of having to read or skim through a lengthy paper.

Abstracts have a specific form even though it is generally assumed that they are merely short paragraphs that tell what the full paper is about. An effective abstract will answer questions such as the following:

- What is the problem, or what is the subject of the paper?

- What is the solution to the problem, or what is the purpose of discussing this subject?

- What are the general results of applying this solution to this problem, or what new information has this article contributed to the subject under discussion?

As discussed earlier, American readers like to know crucial information up front and sometimes that information is gleaned from the abstract; however, the abstract serves only to whet the reader's appetite and should not provide details about any of the questions mentioned above. This is where concise writing skills are most needed. Generally, an abstract tells readers the *scope* of the paper as well, which means it tells readers what will or will not be covered in the document. Here is an example abstract for a research paper:

> Employers spend billions of dollars annually to improve employee writing skills. Higher education's response to this problem has been to add a subsequent writing course to freshman composition in many degree programs, most in the form of introductory business or technical writing. In the hopes of giving students one more chance at learning much needed writing skills, the business or technical writing course has a tall order to fill. Further, these introductory courses are becoming a catchall to prepare students for every form of writing known in the workplace regardless of career. The inevitable fallout of a course that tries to put all workplace writing under one umbrella will be students who are inundated with forms and styles and will still fail to be proficient writers in their distinct career fields.
>
> A sequence of interdisciplinary advanced writing classes—beyond freshman composition and business or technical writing—is needed to adequately prepare students for workplace writing. The objective is not to simply increase the number of writing courses, but to sequence classes so they build on the writing demands of a particular career. This paper discusses how an interdisciplinary approach to writing instruction produces graduates who are better prepared for writing on the job than those who learn writing separate from their content courses.

LONGER, COMPLEX FORMS OF WRITING DEFINED

As noted in the beginning of this book, part I is composed with beginning writers in mind. The two-part feature of this book is meant to provide beginning writers with basic introductory information relevant to technical communication without overwhelming them with the intricate and voluminous details that can be inherent to technical writing. In keeping with this concept, the following forms of writing are generally long and complex, and sometimes can take months or even up to a year to write depending on the situation. The purpose of this part of the chapter on communication forms is to provide beginning writers with a working definition of these various documents. Each document type is covered in ample detail in chapters 10 and 11.

Proposals

Proposals may be written for a variety of reasons, but all proposals have the same basic definition: a document that requests approval or funding for a project. Proposals can be complex, such as a billion-dollar missile defense contract for the government that would employ thousands of people in several locations throughout the United States and in foreign countries as well. But, on a smaller scale, consider the following example:

> A technology manager for a small university writes up a document explaining the benefits of using *Second Life* in classroom instruction. Included in the document is the cost, how the program can be integrated into the classroom, the benefits of using *Second Life,* and a persuasive statement encouraging the administration to use this program. Also outlined is a request for the writer to begin work on the project.

This document also is considered a proposal because it includes a section asking the administration to approve using *Second Life* in classroom instruction and for the technology manager to move forward and begin work on the project. A proposal must convince the audience of the project's value as well as the credibility and capability of the individual (or organization) who will complete the work.

As discussed earlier, two major types of proposals are solicited and unsolicited proposals. A *solicited proposal* is a response to a request. Commonly, an organization will send out an RFP by mail or publish it through another media source. A billion-dollar missile defense project is an example of a proposal that would respond to a government RFP. A solicited proposal may be completed on a local level as well. For example, an employer may ask employees to write a proposal for adding a health club near the office.

An *unsolicited proposal* is written, although the recipient has not requested the proposal. This type of proposal often must first convince the recipient that a problem or need exists. For example, an employee may write an unsolicited proposal to a supervisor outlining the need for additional employee parking even though the supervisor did not ask for this information. Writing an unsolicited proposal brings the parking problem to the attention of the manager and also offers a solution to a problematic situation.

The contents of a proposal are extensive and change according to the audience and subject of the document, which will be discussed in ample detail in chapter 11; however, the six basic sections of a proposal are the following:

1. **Executive summary.** This is a one-page summary of the proposal that briefly states the problem, solution, and why the company or individual that is putting forth the proposal is the best in what it is offering.

2. **Need statement.** This statement defines and describes all aspects of the problem relevant to the interests of the audience.

3. **Project description.** This discusses the solution as put forth in the proposal and how it meets all of the needs of the audience.

4. **Budget.** The resources the company or individual will need to implement the proposed solution is outlined in this section.

5. **Organizational information.** This section includes either a company profile, the biographies of the individuals who will work on the project, or both.

6. **Conclusion.** This wraps up the entire proposal, which can be a recap of the problem, the proposed solution, and the credentials of the organization or individuals involved in the proposed project.

Technical Reports

Technical communication most often is associated with the "technical report." But just what is a technical report? It comes in various formats depending on the purpose, audience, and writer. Defined below are four common types of technical reports: the feasibility, recommendation, progress, and empirical research report. All are covered extensively in chapter 10.

Feasibility Study and Report. Feasibility studies serve two functions. First, a feasibility study can determine if a proposed solution to an identified problem is possible given certain guidelines; and second, it can help determine the best solution when several possibilities are being considered. A typical situation is shown in the following example:

> American Insurance Company (AIC) recently looked at its employee leave and attrition statistics and found an increase in the number of days employees are taking for sick and personal time off, as well as an increase in job turnover, both of which cost the company more money each year. The other trend noticed within the company is the changing demographics of more employees having young or school-aged children. Through an employee survey, it was discovered that over 50 percent of the leave taken was due to child illness or the employee being unable to find childcare for one reason or another. This also was stated as a top reason for why employees had to find jobs elsewhere. After much discussion, AIC now faces a couple of viable options: 1) open and fund an on-site day care, or 2) work with a private day care to help meet employee needs regarding their children so that employees take less time off from work.

American Insurance Company knows it wants to do something, but what it needs to learn is which option is best in terms of overall profit for the company, and furthermore, whether that solution would actually be possible to implement within the next six months. What AIC needs is a detailed feasibility study.

First, the company would weigh both solutions against a set of *criteria* to decide which one is best for the company's overall profit margin. Criteria in a feasibility study are the guidelines that one must work within to implement a solution. They can include money, a timeline, health department guidelines, office space, and certifications. In the case above with AIC, the company would conduct a feasibility study to determine which of the two options can meet all or most of its guidelines. Given its money and time constraints (the criteria), AIC has to decide if it is in the company's best interest to build a day care or would contracting with an existing day care meet its needs now and in the long run. The subsequent feasibility report is the document that presents decision makers with the results of the feasibility study and includes a recommendation. By using this report, decision makers can decide which option they want to approve and go forward with. Often, the recommended solution ends up being the subject of a full-length proposal.

The structure of a feasibility report will vary depending on the subject and audience; however, the following five sections are almost always included:

1. **Introduction.** This clearly defines and describes the problem as it relates to the values of the audience. Each possible solution should also be described briefly. Tell the audience what this report will do and give the bottom line.

2. **Criteria and discussion.** These are found within the body of the report. Criteria are the factors by which all solutions are measured against. Discussion explains how the criteria were applied against each possible solution.

3. **Results.** This section that tells how each solution stood up to the list of criteria.

4. **Recommendation.** Unlike the results section, this area advises readers to choose one particular solution.

5. **Conclusion.** All reports should end with a formal conclusion that wraps up the report, which in this case can be reiterating the recommendation with a brief explanation.

It may seem like there is a lot of repetition in the sections as described above, and in truth, there is. The reason for this is that decision makers may look at only certain sections of reports because they only want to know select information, and they expect to find the answers in those sections. Repetition should never be word-for-word from one section to the next, but rather the same idea carried throughout the report and written in various ways.

Recommendation Report. A recommendation report is just that—a report that tells decision makers that a particular course of action should be taken. What precedes this report is usually a feasibility study and possibly a feasibility report; however, a recommendation report often bypasses the feasibility report and shortcuts right to the recommendation. This type of report is typically submitted to high-level or executive management who may not have the time to consider all of the options presented in a feasibility study, but who delegate that task to someone else. Oftentimes, high-level or executive management only wants to know the recommendation of those they put in charge. In this case, a recommendation report can contain the following three elements:

1. **Introduction.** The problem is clearly defined and described as it relates to the values of the audience. A recommendation for one particular course of action is given in this introduction.

2. **Criteria and discussion.** Brief discussion about criteria and other possible solutions can be included here, but the emphasis is on how the recommended course of action fits the needs of the company.

3. **Conclusion.** This wraps up the report, which in this case can be reiterating the recommendation with a brief explanation.

Progress Report. A progress report is meant to inform readers about the status of a project. Such a report usually is required when projects are complex and take a considerable amount of time to complete.

In the case of AIC, mentioned under the feasibility report section, the time frame is six months to implement the new day care solution. If the company decides to build an on-site day care facility, there is a tremendous amount of work to be done. A progress report would keep decision makers informed about space renovations, certifications on the space, hiring certified staff, health department concerns, equipment purchases, daily operations, and anything else related to the project until it is complete. Progress reports tell readers (usually those who funded or approved the project) what work has to be done, what has been completed to date, what is left to be completed, and if new issues or problems have been encountered. Readers of progress reports often are familiar with the project, and because of this, the following four elements are usually part of these reports:

1. **Introduction.** This section tells readers what project is being reported on and the time frame covered in the report.

2. **Body.** The body includes three sections: 1) work that has been completed to date; 2) work yet to be completed; and 3) problems encountered along the way.

3. **Recommendation.** This is based off of the body sections in that a writer would possibly recommend a new course of action or new timeline based on the progress of the work thus far and what problems, if any, have to be dealt with.

4. **Conclusion.** A formal conclusion should wrap up the report, which in this case could be reiterating any changes in the work plan since the last report.

Empirical Research Report. This type of report is often used in the sciences, such as engineering, biology, chemistry, and geology, to prove a scientific hypothesis and relay information about how an experiment was conducted, while also providing results, recommendations, or conclusions. The final report is the result of original scientific research.

Empirical research reports are usually generated for technical expert audiences who are interested in the validity of scientific studies in their field. To them, the methodology, which explains the methods of setting up the experiment, is as important as the results and conclusions. An empirical research report gives historical or background information about a subject, explains how an original research study was conducted, and reports the findings of the experiment. With that in mind, the following five sections are usually included in empirical research reports:

1. **Introduction.** This states the problem and hypothesis of the research study. Background is also part of the introduction, which includes the history of the problem, the original research presented in the report, and other studies on the subject.

2. **Methodology.** This section describes how the experiment was set up, and can give clues as to how certain results were obtained.

3. **Results.** This section reports results according to how the research was set up. For instance, if the methodology section describes a control group, group A, and then group B, the results section should report findings first for the control group, then for group A, and lastly for group B.

4. **Recommendation.** While a recommendation is not always part of an empirical report, if it is, a writer would state what course of action is recommended using information from the methodology and results section as support for the writer's suggestion. This section also may note where further research needs to be done going forward.

5. **Conclusion.** This wraps up the report. This section could restate special results that were obtained in the experiment, indicate a lack of unique results, or further emphasize a recommendation if one was given.

Policy and Procedure Manuals

A policy and procedure manual addresses both the needs of the company or organization and the employee or member by clearly stating the rules that everyone is to follow; it also details the consequences for not following those rules. In turn, employees do not have to guess as to what is expected, while managers have grounds for enforcing recognized protocols.

A policy and procedure manual can extend well beyond just explaining rules, though. It can be a means of welcoming a new employee to the company, while keeping established employees well informed. Furthermore, it is a resource for information on a variety of issues that all employees encounter. A list of suggested topics to cover in a policy and procedure manual is shown in figure 3.8.

FIGURE 3.8 *Policy and Procedure Manual Topics*

Policies	Procedures	Other
Expected Work Hours	Entering the Building	Benefits
Appropriate Attire	Accessing Information	Facilities
Taking Vacation/Sick Days	Contacting Managers	Holiday/Payday Calendar
Disability	Logging On to Computer	List of Contacts

Every policy and procedure manual differs with respect to the extent of information covered. What to include and exclude is often dictated by management and the needs of the company. Minimally, the eight sections listed below should be included:

1. **Introduction.** This section should clearly set the tone for the manual and the company as a whole.

2. **Table of contents.** This allows readers to easily navigate to the information most pertinent to their needs.

3. **Contact information.** This section should be listed logically so an employee knows who to contact for further information on a given topic.

4. **Policies.** This section details policies that are necessary to document along with the consequences for not adhering to these policies.

5. **Procedures.** This defines the procedures related to tasks that employees are likely to undertake while with the company.

6. **Employee benefits.** This details benefits and additional information not included in the previous sections.

7. **Conclusion.** This should leave a positive impression on the reader.

8. **Sign-off verification form.** This is a form that each employee must sign after reading and understanding the policy and procedure manual.

Chapter 10 covers the above sections in more detail, along with other sections that might be of interest to various companies. Once each section is written, it needs to be reviewed and authorized by legal and human resources representatives, along with anyone in management who will need to enforce the policies. Furthermore, careful consideration needs to be given to how each section will be displayed in the manual.

It is best to establish a standard design and use it on every page of the manual. This design might be based on standards previously developed by the company, including colors, fonts, and layout, or it may be an altogether original format. If there is flexibility in what design can be used, the manual should have clear organization with proper use of headings and subheadings. Although not required, a numbering system for each section is an ideal way to help the reader easily navigate through the manual. White space should be used effectively to allow a reader's eyes to rest, but not so much so that it looks like content is missing. Finally, it is important to consider how the manual will be printed or displayed electronically. This will impact decisions about where to put content and which colors to use.

A writer needs to create the policy and procedure manual to be inviting and readable, yet full of content needed by the reader. Although most readers may not read the manual from cover to cover, it is the best means to establish common ground about expectations and benefits associated with the company.

Technical Instructions

A set of instructions can be simple, such as installing a general purpose lightbulb, or complex, such as installing a home theater. In all cases, though, the instructions need to be straightforward and usable, because the reader is likely to be frustrated by the time he or she resorts to reading the instructions. Knowing the intended reader's possible state of mind will compel the writer to design the document to meet anticipated needs. A general list of characteristics that should be reflected in a set of instructions is shown in figure 3.9; more in-depth explanations of required and optional characteristics are covered in chapter 10.

Although audience analysis dictates what is truly required in a set of instructions, a writer can begin the writing process with a general idea of

FIGURE 3.9 *Instruction Set Characteristics*

Design	Writing
• Numbered steps • Clear visuals, including tables, charts, and graphics • Bold and obvious warnings and cautions • Prominent headings and subheadings	• Begin each step with an action verb (or direct order) • Use parallelism when phrasing a step • Keep explanatory material separate from direction material • Write with a formal or informal tone throughout, as dictated by audience analysis • Be confident in every step written

what is expected in the document. There are standard sections that most readers will either expect to see or will benefit from, even if they are not expected sections. Below are five sections that should be included in a basic set of instructions:

1. **Title.** This should specifically and briefly describe what the document is covering.

2. **Introduction.** This expands on the title, and clearly tells the reader what the expectations and outcomes of the process are.

3. **List of tools.** This should encompass the tools or other required materials a reader will need while executing the instructions.

4. **Steps.** This should list the actual steps or instructions of the process.

5. **Conclusion.** This will help the reader know the process is complete and what outcome the reader should be experiencing at this point.

There is a variety of other sections that can be included in a set of instructions—these are covered in chapter 10—but the sections listed above are a good basis to begin with. To make each section really meaningful to a reader, thorough research on the topic needs to be done.

Research for a set of instructions should begin with previously written material so that the writer can learn from that material's strengths and weaknesses. The research then will move toward accessing relevant material from subject matter experts, either in published form or through interviews. The writer needs to be confident in his or her own understanding of the process, because the reader is completely dependent on the information in the instructions. To find this confidence, a writer can do more than research publications and conduct interviews; if doing or watching the process being done is a viable option, then a writer should capitalize on that opportunity. This will lead to an accurate and reliable document for the intended reader.

Overall, a writer needs to approach instruction writing with patience. Define the intended readers so that the instructions are tailored to their expectations. Research needs to be accountable. A step cannot be missed or inaccurate, and the document's design should be engaging and easy to follow. It is the writer's responsibility to create and uphold a set of instructions with integrity and reliability.

User Guides

A user guide is required documentation for products and services that typically seem complex to customers. This guide is a means to explain every feature and effective use of the product. Although a set of instructions may be written to explain processes involved with using the product, a user guide presents those instructions along with extensive details about every aspect of the product. This guide is the documentation customers turn to when looking for in-depth insights about the product they have purchased.

With all this in mind, writing a user guide is a large task for any writer to produce. Taken a step at a time, the guide can be effectively created to meet the needs of target readers. The first step is researching the required content of the guide. The easiest research effort generally entails tracking down what already has been written about the product, including finding previously written guides, product development proposals, technical specifications, and marketing materials. This will help set a baseline to begin writing with. Even more important than previous documents are interviews with subject matter experts, including those who worked on developing the product and customer support representatives who will respond to concerns about the product. These individuals can provide insight into the nuances of the product and any processes involved in owning the product. Keep in mind that the research endeavor may continue as the writing process begins and further clarification or details are needed to give a detailed written description of the product.

The content of the guide needs to be detailed and visual. If few or no graphics are available for certain aspects, then the text should give the reader a clear sense of what should be seen when viewing and using the product. Whenever possible, though, use clear graphics or photos to help the reader with the visualization process while reading the guide. Each graphic must be labeled and located near the supporting text explaining the graphic.

Beyond including graphics, consider including the eight sections noted below; more sections can be included and are covered further in chapter 10:

1. **Title.** This should be specific for the product.

2. **Preface.** This is a product overview to introduce the product to the reader in a general manner, while still giving a clear idea of what can be expected from the product during use.

3. **Table of contents.** This is a listing of all sections and subsections in the guide.

4. **List of materials.** This lists all materials, either included or required, and appear at the beginning of the guide.

5. **Product description.** This describes the product and includes related graphics to help the reader understand the product from every angle and function.

6. **Operating procedures.** This details any steps for setting up and using the product, and also reviews precautionary measures the reader needs to keep in mind while using the product.

7. **Troubleshooting.** This section describes some potential negative situations a reader might encounter when setting up or using the product and possible solutions.

8. **Contact information.** Information for customer and technical support should be listed, including email addresses, websites, telephone numbers, and addresses (if applicable).

Every section is developed to meet the needs of the intended reader and reduce any point of confusion about the product. If a customer cannot understand a product, the customer is more likely to return the product or not purchase future products from the company. Another way to keep a customer loyal by way of the user guide is to design the document to be easy to use and visually inviting.

The overall design needs to take into account what size the guide will be published, because this will affect the margins, line length, and graphic placement. The writer must consciously write paragraphs that are short and easy to read, no matter at what size the guide is ultimately printed. Readers have difficulty following and remembering long paragraphs, which makes them more likely to skim the text. Important information might be missed when the reader begins skimming. It is the writer's responsibility to design a guide that discourages skimming, while still highlighting the most important aspects that the reader needs to walk away with. Beyond writing concise sentences and paragraphs, the use of headings, graphics, and text boxes are means to achieve this goal.

The patience and persistence of the writer developing a user guide will be rewarded with customer loyalty and fewer complaints by customers using the product. Clear, detailed, and well-organized writing is the best means to develop a user guide that customers will use and appreciate.

CHAPTER 4

Research

R esearch is part of the writing process that does not change when moving from composition to more functional writing like technical communication. Research in technical communication is used for various purposes, such as supporting claims, developing hypotheses, and providing background, specifications, or cost information. With the overload of information available in electronic format, especially via the Internet, discussions on research have grown exponentially, too. This chapter focuses on where to find information, how to evaluate sources, and how to integrate research into reports or other forms of communication used in technical writing and presentations.

Before beginning to research, it is important that a writer clearly understand what sources can be used and how to employ them appropriately. There are two major types of research: primary and secondary. *Primary* research is considered firsthand or original source information. For instance, a witness is a primary source, as is original research (when the person who actually conducts the research writes up the results). *Secondary* research is when the information has been filtered from a primary source into another medium for others to use and interpret. Newspaper stories and some books or journal articles that refer to others' research are considered secondary sources. Depending on the subject, there are times when primary research is deemed more credible than secondary information. Likewise, secondary research has its benefits in that it has stood the test of time and peer review. Both source types can be found in multiple places, such as traditional libraries or the Internet.

TRADITIONAL LIBRARIES

Traditional brick-and-mortar libraries now have most, if not all, of their resources in an electronic database known as an *online catalog*. This should not be confused with an online database, which is part of the electronic resources offered through both traditional and online libraries. An online catalog is a computerized listing of all resources available through that library branch—it replaces the old card-catalog system. Online catalogs give location and basic source information for books, periodicals, CDs, DVDs, newspapers, and any other sources stored or available through that library. The catalog is usually accessed through library computers available upon entering the building or by the reference desk, though universities and larger libraries often allow students and patrons to access these services remotely.

Traditional libraries offer complete library services to the community, and they still have a few resources that are not available online. For instance, they house historical collections and books and other materials that are not yet available in digital format. While many publishers are offering ebook options for newer publications, there are still books and other resources that have not yet made their way into electronic format; however, they are available through brick-and-mortar community libraries or school libraries. The benefits of going to a traditional library to check out materials are that, if available, the resources are obtained immediately, and, if one cannot find information readily, a reference librarian is available to offer assistance. Two other services most often associated with brick-and-mortar libraries are the reference books section and interlibrary loan, although both now are available through online libraries as well.

Reference Books

Reference books usually contain compiled statistical or factual information, such as encyclopedias, dictionaries, bibliographies, almanacs, yearbooks, atlases, and indexes. They usually cannot be checked out of a library because they are meant to be used to look up or cross-reference specific information and not read from cover to cover like other books. Some reference books, such as almanacs and atlases, also are available online, so the traditional reference library section is not the only place where these resources can be found. For technical communicators, some important reference books include style guides, grammar books, technical writing handbooks, and other guides for the field in which the technical communicator works, such as standards and specifications or glossaries.

Interlibrary Loan

This service is available when libraries collaborate with one another and share resources. Budget constraints affect how many books or other resources a library can purchase, and building constraints dictate how many resources a library can physically hold. These constraints limit what is available to patrons in one location; however, an interlibrary loan service allows library members to order books, copies of periodical articles, or other resources from another library within the vicinity, or nationwide, and have any of these research items shipped to their local library. Because items have to be mailed, there is usually a waiting period anywhere from a few days to a few weeks, so timing and planning are essential when using this service. Some libraries also might charge a fee for shipping the book from out of state. Interlibrary loan now is available through online libraries as well.

USING THE INTERNET

Many people like the convenience of using the Internet to conduct research because they do not have to leave their home or office to go to a library. While the Internet is valuable for research, the key to finding appropriate and credible sources is to use the tools on the Internet appropriately. The Internet is not one giant entity that has one search engine; it is actually a system of worldwide networks with numerous tools available to help users search for and find information in these networks, as well as communicate with one another.

Search Engines

Most users are familiar with *search engines*. Basically, a search engine is a software program that allows users to search a database of websites. There are numerous search engines available for anyone to use. The key is to know which one to use depending on the focus of the research. The examples below are by no means a comprehensive list of search engines and directories, nor are certain sites recommended over others; they are included to give readers an idea of the variety of general search engines and specialized directories available. Some general all purpose search engines include the following:

- Alltheweb.com
- Ask.com
- Dogpile.com
- Google.com
- MSN.com
- Yahoo.com

Specialized directories use the larger search engines and filter the information to give more focused results. Examples of the various types of directories and specialized search engines include the following:

- **Findarticles.com** for a list of articles on multiple subjects. Some articles are free and others require a fee.

- **Findlaw.com** for legal information

- **Healthfind.com** for health and medical information

- **Hotbot.com** and **infoseek.com** for academic searches

- **Scholar.google.com** for materials such as technical abstracts, research reports, peer-reviewed journal articles, and a host of other academic resources

- **Scirus.com** for scientific information only

- **Usa.gov** for a list of government agencies and other related websites

Credible Information

Search engines are tools to help users find relevant websites for whatever words they type into the search box; however, results are not guaranteed regarding

Internet Searching

Google and other major search engines have begun essentially policing the content on the Internet to a certain extent. These search engines are not writing legally binding citations for the offenders or in any way flagging bad websites. Rather, websites that have suspicious content typically do not make it into the beginning ranks of search results for users. Popular search engines have realized that users do not need or want every single website related to a search term; instead, users want the best websites pertinent to a search term. If users continually encounter lists of websites with bad or irrelevant content, the users will turn to other search engines with hopes of better results.

What users do not see during the search process are the algorithms continually employed to rank Web pages and assign values to them. Along with the ranking system, search engines use text-matching to produce results that are high ranking and relevant to the search term. The specifics of how this process is implemented are kept secret by Google and other search engines as a means to keep their stakes in the industry, yet their effectiveness can be seen with every Internet search.

the credibility of the site or the information. Anyone can put up a website and say anything he or she wants, and generally, search engines do not filter sites for trustworthy information, although this technology is evolving (see sidebar). Besides, what one person considers trustworthy, someone else might consider a hoax. When it comes to academic and professional writing, credibility is directly linked to *accuracy*. Accurate information is unbiased, objective, factual material. *Unbiased* means that there is no particular motivation for reporting certain ideas or results; *objective* means no personal bias is present in the information; and *factual* means that the material has gone through experimental processes or has been peer reviewed. *Theoretical* material also is considered credible only when it is based off of other credible research. To find credible information on the Internet means researchers have to know what purpose certain domains serve, as well as understand the concepts behind the forms and resources available through this medium.

Online Databases. Electronic or *online databases* are indexes of periodical or newspaper articles, citations, and abstracts that are retrievable through the Internet. They can be accessed through membership at school libraries or community libraries. Online databases are either interdisciplinary or discipline-specific for professions in medicine, law, psychology, business, education, communications, and more. Technical communicators especially may use databases such as the following:

- **Academic Search Elite** for interdisciplinary scholarly articles

- **Business Source Premier** for discipline-specific articles on commerce and industry

- **Communication and Mass Media Complete (CMMC)** for discipline-specific articles in communications and mass media

- **Lexis-Nexis Academic** for interdisciplinary articles on news, business, medical, and legal issues

- **Master File Premier** for interdisciplinary articles on general references, health, education, and science

Access to these and all other databases is determined by the library used. Libraries pay annual fees to grant their patrons access to these databases, but not all libraries have subscriptions to all available databases. Furthermore, a user may not be able to access anything more than the abstract or citation if the library does not have a subscription to the relevant periodical.

Commercial Sites (.com)

Commercial websites serve a purpose—they sell products or services. In order to sell products and services, companies have a variety of strategies. One strategy is to use research to prove their product or service is better than all others. This research is sometimes displayed as an article or what otherwise looks like empirical research reports. There are two main problems when using research found on commercial sites. The first is that some companies will claim they have conducted "independent studies" to create results that most likely will be in favor of the product they are marketing. However, because no one outside the company knows the particulars of how the study was designed, the results from such studies may be biased or contrived. As previously discussed in chapter 3, the methods of such studies are essential when analyzing empirical research reports for their accuracy and validity. The second problem with conducting research using these sites is that commercial sites usually have biased information, considering that the motivating factor behind what they report is the sale of their product and the company's profit margin. When conducting research for school or work, reasons for referencing commercial sites should be pinpointed to a particular use and not to obtain general information about a subject.

Wikis. A wiki is a virtual and dynamic source where anyone who registers on a wiki site becomes an "editor" and can alter the information on that site. This kind of open access allows registered users to post a wide range of material, which can include personal experiences that might go outside the scope of the general definition of a word or concept. This openness can give readers a more comprehensive or realistic understanding of the subject being searched. While these sites are heavily monitored and guarded by those involved in a particular subject, the problem with using these sites is that faulty or cynical information can be posted. In the time that it takes for another registered user to spot the addition of this material and go back in and change it, another unsuspecting or naive user who knows little to nothing about the subject can access the site, read the false information, and leave the site thinking the information is accurate. For instance, on wiki dictionary sites, it is not unusual to find satirical definitions, such as using politicians' names under words such as "hypocrite" or "liar." While these examples seem tame and innocent on one hand, it is the dynamic concept behind wikis that makes these sites generally unreliable as accurate research sources for school and work.

Newsgroups. A newsgroup is a forum where the general public can post articles about any subject and have discussions about them. The benefit of newsgroups is that, when searching for information, users can post questions and usually within minutes have a response from someone around the world. As with wikis, this information is often personal or opinionated and cannot be considered unbiased, objective, or factual. While articles posted on newsgroups can be used as research sources, it is wise to consider the source of the article. Just because it is deemed an article or report does not mean it is credible information. One thing a newsgroup can do is give users ideas for how to narrow the focus of their research subject.

RSS Feeds Offer New Ways to Receive News, Blog, or Other Electronic Updates

A Really Simple Syndication or Rich Site Summary (RSS) feed is a new way to receive news, blogs, or journal updates. RSS feeds can even be customized to download content relevant to certain search criteria. Although some browsers or email programs can accommodate feeds, sometimes certain readers have to be downloaded in order to view RSS content. Yahoo! Bloglines and Google allow users to add feeds from various websites to their home page. The following three professional websites have RSS feeds for technical *communications* articles:

- *http://tc.eserver.org/*
- *http://stc-on.org/online/*
- *www.techwr-l.com/*

Listservs. A listserv is an electronic discussion group similar to a newsgroup. People become members of listservs that are dedicated to the discussion of certain topics, such as technical writing, mass communications, certain aspects of the health and legal fields, and many other subjects. Discussion on listservs is distributed via email to all members of the group. One benefit of belonging to listservs is that, depending on the subject, other members could be working experts in a particular field and provide inquiring members with ideas about where to obtain credible information regarding a query. Once again, it is not the individual replies that should be used as research sources because these often contain personal opinions; however, a member of a listserv can certainly generate leads for finding other credible sources.

Blogs. A blog is an electronic personal diary. Like anything else on the Internet, blogs can be about any subject. They are, however, personal even if they are about a company or an otherwise objective subject, such as geology or medicine, because they are one person's view, experience, or opinion. The most important thing to remember about a blog is that it is one person's experience published for the world to read. Soldiers in conflicts or wars often blog their daily activities in combat. Employees blog their daily activities on the job. By saying that a blog is not a reliable research source in no way is a reflection on the individual posting the blog. Like a wiki, it is the nature of the medium, and in this case that means it is a personal forum, which makes it biased information.

Other Sites. Noncommercial websites (.gov, .edu, and .org) are usually thought to have more reliable information. While these sites are not selling a product or service per se, and are not generally viewed as being financially vested in promoting anything in particular, they do have an agenda. These sites can be used to explore information about the government, a college, or an organization; however, material posted on these sites is generally favorable because, even though they are not commercial, they still have an image to uphold, and that influences what material is posted. Presenting biased material is somewhat lessened though because credible organizations have guidelines they must adhere to in order to exist. These standards affect what they allow on their websites as well. In some instances, these sites even will offer community services, such as providing databases of publications, in which case it is not the site itself that should be evaluated, but each individual article retrieved from its database.

When it comes to using the Internet for research, users want to consider the source as well as the medium in which information is found. Like any form of media, the Internet is a portal for communication and has its own forms. The nature or concepts behind these forms (such as newsgroups, listservs, and blogs) make the information sometimes rather dubious. As mentioned in several of the categories above, many of these forms are a great way to help narrow a search or get new ideas for a research subject; however, given that much of this information is not presented in what is considered an official format, such as publication in a peer-reviewed journal, the material can be considered questionable.

So what is credible information? In most cases, readers expect to see information that has gone through some form of peer review, such as articles from professional journals, discipline-specific magazines, books, newspapers (to some extent), and interviews with experts in a field. This information can be found in various places on the Internet, so when this type of material is retrieved over the Internet, the next step is to evaluate the source individually.

EVALUATING SOURCES

Sources obtained from online databases or publications found in a library, such as in the periodical section or even a book, are generally considered more credible than most Internet sources. While this is a general rule that can be taken for granted to some extent, it is always a good idea to evaluate the relevance, usefulness, and even the credibility of the source itself. A few things to consider when evaluating a source are the credibility of the author and the author's expertise with the subject matter, timeliness of publication, and integrity of the content.

Credibility of the Author

Just because someone is a published author does not automatically give that person credibility for what he or she writes. Professionals have areas of expertise, and while they can certainly cross over into other fields, their knowledge and experience with a subject are what matter most. Here is where the Internet would be a good tool to use to research the author and the author's background regarding his or her subject expertise. If no information is readily found, that does not mean the author is a fake; it might mean the author is relatively new to the field. In that case, check to see what sources are being cited and how the author is using this information. If someone with no other credentials besides a single book or article is dismissing established professionals who have been in the field for a long time, then it is a good idea to keep that resource in reserve until the claims can be verified. This is not to say that anyone who disagrees with traditional theories or otherwise accepted facts is not credible; still, it is prudent to research the claims of such a person in detail before accepting them as credible. Even if such an article appears in a peer-reviewed journal, determine what the agenda of the journal is and how the article plays into furthering that agenda.

Timeliness of Publication

A good rule of thumb is to include research that is no more than 10 years old; but, like any document, this depends on the subject, audience, and purpose. There are sometimes very good reasons to include research that is much older than 10 years, as well as good reasons to include research that is no more than a week old. In most cases, readers want to know that writers have the most current information to substantiate their ideas. Ten years is a good time frame to work with in order to see the changes that can evolve with a given subject matter; however, writers may want to use information that is more than 10 years old when they want to give a historical perspective or report the

Checklist for Evaluating Sources on the Internet

☐ If the information is found on the Internet, what domain does the source reside on (.com, .edu, .gov, .org)?

☐ How does the subject matter relate to other information on the website? What bias could be present in the article given the domain in which it was found?

☐ Is there an author? If so, what are the person's credentials? Does the author(s) show up as being who he or she claims when cross-referencing other sites or publications? For instance, if a person claims to be a Ph.D. in physics at Johns Hopkins University, does that person show up in the list of faculty on Johns Hopkins University website?

☐ If there is no author, does an organization or company take credit for writing the article? If so, research the reputation of the organization if unknown. A more reputable organization like National Geographic generally can stand on its own; however, consider where the information was found on the Internet. Usually such high-profile organizations do not scatter their documents on the Internet, but somehow have them linked to one of their official websites.

☐ Is there a date of publication? If so, does it fall into an acceptable time frame for the topic being researched?

☐ Is the content reliable and valid? Are there incredible claims that do not show up in any other research on the subject?

history of a subject. Conversely, certain subjects demand writers use only the most current information that can be anywhere from only a few weeks to no more than a year old, as when reporting financial information such as stock prices or mortgage rates, or when researching equipment for purchase.

Integrity of the Content

To evaluate content means that a researcher has to read more than one or two articles, books, or reports on the subject, especially if the researcher is not familiar with it. The reason for this is to gain a fundamental understanding of a subject by learning about facts and theories, who the experts are in a field, and where the experts stand on certain issues. After becoming familiar with the material, it is easier to spot incredible or unsubstantiated claims. Without doing this kind of background work, a researcher has no idea of what is considered fact, theory, or outrageous. Other things to consider when evaluating content include determining if the information is reliable and valid. *Reliability* refers to whether bias is present. *Validity* refers to the correctness of the information. Always determine whether the material is accurate, factual, or simply the author's opinion.

INTEGRATING RESEARCH INTO WRITING

Gathering research before drafting is usually a good idea so that supporting information is available when it is time to write. But, research is not a separate entity outside of the realm of writing; in fact, it is part of the process from start to finish.

Research and the Writing Process

Research and the writing process go hand-in-hand. To begin writing a report or paper, it is important to read about a subject to gain a clear understanding of it, as well as narrow the scope of a paper. The *scope* defines the boundaries of the subject that will be covered in a paper. For instance, if a person were asked to write a paper about technical communication, they would quickly realize that it is a huge topic. Should the paper cover the history of technical communication, what technical communication means today, what it meant 50 years ago, or which professions use technical communicators? The scope of a paper generally focuses on one aspect of a topic, which can be part of a thesis statement, such as the following:

> Technical writing underwent major changes in how it was defined and taught between 1930 and 1980.

In this example, the scope of the paper is that technical writing will be discussed in terms of how it was defined and taught for only the years between 1930 and 1980.

To develop even a short thesis, as in the example above, usually requires research. Consulting research sources does not mean only reading them; a researcher has to be an active reader and become involved with the subject. This is achieved by annotating a text.

Annotations

Reading is not a solitary act separate from writing. In fact, it should be integral in that an active reader will annotate texts. *To annotate* means to highlight, underline, circle, jot down notes in the margins, or create a separate sheet of paper with notes that pertain to the reading. Annotations are the ideas generated by readers who are involved with a subject as they read the research. An example of an annotated passage is shown below:

Does this include only words or body language, too?	"What is spoken in the context of gossip unconsciously reveals intricacies about the speaker by what is added, deleted, and interpreted.
This is interesting; however, how are these motivations revealed? Do I have to psychoanalyze every bit of gossip?	Gossip highlights unconscious motivations in the speaker.
Isn't this because there is an element of trust or familiarity with the person?	'It is often information that is rendered without the façade of social formality or the need for appearances. It deals with a situation unmasked and is often transmitted in a situation of a certain intimacy' (Medini & Rosenberg 1976). Because gossip is generally exchanged in a comfortable setting, the talk is unguarded and unchecked by the speaker.
We normally take some people's word as being the truth.	Whether gossip is altered unconsciously or in order to make the topic more interesting, gossip is a manifestation of the person's psyche" (Hannigan 2007).

Annotations generally are part of what is termed prewriting. *Prewriting* is a step in the writing process where ideas are generated that will form either a subject or a thesis. This is where annotations come in. Through reading, a researcher discovers the various sides to a topic, explores unknown areas, and confirms prior knowledge. By asking questions and annotating, a researcher focuses on what to look for in other sources or gains an understanding of what direction the paper can take.

Summary

A summary is a synopsis of someone else's work or writing. There is no original thought put into writing a summary; it is simply a recap of an article, book, or excerpt. Summaries are good for annotated bibliographies (see chapter 14) or as a reminder of the content of certain sources; however, they are generally not used in reports or papers unless there is a section that is specifically meant to summarize relevant research.

Quotations

Quotations are word-for-word passages borrowed from someone else's writing. Generally, they are used as evidence. What this means is that quotations are used to support a writer's original ideas. The whole purpose of writing an essay or report is to contribute to the body of knowledge on a subject, which is why summaries generally are not used. The essence of most essays or reports is the claims made. *Claims* are derived from research, usually in the prewriting phase, and are statements that have to be proven. For instance, when writing a paper on how gossip is used in the workplace, the following claim may be made:

> Gossip goes beyond the stereotypical caution of it not being nice to talk about someone behind his or her back, and in some cases can be useful.

This statement cannot stand on its own as being fact; the writer has to prove this statement. This would be done, in part, by using quotes from credible research where experts on the subject make similar claims, such as in the following example:

> Gossip goes beyond the stereotypical caution of it not being nice to talk about someone behind his or her back, and in some cases can be useful. Hannigan (2007) even suggests that gossip has societal implications because "gossip is an exchange of information that can lead to building relationships and influencing

society. The communication of information may not always have an innocent tone when guised as gossip, yet individuals rely on the dispersion of this information" (p. 4).

In this passage, the writer begins with his or her claim, and then finds other research that makes a similar claim. The research is used as *support* for the original claim by the writer.

When integrating quotes into one's own writing, simply inserting them after a claim can make the reading choppy, boring, or seem like an interruption in the sentence. The best way to integrate quotes is to make them flow with the rest of the paragraph text. This is usually done by using signal phrases. *Signal phrases* are words or phrases that help put quotes in the right context and also provide meaning for how the quote is being used or interpreted. Signal phrases are verbs or verb phrases. Common verbs in signal phrases include the following:

Acknowledges	Comments	Observes
Agrees	Declares	Points out
Argues	Disputes	Refutes
Asserts	Illustrates	Reports
Claims	Notes	Suggests

In the example above, the signal phrase "Hannigan (2007) even suggests that gossip has societal implications because" helps to bring in Hannigan's main idea so that it flows with the rest of the paragraph. When quoting, the entire sentence does not have to be used as long as an appropriate signal phrase marks the integration of the quote, and the correct context and meaning are retained. The signal phrase may not be able to maintain the context of a quote all by itself, so many times an explanation may follow a quote, as in the following passage:

Gossip goes beyond the stereotypical caution of it not being nice to talk about someone behind his or her back, and in some cases can be useful. Hannigan (2007) even suggests that gossip has societal implications because "gossip is an exchange of information that can lead to building relationships and influencing society. The communication of information may not always have an innocent tone when guised as gossip, yet individuals rely on the dispersion of this information" (p. 4). What Hannigan points out is that sometimes gossip may be used to relay norms in society, such as common practices at work.

The follow-up to the quote explains what the quote refers to, further retains the context and message of the quotation, and gives an example of the idea being expressed.

Paraphrases also are used to support claims (see paraphrasing below) because quotations should be used sparingly. Overusing quotations gives a document the feeling of being a summary in lieu of the original ideas of the writer, which might be overlooked. There are three general guidelines for when to use a quotation:

1. When the original words are so precise that to rewrite them would skew the meaning

2. When referring to dialogue

3. When critiquing what someone else has said

In addition to making sure a quotation is not taken out of context or misused, it is essential to properly give credit to the author of the quote by using an appropriate citation method, which is elaborated on further below and shown in appendix B. A reader should be able to continue further research on the topic by using the citation as a beginning point.

Paraphrasing

Paraphrasing occurs when only an idea is borrowed from someone else's writing, and the writer puts that idea into his or her own words. Contrary to what some may think, changing just a few words or switching the words around is not considered paraphrasing. In fact, that can be considered plagiarism. Paraphrases only borrow ideas; the words should be entirely those of the writer. The only exceptions to this rule are when technical terms or jargon from the original text are used; then it is permissible to use only those certain terms in a paraphrase. As noted above, quotations should be used only for specific reasons, but there are many more times when writers want to borrow ideas from others. To do so correctly entails paraphrasing those ideas.

When paraphrasing, maintain the original quote's meaning and context. *Context* refers to the situation or background surrounding a statement and how it is used. This can be achieved by following these five steps:

1. Read the original passage several times before attempting to paraphrase. Be sure to understand completely and clearly the idea being expressed and the context in which the material is being used.

2. Write down, in one's own words, the idea of the passage without looking back at the original. Looking back can sometimes make a writer want to use the same words.

3. Determine if the wording in the paraphrase captures the exact meaning as the original.

4. Ask, is the paraphrase used in the same context as the original? Is the borrowed idea used in the same manner that it was used in the original or has it been altered so that it serves a completely different purpose? Taking an idea out of context is faulty research and damages one's argument.

5. Ask someone else to read the original, then read the paraphrase, and then compare the meaning and context between the two.

The following examples show acceptable and unacceptable paraphrases:

Original passage: "Educational leaders posed with the task of integrating ethics into the undergraduate general education curriculum are faced with multiple challenges. They must first seek out faculty members truly interested in the topic, and those that see value in integrating ethics into the curriculum. Questions that need to be asked include: How will ethics be integrated into the curriculum? Should a formal course in ethics be offered or integrated across the curriculum? What are the ethical issues challenging today's undergraduate students? Educational leaders such as deans or program directors should encourage faculty members interested in this topic, but should not force integrating ethics in all general education courses. Student concerns need to be explained and suggestions for integrating ethics into the curriculum need to be offered" (Stevenson 2007).

Acceptable paraphrase: Addressing ethics in higher education is not an easy task. Developing a separate course or having ethics integrated into existing courses are challenges faced by faculty and administrators. Furthermore, only faculty members who sincerely value the addition of ethics to a college curriculum should teach this content because the topic, as it applies to any discipline, cannot be forced on someone to teach and teach it well (Stevenson 2007).

Unacceptable paraphrase: Educational leaders have to decide to integrate ethics into the undergraduate general education curriculum. They are faced with many challenges. The first is to seek out faculty members truly interested in the topic, and those that see value in integrating ethics into the curriculum. Questions that need to be asked include: How will ethics be integrated into the curriculum? Should a formal course in ethics be offered or integrated across the curriculum? What are the ethical issues challenging today's undergraduate students? Educational leaders should encourage faculty members interested in this topic, but should not force them. Student concerns need to be explained and suggestions for integrating ethics into the curriculum need to be offered (Stevenson 2007).

In the first paraphrase, the main idea of the quote is retained, yet it is in the author's own words. In the second paraphrase, too many of the original source's words are used, and therefore, it could be construed as plagiarism because the whole quote was not used and put in quotation marks.

Paraphrasing implies that the writer has used his or her own words and not simply rearranged someone else's.

Additionally, in-text citations are shown in the examples above. An *in-text citation* or *parenthetical citation* is a type of shorthand that lets readers know where the information came from. Longer citations are included on a references or works cited page. (Style and format for in-text and reference page citations are included in appendix B.) In-text and reference page citations should be correlated. Because paraphrasing involves borrowing someone else's idea, attribution has to be given to the person or text where the idea came from. Not citing a paraphrase is considered plagiarism.

Plagiarism

Plagiarism occurs when an author uses someone else's words or ideas and does not give appropriate credit. There are a couple of reasons why authors plagiarize. The first is unintentional in that an author may not know what is considered plagiarism, and the second is intentional in that the author simply does not give credit for borrowed words or ideas. In the latter case, the words or ideas are simply stolen. But, even if it is unintentional, plagiarism is a crime and carries with it some serious consequences as in the case below.

> "A CBS News producer was fired and the network apologized after a Katie Couric video essay on libraries was found to be plagiarized from *The Wall Street Journal*" ("CBS News Fires" 2007).

Strategies to avoid plagiarism are described below, but the main point to keep in mind is that if the idea or words are not original and did not come from the writer's own head, then the words or ideas have to be cited showing where they did come from. Sometimes, writers will become so familiar with a topic after reading through the research that when it comes time to write they may wonder if they actually thought of the idea themselves or if it came from one of the sources read. Below are some ways to avoid this problem:

- Write down the source's bibliographic information first and then compile notes under that heading.

- Keep track of page numbers in notes, whether quoting or paraphrasing.

- Double-check all quotes and paraphrases once integrated into the paper to make sure the accurate source is being cited.

Style Guides. A style guide is a set of rules that govern how material should be cited in the body of a paper as well as in the list of references or works cited page. Different professions use different style guides. Technical communicators should be familiar with several styles because they work in various fields. The most commonly used style guides are the American Psychological Association (APA), Chicago Manual of Style, and Modern Language Association (MLA). Generally, the sciences use APA; news or popular culture use Chicago Manual of Style; and liberal arts, such as English, use MLA. Appendix B contains information and example citations for each of these style guides.

Other Resources

Chapter 14 focuses on research in the workplace. It covers how to obtain and use research from more complex sources, such as government documents, company publications, letters, meeting minutes, emails, interviews, and surveys. Additionally, copyright and fair use, as well as annotated bibliographies, are discussed.

REFERENCE

The Associated Press. 2007. "CBS Fires Producer for Plagiarism." 8 November 2007. *http://abcnews.go.com/Entertainment/wireStory?id = 3028148.*

CHAPTER 5

Planning, Organizing, Drafting, and Style

When faced with an in-box full of projects and what feels like a limited amount of time, it is easy for a technical writer to feel like the best course of action is to jump in with both feet and begin cranking out documents. However, taking the time to craft a plan, organize one's thoughts, and draft out a project will not only result in a stronger, cleaner, more effective document, it actually will save time in the long run. This chapter will discuss how to plan, organize, and draft a project to do just that.

PLANNING, ORGANIZING, AND DRAFTING

A technical communicator should always create a plan before beginning to compose a document or presentation. Just as it would be reckless to take off on a vacation with no plane tickets, hotel reservations, or idea of where one would end up, it would be equally reckless to try to compose a document of any value without first reviewing the end goal and how to achieve it.

Timelines

An important part of any technical writing project is meeting deadlines. With project assignments come deadlines that must be met. Additionally, technical communicators often are asked to balance multiple projects at once, so good time management is essential to success. In the workplace, failing to meet a deadline results in serious consequences that can include the potential failure of the project or even termination. Taking the time to create a timeline allows deadlines to be met. An example timeline is shown in figure 5.1.

Timelines should identify all of the specific tasks that must be completed for the project to be finished. It is important to examine the whole scope of a project and not just focus on the idea of the end product. A writer should set smaller deadlines when creating a timeline. This makes the overall deadline more manageable. Ample time should be allowed for each step of the writing process, including prewriting, drafting, revising, and proofreading. Listing out the individual tasks that must be completed will make the timeline more effective and also allow the writer to better estimate how much time is needed for each step. Failing to consider all individual tasks may result in costly delays or last minute cramming.

Timelines should be realistic. It is easy to try to rush through a project when faced with a deadline, but each step of the writing process deserves adequate attention. It is also easy for a writer to underestimate the amount of time that should be devoted to a step such as revision. Many writers will

FIGURE 5.1 *Timeline*

Timeline for Green Audio Memo Proposal

Assigned: January 15, 2007
Final Due Date: January 30, 2007

Time	Task	Completed
1/15	Write statement of purpose	1/15
1/16–1/17	Identify and research primary audience	1/16
1/18–1/19	Outline proposal	1/18
1/22	Write draft	1/22
1/23	Send to Lee for comments	1/22
1/25–1/26	Revise draft	1/26
1/29	Edit and proofread proposal	1/29
1/30	Deliver proposal to client	1/30

attempt to create a perfect document on the first try and leave themselves very little time for revision. However, revision is one of the most important steps in any writer's process and it deserves a significant amount of time. A cooling period before revising is also important for most writers. Once again, a realistic timeline reflects this. A writer should always set aside time that is devoted exclusively to writing or revising. Attempting to multitask during the writing process will result in a lack of focus and possibly sloppy work.

Statement of Purpose

As discussed in chapter 2, a technical communicator must know the purpose of the document or presentation being created. Statements of purpose clearly identify what a document or presentation is designed to achieve, as in the following example:

> **Statement of purpose:** This proposal will recommend the implementation of a county-wide recycling program in order to reduce the amount of waste being deposited in the Sandberg County Landfill, which is nearing capacity.

The statement of purpose is an effective planning tool. A writer can use the statement of purpose as a jumping off point to begin the project. To help generate ideas, a writer can place the statement of purpose at the top of a blank page, and then begin listing what will need to be included to achieve that purpose. These notes can then be translated into a more organized format—the outline. The statement of purpose serves in a similar capacity as a thesis statement in an essay. The statement of purpose is the foundation of the document and gives it direction. Everything else in the document will build from this statement of purpose.

Organizing

Before a writer actually prepares an outline, it is important to consider how the information will need to be organized. Some forms of documents have an inherent organization. For example, technical instructions need to be arranged sequentially so the reader can perform the steps in the proper order. However, sometimes organization will vary with the type of material being presented. Following is a list of and brief explanations for the most commonly used organizational styles:

- **Chronological.** This organizational pattern lists steps or events in the order that they happened or should occur. This pattern is directly related to time. Scientific papers that describe experiments are generally arranged in chronological order.

- **Sequential.** Sequential organization also presents steps in a particular order, but they are not associated with any specific time. Technical instructions usually are arranged sequentially.

- **Alphabetical.** This pattern organizes terms or items alphabetically for easy reference. For example, indexes often are ordered alphabetically.

- **Spatial.** The spatial method of organization describes an object based on its physical characteristics or arrangement. For example, a product can be described from top to bottom or from left to right as in a user guide.

- **Comparison.** This organizational style evaluates two or more items by reviewing them side by side. A proposal recommending one product over another may choose to use this style to present the argument.

- **Problem and solution.** Organizing information in this way begins by establishing and explaining a predicament and then detailing the resolution for said issue. A recommendation report may be organized by problem and solution.

- **Cause and effect.** This method of organization identifies the root of an issue or problem and details the potential or actual repercussions. Environmental impact reports often use cause and effect organization.

- **Increasing order of importance.** This organizational style lists information from least to most important. Memo proposals often are arranged in this order because it leaves the reader pondering the most important point. This is a good method for any persuasive document.

- **Decreasing order of importance.** In contrast to the style above, this method lists information from most to least important. This method may be used in technical reports to allow readers to immediately find the central idea of the document.

- **Inductive.** This organizational pattern utilizes examples or illustrations to lead the reader to a particular conclusion. This method is often used in presentations.

- **Deductive.** Deductive organization opens with a generality and then substantiates that generality with evidence. This method often is used in scientific papers, such as an empirical research report.

- **General to specific.** As the title implies, this organizational style leads with a broad statement and moves toward a more detailed discussion. Proposals often open with a general statement that is then proved with specific information in the body of the proposal.

- **Specific to general.** Conversely, this method begins with a very detailed discussion of an issue, product, or problem and then progresses to a general conclusion. This can be very useful if the audience needs a great deal of background information before being confronted with the central issue at hand, as may be the case with some technical reports.

The following questions can assist a writer in choosing the appropriate strategy for organizing a document:

- Is time important in the presentation of the material?
  Corresponding organizational style: Chronological

- Will the document include steps that must be performed in a particular order?
  Corresponding organizational style: Sequential

- Does the document reference a physical object or event that the reader needs to visualize?
  Corresponding organizational style: Spatial

- Does the document present a list of information that will need to be quickly referenced by the reader?
  Corresponding organizational style: Alphabetical

- Will the document include two or more products, concepts, or solutions?
  Corresponding organizational style: Comparison

- Is the document offering the answer to a previous question or issue?
  Corresponding organizational style: Problem/solution

- Does the document discuss a complex subject that would be easier explained in smaller parts?
  Corresponding organizational style: Division/classification

- Will the document be assessing potential repercussions of a known issue?
  Corresponding organizational style: Cause/effect

- Does the writer wish to leave the reader with the most important point at the forefront of the reader's mind?
  Corresponding organizational style: Increasing order of importance

- Is it important for the reader to find the main point immediately upon viewing the document?
  Corresponding organizational style: Decreasing order of importance

- Will the information contained in the document be leading the reader to a logical conclusion?
  Corresponding organizational style: Deductive

- Is the body of the document designed to prove or support one main idea or recommendation to the reader?
  Corresponding organizational style: General to specific

- Will the audience need a great deal of background information before being introduced to the main idea or recommendation?
  Corresponding organizational style: Specific to general

Sometimes, a document will require the use of more than one organizational strategy. For example, a user guide for a home computer may include both a chronologically ordered set of instructions and a spatially organized description of the parts of the computer. Using the questions above will help the writer determine if multiple strategies need to be used as well as identify which ones are appropriate.

Writing for International Audiences. Organizational expectations vary across cultures. Americans are accustomed to a linear progression that begins with the main point and then supports that point. However, in other countries, non-linear patterns are preferred. For example, in Japan it is considered rude to get directly to the point. Instead, the Japanese prefer an indirect approach that circles around the issue, getting to the main point at the end of the document. Because of these varied expectations, the technical communicator must consider what the reader will expect to find and provide that whenever possible.

Outlining

An outline is one of the most common and effective methods for organizing thoughts and ideas before composing a draft. An outline acts as a road map for the writer. It gives direction and keeps the writer on course. Using an outline also can make a large project seem more manageable by breaking it down into smaller pieces. For example, a user manual can be a long, intimidating document to create, but using an outline can help the writer separate it into individual topics that can be tackled one at a time.

Outlines also allow the writer to make choices about the organization of a document. By dividing up the topics to be covered, as in the example of the user manual above, the writer can see how the separate parts of the document will work together to create the whole or fulfill the statement of purpose. If sections need to be rearranged or reorganized, the outline will show that. It also may point out areas that need further support or explanation.

Outlines can be formal or informal depending on the length or complexity of the project. A memo probably does not require a formal outline. However, a lengthier document like a feasibility report would benefit from one. There are two main styles of formal outlines: Roman numeral outlines and decimal numbering outlines. Both lay out the document in a hierarchical fashion, moving from main points to various levels of supporting points, and both accomplish the same task. The only real difference between them is in how they identify that hierarchy within the outline. A traditional Roman numeral style outline (see figure 5.2) uses a mixture of Roman numerals, Arabic numbers, and letters, while a decimal numbered outline (see figure 5.3) uses only Arabic numbers. Some scientific fields favor the decimal numbering outline, but it is really just a matter of preference because the outline is just for the writer's use.

FIGURE 5.2 *Roman Numeral Outline*

I. First main idea
    A. First supporting point for I
        1. First detail for A
           a. First detail for 1
        2. Second detail for A
    B. Second supporting point for I
        1. First detail for B
        2. Second detail for B
           a. First detail for 2
              1) First detail for a
II. Second main idea
    A. First supporting point for II
        1. First detail for A
        2. Second detail for A
    B. Second supporting point for II
        1. First detail for B
        2. Second detail for B
III. Third main idea
    A. First supporting point for III
        1. First detail for A
           a. First detail for 1
        2. Second supporting point for A

FIGURE 5.3 *Decimal Numbered Outline*

Purpose Statement: To prove gossip perpetuates a healthy work environment and should be controlled and even facilitated by managers through productive strategies.

1. Gossip has an inherent place in the psyches of humans.

    1.1 Gossip provides intimate insights that should not be underestimated.

        1.1.1 "Gossip is never as trivial as people think it is. It is the common man's closet approach to philosophy" (as cited in Medini and Rosenberg 1976).

        1.1.2 The intellectual and emotional threads of gossip run deeply through the human psyche, leading researchers to make the connection between gossip and psychoanalysis.

            1.1.2.1 Reflecting on gossip helps bring humanity closer to understanding itself by revealing "issues of the human condition, the human community and kinship, issues of secrecy, self-esteem, pride, voyeurism, intimacy, and the search for security" (Medini and Rosenberg 1976).

    1.2 Gossip highlights unconscious motivations in the speaker.

        1.2.1 "It is often information that is rendered without the façade of social formality or the need for appearances. It deals with a situation unmasked and is often transmitted in a situation of a certain intimacy" (Medini and Rosenberg 1976).

2. Gossip is an exchange of information that can lead to building relationships and influencing society.

    2.1 "Even gossip that doesn't necessarily increase productivity can help workers understand workplace etiquette" (as cited in Soste 2006).

It is important to keep in mind that outlines are just a form of prewriting. They are not concrete and can be changed. In fact, they should be adjusted as needed in order to help the writer create the strongest draft and, eventually, final document, possible.

To further assist the writer in choosing the appropriate order of organization, a collection of partial outlines for some of the commonly used styles follows:

Chronological

I. Test subjects gathered.
   A. Gathered at 9:00 PM, after dark, when they appeared to be most active.
      1. Five specimens captured outside of Hall 3.
      2. Three specimens captured on the quad.
      3. Two specimens captured by the Communications building.
II. Test subjects held.
   A. Kept in a dark box for 24 hours.
   B. Food and water was provided.
III. Trials
   A. 9:00 AM
      1. All test subjects were removed and allowed to run.
      2. Distance traveled was measured and recorded for each specimen.
   B. 3:00 PM
      1. All test subjects were removed and allowed to run.
      2. Distance traveled was measured and recorded for each specimen.
   C. 9:00 PM
      1. All test subjects were removed and allowed to run.
      2. Distance traveled was measured and recorded for each specimen.

Sequential

I. Gather all ingredients.
   A. 2 cups flour
   B. 1 cup sugar
   C. 2 eggs
   D. ¼ teaspoon salt
   E. 1 stick butter, melted

II. Combine all ingredients.

    A. Mix together dry ingredients in medium bowl.

    B. Add melted butter and stir well.

    C. Add eggs one at a time, combining after each addition.

III. Prepare dough for baking.

    A. Roll dough into 1-inch rounds.

    B. Place on well-greased baking sheet.

Spatial

I. Computer monitor

    A. Screen

    B. Stand

    C. A/C power supply plug

    D. USB port

    E. Power switch

II. Computer tower

    A. Power switch

    B. Printer port

    C. USB port (3)

Comparison

I. UHA 2000

    A. Cost

    B. Availability

    C. Ease of use

II. Copy Master HI3

    A. Cost

    B. Availability

    C. Ease of use

III. Recommendations

Problem and Solution

I. Problem

    A. There is a shortage of parking for day-shift employees.

        1. There are fewer spots than employees.

  2. Must compete for spots with vendors and other nearby businesses.

 B. Some employees are being forced to pay for parking off-site and walk several blocks.

  1. This additional cost is a hardship for some.

  2. The lengthy process is causing some employees to be late.

II. Solution

 A. Short term

  1. Institute company-wide carpooling and vanpooling program.

 B. Long term

  1. Convene a taskforce to find a permanent solution for the parking problem.

Cause and Effect

I. Causes of global warming

 A. Car emissions

  1. Scientific support

 B. Methane gas

  1. Scientific support

 C. Factory emissions

  1. Scientific support

II. Effects of global warming

 A. Increased air temperatures

  1. Melting polar ice caps

 B. Increased ocean temperatures

  1. Changing ocean habitats

Increasing Order of Importance

I. Writing placement exam was recently revised.

 A. It is now auto-graded for prompt results.

 B. It is now conveniently located where all students can access it.

II. Students are being incorrectly placed in advanced writing courses.

 A. Students are not taking the writing placement exam because it is not mandatory.

B. Advisors are assigning students based on student scheduling preferences.

III. The writing placement exam must be mandatory.

  A. It will improve retention by ensuring students are enrolled in the proper course.

Decreasing Order of Importance

I. Copy Master HI3 is the best choice for a new office copier.

  A. Positive features

    1. It is economically priced at $5,999.

    2. It comes with a five-year warranty.

    3. The service center is located nearby.

  B. Negative features

    1. The toner for this model is more expensive than the one currently in use.

II. The other option is the UHA 2000.

  A. Positive features

    1. It comes with a two-year warranty.

  B. Negative features

    1. Closest service center is two hours away.

    2. Standard warranty is extremely limited in coverage.

General to Specific

I. The company picnic must be rescheduled due to several unforeseen events.

  A. The location previously reserved for the picnic sustained weather damage and is closed for remodeling on the current date.

  B. The previous day/time for the picnic conflicts with an important meeting that a significant number of employees are obligated to attend.

  C. The predicted forecast for the current day calls for severe weather.

Specific to General

I. According to the National Highway Traffic Safety Administration (2007), 55 percent of all those killed in traffic accidents in 2006 were not wearing a seatbelt.

II. Most school buses still do not have seat belts installed.

III. Seatbelts should be installed on all California state school buses.

Once a writer has decided how the information should be organized and has composed an outline, it is time to draft the document. A *draft* expands on what the outline began. It takes those single sentences and turns them into well-supported paragraphs.

Writing is a process, and the draft plays a specific role in that process. The draft functions to get the main ideas down on paper. Therefore, the focus of a draft should be the content. Revision, editing, and proofreading will come later. It is imperative that a writer not attempt to edit at the same time as the draft is being composed. Taking time to edit at this stage of the process will disrupt the flow of writing and may result in valuable ideas being lost or forgotten. It also can put undo pressure on the writer to create a perfect piece on the first attempt. This is both a daunting and unrealistic task. Instead, the writer should focus solely on getting those primary ideas down on paper. It ultimately will save time and create a stronger document or presentation.

When drafting, any summaries of sections of the entire document should be drafted last. That way, the summary can be accurate and complete. The material that will be summarized should be drafted first so that no important information is left out. Beginning with the summary may result in valuable information being left out as the writer may include text that was not covered in the original outline.

Although summaries should be written at the end of the drafting process, there is no other particular order in which a draft must be written. Some writers prefer to follow the chronological order of the outline. However, if a writer finds himself or herself staring at a blank screen, it may be best to start with the easiest section of the document. There are no rules that demand a draft be written in order, so it is best to stick with what is most comfortable for the writer.

Finally, it is important that the writer set aside enough time to complete the draft and any subsequent revisions of the initial draft. Drafting is an important part of the overall writing process, and the writer must allocate time to drafting when establishing the timeline for completing a project. Proper planning is critical to the success of any writing endeavor.

REFERENCE

National Highway Traffic Safety Administration. 2007. "2006 Annual Assessment Final Report." *NHTSA.* 7 December 2007. *www.nhtsa.dot.gov/ portal/site/nhtsa/.*

CHAPTER 6

Page Design and Visuals

The goal of effective writing involves ensuring that readers understand the ideas, words, and language presented in a document. It is important that the reader has a clear understanding of the material as well as an interest in reading the material. In addition to the written text, consider the visual appearance of technical documents. A reader who sees large blocks of texts in a font size too small to easily read may skim the material. When complex information, such as in an instruction manual, is presented without the use of such visuals as photographs or drawings, the reader may become confused and find the information difficult to follow. Documents need to include effective page design and use of visuals to assist readers in understanding the material presented as well as to engage them in the written text.

Technical communicators need to consider design and visual appeal for enhancing readability. When designing the text portion of a document, white space, headings, subheadings, and use of contrast are elements that need to be considered. Visuals may be selected to enhance or supplement text. Common visuals include tables, graphs, charts, drawings, and illustrations. This section provides an overview of page design including use of white space, font styles, and use of design techniques for comparison/contrast. An introduction to the use of visuals, such as charts, tables, and graphs, in technical documents is also provided. Chapter 15 expands on this discussion to include the use of visuals in various types of documents and presentations and also provides a more detailed discussion of page and document design.

PAGE DESIGN

When planning, revising, and writing documents, the writer should consider page design and visuals for increasing reader understanding of the material. Page design and use of visuals are important for several reasons, specifically the following:

- **To gain the attention of the reader.** The visual appearance of a document has an impact on the reader. Many people are attracted to the design of a document. Attention of the reader is gained if the information is visually appealing and provides use of visuals to aid in the understanding of the material. For example, consider a car owner's manual. The manual contains information about the engine, brakes, steering, maintenance, troubleshooting, and much more. If the manual refers to the steering column, but does not include an illustration, the reader may be confused as to the location of this part. Reading 100 pages of text in a manual can be confusing as well as overwhelming to the reader. Including visuals assists in understanding the location of the car parts and aids in understanding how to perform the task.

- **To show connections.** Readers often are presented with a great deal of information and need to see how the process or parts fit into a larger picture. Elements of effective page design can be used to emphasize key points for readers. Relationships and connections also can be seen easily through use of effective page design. For example, an annual report is written to present the state of a company for the current year. The amount of revenue generated from the past five years is included as a graph in the report to show a steady increase in the amount of profit the company has earned through the years. Use of a visual assists the reader in quickly seeing the comparison of profit over the years rather than skimming through pages of text.

- **To appeal to visual learners.** Websites, television, film, and electronic communication have changed the way readers view documents. Readers are more visually oriented and are used to being engaged in the visual elements of text. Today's visually oriented society places a high value on the appearance of documents. A poorly designed document is not likely to be read by visually oriented readers. For example, consider the amount of information presented on an Internet site such as *The New York Times* website. The use of color, page design, and appearance are all taken into consideration when designing a website. Those designing print publications have these same considerations.

White Space

White space, which is the amount of space allowed between text, provides readers with a visually appealing document. A document that has no white space may seem complicated or boring to readers. Effective use of white space breaks up large blocks of text and also provides division between segments or sections in the text. Examples 1 and 2 below illustrate the difference between ineffective and effective use of white space. Margins and indentations are examples of using white space. Indenting the text when there is a new paragraph alerts the reader that new information will be presented. Technical documents typically use white space between headings and subheadings and also allow space between paragraphs. Brochures and newsletters break up large amounts of text with photographs and color along with inclusion of white space by chunking the text. Consider the use of white space in the following examples:

Ineffective Use of White Space

The purpose of this study was to describe and explain selected deans', academic technology directors', and faculty members' perspectives on instructional technology use in the curriculum of undergraduate general education programs. The exploratory questions that guided the study were: What elements constitute perspectives in technology use in the undergraduate general education curriculum? What variables influence this perspective on technology use? What beliefs do these educational leaders hold that support or negate this perspective? As noted in chapter three, the data collection strategies used in this study were transcribed interviews, observations, researcher field notes, researcher's reflective journal, and documents and artifacts.

Effective Use of White Space

The purpose of this study was to describe and explain selected deans', academic technology directors', and faculty members' perspectives on instructional technology use in the curriculum of undergraduate general education programs. The exploratory questions that guided the study were:

- What elements constitute perspectives in technology used in the undergraduate general education curriculum?

- What variables influence this perspective on technology use?

- What beliefs do these educational leaders hold that support or negate this perspective?

The first example does not effectively use white space because the text is cluttered and difficult to read. There is no variation between line spacing and no features that call attention to important elements for the reader. The text is set flush left with no indentation introducing a new paragraph. The second example shows an effective use of white space because there is space between main concepts and ideas. The text is double-spaced creating a strong readability effect. The reader can easily see the transition to a new topic and key points are indented and bulleted.

Headings and Subheadings

Headings and subheadings provide introductions to new topics and emphasize important information. A *heading* is used when a new idea is presented in the document and is a major point. *Subheadings* are used to show connections of related material to the heading. Following are some general guidelines for using headings and subheadings:

- Limit words in a heading or subheading.

- Include descriptive words. Select words that capture the main points of the heading or subheading.

- Use bold font, color, or italics to draw attention to headings or subheadings.

- Consider varying font sizes to show hierarchy between headings and subheadings.

- Determine if mixed or uniform font types should be used between headings, subheadings, and text, such as the following:

  - Emphasis comes from mixing font types between headings, subheadings, and the text:

  ## Heading

  ### Subheading

  Text

  - Uniformity is created by using the same font family (e.g., Arial Black and Arial):

  ## Heading

  ### Subheading

  Text

The following example shows heading and related subheadings for use in a document on professional writing:

Documents for the Public

Writing Documents for the Public

Business Letters

Memos

E-mail

Newsletters and Brochures

Contrast

Contrast is used for emphasizing key points or differences between concepts. For example, using a different size type, bold, italics, or color can indicate which concept is more important and which concept is less important. While use of bold type can indicate contrast and draw attention to the emphasized points, be careful not to overuse it. Too much bold type on one page can make the text look heavy and cluttered, and it can distract the reader from the important points. On a similar note, italicized or underlined text can be difficult to read when used for long passages of text, so these types of contrast also should be used carefully. Other techniques for using contrast include background shading and coloring, white space, indentation, and visuals. figure 6.1 illustrates contrast using shading, bolding, and a visual (comment box).

Contrast also can be achieved by increasing or decreasing the size of type. In the previous heading and subheading example, a large type size was used for the heading to distinguish importance over the subheadings written in a smaller type size. When designing a page, avoid using too many variations in type size because it will distract readers from the main points presented in the document. Common type sizes range from 10 to 12 point for regular text to 16 point for main headings. A sample of the variety of type sizes measured in points is shown in figure 6.2.

FIGURE 6.1 *Effective Use of Contrast*

Remember to **proofread** all documents to avoid grammatical errors. Spellcheck is a useful tool. However, spellcheck does not catch every error. A document with grammatical errors takes away from the credibility of the writer and the document. If possible, have an outside reader review written documents before submitting the final project.

FIGURE 6.2 *Sizes of Type*

C	C	C	C	C	C	C	C	C	C	C	C
8	10	12	14	16	18	20	22	24	36	48	72

Different styles of typeface also may be used to create contrast in a document. In order for differing typefaces to be effective as a contrast, there has to be enough difference between the styles so that the reader can see the distinction between the two. For example, Century Schoolbook and Bookman Old Style do not provide contrast between the typefaces. An effective use of contrasting typefaces is seen between Century and **Arial Black**.

Font Types

There are two basic types of fonts: serif and sans serif. *Serif* fonts are those that have "feet," or marks, at the bottom of the letter, such as Times New Roman. Sans means "without," so *sans serif* fonts are those that do not have feet at the bottom, for example, Arial. Choosing which font type to use depends on ease of reading. Generally, serif fonts are used for print publications, especially long technical documents. It is a more traditional font, and the feet actually act as a guide for the eye to move from one word to the next. Common serif fonts used in print publications include Times New Roman, Book Antigua, Century, and Georgia. Sans serif fonts are more modern and are used to convey this image, but another important thing about this font type is that it is easier to read on a screen; therefore, online publications and websites usually use some sort of sans serif font, such as Arial, Century Gothic, Comic Sans MS, Tahoma, or Verdana.

While there are many typefaces to choose from when designing a document, technical documents need a typeface that is easy to read. Avoid using fancy or script fonts that are difficult to read. Select a typeface that is easy on the eyes and does not distract the reader from the information presented in the document. Use no more than two font types to avoid a cluttered look. Using more than two fonts actually becomes a distraction for the reader, and it is difficult to see the importance of the headings and subheadings. Listed below are example fonts to use and fonts to avoid for technical documentation:

Example fonts to use in technical documents:

- Times New Roman
- Helvetica
- Century
- Arial
- Century Schoolbook
- Bookman Old Style

Example fonts to avoid in technical documents:

- *Script MT Bold*
- BERMUDA LP
- Giddyup
- Fette Fraktur
- Park Avenue

VISUALS

Tables are used to display numerical data in a visually appealing and readable format or to summarize long or complex text. Numerical information can be especially complex and difficult to comprehend when it is written in textual and paragraph form. It is much easier to see the numbers in a table. When designing tables, include explanatory titles and provide a heading for each column. Table 6.1 shows an example of a table that displays numerical data for easy reading.

A *word table* is often used to summarize key points of narrative text. An example word table outlining the proposal process in shown in table 6.2.

TABLE 6.1 *Table Showing Numerical Data*

Road Trip Analysis

Location To–From	Highway Route (in miles)	Back Roads Route (in miles)	Scenic Route (in miles)
Denver–Dallas	879	892	930
Dallas–Ft. Lauderdale	1,291	1,304	1,363

TABLE 6.2 *Word Table*

Steps to the Proposal Writing Process

1. Set funding priorities
2. Develop the master proposal
3. Develop the budget
4. Research potential funders
5. Cultivate potential funders
6. Administer the grant or rejection

Charts are visual representations of complex information. Charts are used to effectively display a large amount of information to the reader in a clear and concise manner. A *flow chart* uses symbols or lines to connect parts of the information process. An example information chart is shown in figure 6.3.

An *organizational chart* is commonly used to show the flow of authority or chain of command in a company. A sample organizational chart for a publishing company is shown in figure 6.4.

Graphs are frequently used visuals that compare information. Often, graphs are used in technical documents to show change over a period of time or to compare items. If there is more than one set of lines on the graph, it is beneficial to use a separate color to distinguish one from the other. Bar graphs,

FIGURE 6.3 *Flow Chart*

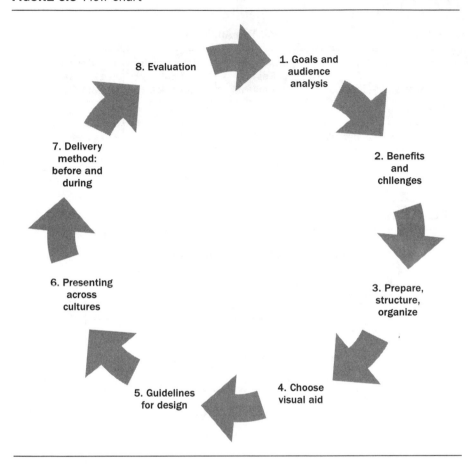

line charts, and pie charts are commonly used graphs in technical communications. None of these three graph types are interchangeable, so carefully select one graph based on the information that needs to be visually displayed.

A *bar graph* presents information using a series of horizontal or vertical lines. When designing bar graphs, it is important to convey an accurate visual impression for the reader. If one bar looks misleadingly large, the graph should be adjusted to portray an accurate impression. Figure 6.5 shows an example bar graph that represents the type of careers available in the communication field.

FIGURE 6.4 *Organizational Chart for a Publishing Company*

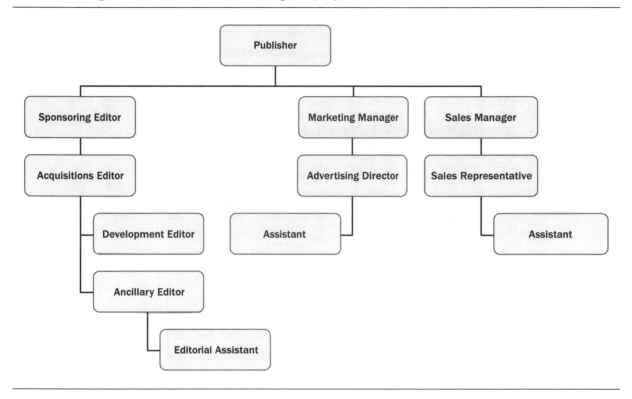

A *line chart* is used to show changes over a period of time. For example, figure 6.6 shows the same information as the bar chart (sample only) but represented in a line graph.

Pie charts are used to create a visual that compares parts to a whole or to show a relationship among these parts. Figure 6.7 represents a sample chart of the percentage of the type of fruit sold for a local grocery store in one year.

Photographs are useful visuals to consider when the purpose is to show readers how to perform a task, locate an object, or see the way something looks. It is important that photographs are clear and capture only the information needed to explain the text. Unrelated images captured in the photograph should be cropped to avoid confusion by the reader. Each photograph should be labeled and cited if it is taken from a source.

FIGURE 6.5 *Bar Graph*

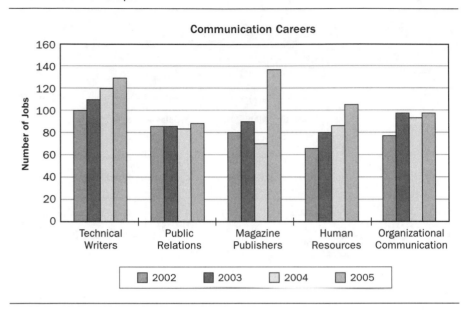

FIGURE 6.6 *Line Graph*

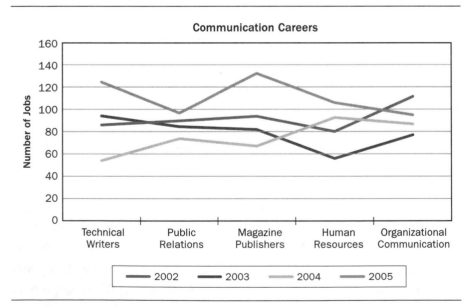

*Statistics are for demonstration purposes only and do not represent actual numbers.

FIGURE 6.7 *Pie Chart*

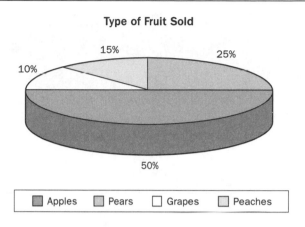

Type of Fruit Sold

15%

25%

10%

50%

☐ Apples ☐ Pears ☐ Grapes ☐ Peaches

Drawings and illustrations also may be used to show how to do something or how something is constructed. For example, a drawing would be useful in an instruction manual describing ways to install a dishwasher. Parts of the dishwasher would be labeled with a visual representation of what these parts look like.

To truly benefit the reader, drawings and illustrations need to appear in the appropriate proportioned size. A distorted image, such as the one shown in figure 6.8, creates confusion and distracts the reader from the text. Effective visuals should be a representation of the scale of the actual object as illustrated in figure 6.9.

A *screen shot,* which is a visual picture taken from a website or software, is used to help readers perform a computer-related task. A screen shot involves capturing the text from a document the exact way it appears in the original computer screen view. This technique is especially useful when directing readers on how to do something. For example, if searching for a specific career on the Bureau of Labor Statistics website, showing a screen shot of the search area creates a clear picture for readers on how to perform the search. Figure 6.10 shows a screen shot from the Bureau of Labor Statistics website.

FIGURE 6.8 *Distorted Image*

FIGURE 6.9 *Effective Image*

Listed below are the steps needed to create a screen shot in Microsoft® Windows:

1. Capture the image of the full screen by pressing the PRINT SCREEN key.
2. To capture a window's image, press PRINT SCREEN and ALT at the same time.
3. Paste the image into the document.

FIGURE 6.10 *Screen Shot of the Bureau of Labor Statistics Website*

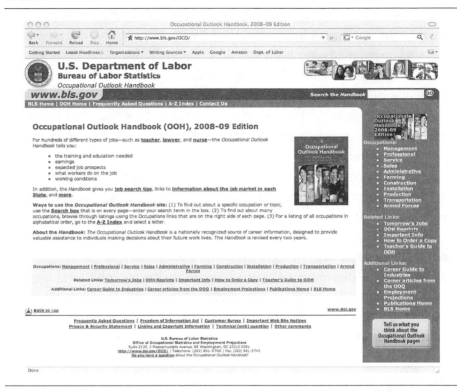

Listed below are the steps needed to create a screen shot in Mac OS:

1. To take a full screen shot, press these keys at the same time: Command, Shift, and 3.

2. To take a cropped screen shot, press these keys at the same time: Command, Shift, and 4. Drag the cursor around the desired area.

3. Place the image in the document by pulling down the Insert Menu and choosing Picture > From File.

When information is too complex or lengthy to place in the body of the text, an *appendix* may be used at the end of a section or document. An appendix may be useful when the information is so detailed that it distracts the attention of the readers, and the main concepts of the information are interrupted with the detailed information. An appendix may include an entire document, photographs, lists, survey questionnaires, responses to surveys, cost estimates, and other supporting materials. If there is only one appendix in the document, it should be labeled "Appendix." If the document includes more than one appendix, use the labels "Appendix A," "Appendix B," and so on. In the written portion of the document, a reference should be made to the appropriate appendix. For example: Survey responses indicate a greater need for funding a community center (see appendix B for a copy of the survey questions and responses).

Ethical considerations need to be taken into account when using visuals in technical documents. Copyright laws treat use of graphics in a different way than "fair use" of text. The "fair use" provision allows for a small amount of written information to be quoted without permission from the author, though proper citations still need to accompany the quoted material. Be aware, however, that permission must be granted for every graphic used from another source, even if using only one out of a thousand graphics featured in the source. The only exceptions are graphics in the *public domain* because they are owned by a government agency or are owned by the writer's employer. Public domain is a creative work that is not copyrighted and that may be used freely by anyone. However, even when using graphics from a public domain, cite the source of the graphic. Permission must also be granted for graphics obtained from websites as well as print documents.

When deciding on the page design and type of visuals to use in a technical document, it is important to refer back to the communication goals of the document. Use of page design elements, such as white space, headings, and subheadings, and contrast, create a more visually appealing document for the reader. Emphasis can be drawn toward key elements using bold, italics, shading, and color. Often, numerical data can be shown more effectively through visuals than through lengthy narrative. Because visuals can clarify complicated statistics, time also can be saved by presenting complex information in a concise way the reader can comprehend. Overall, though, it is important to not overdo or rely on a single design strategy too heavily in any one document.

CHAPTER 7

Revising, Editing, and Proofreading

O nce a writer has created a *draft,* or several drafts, of a project, it is time to clean it up and turn it into the finished product. The *revising, editing,* and *proofreading* processes are designed to do just that. This chapter will focus on those three important final steps that will prepare the document or presentation for circulation, publication, or delivery.

REVISING

All writers need to take the time to revise their work. No one gets it perfect on the first try, including professional writers. Revision is a vital part of the writing process that allows the writer to see what he or she has written with fresh eyes.

To gain that clear perspective, a writer should always take some time to "cool" before beginning to revise. It is vital that the author step back and detach from the project, including the compiled research and brainstorming documents. This break allows the writer to come back to the document with a new outlook. Ideally, a writer wants to try to see the document from the point of view of a reader who is viewing the document for the first time. This different point of view helps the writer to be more objective when reviewing the document. But what should a writer be looking for during the revision process?

Revision and Editing Defined

Revising focuses on evaluating the content of the document while editing focuses on the mechanical aspects of a text. For example, when revising, the author ensures that the document's purpose is well supported by the ideas and evidence presented. During the editing process, the author reviews sentence structure to make certain the purpose is clearly and concisely stated.

Organization and Content

The revision process should focus on the content and organization of a document. The writer should consider the following questions:

- How is the document arranged?
- Was the most effective organizational structure used to present the material?
- Were the appropriate areas highlighted?
- Is there adequate support for all main points?
- Are there accurate citations included for any outside sources that were used?
- Was any important information left out?

All of these questions can help a writer revise the content and organization of a project.

Many writers find it useful to create an outline of the draft in order to thoroughly assess the content and organization of a document. This technique is called *post-draft outlining.* A post-draft outline looks similar to a traditional outline used to organize the writer's thoughts before commencing writing, but this method outlines the paragraphs as they were actually written. The post-draft outline allows the writer to view the document in an abbreviated version, boiled down to its essence, and it also can be compared to the original outline to ensure that the writer covered all of the intended information. An example is shown in the sidebar Post-draft Outline of a Letter of Appeal.

Post-draft Outline of a Letter of Appeal

I. Please reconsider denying Susan Smith's appeal to be released from her 2007 housing contract.

II. She cannot afford the current rent and has found other accommodations that would financially allow her to continue attending school.

III. Yes, contracts should be honored, but if the alternative is dropping out of school altogether, can't an exception be made?

In looking at this post-draft outline, it becomes apparent that there is no real conclusion to this letter. The author should consider including an additional paragraph that summarizes the request and again asks for consideration of the appeal.

When revising for content and organization, it is also important that the author examine whether the purpose of the document is clear and speaks to the intended audience. As discussed in chapter 2, if the purpose is not clear and does not reach the intended audience, then the writer has failed to do the job. Taking the time to be objective and ask the questions listed above will allow the author to deliver an effective document.

EDITING

There are several aspects of a document that need to be examined during the editing process. Because of that, it is recommended that a writer make several passes at editing, focusing on different areas with each reading. This is the most effective method for editing a document of any length. It ensures that the maximum number of errors are caught and addressed, and it also prevents the editing process from becoming overwhelming. It is much easier to read over a document looking for one type of error than it is to look for six or seven. Each area that should be examined during the editing process is discussed in detail below. All are equally important, and careful consideration should be given to each aspect of the writing.

Format

As previously discussed, technical writing uses specific *formats* for different types of documents. Some of the most commonly used formats were discussed in chapter 3. During the editing process, the writer should review the format used to compose the document in question to ensure that the proscribed form has been followed. For example, if the audience expects to see an abstract, has that been included? In technical communication, the writer should strive to give the readers what they need as well as what they expect. The format of a given document can be a part of those expectations.

Style

As it pertains to writing, *style* refers to the way something is written, including things such as word choice, syntax, sentence length, and voice. The intended audience and context of the document often determine the style used by the author. For instance, an email to a coworker may be composed in an informal style using first person and including contractions. However, a business proposal would likely be arranged in a much more formal style that uses third person and avoids contractions. That writer must have a clear understanding of both purpose and audience in order to determine the appropriate style for a document. *Style guides,* which are exclusive to some companies and organizations, will be discussed later in the chapter. When editing a document for style, there are several elements that must be reviewed.

Coherence. *Coherence* ensures that there is a smooth flow of ideas within a document. The reader should be able to clearly identify the connection between all of the primary concepts.

This connection means that each paragraph must be unified in its purpose. A paragraph should clearly state an idea, generally in the form of a topic sentence, and then offer support for that idea. When the topic changes, a new paragraph should begin. While editing, a writer should check to see that each paragraph has a single, central focus.

Additionally, a writer should include transitions that help propel the reader from one paragraph or idea to the next. Transitions improve the flow and readability of a document by connecting ideas. A list of common transitional words and phrases can be found in table 7.1.

TABLE 7.1 *Common Transitions*

To Add Information	To Compare or Contrast	To Conclude	To Show Time	To Show a Logical Relationship	To Show Examples
and	also	in other words	after	if	for example
also	in the same manner	in short	as	so	for instance
besides	similarly	in summary	before	therefore	to illustrate
further	likewise	to sum up	next	consequently	in fact
furthermore	but	that is	during	thus	specifically
in addition	however	therefore	later	as a result	
moreover	on the other hand		finally	for this reason	
next	in contrast		meanwhile	because	
too	nevertheless		then		
first	still		when		
second	even though		while		
	on the contrary		immediately		
	yet				
	although				

Voice. One way a writer can edit his or her writing to be stronger and more effective is to edit out the use of passive *voice* in favor of active writing. Active voice means the subject of the sentence is performing the action. In contrast, with passive voice the subject is receiving the action or being acted upon, as noted in the following example:

Active: Theresa Lane prepared the document.

Passive: The document was prepared by Theresa Lane.

While passive voice is not grammatically incorrect, active voice is more direct and usually more concise. For that reason, it is often the preferred voice of technical and business writing. But passive voice also has its place in these forms of writing. For instance, passive voice should be used when there is no need to know who performed the action in the sentence. Passive voice is also appropriate when the writer wants to emphasize the person receiving the action rather than the action itself. Scientific writing often uses the passive voice when describing research.

Clarity. The words that a writer chooses to use should always be carefully considered. Words are powerful tools, and a good writer wants to use the words that will most effectively deliver the message to the audience. A writer must ensure that the chosen words truly deliver the intended message. Knowing the literal and contextual meaning of words can help prevent embarrassing misunderstandings. For example, when writing an instruction set for a DVD player, it is important to clearly identify the parts of the appliance so the reader does not misunderstand the directions and hook up the device incorrectly. Using a word like *thing* is vague and does not give clear direction to the reader. Precise, accurate word choice guarantees the correct message is conveyed. During the editing process, a writer should review word choice and adjust as needed to ensure clarity.

Conciseness. The use of concise language is also important in technical writing. As noted in chapter 1, technical writing should get right to the point. There is no need for long, flowery language in a technical or business document, unless it will specifically be used for marketing. A writer should take the time to edit out any unnecessary or redundant words or phrases that are taking up space without delivering any usable information. For example, the phrase "if and when" says the same thing twice. A writer should choose one of those words rather than including both. Avoid using 30 words to say what can be accomplished using 15 instead. Each word should count by contributing to the purpose of the document. Sentences that are not contributing to the meaning of the paragraph or overall document should also be removed. Readers should not have to sift through flowery or pretentious writing to find the information that they need. Concise writing is far more effective at delivering a message in the context of the workplace and fields of technical and business writing.

Unbiased Language. A writer also must be sure to avoid biased language that may offend the readers. Biased language is offensive because it makes assumptions or generalizations based on age, gender, sexual preference, ethnicity, or physical disabilities. This type of language alienates and isolates some readers, while preventing the message from reaching the intended audience. Biased language does not have to be intentional to be offensive. For this reason, a writer also should be careful to edit out any language that could be perceived as offensive.

Sexist language is one of the most common forms of biased language. For example, the pronoun *he* historically was an acceptable generic pronoun often used to refer to a subject. However, *he* is a masculine pronoun, and using it to refer to a subject where gender is unknown is biased. It assumes that the subject is likely male or that masculine pronouns are somehow superior or preferable to feminine pronouns. For that reason, writers now use *he or she* to reference a subject with unknown gender.

Inappropriate references to a subject's age, race, or ability can be equally offensive and have no place in professional, technical, or business writing. Unless it is relevant information (as in the case of a scientific study where age was one of the factors being observed), these types of references should be edited out.

International Audiences

If a document is going to be used by an international or intercultural audience, some additional considerations should be made during the editing process. First, a writer targeting this kind of audience must be culturally aware of beliefs or practices that may affect how a group of readers interpret a document. Avoiding clichés, American jargon, and humor can help prevent misunderstanding and reduce the possibility of offending an international reader. For instance, sarcasm, while popular in American humor, does not translate very well for non-native speakers. Additionally, a non-native speaker may not understand a phrase like "going against the grain." For this reason, clear, concise, Standard American English is the best choice.

It is also a good idea to keep sentences and paragraphs short when writing for an international audience. Including one thought per sentence is important if the audience comprises non-native speakers. For that reason, a writer should use active voice when writing for an international audience. Limiting the number of modifiers also will help keep sentences clear and manageable for the reader.

PROOFREADING

Proofreading is the final step in the writing process. In this step, the writer reviews the document to find and correct mechanical errors. Severe grammatical or mechanical errors can yield a document unreadable and prevent the message from being conveyed. In less extreme cases, the file may still be readable, but it certainly sends a negative message to the reader about the writer and about the organization that produced the document. Careful proofreading ensures that the message is clearly conveyed, and it also improves the writer's credibility with the reader.

Proofreading requires both an eye for detail and knowledge of the rules for grammar, punctuation, spelling, capitalization, and other mechanical considerations. A full review of these rules and expectations can be found in appendix A.

Style Guides

Many companies and organizations have style guides that they use to ensure standard usage and formatting in all company-produced documents. A technical communicator should receive such a guide upon being employed if it already exists. However, sometimes a technical communicator may be asked to help create a style guide for the company or organization. The style guide should include the company's standards on everything from how to write out numbers to preferred formatting. The guide also might include standards for grammar usage on rules that are flexible (e.g., certain rules of comma usage). A style guide ensures that all documents produced by that company or organization are mechanically consistent. If one exists, a style guide should be adhered to unless an author is otherwise directed. Refer to appendix B for information on popular style guides.

CHAPTER 8

Presentations

Computer-generated presentations are common in the modern workforce and the expectations of well-delivered presentations have increased along with the advancements in technology. As such, verbal presentations are often as important to the client as the written document. The technical communicator is frequently called upon to deliver information via a live presentation. Even the most thoroughly articulated document may fall short of the client's expectations if the presentation does not capture the key components of the written document. To achieve the outcome of delivering an effective presentation, the following three areas need to be addressed:

1. Define presentation goals and audience analysis.

2. Prepare, structure, and organize the presentation.

3. Recognize the benefits of presentation visual aids.

This section will provide an overview of the presentation process and the benefits of using visual aids in presentations. Detailed discussion about the selection of appropriate visual aids and designing effective visual aids is covered extensively in chapter 15.

PRESENTATION GOALS AND AUDIENCE ANALYSIS

Presentation goals and audience analysis are the first areas that need to be addressed when organizing a professional presentation. Goals are either informative or persuasive depending on the task assigned to the technical communicator. The audience may range from potential client, current client, or members of a workgroup. Knowledge of the audience may vary between decision makers on the project who have extensive knowledge of the topic to individuals with limited knowledge of the technical aspects of the project. Successful presentations begin with these two components.

First, a presentation goal needs to be clearly stated to the audience and should be expressed in a one-sentence statement. Goals may be informative or persuasive. Informative presentations fulfill three goals. The audience wants to know, understand, and use information. Persuasive presentations involve the process of influencing another person's values, beliefs, attitudes, or behaviors (Grice and Skinner 2004).

The following are examples of informative goals:

As a result of this presentation,

. . . engineers will understand new design techniques for the car engine.

. . . managers will learn the results of the feasibility study on employee satisfaction.

. . . consumers will understand the ways to invest in real estate.

Examples of persuasive goals include:

As a result of this presentation,

. . . the company will adopt a new user guide for the product.

. . . the funder will accept the proposal for funding of an arts program for a local grade school.

. . . the potential client will accept the proposal for conducting a feasibility study on implementing new call center procedures.

Once the goals of the presentation have been set, the second step is to analyze what the audience already knows and wants to know. The audience of a technical presentation is an important consideration when planning, organizing, and preparing visual presentation aids. Failure to analyze and adapt to the considerations of the audience is a major cause for ineffective presentations in technical settings.

Identifying the type of audience the presentation is geared toward is the first step. Often, there may be multiple audiences for the presentation. Categories for audiences include the following:

- **Experts.** These individuals have a strong understanding of the product. The communication challenge is presenting the information at a level of expertise that will engage the expert at a technical level of understanding.

- **Future clients.** The goal of presenting to this audience is to sell a future service or pitch a proposal. The presentation needs to provide detailed information about the benefits of pursuing the project to the next level and is persuasive in tone.

- **Non-specialists.** These individuals have the least amount of technical knowledge and involvement if the project is practical in nature. Often non-specialists are interested in the ways the product or service can improve tasks. Because technical knowledge may be limited, information needs to be presented in everyday, common language.

Prior to designing the presentation, discover the audience's attitude toward the topic. A current client may be looking for a progress report on the project. A future client may be looking for the benefits of pursuing the project further. Consider these questions prior to starting:

- What is the current interest level of the audience? Is the project of low or high priority?

- What is the presentation preference for the audience? Does the audience prefer slides? multimedia presentations? handouts?

- Will the outcome of the presentation be easy or difficult to achieve? Will the recommendations presented be widely accepted by the audience?

- Will the recommendation be difficult to accept and require follow-up information?

Benefits of Presentation Aids

Technical communicators often work with complex information. In an effort to present the information in a clear and concise manner, it is beneficial for the audience to both see and hear the information. Benefits of using presentation aids, such as PowerPoint slides or a whiteboard, include adding speaker credibility, improving listener memory, and increasing comprehension of the material presented.

Using presentation aids provides the audience with a perception that the presenter has spent considerable time researching and organizing the information. Instead of speaking "off the cuff," the presentation has visual support for the information. An added benefit to the presenter is that there is a natural flow for the presentation because the information may be written in an agenda or prepared on slides. Additionally, the presenter gains confidence by ensuring that all necessary information will be covered because the presentation aids include critical points.

Research on listening (Wolff et al. 1983) reveals that most listeners remember 10 percent of the information of a presentation for only a few days. Additionally, information retained may not be accurate because of the audience's personal interpretation of the material. Hamilton (2008) found that improved organization, vivid examples, and a dynamic delivery will not necessarily improve these statistics. However, use of presentation aids will increase what the audience remembers. Mayer (2001) discusses two principles related to the importance of visual aids. The *coherence principle* explains that people learn better when words and pictures are used together. The *contiguity principle* states that people learn better when the pictures are next to the words they illustrate.

Additional research conducted by the University of Minnesota and 3M Corporation found that a persuasive presentation incorporating presentation aids (especially color visuals) improved the audience's immediate recall by

8.5 percent and improved delayed recall by 10.1 percent (Vogel, Dickson, and Lehman 1986). In another study, Hamilton (1999) found that audience recall on an informative presentation improved by 18 percent when presentation aids were used for delivery. High-quality color visuals produced the greatest impact on recall, while poor-quality color visuals were the least effective, ranking lower than either high-quality or low-quality black-and-white visuals.

Use of presentation aids also increases the audience's comprehension of the technical material. Most listeners comprehend quicker when presentation aids are used. Therefore, the technical communicator can present information in less time. A study by University of Minnesota and 3M Corporation found that use of presentation aids, specifically visuals aids, potentially reduce the length of the average business meeting by 28 percent (Antonoff 1990). Because technical communicators often are involved in time-sensitive projects, using presentation aids allows the audience to comprehend information quicker, reducing the amount of time presenting information to the audience.

Preparing, Structuring, and Organizing the Presentation

When preparing, structuring, and organizing a presentation, search actively for places where appropriate graphics can be used for achieving presentation objectives. In today's visually orientated world, more people can gain and retain information from visual images. It is critical to include the opportunity for increasing communication effectiveness by reinforcing words of the presentation with visuals.

Preparing and structuring a presentation involves gathering information on the topic. Additional research may need to be gathered, such as statistics, expert opinion, interviews, Internet resources, databases, and other sources. When presenting a proposal, information can be gathered directly from the written document and included in the presentation. The same is true for presenting key components of a report, such as a feasibility report. Because the information has already been compiled in written format, key elements can be pulled from the document and included in the presentation aid. Caution: The presentation should not simply repeat the same information as stated in the document. Copying and pasting information from the document does not make an effective presentation.

Organization of the presentation may be drafted on note cards or slides if a PowerPoint presentation will be used. Develop an overview of the key points of the presentation. Often, it is useful to use a schematic or flow chart to organize main points of the presentation. An example of an organizational chart of this type is shown in figure 8.1.

When organizing presentations, keep in mind the following:

- **Stay within the specified time limit.** It is critical to both the credibility of the presenter as well as respect for the client's time to stay within the specified time limit. Furthermore, the presentation should

FIGURE 8.1 *Chart for a Presentation on Oral Presentations*

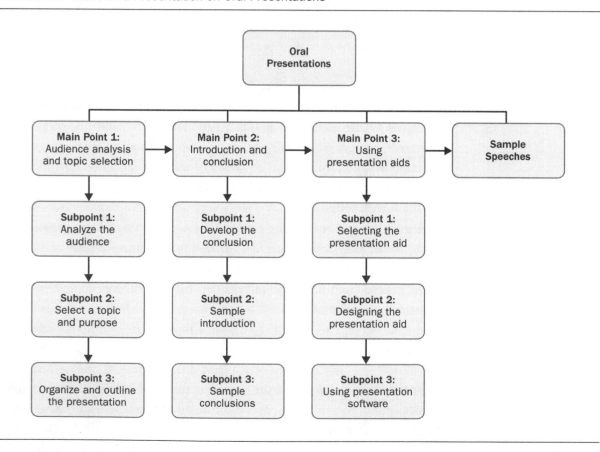

not end too early and leave the audience wondering if content was missed or skipped. Practice and time the presentation prior to the live session.

- **Use visuals effectively.** Use visuals to enhance the information in the presentation. If a visual does not add to the written text, do not include it. Also, ensure that information presented in the visual is accurate and clear. A confusing visual can be a major cause for an ineffective presentation.

- **Decide what information needs to be included.** Using a presentation organizational chart assists in organizing important points.

- **Provide an effective introduction.** Include an overview of the presentation that provides a brief summary of main points and an agenda. Provide an attention grabber to gain the attention of the audience. Example opening techniques include a rhetorical question, personal story, statistic, or quote.

- **Discuss audience benefits.** Clearly present what the audience can gain from the presentation.

- **Build credibility for the speaker and project.** Discuss presenter qualifications for personal credibility. Use statistics and other references to establish credibility.

- **Use transitions between slides or main ideas.** Explicit verbal transitions need to be used in the presentation. Example transitions include next, the third point, finally, and in summary. Do not just jump from one topic to the next without clearly noting connections.

- **Provide a strong conclusion.** Include a summary of key points of the presentation or take aways for the audience. Include any action items that need to be completed by members of the audience or project team. Concentrate on main ideas. If time has expired, do not rush through every detail of the presentation. Instead, use the limited time wisely and cover main points.

A Special Note on PowerPoint

Effective use of PowerPoint can enhance a presentation. However, too often, presenters use PowerPoint slides as "a substitute for real planning, thoughtful discussion, and cogent analysis" (Woodridge 2004, p. 85). As a technical communicator, it is important to keep in mind the purpose of using PowerPoint as a presentation aid: to enhance, not detract from, the value of information presented. Simons (2004) points out two serious mistakes made by presenters using PowerPoint:

1. **The purpose for using visual aids has been forgotten.** The core reason for using visual aids is to assist a listener in understanding the material. If a listener cannot grasp the content of a visual in approximately six seconds, the audience is forced out of active listening mode into reading mode. Audiences cannot do both at once. If the audience is reading, attention is not being paid to the presenter. When designing a PowerPoint presentation, limit words in the title (use a subtitle if needed), words per line, and number of lines. In addition, nothing on the slide should be random—not the colors, fonts, or number of slides, animation, or sounds. What to use on the slides depends on the audience, so begin by keeping the goals of the audience in mind.

2. **The delivery of the visuals is ineffective.** Many presenters make the mistake of giving PowerPoint presentations in a dark room where the audience can barely see the speaker. Effective presenters need to be in some light (even from a simple can light in the ceiling) so that eye contact, facial expressions, and gestures may be visible to the audience. These nonverbal expressions add both interest and clarity to the presentation. Presenters also make the mistake of reading from the slides—a sure way to put the audience to sleep. PowerPoint slides should "aid" and reinforce the goal of the presentation. If everything the audience needs to know is written on the slides, the audience does not need the presenter.

Choosing Text or Graphics

Careful design of PowerPoint slides is critical to the success of a presentation. The presenter must first decide if text or graphics need to be used. Graphics common to technical presentations using PowerPoint slides include diagrams and schematics, charts, maps, graphs, and drawings. Visual aspects, such as number of graphics, typeface, and font size, use of color, and general design principles, need to be considered.

Visuals used in PowerPoint presentations may be in one of two formats: text or graphic. *Text visuals* are mainly text or printed words. The majority of material in a PowerPoint presentation is text. *Graphic visuals* either emphasize the text or show a different representation of textual material (not always included on the slide), such as a chart, graph, or drawing. Deciding on the type of graphic depends on the ideas explained in the PowerPoint presentation. Graphics can increase an audience's understanding by providing a visual explanation, allowing the audience to "see" the information. Text is a better choice when presenting steps in a process, including call to action items, and outlining main points of a written document.

The decision to use specific graphics or pictures in a PowerPoint presentation depends on the purpose. Graphics can assist audience members' understanding of the use of information in the presentation. The main purposes for including graphics in a presentation are to:

- Show readers how something looks
- Show readers how to do something
- Explain a process
- Show how something is constructed
- Show trends or other numerical relationships
- Present information

Diagrams and schematics provide effective visuals and are available through templates or the drawing toolbar in Microsoft Word or PowerPoint. To access sample diagrams in either of these software programs, go to Insert/ Diagram on the menu bar. If complicated diagrams or schematics are needed, a graphic designer or graphic artist can assist in the creation of these more complex visuals.

Visual considerations, such as the number of graphics, typeface, and font size, use of color, and general design principles, need to be thought about

A Word about Clipart

While clipart is provided in Microsoft Office© programs and other publishing software, there are special considerations one should think through before inserting these graphics into a presentation or document. The first thing to note is that clipart is generic and the message it sends is generic as well. There are also restrictions on how one can use clipart.

Appropriate and Inappropriate Uses of Clipart

One key to successfully using clipart is to find a picture that captures an idea presented by the text on the slide. This is not easy to do because clipart is designed to be rather generic or standard. Once in a while, however, a picture will be exactly what one is looking for to enhance the message. It is important though to find that thin line between inspiring and ridiculous. For instance, symbols can be relevant and meaningful to certain presentations, and the graphic provides a lasting image regarding the message; however, inserting clipart for the purpose of just having a graphic is not a good reason to use it. In fact, this kind of thinking can backfire and make the presenter look amateur, which affects how the audience will view the information in the presentation as well. Clipart is often cartoon drawings, although actual photos now also are included, but even so, the images are nondescript and there is essentially no real message that can be obtained from clipart. Furthermore, clipart generally does not explain or enhance textual information. For instance, inserting stickmen figures into a business meeting presentation is probably not a good idea. Stickmen figures add no value other than entertainment, which is not

when planning a presentation using PowerPoint. These presentations require additional considerations, including the appropriate number of slides and amount of text used on each slide. In an effort to avoid subjecting the audience to "death by PowerPoint" or "PowerPoint Poisoning," it is critical to observe these guidelines.

When designing a PowerPoint presentation, it is imperative that the goal of the presentation is met, mainly providing the intended audience with information. For example, while the color yellow may be bright and cheerful, it may be difficult to view in a visual presentation. Typically, darker colors, such as blues, dark greens, and black, are best selections for font color. When contrasted with a lighter background, the audience can clearly see the text.

usually why an audience is sitting through a business meeting. Besides, the stickmen are so common they are not really all that funny or entertaining anyways. This is not to say that audiences do not want to be entertained, but this will not happen in a business meeting by using a stickman figure that has a light bulb above its head.

So why would someone use clipart? Borders and holiday images can make educational materials more visually entertaining for the intended audience of students. And students can find clipart that creates a lasting image about a particular subject they may be writing on, which is actually the first step in learning how to use graphics in documents. For business situations, however, clipart has limitations and presenters should seriously analyze their reasons for including such generic images and whether the image actually serves a purpose other than taking up space. The result of adding clipart to some presentations could be disastrous, while for other less formal situations, such as school, the inclusion of such artwork is certainly acceptable and somewhat entertaining.

Restrictions on Clipart

Clipart is not part of the public domain. It is owned by whomever puts it out and there are usually guidelines or restrictions attached to its use. For example, the clipart found in the suite of Microsoft Office programs, according to information found on *www.microsoft.com,* can be used for school or church, but it cannot be used for commercial purposes. It cannot be part of a company's logo or used to advertise a business or product.

Holcombe and Stein (1996) offer specific guidelines for designing Power-Point slides, illustrated in figure 8.2. When reading the slide, think about how many of the design tips are followed. Additionally, what design guidelines are not followed? How does this impact the quality of the visual? Effective use of text and design tips for PowerPoint slides are shown in figures 8.3 and 8.4.

When using PowerPoint, these guidelines should be followed when creating slides:

- **Title:** Use a 30- to 36-point font.
- **Subtitle:** Use a 24-point font.
- **Text:** Use an 18-point font (can use a 24-point font if not a subtitle).

FIGURE 8.2 *Ineffective Use of Design Tips for PowerPoint Slides*

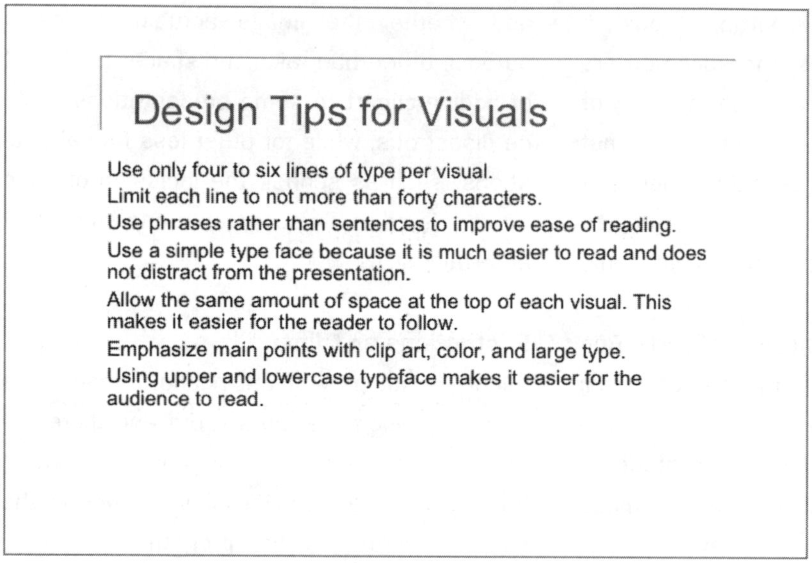

Design Tips for Visuals

Use only four to six lines of type per visual.

Limit each line to not more than forty characters.

Use phrases rather than sentences to improve ease of reading.

Use a simple type face because it is much easier to read and does not distract from the presentation.

Allow the same amount of space at the top of each visual. This makes it easier for the reader to follow.

Emphasize main points with clip art, color, and large type.

Using upper and lowercase typeface makes it easier for the audience to read.

FIGURE 8.3 *Effective Use of Text in a PowerPoint Slide*

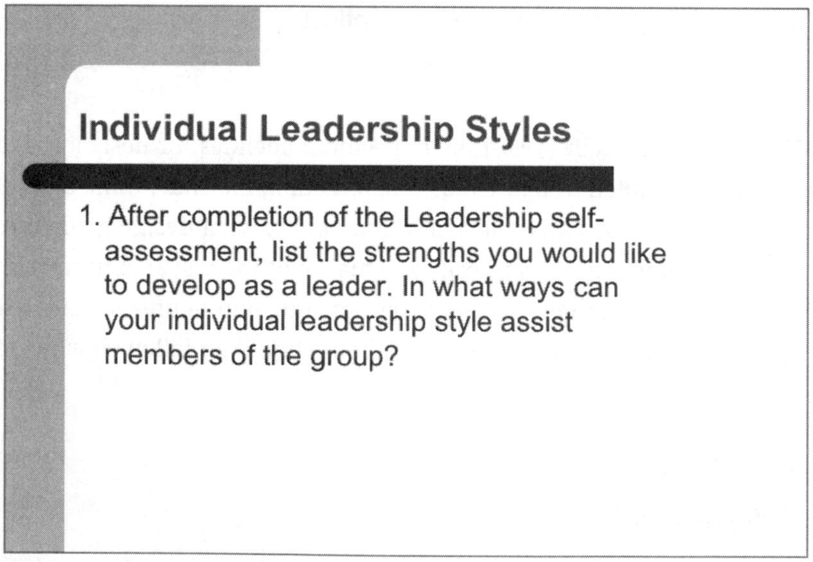

Individual Leadership Styles

1. After completion of the Leadership self-assessment, list the strengths you would like to develop as a leader. In what ways can your individual leadership style assist members of the group?

FIGURE 8.4 *Effective Use of Design Tips with Graphic and Text*

Stages of Group Development

Team development experts define four stages of progression in professional collaboration:
•Forming: Orientation
•Storming: Conflict in professional collaboration
•Norming: Creating cohesion in the group
•Performing: making decisions and solving problems

Typefaces can affect the readability of PowerPoint slides and should be considered carefully when preparing presentations. Suggested typefaces, compiled from Buchanan (1993), Dewsnap (1992), and Williams (2004 and 2006), are listed below:

- Times New Roman (official)
- **Arial** (professional)
- Century (friendly)
- Garamond (sophisticated)
- Palatino (upbeat)
- Veranda (modern)
- Bodoni (trendy)
- **Poster Bodoni** (playful)

Avoid using a fancy or script typeface because it is difficult to read. The following typefaces should not be used in presentations:

- *Freestyle Script*
- **Brush Script**
- *Shelley Script*
- *Kunstler Script*
- *Park Avenue*

PowerPoint may be an effective presentation tool. However, it is important that the presentation be clear, concise, and designed in a way the audience can read and understand. Avoid copying and pasting blocks of text from written papers. Include key phrases that underscore the main point of the presentation. As with any written documents, sources need to be documented for any thought, idea, or expression borrowed from another source.

REFERENCES

Antonoff, M. 1990. Presentations that persuade. *Personal commuting,* 14:62–68.

Buchanan, C. 1993. *Quick solutions for great type combinations.* Cincinnati, OH: North Light Books.

Dewsnap, D. 1992. *Desktop publisher's easy type guide: The 150 most important typefaces.* Rockport, ME: Rockport Publishers.

Grice, G. L., and J. F. Skinner. 2004. *Mastering public speaking.* 5th ed. Boston, MA: Pearson.

Hamilton, C. 2008. *Communicating for results: A guide for business and the professions.* 8th ed. Belmont, CA: Thompson Higher Education.

Holcombe, M. W., and J. K. Stein. 1996. *Presentations for decision makers.* 3d ed. New York, NY: Wiley.

Mayer, R. E. 2001. *Multimedia learning.* New York, NY: Cambridge University Press.

Simons, T. 2004. *Bullets may be dangerous, but don't blame PowerPoint.* From presentations.com. Retrieved 17 July 2007 at *www.presentations.com/presentations/search/search_display.jsp?vnu_content_id = 2063909.*

Vogel, D. R., G. W. Dickson, and J. A. Lehamn. 1986. *Persuasion and the role of visual presentation support: The UM/3M study* (in-house publication, pp. 1–20). St. Paul, MN: 3M Corporation.

Vogel, D. R., G. W. Dickson, and J. A. Lehamn. 1990. *Persuasion and the role of visual presentation support: The UM/3M study.* In: M. Antonoff: Presentations that persuade. *Personal commuting,* 14.

Williams, R. 2004. *The non-designer's design book: Design and typographic principles for the visual novice.* 2d ed. Berkeley, CA: Peachpit.

—2006. *Robin Williams design workshop.* 2d ed. Berkeley, CA: Peachpit.

Wolff, F. I., et al. 1983. *Perceptive listening.* New York, NY: Holt, Rinehart, & Winston.

Woodridge, E. T. III. 2004. *Order a PowerPoint stand-down.* Proceedings of the United State Naval Institute, 130, 85.

PART II

TECHNICAL COMMUNICATION IN THE WORKPLACE

CHAPTER 9

Collaboration in the Workplace

Turn on the television news any day of the week and there will be a celebration of teamwork on a football field, basketball court, baseball diamond, hockey rink, or soccer field as fans cheer their favorite teams. As much as the American culture values independence in life and the workplace, teams and their collective victories are honored. Working with others allows individuals to promote their strengths and complement any weaknesses while building on the ideas and research of others.

WORKING AS PART OF A TEAM

Whether bouncing ideas off of colleagues, passing a document by a supervisor, or collaborating with larger groups of writers and subject matter experts, technical communicators often find themselves as part of a document design team. As a member of a project team acting as a collective group with a joint objective or final goal, individuals must communicate effectively, in a timely manner, and work collaboratively with others to complete the project.

Being a Team Member

When chosen as a team member for a technical communication project, individuals may have extremely different ideas about the project, goals, or even the other team members. To work effectively together, differences, sometimes substantial, need to be put aside. As with all types of technical communication, the purpose remains the key element, giving group members a clear focus and reason behind their efforts. Developing objectives, goals, schedules, and deadlines becomes easier when everyone is aware of the purpose behind the project.

Top Five Tips for Working in Groups

1. Remember that group work is about creating a solid final product, not competition.
2. Respect the ideas of others, but feel free to disagree.
3. Offer encouragement and potential solutions when introducing a problem or difficulty.
4. Do not procrastinate.
5. Communicate difficulties as soon as possible to avoid creating additional issues.

Even with a clear purpose, teamwork can be riddled with opportunities as well as challenges, such as the following:

- Teams in the workplace at times form with members from a number of different departments, offices, or branches within a company, and occasionally from a number of companies.

- Technical communicators may comprise an entire project team, or they may be joined by subject matter experts, such as engineers, computer programmers, or others with specialized knowledge.

- Members of financial departments may be involved to keep the task on budget, and human resources specialists often are included when projects involve the welfare of company personnel, such as policy manuals or training materials.

- Target audience members, for example, clients, may hold specific roles in the process as well.

- A number of supervisory or administrative levels may be represented.

All of these differences, including those normally faced in the workplace, such as cultural, racial, religious, gender, and age variations, can make working as a team challenging or rewarding.

Overcoming differences is a must if a team plans for success. The ability to share ideas, communicate suggestions, and feel comfortable with each other's efforts allows a team to create a high-quality final product. To accomplish this, team members must know their individual role, how their participation will be evaluated, and the expectations of the other members. Working in the true spirit of collaboration, sharing, encouraging, and learning from one another, also allows for unique opportunities. Seeing team members as resources rather than competition brings about a community atmosphere and promotes the exchange of ideas. An open exchange of information in return allows for higher levels of creativity and increased team morale. After all, a team who enjoys the collaborative process is more likely to create a top-quality product and leave the group with positive experiences. *Synergy,* which is the ability to work together and create a sense of energy within the team, is a key factor to the team and product's success.

In the Spirit of Collaboration

Working together and sharing ideas allows for brainstorming, group editing and revision, and a delegation of tasks. Creating a superior final product becomes the goal of the entire team, not merely one writer, and additional insights, strategies, techniques, and areas of expertise are shared across the entire group. Collaborative efforts can reward team members by way of creating social and professional ties as well.

However, as individuals, it can be difficult to suppress individual wants and goals for the good of the team. This is when collaborative groups often disband. Individuals may join together to counteract a team design, and while it need not be as dramatic as a government coup, it will cause distinct separation of goals, objectives, and products. When working as a team, group members

Benefits of Working in a Group

Working in a group may seem awkward or frustrating to some as it can place additional constraints on ideas or time. However, teamwork allows for a number of benefits such as those listed below:

- Collaboration gives participants a chance to learn from each other and use the other team members as resources.
- In large companies especially, working in smaller groups that span departments can forge new relationships and also build a sense of unity.
- Breaking a large project into smaller pieces allows each team member to specialize on tasks rather than become overwhelmed with an entire project.
- Working in a group gives each member a chance to reach out for assistance if there are issues or problems.
- New ideas are created when participants work to build on an initial thought.

occasionally may be distracted from the overall goal. Individual personalities or insecurities may emerge. When this occurs, the spirit of collaboration may be evaded for personal gain or interest. Team members may insult the work and ideas of others, attempt to take on large portions of the project on their own, convince other group members of their own superiority, or even refuse to share information as a form of self-preservation, or in an attempt to control the project. However, a number of team-building strategies can help in keeping the community environment growing in collaborative efforts.

While these negative interactions may not be completely avoidable, by ensuring that roles within the team are delineated and that lines of communication remain open, even the worst conflicts can be worked through.

Roles within a Team

Occasionally, teams find themselves working with a clear structure or hierarchy. This happens most often when someone of a supervisory level acts as the team leader or coordinator. At other times, determining the team structure is not as easy. For instance, if there are a number of participants who share the same position, experiences, or levels of supervision, determining a leader may be more difficult. At this point, a supervisor or other individual outside of the group may appoint a leader. If this is not the case and it is not clear who will act as the team leader, the group may elect one, or one may emerge based on personality. Regardless of whom the team coordinator happens to be, everyone on the team, and those the team may contact or work with, should be aware of the coordinator's role and contact information.

Other common roles within a team include publicist, scheduler, accountant, editor, researcher, legal advisor, and subject matter expert. Further roles may emerge or be called for due to the specialization of a team. Each role aligns with specific tasks and requires varying degrees of expertise. However, one individual might take on more than one role during the collaborative process. The roles are defined as follows:

Publicist. The publicist, sometimes called a secretary or group historian, is responsible for recording the group activities. This person takes minutes and attendance and is charged with distributing them after meetings. The publicist may be tasked with group communication, such as distribution of files, standards, and schedules. The publicist compiles pieces of the project and formats the final document as well. Also, any information that fits the task of public relations and informs those outside the group of their progress is usually written and dispersed by the publicist.

Scheduler. A team's scheduler creates a schedule of deadlines and assists in maintaining the project timeline. Deadlines are managed by the scheduler, although they are normally determined by the group as a whole. Often, general deadlines for large parts of the project are set by mutual agreement and the scheduler works to determine target dates for the pieces or tasks that comprise the larger deadline. For instance, if the first portion of a project consists of eight chapters and needs to be finished in 10 weeks, the scheduler would set the primary copy, review, and editing deadlines to fit within that 10-week time constraint. The scheduler needs to be apprised of any setbacks, including those at the individual level, in order to keep the team on task and on time.

Accountant. A team accountant may be appointed by a company or client to ensure the project remains within the designated budget. The budget may come from the estimated cost the group determines, or it may be established by a department not represented in the collaborative team. Regardless from where the project budget stems, the accountant estimates costs, tracks expenditures, makes the majority of product or supply purchases, and reports any needed financial information to the group or other entities requiring it. Unlike many roles, the accountant position may be filled by someone outside the group to whom the group reports or who acts as a comptroller.

Editor. Editors face the task of finalizing documents. Like editors in many scenarios, the group editor has final mandate on all written material. This means that editorial decisions regarding wording, format, style, tone, mechanics, and other writing-oriented judgments eventually fall to the authority of the editor. The editor also may review the material as it becomes due, make comments on graphics and text, and set the style templates for the product. The level of editing, or the amount the editor is allowed to change the document, should be determined by the group or announced by the team leader at the beginning of the project. This allows team members to feel a degree of comfort in the integrity of their work, ensuring it will not be misrepresented. The position of editor is often held by an individual who writes a section of the project. Having more than one editor allows for group review and decisions. If there is only one technical communicator in the group, this task usually falls to that person.

Group Researcher. Group researchers can fill two roles, completing the primary research required for the project and checking facts or specialized information for accuracy. Researchers may conduct interviews, construct citations, and ensure factual accuracy for the project as a whole. This role does not have to be given to one member of the team; instead, each writer may be responsible for his or her own material.

Legal Advisor. Legal advisors hold a rather specific role and not all groups will have a need for one. When there is a need for a legal advisor, this person normally acts as a consultant rather than a full-time group member. However, the role of the legal advisor can change the content of the document entirely as the advisor is generally in charge of whether specific information can be included. The legal advisor may be charged with obtaining permissions for information that is to be referenced or may determine that information is confidential, a liability, or not supported enough to publish.

Expert. Subject matter experts will differ depending on the type of project. These individuals are able to offer specific knowledge regarding the subject matter of the project, yet they may not be familiar with creating the type of documents needed. For example, while software programmers created the program, they often are not the most qualified to create a user manual. This task may be given to a group of technical communicators who are asked to work with the programmers to learn how the program works and what information needs to be conveyed. Other experts would include physicians, engineers, product leads or coordinators, human resources specialists, legal advisors, researchers, and political analysts. Subject matter experts may be employed by the team's company, or work on a consulting basis, but they will be the authorities on the technical or scientific elements of the project and should be heeded. While these individuals are the professional specialists, commonly they do not hold other positions within the group. While editors and researchers may be one in the same, subject matter experts concentrate on their content focus and generally do not contribute to other areas of the project.

Team Dynamics

Interpersonal relationships and how team members interact does quite a bit to define how a project will culminate. Creating a team identity and defining who the group is can help promote interdependence and communication. Part of a group's identity will be defined by the culture of which it is a part. For example, a collaborative group in an industry will have a different product, process, and relationship than a group working in a nonprofit organization. The policies, guidelines, and general philosophy of the surrounding organization can change how team members communicate as well as their expectations of others.

Another influence on a team's dynamics is the purpose of the group and the nature of the group's product. What tasks is the group collaborating on?

Will the group work together throughout the entire project or work independently unless determining deadlines and budgets? How much of the project will be decided by the group rather than controlled by others? The answers to these questions shape the amount of collaboration that will be done, as well as how often the group will meet or if there will be a peer-review process implemented.

Interaction. How and when a group interacts needs to be determined at the beginning of the project. Determining whether the group will share information by email, group meetings held in person, web conferences, telephone, or through use of a web bulletin board or shared web space or office intranet, also changes how the group collaborates.

Deciding on the type of predominant communication can depend on a number of issues. Geographic location, time constraints, and cost can limit the number of face-to-face meetings that can be held during the course of a project. As more virtual collaboration efforts enter the workplace (discussed later in this chapter), these factors come further into play, and have both positive and negative aspects. Even if teammates are in the same office, time constraints and additional projects may interfere with an ideal meeting schedule. Because of this, other avenues need to be taken.

The way the team will interact and communicate can be determined by a supervisor or group leader. However, to make all group members feel comfortable with the method of communication, it is advisable that the group determine the method, if at all possible.

Interdependence. The actions and outcomes of each individual are at least partly determined by the actions of others in the group. One task not being completed by deadline has the potential to change other deadlines and tasks entirely. One piece of a project coming in over budget can potentially eliminate other items. In this way, all tasks and group members depend on each other and are connected in a web-like way.

It is this web that allows for true collaboration. Working together and being dependent on other members of the team works to eliminate competition and individual feelings of superiority. Also, the ability to communicate conflicts or issues without fear of condemnation encourages team members to work together, offer each other solutions, and take on additional tasks when they cannot be completed as assigned.

Assigning Tasks. While working with predetermined roles within a team can assist with the designation of specific tasks, there generally will be some tasks that do not fit into a role neatly. Initially, tasks can be outlined based on the profession of each group member. For instance, the software programmer would act as subject matter expert and offer technical particulars, while the hired technical communicator would act as researcher, editor, and publicist.

When the profession of the team members does not designate roles or tasks, they need to be assigned. This can be a supervisory task or one determined by the group. It is recommended that the group make as many decisions together as possible to encourage interaction and ensure each member has a voice in the decisions.

Make Decisions as a Team

Any decisions that can be made as a group, should be. This encourages collaboration and gives members a voice. Often, when each participant feels comfortable sharing concerns and ideas, communication is at its peak. However, a system should be put in place to deal with any discrepancies that come up in the decision-making process. Designating a process or a final decision maker within the group early on can help eliminate any issues that arise when the group cannot make a joint decision.

Regardless of how tasks are assigned, all tasks need to be delegated as soon as possible with the majority designated at the beginning of the project. Deadlines also should be assigned at the same time if at all possible.

Evaluations. It needs to be made clear to team members if and how their participation or individual parts of the project will be evaluated. Peer evaluations are common in projects, but this is not always necessary.

These evaluations allow group members to report on the participation and effectiveness of others throughout the project. This makes each member accountable to the others for his or her own actions and efforts.

Regardless of whether the group participates in formal evaluations, the group leader or coordinator should be prepared in the case that evaluations need to be assessed for the group as a whole or for the individuals taking part. To complete formal evaluations, task-specific objectives need to be set at the beginning of the project. These expectations must be communicated to the group members. Evaluations, especially those conducted by supervisors or group leaders, may be included in overall job performance appraisals, thereby influencing raises or bonuses based on these appraisals.

Setting Deadlines

While the task of setting deadlines may belong to one team member, the scheduler, more often the final deadline is set by an outside organization. This leaves the team to create its own sub-deadlines to complete the project on time. When setting these internal deadlines, all steps of the process should be considered. For example, the conception process, the phase where the group works together to determine roles and tasks, what the final product will be, and how they will create it, should have a finite deadline. Without a concrete deadline for this process, concepts can continue to generate and complicate the creation of the product. This may be the most inflexible deadline of the creation process, yet without it, the project never begins. The team must get out of the concept phase in order to progress to creation.

Team members work as individuals on many project components. They can be made responsible for their own deadlines as long as they know when their pieces should be in the hands of the group. The review process needs to be determined as well. If the team will use an internal review method, with members reviewing the work of others, this needs to be factored into the project schedule, as does enough time for members to revise their pieces.

All deadlines should be clearly communicated to team members and formally documented. Individuals also need to know who to contact if there is a problem meeting the deadline. Having regularly scheduled status meetings will help keep individuals accountable for their tasks, while continually facilitating communication between all group members.

LEADING A TEAM

While it has been said that no man is an island, the same may be true about technical communicators. Because so many are involved in collaborative work, a number will find themselves leading a team through a project at one time or another. They may head a team of only fellow writers, or the group may be more heterogeneous and involve those with other backgrounds and professions. Regardless of the team's makeup, there are a number of responsibilities a team leader must face.

Choose the Participants

In a perfect scenario, a group leader hand selects the people he or she wants as part of the project team. In the less-than-perfect world where most work, teams are formed by availability and job-related tasks involved in the project. Team members may be assigned or offered up when departments find they need to contribute to the team. The team members may not be those best suited for the project, but rather those the departments felt they could spare.

However, when team leaders are able to choose group participants, the task associated with the project should be the focus. To select the best suited individuals, the team leader must think ahead to the final product in order to choose those who will complete it most efficiently. Making sure the right people are assigned to the right jobs is a clear way to create a good team dynamic. When team members feel assigned to tasks that allow them to stretch, but do not require a large learning curve, the team can work to create ideas and learn from one another instead of focusing on catching up with the information they should know. Regardless of who is on the team, it is the mission of the team leader to use team members in the best, most productive way.

Build a Team

Once members are selected or assigned, team building begins. Motivating team members and creating a sense of community is a large part of structuring a team. Recognizing the team members as the experts they are goes a long way in developing trust between group members and their leader. This also encourages others to look at the team as resources and individuals with valid ideas. In this type of environment, ideas and new information are more apt to be welcomed than scorned and competition can be kept to a minimum.

Managing Conflict

Group leaders are often the mediators when dealing with group conflicts, be they based on actual issues or personality. To assist in these situations, it may be necessary to speak to those involved individually. However, if the conflict can be addressed within the group, that is generally the best way to handle the situation while keeping all members informed. For instance, if the conflict first comes to light during a meeting, addressing it immediately may keep it from escalating further. If the conflict is brought to the leader's attention on an individual basis, the dynamic has changed. Instead of addressing it as it occurs, the leader must first decide what the true issue is because it was not witnessed firsthand. Researching the conflict at this point can be an important part of the mediation and should not be avoided.

Ensuring that team members know what is expected of them is another way to make them feel comfortable with the interaction. Clearly defined goals and deadlines give the team a chance to manage their time and other tasks. Setting these expectations early works best and changes must be communicated immediately to ensure they all have the same information and time to adjust.

Another consideration of building a strong team is to determine the rules of communication immediately after the group is formed. This lets team members know who to contact about specific issues and the most appropriate ways to communicate. No member should feel insecure or apprehensive about reaching out to other members for information. Thus, setting clear communication methods will help ease tension between members.

Build Ideas

Giving the team a chance to form ideas as a group is important. A leader should avoid piloting the team and presenting personal ideas as rules or policy. Instead, the team should be able to brainstorm and polish ideas. While the leader may bring up basic plans, introducing finished products does not allow the members to work together, nor does it validate their experience. This process may take longer, but dictating the information to the group will have devastating effects. It is worth taking the extra time to hear and document all group members' ideas.

Assign Tasks

Specific roles and associated tasks often take shape in a team. However, there are occasions when team leaders must assign tasks. This happens when tasks do not match the expertise of the team members, or when no one in the group volunteers for a specific part of the project.

In order to assign tasks, they first need to be determined. Doing this as a group can be beneficial because team members can contribute their ideas to what needs to be done and how to accomplish it. This collaboration requires a clear purpose and a team willing to share ideas, while it also requires a strong leader to help guide the discussion to meet the specific needs of the project.

Asking for task-specific comfort levels can assist in the assignment of undesignated tasks. Above all, a leader must use his or her best judgment when determining what tasks need to be assigned and must consider the time constraints, number of tasks assigned, ability of each team member, and how much time the individual has to dedicate to the project.

Negotiate Conflict

Difficulties most likely will emerge during any project, whether or not they are completed collaboratively. Of course, the more people involved in a project, the greater the risk of personality conflicts, competition, and conflicting ideas. The role of conflict negotiator lies with the leader.

Determining the type of conflict becomes a priority because it can be easier to deal with time management conflicts than personality conflicts. In one scenario, the leader could reassign a task. When dealing with personality issues, a strong leader must handle the conflict while respecting each member's rights to their own beliefs, work habits, ethics, morals, and overall personality. Any type of conflict can work against the group's morale or product creation, so each conflict needs to be taken care of with haste.

Personal disputes are not always about the project at hand. Instead they can stem from a number of cultural or social issues. Differences in personality, work habits, or ideas can promote conflict that originated with the project. However, once these divergences hit a personal level, they are harder to deal with and those involved are likely to become defensive and critical. Handling issues before they escalate often can keep the focus on the project and off the personal differences of the team members.

Other conflicts may involve individuals outside the team, including clients, subject matter experts, and supervisors. At this point, a team leader is generally responsible for speaking for the team and upholding the goals and objectives the team deemed important.

CONDUCTING MEETINGS

"Meetings: None of us is as dumb as all of us." This caption appears on a faux inspirational poster created by Demotivators (*www.despair.com*). While the poster is designed to be humorous, the reality is that many people in the workplace feel just this way. Employees often cringe at the thought of attending yet another meeting in their already full workweek. But why do meetings elicit such a response in so many? It is the poorly planned and poorly executed meetings that leave employees feeling like their time has been squandered. They also waste countless work hours and thousands of dollars each year. According to Merrick Rosenberg (2006), "A single weekly staff meeting costs hundreds of dollars per meeting and tens of thousands of dollars each year" (p. 14). This is fine if the meeting is accomplishing something substantial, but if it is not, then it is just wasting time and money while irritating employees. However, taking the time to plan and then following through with good management can produce happier employees and more productive meetings.

Identify the Purpose

The first step to ensuring an industrious meeting is to clearly define the *purpose* of the gathering. There are generally three reasons for holding a meeting: to brainstorm ideas, to convey important information, or to make decisions. Sometimes one or more of these will overlap in a single meeting. For example, a committee may meet to generate ideas, and then make a decision at the end as to which ideas will be further developed. Still, the organizer should take the time to define what needs to take place. It is a good idea to draft out a statement of purpose, just as a writer would before beginning any other project. Knowing the purpose will allow the organizer to create an agenda.

Knowing the purpose also allows the facilitator to decide whether a meeting is truly necessary. Meetings take time out of everyone's day, and it is important to consider whether a meeting is indeed the best course of action. Some information can be passed on in an email or memo rather than in a meeting. A facilitator never needs to waste employees' time. Additionally, some meetings may be easier to hold over the phone or via video conference. These options will be discussed later in the chapter.

Create an Agenda

Once the purpose is clearly established, an *agenda* can be created. The agenda is a formal listing of what needs to take place at the meeting and in what order. It also should include the amount of time dedicated to each agenda item and a start and end time for the meeting. This will give attendees an idea of how much time they need to set aside for the meeting. If there will be multiple speakers or presenters, that information also should be included. To further accommodate attendees, the agenda should also include the location of the meeting, the call-in telephone number (when available), and a link to the meeting's Internet-based component (when available). The agenda should be sent out to all participants at least 24 hours in advance, though allowing more time is preferable. Early distribution of the agenda allows those who will attend the meeting to come prepared. Additionally, making a printed agenda available can help keep the meeting on task and on time. Figure 9.1 shows an example agenda.

Choose the Attendees

After the purpose and agenda have been set, it is time to decide who needs to attend the meeting. It is easy to assume that everyone needs to be there. However, the reality may be that only a few key players actually need to be in attendance. Only those persons who require the information being discussed or need to be present for a decision to be made should be invited. Inviting excess people wastes time and money, irritates employees, and can bog down the meeting. For instance, if a meeting is arranged to discuss a standard operating procedure that involves only the accounting department, but the entire office is in attendance, the non-accounting audience members may ask a number of questions that do not apply to the topic at hand simply because they lack an understanding of the basic procedures used in the department. The organizer will end up wasting a great deal of time answering these questions. Taking the time to analyze who truly needs to attend a meeting will make the entire experience more effective for all involved.

FIGURE 9.1 *Meeting Agenda*

AGENDA

Purpose: To review the curriculum revisions made in ENG 301 to run in the fall

Date: August 3, 2007

Time: 1:00 PM–2:00 PM

Location: Third floor conference room

Attendees: Ann Baker, Sally Smith, John Rogers, Alicia Lee, Samuel Ray, Troy Barton, Alan MacArthur, Leanne Jones

Discussion:

1:00–1:20 PM	Review the narrative essay assignment for clarity and relevance.
1:20–1:40 PM	Review the research essay assignment for clarity and relevance.

Decisions:

1:40–2:00 PM	Decide whether the course is ready to run in the fall semester.

Choose Where, When, and How

Deciding the time and location are equally important to the success and effectiveness of the meeting. A poor location or an inappropriate time can adversely affect the meeting's outcome. When choosing a location, make sure the room will comfortably hold all of the attendees. It should be in a convenient location that is easily accessible to all participants. There should be adequate seating for all attendees, and if note-taking is expected or required, tables should be provided. The room also should be fully equipped with whatever additional tools the meeting facilitator will need (e.g., projector, screen, lectern). The meeting room should be set up and ready to go well before the meeting participants begin arriving, which may mean that the meeting facilitator needs to arrive and check the room personally 10 minutes or so before the scheduled start.

When choosing the time, it is important to be considerate of other people's time and schedules. Early morning meetings (before 9:00 AM) should generally be avoided in order to allow employees to begin their day and get organized. Conversely, meetings should not be held late in the afternoon right before people begin leaving for the day. A meeting held at 4:00 PM on a Friday will probably not be very effective. It also does not leave much time to act or follow up on anything that was decided during the meeting. If employees are calling in from different sites, be mindful of the different time zones and office hours for those individuals. Likewise, the facilitator must consider the needs of attendees who are traveling from other locations to attend the meeting; leave enough time for them to arrive from the airport and get settled, while also leaving enough time for them to leave the office to return to the airport. Meeting times should be as unobtrusive as possible.

Technology also gives meeting facilitators some options regarding how a meeting takes place. Sometimes meeting in a physical location is not possible, practical, or cost effective. In those cases, several other options are available. Audio, video, and computer-assisted meetings can allow people from around the globe to meet, discuss, and make decisions from the comfort of their respective offices. They can help keep costs down and are very convenient in many instances.

However, they also come with a unique set of challenges. Technology does not always work like it is supposed to, whether due to operator error or technical malfunction. Additionally, some participants may not be comfortable using unfamiliar tools or systems. Taking time to test out all systems ahead of time can help prevent technical problems. Additionally, making sure that all attendees have been trained to use the technology and that they have all required tools can prevent any discomfort on the part of the participants.

Audio Conference. Audio conferences are held using telephone bridges. These conference calls can be used to hold meetings for parties who are not in the same physical location. This can be a great solution if the funds are not available to bring everyone together for a face-to-face meeting.

When hosting an audio conference, the rules are the same as for a meeting held in person. The same considerations for time, attendees, and agenda should be observed. Additionally, attendance should be taken at the start of the call because the facilitator does not have the benefit of seeing who is present. It is also a good idea to ask participants to have the agenda in front of them because the facilitator will not be able to put a copy up on a projection screen for everyone to see. Finally, the facilitator should ensure that all participants know how to use all of the audio features, such as the mute button. When the audio conference concludes, a summary of the call or meeting minutes should be sent out to everyone originally invited to the meeting.

Video Conference. Video conferencing is another popular option when a face-to-face meeting is not feasible. Video conferencing operates similarly to an audio conference except that the participants can see one another on a specially designed phone unit or via a website. Because specialized equipment and connections are needed for video conferencing, this option may not be readily available at all companies.

The ground rules for hosting a video conference are similar to those for a face-to-face meeting. However, some additional considerations should be made. For example, the facilitator should introduce all participants (or have them introduce themselves) so that everyone knows who is in attendance and to whom they should direct their questions. This is an important step given that some of the participants may have never met and might not recognize one another. The facilitator also should be aware, and make everyone else aware, that there may be a slight delay in the transmission of audio or video. As with a face-to-face meeting, eye contact and personal appearance count in a video conference. The facilitator should ensure that his or her focus remains on the camera and that he or she is dressed professionally and prepared to lead the meeting.

Web-assisted Conference. One of the more popular interactive venues in which to hold long-distance meetings is the web-assisted conference. This method combines the audio conference call with a visual, web-based component that allows participants to view a presentation or screen simultaneously. For example, the program Adobe® Connect™ allows all participants to view the same screen that is under the control of a presenter, or multiple presenters, while listening to a live audio feed or calling in to a conference call. Many of these programs allow the facilitator to easily see who is online, and thus in attendance, while ensuring that everyone is looking at the same page. The considerations for holding an audio conference apply to this style of meeting as well.

Facilitate the Meeting

Once the details of arranging the meeting have been set, it is time for the facilitator to actually lead the meeting. It is always wise to open the meeting with a review of the purpose and goals established in the agenda as well as a reminder of the time allotted to each topic. It is the facilitator's job to ensure that these goals are met, and that the meeting is run so that the focus is not lost. Below is a list of important points to keep in mind when leading a meeting:

- **Get people involved.** Make sure attendees partake in the meeting and any discussion that needs to take place. A successful meeting is one where the attendees are actually contributing to the discussion and helping to generate ideas and solve problems. A facilitator can encourage greater participation by asking questions that require more than a yes or no answer.

- **Do not let one or two people dominate the meeting.** In every group there is at least one person who always tends to jump in and take control of a discussion. While that can be useful up to a point, a good facilitator will never let one or two people take over the discussion and keep others from participating. The facilitator should jump in and invite others to give their opinions. The facilitator even may need to gently and politely remind the dominating individual(s) that everyone's voice needs to be heard.

- **Do not talk over everyone else.** If a facilitator wants attendees to get involved in the meeting, he or she should not make a habit of interrupting or talking over others. While it may occasionally be necessary to break in and keep the discussion moving, a facilitator should not frequently interrupt to make his or her own ideas heard. This type of behavior eventually will result in a drop in participation by attendees. Also, keep in mind that it is especially difficult for attendees who are conferencing in over the telephone to follow conversations when they are overlapping.

- **Manage conflict between participants.** There may be times during a meeting where two or more participants disagree, sometimes vehemently, about an idea or course of action. While conflict can be

Avoid Meeting Chaos

Meetings can generate great ideas and intense energy about topics and projects. There are times, though, when the ideas and energy can turn into chaos with everyone talking at once and no one being heard. A leader needs to be prepared to adeptly handle this type of situation, whether it is positive or negative, before it breaks up the flow of the meeting and upsets attendees. One effective method to handle this type of situation is to create a Parking Lot for ideas, comments, questions, or complaints that are not quite in line with the agenda. Before the meeting begins, set up a whiteboard or easel that can be seen by those attending the meeting. Clearly put the heading Parking Lot at the top of the whiteboard or paper, so that everyone can see it. As topics are brought up that are not related to the agenda, suggest adding those topics to the Parking Lot for later discussion. It is extremely important to leave time at the end of the meeting to address the items in the Parking Lot; the leader should determine which items need separate meetings and which can be addressed through email or other communications. The logic behind creating the Parking Lot is that attendees feel their ideas and concerns do not go unheard, even if they are not completely in line with the agenda.

redirected to generate new, creative solutions, the facilitator must also ensure that it does not obstruct accomplishing the meeting's purpose and that it does not get out of hand. The facilitator should emphasize any areas of agreement while minimizing the point of contention in order to diffuse any tension, and push toward a solution rather than letting participants focus on differences. The facilitator also should keep the discussion focused on the ideas being discussed to keep the conflict from turning personal. In situations of conflict, the facilitator needs to suggest that the discussion be continued after the meeting or propose to schedule another meeting to specifically cover the topic that the participants cannot agree upon.

Record Meeting Minutes

Unless it is an extremely informal gathering, *minutes* should be recorded for all meetings. Meeting minutes create a permanent record of the meeting's proceedings. They are a written record of who was there, what was said, who said it, and what resolutions were reached. Minutes provide a great summary of the meeting for anyone who was unable to attend. They also can be used for follow-up purposes and to guide future meeting agendas. Next steps for attendees and the facilitator should be prominently noted in the minutes.

Meeting minutes can be formal or informal in nature. Formal minutes should follow the format set out in an organization's procedure manual when available. Informal meeting minutes can take the form of a memo or outline highlighting the main topics and subsequent ideas generated. Regardless of the style, minutes always should be composed using correct grammar, spelling, and usage. Minutes should not include slang or overly informal language. They should be written in concise, complete sentences, and personal opinions or judgments should not be included as minutes are to be an objective record of what was said.

Because meeting minutes create a permanent record, they must be accurate. One person should be responsible for taking notes during the meeting and typing up the minutes so there are not multiple versions floating about. It is often most efficient if someone other than the facilitator takes notes so that the process does not distract the facilitator and interrupt the flow of the meeting. To further ensure accuracy, the minutes should be sent out to everyone who was in attendance so that any discrepancies can be noted and corrected. An example of meeting minutes is shown in figure 9.2.

WORKING IN VIRTUAL TEAMS

Collaboration with others is part of living and working in the professional world. A high portion of our daily communication occurs in groups, such as family, coworkers, and friends. Regardless of career choice, it is likely that individuals will spend a considerable part of their personal and professional lives working in collaboration with others. The changing environment of the workplace has caused an increase in the use of virtual teams for collaborative projects. The major difference between a virtual team and a team that meets face-to-face is the distance that lies between members. It is distance that affects the interaction between group members. Technologies, such as teleconferencing, email, Web-enabled chat, groupware, and shared file programs, have made communication at a distance and virtual collaboration possible. Through technology, virtual teams are able to interact, complete projects, and resolve conflicts.

FIGURE 9.2 *Meeting Minutes*

Minutes of the Biannual Meeting of the Curriculum Board
August 16, 2007

Present: Ann Baker, Sally Smith, John Rogers, Alicia Lee, Samuel Ray, Troy Barton, Alan MacArthur, Leanne Jones

Ann Baker called the meeting to order at 1:00 PM. The previous meeting minutes were read and approved with no corrections.

Old Business
None

New Business
The revised narrative essay assignment was reviewed and compared to the previous version. Samuel Ray made a motion that the page requirement be increased to six pages instead of four in order to facilitate a more in-depth writing experience. Alicia Lee seconded and the motion passed.

The research essay assignment was reviewed and discussed with special attention to source requirements and topic suggestions. Leanne Jones motioned to remove the topic suggestions from the assignment. After debate, the motion was withdrawn.

Ann Baker motioned that we adopt the new version of ENG 301 for the upcoming fall semester. Troy Barton seconded and the motion passed.

Announcement
Ann announced that the next meeting would be held on February 3, 2008, at 1:00 PM.

Samuel Ray made a motion to adjourn the meeting. John Rogers seconded. The motion carried, and the meeting adjourned at 2:04 PM.

Respectfully submitted,

Sally Smith

Sally Smith, Corresponding Secretary

Reaching beyond technology, virtual teams are similar to traditional teams in many ways. Teams, in general, are formed to resolve problems or complete a project. Virtual teams may be formed for a specific project, such as writing a user guide, or may be more long term in the example of employees working from home or telecommuting. It is important to learn ways to promote effective communication within virtual teams and to become knowledgeable of the practices that make working in virtual teams both productive and enjoyable.

The concept of working in virtual teams has grown in importance as the world of work has reached beyond the boundaries of the cubicle to a more global perspective. There are many benefits associated with virtual teams, including the ability to work with a wide range of individuals in remote locations (both nationally and internationally); reduction in cost for organizations as communication occurs through electronic means; and, the ability for technical communicators to work on projects from a virtual location. For example, virtual teamwork allows employees to work on team projects with individuals in other off-site locations or branch offices. For some corporations, this includes both national offices as well as offices at the international level. There is a cost reduction for the organization because travel expenses are eliminated as virtual team members communicate through various technological means. Virtual teamwork also allows opportunities for virtual team members to work from home or telecommute. Travel time is reduced, allowing for more time to work on the virtual team project. Additionally, employees have flexibility to control their own work time, thus reducing the stress often associated with commuting.

There are also challenges to collaboration involving virtual teams, including ensuring that multiple voices are heard, creating equal distribution of work among team members, and establishing a pattern for communication at a distance. There may be uncertainty among group members about when to use the various communication channels. For example, is it appropriate to discuss issues via phone, or is email the only form of communication? A strong system for managing the flow of information needs to be in place. Virtual team members need a means of exchanging documents, allowing for revisions and review of information. The absence of nonverbal communication also creates the need for frequent clarification in electronic correspondence. For example, the tone of an email may seem abrupt to the reader; however, the writer of the email may have a direct style unfamiliar

The Role of Cultural Differences in Virtual Teams

It is important to realize that not all cultures view or solve problems in the same way (Adler 2002; Ivancevich and Matteson 2002; Triandis and Albert 1987). Managers in the United States expect problems to occur, and quickly identify them when they do. Managers in Asian countries, such as Thailand, Malaysia, and Indonesia, are more likely to accept situations for what they are and take longer to identify problems. Also, in the United States, a single individual (usually a manager) assumes the final responsibility for decisions. In Sweden, the responsibility for decisions also rests with an individual, but that individual may be a low-level employee. On the other hand, in Japan, it is a team that makes and assumes responsibility for decisions (Hamilton 2008, p. 255).

to the reader. Without the nonverbal expression present, it may be difficult to interpret the true meaning of the message without asking for clarification. A challenge also may exist in software or hardware incompatibility issues between team members. It is important that technology issues are addressed prior to beginning work on the project.

Before making a decision to work on a project involving virtual teams, cultural diversity among group members needs to be considered. In a globally diverse workplace, individuals encounter decision-making situations with people from diverse cultural backgrounds.

Although various cultures view problem solving differently, research discussed by Nancy Adler (2002) shows that multicultural groups have definite advantages because of their different backgrounds, the members are less susceptible to "groupthink," and they are more likely to produce a creative range of alternatives. These advantages are especially important when problems are complex. Adler (2002) notes that successful teams do not ignore their diversity; they manage it. This is especially important for virtual teams. To manage diversity, Adler (2002) recommends that multicultural groups do the following:

- Recognize differences by describing the range of cultures present.
- Elect members for their task-related abilities.

- Find a purpose, vision, or ultimate goal that "transcends individual differences."

- Avoid cultural dominance and encourage equal participation.

- Develop mutual respect for each other.

- Seek a high level of feedback from each other and the leader.

Both virtual and traditional teams undergo various stages of development. Understanding these stages will assist in improving communication and resolving conflict among virtual team members. Tuckman's (1965) model has been widely accepted because it identifies the central issues a group faces at each stage of the development process. Tuckman named these stages forming, storming, norming, performing, and adjourning. Wheelen and Hochberger (1996) confirmed that groups can be observed moving through each of these stages.

Tuckman's (1965) stages of group development may be described as the following:

- **Forming** is the initial stage of group development during which people come to feel valued and accepted so that they can identify with the group. At the beginning of any group, individual members will experience feelings of discomfort caused by the uncertainty they are facing in this new social situation.

- **Storming** is the stage of group development during which the group clarifies its goals and determines the roles each member will have in the group power structure. The stress and strain that arise when groups begin to make decisions are a natural result of the conflicting ideas, opinions, and personalities that begin to emerge during decision making. There may be underlying or expressed tension as members struggle to determine each other's status and role in the group. Although storming will occur in all groups, some groups will mange it better than others.

- **Norming** is the stage of group development during which the group solidifies its rules for behavior, especially those that relate to how conflict will be managed. As the group successfully completes a storming phase, it moves into a phase where its members begin to apply more pressure on each other to confirm the direction and goals of the project. During this phase, the norms or standards of the group become clear. Members for the most part comply with norms. Slight conflicts may occur based on differing opinions, but a consensus is quickly reached during this phase.

- **Performing** is the stage of group development when the skills, knowledge, and abilities of all members are combined to overcome obstacles and meet goals successfully. Through each of the stages, groups are working to accomplish their goals. During the performing stage, conversations are focused on problem solving and sharing task-related information, with little energy directed on relationship building. In this stage, members freely share information, solicit ideas from others, and work to solve problems.

- **Adjourning** is the stage of group development in which members assign meaning to what they have done and determine how to end or maintain interpersonal relations they have developed. Regardless of whether a group is short-term or ongoing, all groups experience endings. As groups move through the various stages, group leaders must be ready to intervene and provide support for moving the teams to the next level.

When organizing a virtual team for a technical project, the following factors need to be considered:

- **Project design.** The project must be collaborative in nature, calling for multiple individuals to complete it. A file management system needs to be in place that allows individual group members to work on the project simultaneously. For example, many organizations have groupware or a file sharing system for virtual team work. This software allows for documents to be "checked out" electronically by only one person at a time. Working with collaborative software avoids repetition by not allowing more than one person to work on a document at one time. Use of editing tools, such as the track changes feature in Microsoft Word, allows for members of the team to view changes made and comments suggested by other team members. A timeline needs to be established for completion of the project and each virtual team member needs to be committed to completion of the project in the timeframe decided by the group. Checkpoints throughout the process need to be in place to ensure that the virtual team members are moving forward with the project and completing the assigned tasks according to deadline.

- **Communication.** Communication systems need to be established that encourage ideas, questions, and concerns to be directed to the virtual team members.

- **Virtual team member roles.** A virtual team project needs to be organized around a set of team roles and responsibilities. Roles need to be created that address both the talents and interests of the team members. The roles also must take into consideration the work distribution by each member. An equal amount of work and responsibility needs to be established among the varying roles played by the virtual team members.

- **Clear instructions and expectations.** It is important to clearly provide instructions for virtual group members that outline a timeline for completion, clear instructions for communication, an action plan if a member does not adequately participate, steps required for completion of the project, and a reassurance of equal distribution of the workload.

- **Training.** Prior to assigning an individual to work on a virtual team project, it is important to train group members on the use of the collaborative tools for communication. For example, all group members need to be trained on using editing tools, such as track changes, or learn file sharing software.

- **Group membership.** Criteria need to be established by the manager or team leader for managing group membership. Virtual team members must establish guidelines for handling disruptive or non-engaging group members and develop guidelines for handling these situations. Examples of common conflicts and resolutions that occur in virtual teams are presented in the sidebar.

Examples of Conflicts and Resolutions in Virtual Teams

Conflict: Lack of performance by a group member
Resolution: Meet individually with group member to reaffirm the goals of the project, time frame, and responsibilities of the group member. Do not publicly discuss poor work performance in front of the entire group. The group leader or project manager should hold a private conversation with the individual group member regarding performance issues.

Conflict: Misunderstanding of project goals or individual responsibilities
Resolution: Clarify perceptions of project goals and individual responsibilities. If information is conveyed in an email and an individual is unclear as to the goals or responsibilities, provide another form of communication. Often, a phone call may clarify confusion. Establish a supportive, not defensive, climate for the virtual team. Keep communication lines open.

Conflict: Individual differences in ideas
Resolution: Apply the active listening skills: stop, look, listen, question, paraphrase content, and paraphrase feelings. Clarify goals of the project to all group members.

Conflict: Individual group member feels he or she is being personally attacked
Resolution: Allow group members to express personal opinions, but do not allow personal attacks on individual members. Keep the discussion focused on the issues. Use a problem-solving approach to managing differences of opinions. This involves discussion of the problem and potential resolutions. Speak in a calm manner. In certain situations when a resolution cannot be reached by all group members, agree to disagree.

Trust. Developing strong interpersonal relationships in any group setting is based on a degree of trust for the members. The greater the level of trust the members have for one another, the greater the cohesiveness of the group. Trust in virtual teams is critical to the success of the team. Because virtual team members work away from the physical setting of one another, developing and maintaining trust is critical to performance. In a physical setting, a group member can see other members working on the project. In contrast, virtual team members must trust that the members are doing the work they say they are.

In a traditional face-to-face team, nonverbal communication can indicate a person's behavior. In virtual teams, trust is built on general behaviors among group members. These behaviors are illustrated through competence, integrity, and respect. Competence involves group members staying on target with completion of individual tasks. Integrity involves ensuring that actions are consistent with words. Additionally, it is important for the virtual team members to support the team and communicate with other team members about the progress of the project. Respect involves helping team members manage conflict and being mindful of the individual impact of one group member's action on the entire team.

As the global workplace becomes increasingly smaller and more diverse, more organizations are incorporating virtual teams into their work groups. When a decision is made to work on the project involving virtual teams, challenges and benefits of virtual group work need to be clearly articulated to the virtual team members. Group members need to establish guidelines for effective virtual team work including defining roles and responsibilities, establishing criteria for managing group conflict, and developing a communication system for exchange of ideas and information. A sense of community needs to be embraced by the virtual team members to ensure that every voice is heard in the virtual group project, and the goals of the virtual team are met.

REFERENCES

Adler, R. B. 1977. *Confidence in communication: A guide to assertive and social skills.* New York, NY: Holt, Rinehart & Winston.

Hamilton, C. 2008. *Communicating for results: A guide for business and the professions.* 8th ed. Belmont, CA: Thomson-Wadsworth.

Rosenberg, M. 2006. 60 minutes you'll never get back. *T + D,* 60(3), 14. Retrieved on 14 November 2007 from Business Source Premier.

Tuckman, B. W. 1965. Developmental sequence in small groups. *Psychological Bulletin,* 6393, 384–399.

CHAPTER 10

Longer Forms in Technical Writing

C hapter 3 covered the shorter, less complicated forms most technical communicators will encounter on the job. As mentioned in that chapter, there is often a crossover between technical and business writing, and this applies to longer forms of communication as well. This chapter covers those longer, complex forms that many technical communicators will find themselves having to compose, edit, or co-create with a team. Technical documents, such as feasibility, recommendation, progress, and empirical research reports are probably some of the more common forms of writing associated with technical communication; however, a technical communicator also may have to write up office policies and procedures manuals or process documentation, sets of instructions, technical specifications, and user guides. This chapter covers each one of these document types in detail and provides a general superstructure for each one.

TECHNICAL REPORTS

Technical reports can be part of any professional's job whether or not he or she is a technical communicator. There are some main report types that all professionals should be aware of because they are used across the disciplines; thus, all professionals will find themselves as writers, contributors, or readers of the reports covered in this section. Whether one is in science, business, medicine, or other professional fields, feasibility, recommendation, progress, and empirical research reports are common forms of documentation. The basic superstructure for each report is the same no matter the field; however, each company or discipline will have slight modifications. This section provides readers with a detailed description of each report type and the basic superstructure that goes with it.

What is a Superstructure?

Superstructure is the basic outline or recommended sections for certain document types. It refers to the general report segments that are included in complex documents, such as technical reports, instructions, and proposals. The superstructure will be modified slightly depending on audience and purpose, but it is provided to give writers a template from which to work.

Feasibility Study and Report

A feasibility report is the result of a feasibility study, which is a study to analyze proposed solutions to a problem. Generally, a feasibility study and the ensuing report precede a full-length proposal and may be considered preliminary documentation. There are two reasons why someone would conduct a feasibility study and then document their findings in a subsequent report. To examine the first reason, consider the following scenario:

> The engineering firm Carla works for has determined that lack of version control and proper archiving of official documentation is the main reason customers have been receiving wrong or out of date publications. This is a concern that must be dealt with right away, so management has given Carla and another software developer, Juan, three months to research and propose a solution. That solution cannot exceed $15,000, and once a decision has been made, the solution has to be in use company-wide within six months.

This is not an easy task, and the first thing Carla and Juan have to do is plan their approach. Because their research findings will be part of a full-length proposal, a good place to start is with a feasibility study and report. They would do this because there are several solutions to version control and archiving, and they have to find the one that best fits their company's needs and budget. In this case, a feasibility study can be conducted to review how each solution they find in their research stands up against their company's criteria, two of which are a specific time frame for implementation and a budget. Each solution will be weighed equally against a set of criteria to see which one is the best option. *Criteria* refer to items or guidelines by which something will be judged. All of this information is reported to management via the feasibility report. The feasibility report will help management determine if the solutions Carla and Juan come up with are worth pursuing or if another route needs to be considered.

The other reason to conduct a feasibility study is to test the probability of one solution against a set of criteria. Consider the following scenario:

> The Safety Office for Wentworth College has been told by administration that it is to purchase bicycle racks and install them in front of all campus buildings so that people will not lock their bicycles along guardrails or create any other hazardous situations with parked bicycles. It has been given a budget of $25,000 to purchase and install the bicycle racks and has been told they must be in place two weeks before the fall term starts.

In this case, the Safety Office has been given one solution to the problem—purchase and install bicycle racks. So, what would be the purpose of doing a feasibility study and presenting such a report to administration? Even when there is only one solution to a problem, a feasibility study can offer important information that may not have been considered when first choosing the solution. In other words, is the solution reasonable? For instance, can the front of each campus building accommodate a bicycle rack? What if there is no place to put it? Will new cement structures have to be created in front of some buildings? If so, that could drive up the price of the whole project, which means the $25,000 may not be enough. When administration thought of this solution, it probably only considered that the budget had to include the price of the bicycle racks times the number needed and the labor hours to install them. It probably did not consider special situations, such as where to place bicycle racks so they do not ruin the aesthetics of the campus, which could involve pouring new concrete slabs. A feasibility report in this case would tell administration details of the project and help determine whether its solution of bicycle racks across campus is really the best possible answer to the problem.

The general superstructure of a feasibility report, no matter whether it has one or multiple solutions, is described below.

Abstract. An abstract to a feasibility report is a short summary that explains the initial problem, the solution(s) that has been researched, and the criteria, and then states the outcome. This is written in brief prose that gives the reader only basic information contained in the rest of the report.

> Mechanical Engineering, Inc. (ME) provides a service of distributing design publications to customers. Lack of version control and an official archiving system have created a recurring problem in that customers are being sent out of date or incorrect files. To solve this problem, a version control and archiving system has to be purchased and implemented. There are multiple systems available, and research has shown that these can be purchased for $8,000 on up. Three systems were chosen and evaluated against a set of criteria. Given the number of employees and files produced at ME, the best solution for this company is a system called Document Management System (DMS) by Information Systems, Inc. The system costs $10,000, and with several training sessions for an additional charge, it can be in use within three months of installation.

This abstract tells the reader that Carla and Juan have found a system they think will fit the needs of ME, and it falls within the budget and timeline given by management. What it does not tell are the set of criteria, what other four systems were reviewed, and why this one was deemed best, except that it had something to do with the number of employees. There is also no mention of budget other than the initial cost. In this way, the abstract is kept brief and focused only on the main point that will motivate the reader to review the report following the abstract. Below is a second example that follows the same standard:

> Wentworth College is dedicated to providing a safe environment across campus, and while parked bicycles do not seem to pose significant challenges in this area, they have become a problem due to lack of bicycle racks campus-wide. Thus, students have been locking their bicycles along guardrails and in doorways, and have even restricted access to buildings or other thoroughfares in some instances. On May 15, 2007, administration gave the Safety Office a budget of $25,000 to purchase and install bicycle racks in front of every building on campus before the fall semester begins. After careful research, it is estimated that the budget to purchase and install bicycle racks across campus will have to be increased to $37,500. This increase is due to the price of the bicycle rack and also space restrictions in front of some campus buildings where new concrete slabs must be poured.

This abstract tells administration that the Safety Office can do as requested, but there are aspects that were not considered when putting a price on the project, which will be discussed in the report. This is one very good reason for doing a feasibility report because many times budget and timelines are decided arbitrarily without knowing all of the facts. A feasibility report makes the idea more concrete.

Introduction. The introduction of a feasibility report most likely will repeat some information from the abstract, but it will expand on anything borrowed from that section. The introduction serves two purposes: 1) It tells readers the problem in terms of why it is important to them, and 2) it tells them that there are one or more solutions to the problem and identifies them. For instance, in the scenario regarding the version control and archiving project, the problem is probably well known throughout the company. Everyone at the company can give an instance of when someone else sent the wrong file to a customer; but, how much has this cost the company in terms of lost revenue? For some people in management, unless the problem can illustrate a concrete negative impact on the company as a whole, their reaction to a short version of the problem description (as seen in the abstract) may be "Oh well. Send them the right file then." How about the company's reputation? Has anyone received feedback from customers about how their out-of-date or wrong files have caused customers added headaches? Has ME had to pay customers compensation for sending faulty files? How many labor hours are spent finding the correct file to send to a customer? All of this information can be turned into concrete numbers or anecdotal evidence and included in an expanded problem description in the introduction. Certainly, all of this should not be in the very first paragraph, but a clear and progressive picture of the problem is described in detail in the introduction. This may take several paragraphs.

In the example of Wentworth College, administration knows what the general problem is. Most likely someone filed a complaint or lawsuit against the college because access was restricted due to a parked bicycle. But, that may be all that it knows. The Safety Office can present a feasibility report using information from police reports and other reported instances of bicycle violations to make sure administration has a clear picture of how widespread the problem is. In addition, the problem of why there are not enough bicycle racks currently can be discussed. This is where writers of the feasibility report can begin to discuss the problem of putting bicycle racks in front of some buildings or maybe how the campus architect has objections to the placement of some racks. This kind of explanation needs to be part of the discussion because the problem and solution, as noted by the budget increase, is beyond just having a bicycle rack in front of every building.

Criteria. A project has many considerations other than a black-and-white problem/solution scenario. Once a problem is clearly defined in the introduction, other project considerations come to light. These considerations are what solutions are measured against. A set of criteria are certain objectives that must be met by any solution chosen. For instance, in the version control and archiving situation, only two criteria were given to Carla and Juan when they were first given this task: time and money. But, once the problem had been clearly defined and preliminary research into various software programs had been undertaken, other considerations came into play. For example, is the $15,000 only start-up money? What about yearly maintenance of licenses for commercial software products that they are looking into buying? Did management realize there would be an annual fee associated with this project? Suddenly, annual maintenance costs become part of the criteria set along with time and the original $15,000 budget. Furthermore, what about the cost and time dedicated to training all company employees? Who will conduct the training? Once again, two more criteria are added to the list: annual license fees and administration of training. Any software program under consideration now has to be compared to other software programs in terms of initial investment, annual license fees, administration of training, and time to implementation. Defining a problem to its fullest and conducting research into possible solutions is where writers gather their supporting criteria.

In this section of the report, each criterion is identified and explained. For instance, just listing "annual fees" may not be clear to those who are unaware or have forgotten about the expense of commercial licenses. It also may be a good idea to explain what is meant by a license and how licenses are distributed within a company. Additionally, explanation about how one criterion affects another criterion can be added. For instance, readers need to know that the original budget of $15,000 is now only considered a start-up cost and is separate from the added criterion of annual license fees.

If only one solution is under consideration, there are still various aspects to look at. In the case of Wentworth College, the Safety Office had to research various bicycle racks to determine which company to purchase from and which model to choose. Considerations such as method of installation, how many bicycles each rack can hold, and aesthetic and theft features of the racks are now part of the criteria set.

Discussion. The discussion section is where each possible solution is given a thorough examination as to how it stood up against the set of criteria. For instance, if Carla and Juan identify three possible software programs that can meet ME's needs, then the details about each program in terms of the criteria are given in this section. This can be set up in various ways, such as by product or by criteria. Consider the following two examples for ME's discussion section:

By Product

Product A: Features of product A are discussed in detail. Additionally, details about this product's initial investment cost, cost and administration of training, time to implementation, and annual maintenance fees are discussed.

Product B: Features of product B are discussed in detail. Additionally, details about this product's initial investment cost, cost and administration of training, time to implementation, and annual maintenance fees are discussed.

Product C: Features of product C are discussed in detail. Additionally, details about this product's initial investment cost, cost and administration of training, time to implementation, and annual maintenance fees are discussed.

By Criteria

Initial investment cost: Details about the initial cost for products A, B, and C are discussed.

Training: Details about the cost and administration of training for products A, B, and C are discussed.

Time to implementation: Details about the time it takes to implement products A, B, and C are discussed.

When only one solution is under consideration, an effective discussion section might list the criteria and then discuss the various choices within that criterion, as in the below example:

Installation: Discuss how there are various installation methods, some of which can be more destructive than others, some which are more secure than others.

How many bicycles each rack can hold: Like any product, there are various models. Working off of the above criterion about installation, the choices are now narrowed down to three possible models. While model A holds more bicycles, it is not as aesthetically pleasing as model B; however, model C is the most secure for the bicycles, but it does not hold as many bicycles as model A.

Aesthetic and theft features of the racks: The campus architect's office has specific criteria themselves that have to be met before any structure can be installed in front of campus buildings. Those criteria and how each model stands up to them are discussed.

In this section, an important detail to tend to is to make sure that each solution or criterion is treated equally. When more than one solution is being measured against the set of criteria, it is not helpful if only three of the four criteria are considered with product A, but all four were looked at when researching product B. This kind of thoroughness shows readers that the information contained in the entire report is professional and reliable.

Results. While at first it may seem like the discussion and results section are the same, this is not entirely true. Yes, much of the information from the discussion will be used in this section, but what happens from the discussion to this results section is that the information from above is condensed. In this section, readers are looking for only results and not discussion. What this means is that, when it comes to each product in the version control and archiving problem, readers are looking to see if product A, B, or C meets all of the criteria. Basically, they want to know the bottom line of how much each product is going to cost now and later, which product failed miserably against the set of criteria, and which one looks most promising. This information usually is given through textual discussion, but visuals can aid in the presentation. An example table is shown in table 10.1.

Recommendation. A recommendation differs from results in that one product now has to be chosen and the rationale for choosing that product is given, and most importantly, the recommendation is predicated on the information

TABLE 10.1 *Visual Aid for Showing Comparisons*

Criteria	Product A	Product B	Product C
Initial investment	$10,000	$8,000	$13,000
Training	$3,000	$4,500	$1,000
Time to implementation	3 months	5 months	1 month
Annual license fees	$4,000	$7,000	$3,000

in the previous sections of the report. Knowing one's audience is crucial when making a recommendation because a decision can be made based off of the results of the study, but it can also be rationalized based on what is important to readers. Money may not always be the determining factor. With ME, start-up money and low annual maintenance fees for licenses were the determining factors because management forgot all about this added annual expense. Conversely, in the case of Wentworth College, the least expensive bicycle rack was the most destructive in the installation process. Administration, knowing it has to adhere to other campus policies, such as the criteria demanded by the campus architect's office, easily can understand that the cheapest bicycle rack may not be the best solution. A detailed and logically explained rationale for the recommendation is probably the most important aspect of this section.

Conclusion. As with any professional report, a conclusion or final wrap-up of the report is necessary to close the document. In the case of a feasibility report, one way to do so might be to reiterate how the recommendation will solve the problem and is the right course of action to take. The next steps in the project lifecycle also can be discussed once a decision, based off of the report, is made.

It may appear as if this report could be used easily in place of a proposal, but that is not often the case. A feasibility report only tells its audience that the proposed solution fits or does not fit the criteria. It is true that much of the information in a feasibility report will be carried over into a recommendation or progress report, and even to the final proposal, but the purpose of this report is to first determine the suitability of a solution for a problem. If this step is missed, a proposal could be midway in progress when researchers find out that the solution is too expensive or it does not meet other essential criteria. All of that information should be sorted out prior to composing a formal proposal.

Recommendation Report

A recommendation report can be used in place of a feasibility report. This choice is often determined by readers. Reasons why readers might want a recommendation report instead of a feasibility report are time constraints, matters of trust, and delegation of tasks, or the level of detail usually addressed in a feasibility report is too much for certain decision makers; they simply want the recommendation for a solution as well as the rationale. This type of report is often given to decision makers in higher management who have a middle manager who can be concerned with the details of a feasibility report. While a recommendation report can be referred to as a shortened version of a feasibility report in some respects, the research and critical thinking involved in a feasibility study should not be skipped. As mentioned in the section above, a comprehensive description of the problem as well as preliminary research will render a great number of perspectives on both the problem and solution that may have not been thought of initially. These details have to be conveyed in a recommendation report as well.

The purpose of a recommendation report is to suggest one solution to solve a problem and explain why it is the best choice. The superstructure, as detailed below, for a recommendation report is fairly basic, and the information is somewhat abbreviated from what one finds in a feasibility report. The basic superstructure for a recommendation report is detailed in the following sections.

Introduction. The introduction for a recommendation report will not differ much from a feasibility report. It will describe, in ample detail, the problem being addressed and why it is of concern to readers. Careful exploration of the problem from different perspectives is crucial to providing the right solution, so it is wise not to rush through this section; instead, bring to light all aspects of the problem for readers. The recommended solution and a brief explanation about why it was chosen should be part of this section as well. For most American decision makers, they would want to know this information in the first paragraph. International readers may not want to digest this information so quickly, so depending on the readers' culture, the rhetorical strategy for that culture should be used instead of the up-front American approach. The introduction also should include discussion about other possible solutions that were looked at to solve the problem, just like in a feasibility report.

Discussion. In this section, a list and explanation of criteria should be included so that readers are aware of how the recommendation was derived. The same detail and care about explaining the criteria in the feasibility report should be followed for this report as well (and can be a separate section if it is extensive). The one difference between this discussion section and the feasibility report discussion is that each solution is not necessarily called out and measured against the set of criteria. Instead, the focus of this section in a recommendation report is on how the suggested solution is the best choice. The rationale for the recommendation is the most important part of this section, which should depend on how the solution stood up against the criteria, as well as any other relevant information. All other options can be addressed together, but without the detail that the recommended solution is given.

Conclusion. The conclusion for the report reiterates the rationale for the recommendation and wraps up the whole document. No new information should be presented at this point. The next steps in the project lifecycle also can be addressed should the decision makers approve the recommendation.

Readers should ascertain from a recommendation report more about the problem than when they first started reading; they also should have a clear understanding of what options were looked at, but most importantly, they should have a definite solution to consider and all of the facts surrounding that recommendation. The trust decision makers place in the hands of those who put together a recommendation report is immense because they are counting on all of the information to be accurate and thought through in the most critical manner. Sometimes millions of dollars can be riding on readers taking the advice given in a recommendation report. So, while the report itself may not be as detailed as a feasibility report, the background research that informs the recommendation should not be any less.

Progress Reports

Progress reports often follow feasibility or recommendation reports, or even proposals because a decision has been made one way or another to move forward on the project. Progress reports provide details about the evolution of a project from start to finish, and are usually delivered in increments throughout the lifecycle of a project (weekly, monthly, quarterly). They are used most often for either complex or lengthy projects so that decision makers or other stakeholders can monitor the development of a project, and also the time and money being spent. These reports should not be taken lightly because decisions can still be made about a project based on the information in a progress report. The basic superstructure for a progress report is detailed in the following sections.

Introduction. The introduction can begin with an initial project description to orient readers about the particular project and remind them about the goal or end result. Readers of progress reports are usually familiar with the project, so the introduction serves to inform readers about only basic information, such as the time frame the report covers as well as a quick assessment about the progress of the project. American readers want to know immediately about any problems encountered, but international readers may find having this information in the introduction too abrupt. Depending on the audience, a writer has to determine where to put such critical information. For American audiences, the introduction can identify problems with the project and provide a brief explanation as well as whether the problem has been resolved or if an answer is expected as a result of reading the report.

Scope of Work. Decision makers and stakeholders need to have a good idea of the scope of work involved in a project. The readers have to know the big picture of all that is involved in completing the task. To say that bicycle racks have to be installed in front of all buildings on campus is actually a false picture of the project because some buildings already have bicycle racks. This section can identify which buildings need bicycle racks, which buildings have special circumstances, such as having to put racks on the side of the building instead of in front of them, or any prep work that has to be done prior to the racks being installed. The scope of the bicycle rack project also includes ordering information, such as what company was used, when the racks are expected to arrive, who is responsible for installing them (the company or the campus grounds crew), and even an overall timeline for the project. The purpose of this section is to illustrate a comprehensive view of the work to be completed from start to finish.

Work Completed. Because progress reports usually are submitted in incremental time frames, such as weekly, monthly, or quarterly, what stakeholders are counting on is that this section of the report will grow as time passes. The information in this section can be written chronologically, or it can use reverse chronology so that the most recent work is reported on first. There are several formats for this, such as using dates or listing by task; it just depends on the preference of the readers and/or the complexity of the project. The format that makes it easier for readers to track the work being done against the scope of work presented in the previous section is the best choice. Most times, work completed includes an explanation of what was done and the date that it was completed, as shown in the following example:

> **June 25.** Prep work on the north side of the English building included clearing away a 10' × 3' Chinese elm hedge. The hedge was cut down and the roots were dug up as well. The 10' × 3' plot was then prepared for a cement slab expected to be poured on July 10, 2007.

It is important to be thorough when reporting work completed, as this is a means for the reader to clearly see how much effort is going into the project. Minimizing the progress may reflect poorly on those working to complete the project.

Work to Be Completed. Just as readers expect the previous section to grow with each subsequent report, they also expect the work to be completed section to shrink. Based on the information under scope of work, this section details the tasks yet to be finished. Identifying the tasks is usually not enough because not all readers will be familiar with what is involved with every job listed; therefore, it is a good idea to include the task, who is responsible

TABLE 10.2 *Table for Work to Be Completed Section*

Task Description	Responsible Party	Expected Date of Completion
Cut out entire 10' × 3' Chinese elm hedge in front of English building	Facilities	June 25
Prep cleared area for 10' × 3' cement slab to be poured	Facilities	July 10

for the task, a description of the work to be done, and an expected date of completion. It also would be helpful to list the items in this section in the order they are slated to be completed. Visuals can help clarify textual discussion of this information, as shown in table 10.2.

Problems Encountered. Hardly any project is completed according to plan, and this is the part of a progress report that lets readers know the following:

- What problems have been encountered along the way

- What has been done to address or fix the problems

- What is being done to mitigate any further problems

- What advice or suggestions the readers have to solve a problem that is out of the writer's hands

This section is a good example of when clear, concise, and precise wording is absolutely necessary. If a writer is unclear about explaining any of the points above, it could result in confusion for readers and leave them thinking the problem is not as bad or is worse than it really is. This can lead to serious consequences down the road. Furthermore, mentioning a problem and then not following up on it by telling readers whether or not the problem has been solved, how it was fixed, and what has been done to alleviate any further complications will only lead to mistrust or doubt in the capability of project managers and staff or crew to complete the entire job successfully. This also could have serious consequences because if readers misunderstand this part of a progress report, it could mean shutting down the entire project whereby many people are negatively affected.

Recommendation. The recommendation section of a progress report is reliant on the previous sections. If work is moving along as planned, with no problems encountered, then this section may end up being only one sentence long: "It is recommended that the project proceed as originally planned." If there are problems to report, then this section is much more significant because readers are expecting to have an informed and well-thought-out suggestion about how to continue with the project despite the difficulties encountered. Readers expect those who are at the site or have hands-on experience with the project to know more than they do about how to move forward. Once again, a recommendation should be written clearly so that there is no mistake or room for misinterpretation about how this project is going to make it to the final completion date.

Conclusion. A conclusion to this type of report generally acknowledges the progress of the project, any problems encountered, and how they have been resolved, and reiterates the recommendation in the previous section. It is almost like a confirmation to readers that says, "Despite being four months behind due to late delivery of the bicycle racks, there is no reason why the racks cannot still be installed at this time."

Empirical Research Reports

When it comes to technical writing, empirical research reports are what most people equate with the term "technical report." It is true that of all of the reports discussed in this section, this report can be construed as one of the most scientific or technical, but this is due mainly to the intended audience and not necessarily the document type. Empirical research reports can be used to report the results of a scientific study or results of analyses. There is certain information that is vital to readers of empirical research reports because generally they are scientific experts themselves, and in order to accept the reported results, they have to have some background information first. The general superstructure for an empirical research report is detailed next.

Abstract. The abstract of an empirical research report follows many of the same guidelines as a feasibility report. It is meant to give readers an abbreviated discussion about the rest of the report. In this sense, it tells readers what the subject is, from what angle it is being considered, and alludes to the results of the study. It does not directly tell the results of the study unless those results are so incredible that readers are immediately intrigued and have to know how such results could be obtained. Generally, methodology is not part of the abstract because of its detailed nature.

Introduction. The introduction of this report type serves several purposes, and is intended to do the following:

- **Introduce the subject of the report.** As with any report, a writer has to introduce the subject to readers. This can be done in several ways depending on what the report is about. For example, if this is the result of a scientific experiment, then stating what prompted the research to begin with is a good place to start. Additionally, a problem description could be part of the introduction.

- **Present the hypothesis.** Readers want to know where researchers started in their thinking and what they were working to prove; therefore, it is important to state what was being tested, why, and what was expected as a result of the experiment or analysis.

- **Provide background.** Background can mean several things. It can be the theoretical background of the research, the project, or other similar studies, or even all three. The scope and amount of background will depend greatly on the intended audience.

Methodology. For expert researchers, this section is probably more important than the results section. Knowing how an experiment was set up gives clues to how certain results were obtained. It is this section that most readers will turn to when citing reasons why the results are valid or invalid; therefore, concise, clear writing is key to composing this section.

It is impossible to list all of the potential scenarios of information that can be included in this section because every experiment and analysis takes on unique characteristics. For purposes of content, basic information includes the following:

- Roles of researchers

- How groups were determined

- How groups were controlled

- Exact description and explanation of what happened within each group

- Setting and conditions of the experimental environment

- How many iterations of the experiment were administered

- Timeline, exceptions, and other pertinent details about the process and progress of the experiment or analysis

Assessment. Before launching into the results of the experiment, researchers want to know how the results will be interpreted. In this section, a list of criteria by which all results will be measured against should be included. Without this, just like in the feasibility report, readers have no clue how the results are being judged. This information can reference the background information or simply include a rubric of some sort. Again, that is determined by the experiment or analysis itself.

Results. The results section not only reports raw data, but it also includes a researcher's interpretation or assessment of the results. If only raw data were given in this section, then it would be up to each reader to interpret the results, which could lead to disastrous consequences. It is up to the researchers writing the report to connect the dots, so to speak, on how the raw data pertains to the theoretical information behind the hypothesis in the first place.

Lessons Learned. This section is not always included in every empirical research report, but it is always a good idea to conduct a lessons learned study after every experiment or analysis. A lessons-learned study and subsequent section is when everyone involved in the project sits down and discusses what went wrong and their successes, what could have been done better, and what they learned this time around that they would do differently next time. As with the methodology section, lessons learned can shed light on how certain results were obtained. This is enlightening information for those conducting the experiment or those reading the report.

Recommendation. The recommendation of an empirical research report is founded on all previous sections. Depending on the purpose, subject, and audience of the report to begin with, this section can take multiple avenues. What is important to remember here is that writers are clear about what they recommend, provide comprehensive rationale for making such a suggestion, and then discuss next steps.

Conclusion. The conclusion usually wraps up the report by restating the original problem or hypothesis and recommendation. It also can comment on the results obtained based on the previous information included in the report.

POLICY AND PROCEDURE MANUAL

Every company and organization requires a well-written policy and procedure manual, or employee handbook. This manual establishes clear and documented understandings of expectations, rules, and general guidelines for employment. It also creates a sense of community and common understanding. Although these manuals are most commonly written for a corporate environment, every organization consisting of employees or members should have a policy and procedure manual. Whether it is a police department, dentist office, university department, or parent/teacher association, none is exempt from the necessity of a policy and procedure manual. This section will describe corporate manuals, though this information can be easily adapted to any organization's needs.

Consider the following situation:

Marla comes into her place of employment, Acme Accounting, every day at 9:15 AM, even though the office opens at 9:00 AM, and she is the receptionist who is responsible for greeting clients. After settling into her desk, she turns on her computer and takes out her breakfast. The next 20 minutes are spent eating her breakfast and checking various email accounts, national news websites, and her friend's blog. By that time, she will generally remember to change the office's main telephone line to stop forwarding calls to the answering service; this is also so that she can receive her 10:00 AM telephone call from her mother.

When the first client of the day, Mr. Jones, comes through the door, he is not sure he is at the right place. This is primarily due to the atmosphere Marla is creating. She has her MP3 player hooked up to small speakers balanced on a filing cabinet so that she can listen to a "Learn Conversational Spanish" podcast. Beyond that, she is dressed in blue jeans, an ill-fitting t-shirt, and flip-flops. Mr. Jones is forced to stand in front of Marla until she is done yelling at her mother on the telephone. As a paying client, Mr. Jones feels that he deserves more respect and a professional atmosphere, so he brings this situation to the attention of the accountant working on his account.

Marla is confronted by her manager about her conduct, yet Marla argues that there is no policy about what conduct is expected of her. Without a policy and procedure manual for Acme Accounting, Marla is right and management is severely limited in what actions it can take against her.

Although a policy and procedure manual can clearly note policies on conduct, dress code, and other day-to-day issues, the manual also should contain information that an employee can use throughout his or her career with the company. Essentially, the overall content of the manual should be based on the expressed needs of the company and all of its employees.

Audience Analysis

Before determining what to include in the manual, the writer should be aware of and research potential readers. Who will be expected to read, understand, and use the manual? New employees, managers, corporate heads? It is likely that every member of the company will need the manual, so the writer needs to research the needs of all potential readers.

Analyze each employee and what he or she will bring to the manual. New employees may have some of the following characteristics to consider when deciding what to include and expand on in the manual:

- Take into account the potential age and experience of the reader; for instance, a recent college graduate versus a veteran in the field. What might someone who has never held a position in a large corporation need to know? What about someone transitioning from working out of his or her house to working on-site? Understand the company's hiring trends in order to predict the characteristics of new employees.

- Determine if the potential reader has undergone any orientation presentations upon starting with the company. If the orientation is thorough, then the manual will only have to review information the reader already should have heard or read. The manual will need to complement this information so as to not contradict it.

Existing employees may have information needs similar to new employees, but there are variations to consider, such as the following:

- Know the information already made available to employees, either through previous manuals, memos, or training. Also, a writer should know if the employees are likely to read a new manual once it is distributed.

- Understand the demographics of the readers in order to focus on what the majority of the employees will have concerns about. For example, are most employees nearing retirement or do they have child care needs?

Writing to meet the needs of every reader is a daunting task, but it is a requirement of writing a manual that will actually be read and used throughout the company. Focusing on the specific needs of the employees will help keep the writing task within reason. Once the needs are determined, a writer can easily move on to the next task—researching the required content of the manual.

Research

A reliable policy and procedure manual is supported with thorough research. Beyond researching the needs of potential readers, a writer must gather other information. Noted in table 10.3 are some suggestions of what a writer may research and possible places to find that information. Initially, Human Resources should have much of the required information, but there are other options beyond that department.

Many policies and procedures are often implied or passed on verbally from one employee to the next; these are not consistent or reliable methods

TABLE 10.3 *Research for a Policy and Procedure Manual*

Research Topics	Suggestions of Where to Research
Company history and facts	• Recently published marketing material and press releases • Employees, though double-check their information • Internal newsletters, intranet
Previous manuals	• Recently hired employees • Established employees who kept material from when they started with the company • Company intranet • Internet, other companies' manuals
Job descriptions	• Company intranet • Internet, job posting websites • Professional organizations related to job positions • Trade magazines and journals
Government regulations and guidelines	• U.S. government offices or websites • State government offices or websites • Company's legal department
Established policies and procedures	• Previous manuals, publications, intranet • Memos concerning new or revised policies • Department-specific managers

Internet Research

When researching on the Internet, here are some suggested websites to look at for ideas and information:

- Human Resources Guide, *www.hr-guide.com/*
- Human Resources Management, *www.managementhelp.org*
- Monster Jobs, *www.monster.com*
- Society for Human Resource Management, *www.shrm.org/*
- U.S. Bureau of Labor Statistics, *www.bls.gov/*
- U.S. Department of Labor, *www.dol.gov/*
- U.S. Government's Official Web Portal, *www.usa.gov/*

of communication in a company. The research process should account for this information. A writer can conduct interviews of employees and managers to discover this unwritten information, and then accurately document the information in the new manual. An employee cannot be expected to inherently know of such undocumented information, whereas the company cannot enforce those undocumented policies and procedures.

Tone and Writing Style

A policy and procedure manual can help build a community within an organization, especially for new employees who are often disorientated and alone for the first few weeks in the company. This type of scenario may compel a writer to take a more informal and casual tone with the manual, so as to put the reader at ease. Informal writing may be acceptable in the introduction and overview sections, but the remaining sections of the manual should rely on a formal tone. The formal tone, especially for the sections covering policies, will ensure that the reader takes the policies seriously and cannot misinterpret what is being represented. The overall tone for the entire document needs to be clear, simple, and accurate.

If it is necessary to use legal terms, industry vocabulary, or company-specific jargon in the document, these terms should be defined in the manual. Readers can be misled or become frustrated when constantly confronted with unfamiliar vocabulary. The reader may then put the manual down without reading through it or trying to determine what message is being conveyed. Whether the terms are defined in footnotes, sidebars, a glossary, or in the text of the sentence, it is the writer's responsibility to not write over the heads of potential readers.

Writing formally and clearly are typical means of not alienating a reader. It is also important to keep in mind that the tone of the writing should not be threatening, whether implied or blatant. The reader should not become fearful or defensive because of the tone used in the manual. The writer must be unbiased and detached while developing the content. Policies and repercussions should be worded in a professional, factual, and straightforward manner.

If the manual is going to be distributed to different international locations of the company, then a writer needs to be especially careful about the tone used in the manual. Research other available policy and procedure manuals in those particular countries to help identify any norms that should be reflected in the manual being developed. Also, a formal tone is generally most appropriate for international readers because it does not use clichés or slang, which are unfamiliar to readers from other countries.

What to Include

The needs of the company and target readers will dictate what should be included in the policy and procedure manual. There are certain sections that are required at a minimum:

- Introduction
- Table of Contents
- Contact Information (e.g., Human Resources)
- Specific Policies
- Relevant Procedures
- Benefits and Other Information
- Conclusion
- Sign-off Verification

Building Templates

A writer may be required to build a template for a policy and procedure manual so that any department in a company or organization can write manuals to follow the same style. For instance, a writer may design a template for the Arts & Sciences Department of a university, thus allowing every division of that department (e.g., English, Mathematics, Philosophy, and History) to put its individual content into the template. Microsoft Word allows a user to create and save templates. Here are some guidelines to remember while developing templates:

- Use company documentation as a guide for building a template, such as inserting a company logo in the proper place. This gives documents a uniform look. Referring to company documentation also gives a writer an idea of what headings/subheadings to include to help build the content.

- Build the style into headings and subheadings. Prepare headings so that all users have to do is either change the wording or begin typing in the space below a heading, which also should be formatted to retain the correct font size and style. Delete all other styles from the template so that there is no confusion. For instance, styles should be set for heading 1, heading 2, heading 3, heading 4, and normal text.

- Build instructions into a template where all a user has to do is overwrite the instructions with appropriate text. Guidelines can be part of a template, such as telling users not to go more than three levels deep with subheadings.

- Insert tables and graphs into a template to show proper format for those items, including how to label and position them.

- Include normal appendixes as part of templates, such as an acronym list that contains normal acronyms used in that line of work, so all the user has to do is update the list with the acronyms used in the actual document.

Beyond the required sections, the writer should consider adding additional information to the manual, such as the following, to create a more complete document:

- Company History, Overview, Goals
- Organization Chart
- Map of Locations

- Holiday Calendar
- Glossary of Terms
- Forms

A writer should be cautious about allowing the manual to become unwieldy with too much information. Every section needs to be considered essential to the company and employee. Including too much information will force the truly important information to become lost within superfluous sections.

The Internet and a multitude of software companies offer completed templates. There are some issues with using templates that a writer should be aware of prior to adopting one. These templates can make a manual seem generic, especially those that are overused in the industry. Also, templates can be copyrighted, so it is important to know if permission is needed to use the template or if modifications can be made to it without contacting the original creator; generally, copyrighted templates need to be purchased.

Introduction. Writing the introduction must be done with great consideration of the impression the company wants to make with not only new employees, but also existing employees receiving the manual for the first time. The introduction will set the tone for the rest of the manual, while it also should work to pull the reader in and make him or her comfortable. Too formal of an introduction may seem detached and cold, while too informal may seem unrefined and awkward. Defined by the company's image and work environment, the tone should meet those standards in an appropriate manner. Figure 10.1 compares an informal introduction with a formal introduction.

The informal introduction includes clichés, slang, exclamation points, and first- and second-person pronouns. All of this together makes the paragraph sound conversational, as if the reader is being greeted by an actual enthusiastic employee of the company. The formal introduction uses unambiguous language while conveying information that the reader needs to know before going any further into the manual.

After introducing the reader to the company, the introduction should note why it is necessary for the reader to review the manual in its entirety. Many readers are likely to skip around the manual and potentially miss

FIGURE 10.1 *Comparison of Informal and Formal Writing*

Informal Introduction	Formal Introduction
Welcome to Sunstar Software! We are excited to have you on board and looking forward to making you a key part of our outstanding team. Already you may be a little overwhelmed and anxious, but don't worry! You will fit right in and be on track in no time. This manual is a great way to get in touch with how things really work around here. Take some time to read through the manual, and then feel free to go find your manager to discuss any questions, comments, or concerns you have. We welcome all feedback from employees. Again, it is great to have you with us!	Welcome to Sunstar Software. The following manual is a means to help orientate new employees in current policies and procedures relevant to the company. Sunstar Software holds employees to the highest standards in order to consistently benefit customers. Thus, every employee is required to know and adhere to the policies detailed below. After reviewing this information thoroughly, bring any questions or concerns to the attention of management.

information that they are not aware is related to them. The reader needs to know that he or she is responsible for understanding the policies and procedures in the manual.

The introduction is also a good place to put statements concerning how the company is committed to honoring the Equal Employment Opportunity Act, the Americans with Disabilities Act, and Affirmative Action. This will help clearly establish that the company has high ethical standards for hiring and continued employment. If these statements are not included here, be sure to insert them in another prominent section of the manual.

Table of Contents. A table of contents is necessary for policy and procedure manuals because of the complex nature of the document. Essentially, the manual is written to provide specific information on a variety of topics and needs. A reader can navigate easily to the information at the moment it is needed if a clear and logical table of contents is available. The numbering system of the table of contents should match the numbering system used on the headings throughout the document; if page numbers are included in the table of contents, then the page the information begins on should be noted. For long manuals, subsections should be included in the table of contents;

short manuals only need to include main sections. Furthermore, a long table of contents needs to be designed for easy reading. Using ellipses (. . .) or lines (___) from the heading to the section number or page number are effective design options.

Contact Information. As a means to help orientate the reader with the company, a list of contacts for further information on various topics should be included in the manual. List the contact's phone number, location, and email address. Because this information is likely to change as employees join and leave the company, it is often most efficient to list general department information. For example, list the contact information for various divisions of Human Resources, but avoid listing actual names of individuals. Other departments that might be listed in this section include the mailroom, security, front desk or reception, payroll, or the cafeteria. Consider putting this information in a table so that it is easy to follow. Also, another option is to put the contact list on heavier paper or even a colored page to make it easier for a reader to quickly access. Even if the list is not extensive, just having some information accessible will help the reader feel more connected to the company.

Specific Policies. Information about specific policies does not need to be an individual section within the manual called "Policies." Rather, the specific policies can be organized and divided in a logical manner throughout the manual. While every company may differ on what policies need to be included, all of them should be written with unquestionable clarity. As for what policies to include in the manual, this is determined by the research done prior to writing the manual. Here are various examples of policy topics that might be included in a manual:

Absenteeism	Computer Usage
Bereavement Leave	Conduct Warnings
Break Times	Confidentiality
Business/Work Hours	Dating Coworkers
Client Interaction	Dress Code
Company Vehicle Use	Discipline

Dismissal	Probation
Expected Conduct	Promotions/Advancement
Family Leave	Safety/OSHA
Flex Scheduling	Sexual Harassment
Gifts, Bribes	Short/Long Term Disability
Hiring	Sick Days
Identification, Name Badges	Smoking
Information Privacy	Substance Abuse
Internet Access	Tardiness
Jury Duty/Witness Leave	Telecommuting
Military Service	Telehone/Cell Phone
Overtime	Travel Reimbursement
Parking	Worker's Compensation
Personal/Vacation Days	

Before writing a policy, realize the importance of wording a policy precisely because it can be legally binding for the employer and employee. To accurately get perspective on a policy, research the problem the policy will solve and in what context it generally will be used. The content of the policy should be simple: topic of the policy, consequences for not following the policy, and any clearly relevant background information to justify the policy and consequences. Write with authority, which means not using such words as should, might, perhaps, or sometimes.

Also write with clarity to make sure the reader understands and remembers the policy. Figure 10.2 provides examples of policies written following these guidelines. The procedure associated with the policy should appear separately. The policy can be followed immediately by a procedure related to said policy, but it needs to be clear what the actual policy is before explaining the procedure.

Relevant Procedures. Based on the policies included in the manual, procedures for responding to the policies should be included. It is also appropriate to include procedures relevant to every employee, whether or not there is a corresponding policy.

FIGURE 10.2 *Policies*

Dress Code Policy

[Taken from a radiology department policy and procedure manual.]

All radiology support staff, including receptionists, schedulers, and file clerks, are required to abide by the department's dress code policy, which is as follows:

Required: White pants, royal blue shirt, white lab coat or cardigan, and white shoes (white gym shoes or white clogs are acceptable)

Unacceptable: Jeans, spandex or knit pants, tight or low-cut shirts, sweatshirts, fleece shirts or jackets, open-toe shoes, shoes with a pronounced heel, or boots

Note, clothing restrictions are not limited to the list above; your manager will ultimately determine if your clothing is appropriate for work. If your manager deems your clothing inappropriate, you will be sent home to change. You will be responsible for making up the time lost while going home to change. If you are sent home more than three times in a six-month period, you will be given a written conduct warning.

Contact your manager for suggested retail locations for purchasing acceptable clothing. You will be given a $100 clothing allowance in your first paycheck, after which you are responsible for all clothing expenses.

Sick Days Policy

[Taken from university humanities department policy and procedure manual.]

Upon hiring, every employee is provided 14 days per year to be used in cases of minor illness. Only two consecutive sick days can be taken, after which a note from your physician is required to confirm illness. Even with a physician's note, no more than seven consecutive days can be taken; if you need more than seven days, then you are required to take short-term disability (see chapter 3, part 4, on how to apply for short-term disability). Sick days cannot be scheduled in advance; personal or vacation days should be scheduled in those cases instead.

Not following this policy will result in first a verbal warning, and then a written warning, to be included in your personnel file. The verbal and written warnings can both be given for the same instance (e.g., a verbal warning is given when three sick days are taken without a physician's note, and the employee continues to take two more sick days without a physician's note, thus resulting in a written warning). After a written warning, further violation of the policy is grounds for termination. Refer to chapter 3, part 2, of this manual for the procedure to use sick days.

FIGURE 10.2 *Policies (continued)*

Internet Access Policy

[Taken from an accounting firm policy and procedure manual.]

Internet usage should be limited to work-related efforts only. All usage will be monitored for time and content; thus, you may be asked to justify your Internet usage if it is deemed extensive or non-work related. Examples of inappropriate internet usage include, but are not limited to: online auctions, email accounts, news sources, or retail websites. Examples of Internet usage that is generally suitable include: client's website, financial websites, or accounting organization websites.

Visiting websites with pornographic or illegal content is grounds for immediate dismal; the police also will be contacted for instances involving child pornography or clearly illegal Internet activity. If you have any questions about this policy, contact your manager for clarification. Email usage is covered in Section 5.3 of this manual.

Travel Reimbursement Policy

[Taken from a software company policy and procedure manual.]

Every employee is eligible for reimbursement for travel expenses. Travel must be approved by a manager prior to making travel plans; otherwise, the employee will not be reimbursed for expenses. Further guidelines are noted below:

- All expenses must be applied for within 30 days of the initial travel date.
- Receipts must accompany all expense reimbursement requests.
- Employees must schedule flights, car rental, and hotel reservations through TravelPro in order to be eligible for reimbursement.
- Expenses must fall within prior approved budget.
- Upgrades in flight seating, hotel room choice, or car rental must be approved by a manager prior to making reservations.
- Travelers are allotted $70 per day for meals (e.g., $10 for breakfast, $20 for lunch, and $40 for dinner).
- Expenses for guests will not be reimbursed by the company.

Please see the detailed explanation of how to apply for travel reimbursement using the company's ExpensePro software in Appendix IV of this manual. Not all travel expenses are eligible for reimbursement; these are detailed in ExpensePro.

Writing procedures is much like writing sets of instructions, where the information is logically organized so the reader can complete every necessary step. Each procedure should be made up of the following three basic elements:

1. **An introduction to the procedure,** which serves as an overview of what the procedure will accomplish;

2. **The steps of the procedure,** including any sub-steps, warnings, or possible variations; and

3. **A conclusion,** to reiterate important factors and outcomes from completing the procedure.

Included procedures can range from how to contact management about policy abuses to how to enter the building using a security identification card. A writer has to write procedures that are relevant to both new and established employees; it is not enough to just focus on procedures relevant to the first few weeks working for the company. This is why the research done prior to writing the manual needs to include existing employees who are familiar with what long-term issues should be covered in the manual. Below is a sample procedure:

> The following procedure details the steps every employee must follow when scheduling vacation or personal days. See Policy 14 on page 75 of this manual for the specific policy regarding using personal and vacation days.
>
> 1. **Contact your manager via email to request a specific set of days.** This email should be sent a minimum of seven days prior to the first day needed off of work. The email will include: your name, title, department, and days (hours) requesting as vacation. It is not necessary to include information as to why the days are needed.

2. **Note the days you need off in the** *Vacation/Personal Days Tracking Spreadsheet.* This spreadsheet is stored at L:/all_company/vacation. Your name will be listed in the left-hand column; note the days and hours you are requesting.

3. **Wait for manager approval.** Your manager will contact you via email within 24 hours of your initial request; he or she will clearly note whether your request has been approved and any reasons for not approving the request. Your manager also will update the *Vacation/Personal Days Tracking Spreadsheet* with an X in either the "Approved" or "Denied" column.

4. **Coordinate with your manager for coverage of your responsibilities.** Either via email or in person, discuss options with your manager as to how your work will be covered in your absence. If there are no resources available for covering your work, then the manager has the authority to deny your vacation request at this point. All coverage decisions should be written in an email and sent to the people responsible for covering your work in your absence.

Benefits and Other Information. Although the policies may overlap with the benefits the company provides, a writer needs to adequately cover all the benefits an employee may expect and at what point he or she is eligible for the benefits. There is also information that does not fit into the categories of policy, procedure, or benefit; this additional information still needs to be conveyed to the reader, and the manual is an appropriate place. When presenting benefits or other information, they should be clear and detailed. They also should be organized in a logical fashion, which is generally by related topic and then alphabetically. See figure 10.3 for examples of additional information to include.

As mentioned earlier, the manual should not be burdened with an excessive amount of unimportant information. Carefully select what is included, and what can be provided in a different means of communication.

FIGURE 10.3 *Additional Information to Include*

Health	Financial	Building	Other
Cobra	Credit Union	Building Hours	Award Opportunities
Dental Insurance	Electronic Funds Transfer	Company Security	Child Care Reimbursement
Eye Care		Exercise Room	
Flexible Spending Account	401(k)	On-site Day Care	Discount Programs
	Pension	Severe Weather	Employee Suggestions
Health Insurance	Profit Sharing		Tuition Reimbursement

Conclusion. The conclusion section is a means to leave a lasting impression on the reader, whether it is reinforcing the company's philosophy or further welcoming the employee to the company's community. It is generally most effective to conclude the manual with the same tone used in the introduction, thus giving the manual a sense of full-circle closure. The conclusion should not contain material not previously covered in the manual because the reader is not likely to read the conclusion carefully.

Sign-off Verification. A policy and procedure manual contains complex and significant information relevant to every employee. A company cannot assume that every employee will read and understand the manual, and yet a company must hold every employee responsible for doing just that. The most effective way to hold the employee responsible is to include a verification form that is required to be signed by the employee and returned to a manager or Human Resources within a given time frame. Essentially, the form needs to inform readers that they are responsible for the contents of the manual and will be held accountable for following the described policies and procedures. An example sign-off verification form is shown in figure 10.4. The form either should be a separate sheet of paper in the manual or it should be perforated for easy removal from the manual. The form then will be kept with employees' records in case there is any question as to whether an employee was adequately informed about a particular policy or procedure.

FIGURE 10.4 *Sign-off Verification*

Smith & Jones Law Firm

Policy & Procedure Manual Sign-off Verification

I, _____ , acknowledge that I have received, read, and understood the *Smith & Jones Law Firm Policy & Procedure Manual.* I agree to follow the policies and procedures as they are described in this manual, and further understand that not following the policies and procedures is grounds for termination from the firm. I also understand that this manual replaces any other verbal or written policies in regards to Smith & Jones Law Firm. At any point in the future I have any questions or concerns about any material in this manual, I know that it is my responsibility to contact my manager immediately for further consultation. Finally, I recognize that this manual is subject to change without prior notification.

_____   _____

Employee Signature   Date

_____

Employee's Name Printed

_____   _____

Human Resources Representative Signature   Date

Optional Sections. Depending on audience analysis and expressed needs from management, there are other sections that can be included in a policy and procedure manual:

- **Company history, overview, goals, or mission statement.** Even if a company does not have a long history, including where the company came from, where it is now, and where it will be in the future, this is a means to create community within a company. The goals and mission statement will set the tone for the policies in the manual, as each policy will serve to support the goals and mission of the company.

- **Organization chart.** Designed like a simple flow chart, an organization chart lists names and positions of upper management while using lines to show the connections between people.

- **Map.** Either a map of the building or of all the company's locations worldwide can be included in the manual. The map should be designed to be clear and visually appealing. Furthermore, explanatory text should accompany the map to ensure the reader understands what is being represented.

- **Holiday calendar.** This calendar lists the holidays the company celebrates by closing the building or paying overtime. It also may be helpful to list pay dates on this calendar.

- **Glossary.** If there are words or phrases included in the manual that the reader is likely to not know or understand, then a glossary can be included to provide definitions.

- **Forms.** Any commonly used or required forms can be included in the manual, along with detailed instructions of when and how to use the forms.

Document Design

Logical and consistent organization and style are required for policy and procedure manuals. The reader should be able to clearly follow the information from one section to the next. The first step to designing a manual is gathering information about the company's standards for internal documentation. Beyond just the company colors and logo, it is ideal the writer adhere to established designs for headers, numbering, fonts, and overall spacing.

If a style guide or expressed standards for the manual are not available, then the writer must consider the following design issues:

- **Functionality.** The manual is not marketing material, so the design's focus is more on how to construct the document in a way that readers can easily access necessary information as needed, rather than simply highlighting the positive aspects of the company. Creating a functional manual includes using tabs on the sides of pages that note new sections, white space to allow for easy reading and note taking, bold headings for skimming, and tables to organize complicated data.

- **Visual appeal.** Although functionality is a concern, also design the manual to be inviting to open and read. If the company's colors are jarring to the reader, use them minimally as a thin colored bar at the top and/or bottom of every page, or only on the cover of the manual. In either case, colors should be used in moderation so as to not distract the reader from the actual content.

- **Logo usage.** If the company has a logo, it should be represented in the manual, either on the cover or on every page. It does not need to be prominent; instead, subtly add the logo by making it small or transparent to the text on the page.

- **Media flexibility.** Policy and procedure manuals can be distributed to employees in a variety of methods, not just in printed format. Consider designing the manual so that it can easily transition from print to PDF to HTML or other possible media. Graphics, fonts, and spacing may not appear as originally intended when reproduced in different formats. Also consider if the printed format will be bound, put in a binder, or just held together with a binder clip.

- **Formatting (Modular).** Policies and procedures evolve as the company changes and employees bring issues up to management. Thus, the manual will need to be altered to accommodate the revisions. Designing the document with clearly delineated section breaks between unrelated content will help ease the revision process. All the pages will not need to be reflowed if minimal information is changed within a section.

Editing and Revising

The editing and revising process needs to be done very carefully with a policy and procedure manual. Employees rely on the accuracy of the content, while simple grammatical errors and typos can jeopardize the trust the reader has in the document overall. Although it is a painstaking process, review each section carefully for errors, inaccuracies, or potentially confusing text. Beyond a writer's review of the draft, it is advisable to send the manual to a larger audience for approval, which should include company lawyers, managers, human resources representatives, and company leaders. These individuals can help guarantee that the manual is effectively reflecting the company's philosophy and direction, while also protecting the company from possible legal repercussions for inaccurate policies or procedures described in the manual. It is also a good idea to have potential readers review the manual prior to finalizing it; refer to chapter 17 for guidance on usability testing. This will help ensure that the manual is easy to read, understand, remember, and follow.

INSTRUCTION WRITING

Written instructions can range from an apple pie recipe to replacing a light bulb to reconfiguring processor resources to reduce power consumption. No matter what the intended outcome is, keep the reader's frame of mind in perspective. A writer cannot be disillusioned into believing that readers always review instructions while calm and open to new ideas. Rather, many readers are likely to be confused and aggravated, and only turning to a set of instructions as a last resort. Readers may doubt their own abilities to successfully complete the task. A writer's goal must be to ease this tension and prevent the reader from pitching the instructions and everything else out a window.

Reaching frustrated readers can be accomplished with clear, precise, and well-organized writing. Base the writing on thorough research of the intended audience and the process being discussed. Graphics and other visual queues also will help draw a reader in and keep the reader reading. Beyond that, the document needs to be edited and revised so that grammar and content issues do not trip up a reader.

Audience Analysis

Carefully consider who the intended reader is prior to sitting down to write instructions for any process. This audience analysis allows a writer to tailor the writing to meet the needs of those readers who are most likely to pick up the set of instructions. It also helps alleviate the frustration average readers may feel if they have to slog through a document written for someone with an advanced degree in biomedical engineering, for example. The questions noted below are just a few things to consider prior to writing instructions for specific readers:

- **Will the reader interact with the process just once?** If the reader will do this process only once, and never need to do it again, then the steps should not be written to teach the reader at a deeper level. The reader is not likely to care about the significance of each step if the process is only done once or even only every once in a while. Do not waste time writing information that is likely to be ignored by a reader who only wants to get the job done quickly.

- **Will the reader need quick access to the instructions?** Often, readers are in the field dealing with a crisis when referring to instructions. These types of readers need to be able to access information quickly, which means that organization and document design will come into play. It also means that it is unlikely that the reader needs details about the process if the details are not specifically relevant to getting the job done quickly.

- **Is the reader already familiar with the steps?** When documenting instructions, do not assume that the reader is new to the process. Many professionals have to learn tasks by jumping right in on their first day and essentially figuring things out as they go. Documentation of those steps might be lacking, missing, or poorly written. Thus, it becomes the task of a writer to present reliable documentation of the process, whether it is for historical sake, standardization of the process, or possible future training needs.

- **What is the age and education of the user?** These factors cannot be ignored, though they often need to be approached delicately. A teenager learns differently than a middle-age adult; one might be open to new ideas, while the other may have vast experience with the existing process. Someone with a college education may learn differently than someone with specific technical training. A writer needs to be sensitive toward the intended reader, and write to meet the different learning curves.

- **Will the reader be familiar with jargon?** A quick way to lose a reader is to insert jargon and acronyms with meanings that cannot be derived from the context of the sentence or preexisting knowledge about the process. Conversely, if the jargon is commonly batted around by the intended reader, then time should not be spent explicitly explaining the terms. Otherwise, make an effort to define jargon, acronyms, or other unfamiliar process-specific terms.

- **Is the reader likely to only skim the instructions?** Aliterate readers know how to read, but choose not to. These readers are often those pressed for time, but also those who are confident in their abilities to figure things out without spending a lot of time reading. If there is anything important for the reader to know, approach it in a way that even the most aliterate reader cannot ignore. Document design can help draw these readers in as needed.

- **Are there other resources for the intended reader to turn to?** This is a difficult realization for writers: Readers are not likely to turn to sets of instructions first. Readers are most likely to first try and figure the process out on their own. Then, they are likely to seek help from peers or others familiar with the process. Finally, they may turn to a set of written instructions. With the increased resources available on the Internet, though, they may try a general search on the internet to find specific answers to questions rather than reading a set of instructions. Keep in mind that readers may have accessed other resources by the time they refer to a printed set of instructions.

- **Will there be vast differences between groups of readers?** If the writer identifies major groups of readers with different needs, more than one document may need to be created. For instance, one group may need detailed graphics with little explanatory text, whereas another group may need a detailed process explanation but no background information.

- **Will the document need to be understood by international readers?** No matter what language the document is written in or translated to, certain considerations ought to be made for international readers. There are cultural norms that need to be respected and understood prior to writing a document for international readers. It is important to not assume that everyone thinks like an American reader, because this will limit the ultimate usability of the document.

If the characteristics and needs of the intended reader are not readily apparent or provided, then it is important to conduct research about the reader prior to beginning to write the instructions.

Research

Research will likely fall into two categories: 1) audience, as noted above; and 2) content support.

Before trying to understand a process and its steps, the intended reader must be understood. This information is gathered by conducting interviews, observing the process as it is completed, and reading existing published information on the process. Beyond this prewriting aspect, the research also will build a list of contacts to refer back to when the documentation needs to be reviewed and tested for usability.

After the readers and their needs are understood, research for writing the content of the document can begin. This research is twofold:

1. **Review previous documentation.** Research what has been written before on this process, who wrote the documentation, why it was originally created, and why it is being revised or completely rewritten now. This creates an opportunity to learn from any past mistakes or accomplishments of the previous document, while creating a base to begin writing the new document.

2. **Understand the process.** Research every aspect of the steps, jargon, and tools/equipment. If needed, cite sources in order to add credibility to the writing. Again, if possible, watch the process as it is being completed by an expert or someone familiar with the nuances of the steps. If access to someone in the field is not possible, then another option is to require usability testing while writing and upon completion of the document; refer to chapter 17 for information on usability testing.

When working with encroaching deadlines, the research process may be cut short. In the end, though, the research will be unavoidable at some point during the writing or reviewing process in order to create a thorough and accurate document. It is best to complete the research up front so that only minimal research needs to be done during the actual writing phase.

Tone and Writing Style

Overall, technical communications all have similar qualities in tone and style: clear, concise, and accurate. This is the same for writing instructions. Beyond that, there are other qualities particular to instruction writing that should not be overlooked:

Articles and Other Little Words. When describing steps in a process, writers often use as few words as possible to keep the writing concise. Although it is important to keep the writing concise, it is important to not remove words that the reader expects to see.

Common words often excluded by writers are *a, an, and, the, then,* and *that.* Skipping these words may cause the reader to stumble over the text, knowing something is missing, but not sure what. Also, if the instructions are going to be translated or used by readers not entirely familiar with English, the small words help with clear and accurate translation and interpretation. Do not trip up the reader by choosing to exclude little words. Instead, work to revise for conciseness by removing words and phrases that are not necessary to the process.

Formal or Informal Tone. If audience analysis does not clearly reveal whether the writing would be more appropriate as formal or informal, go with a formal writing tone. Formal writing maintains a nonoffensive and professional means of communicating to any type of reader, especially international readers. Clichés, slang, and sexist or biased words should be avoided. Also, first and second personal pronouns are inappropriate in formal writing. Informal writing, on the other hand, can work to build a relationship with a reader. A casual and warm tone might set the reader at ease and help the reader to not feel alone in the process. By using first and second personal pronouns, the instructions will seem more like a personalized tutorial on the process.

Verb First/Action Writing. It may seem obvious that the goal of writing each step is to motivate the reader to do something, but it is important that the action is the focal part of the sentence. This can be achieved by beginning the step with a verb. If explanatory information is needed, it can be presented in a text box, sidebar, or small paragraph after the step has been given, so as to not interfere with beginning the step with a verb.

Confident Tone. The reader should feel secure in completing each instruction step, thus the writing needs to sound confident. Informing the reader that a step may not be accurate is not an option. If a writer is not sure about the step, further research and interviews need to be conducted. The reader is relying on the writer to be the authority on the topic.

What to Include

A set of instructions should be designed to meet the needs of the specific reader who will be using the document. Based on an analysis of the target reader, the document will incorporate several pieces relevant to clearly communicating the necessary instructions. This means that a document does not need to include every section noted below; rather, it should include the sections deemed most useful to the reader and most likely to be expected by the reader. For example, if a writer's research shows that the reader knows all the relevant terms, then a glossary is not needed and will only get in the reader's way.

When writing a complete set of instructions, most readers will minimally require the following sections:

- Title
- Introduction
- List of Tools
- Steps or Instructions
- Conclusion

Many readers will appreciate the inclusion of further sections, though they generally are not required in order to understand a process in a minimal sense:

- Table of Contents
- Glossary of Terms
- History
- Troubleshooting or Advanced Tips
- Checklists

- Case Studies or What-if Scenarios
- Bibliography
- Contacts

Interviewing potential readers or contacting clients for detailed information about potential readers will help determine what should be included. Also, relying on industry standards or previously successful documents can provide insights as to what to include.

Title. The title serves to briefly inform readers what they will achieve by completing the steps detailed in the document.

Imagine the document is thrown into a stack of other instructional documents on an already chaotic desk. If all the documents have vague titles, how will the reader know which document is appropriate for the task at hand? *Ultimate Guide to the Process, Instructional Manual, Basic Procedural Steps* . . . none of these titles is insightful. Instead, write titles that clearly state the specific goal or procedure and are intuitive to the reader at a glance: *Updating Website Content Quickly, Manual for the Acme Leaf-blower, Steps to Balancing the Cash Register Drawer Daily.* It is important to recognize that the title is brief so that it can be quickly interpreted by the reader, while the details of the process will be provided in the introduction paragraph.

Introduction. The introduction builds off of the title in the way it explains the goal of the instructions and general information pertinent to completing the tasks. The first sentence is key. It should clearly state what the document covers while also enticing the reader to continue reading the document.

Although it is ideal to keep an introduction brief, often the complexity of the topic and requirements of the reader dictate the need for other sections or information to be included along with the introduction. Potential topics for the introduction include an overview of the process, background or historical information relevant to the process, or product specifications.

Companies and clients may request these sections, or even longer introduction paragraphs, but readers are more likely to skim this information for obvious pertinent information and then move on to get to the bulk of the document. This is not to say that the writing should not have characteristics of quality and depth, rather, be sure what is written is absolutely necessary to enhance the appeal of the document overall.

List of Tools and Materials. A list of tools is an important feature for any set of instructions. This list serves as a means to orientate the reader and give perspective on what the described process will entail. Having a list before the steps begin allows the reader to gather tools and not have to continually start and stop the process.

Forcing readers to gather necessary tools and materials while reading the steps is not an effective use of their time. Imagine baking chocolate chip cookies without a list of ingredients. While initiating the first step of mixing butter, the next ingredient needs to be found and measured. As ingredients are read in the steps, they need to be sought and measured on a continual basis, thus putting the reader in a manic state in order to keep up with the process. What if the ingredient is not readily available? What if it takes several minutes to find an ingredient and measure it? It is likely that the delay will change the outcome of the cookies and, ultimately, frustrate the reader.

Clearly listing anything necessary to complete the given task will help keep the reader clear minded and on track while reading the instructions. The list of tools can actually cover a variety of necessities, not just the traditional ones that come to mind, such as screwdriver. Consider also including the following:

- Skills needed to perform tasks or previous training
- Computer software or hardware or other electrical components
- Time required to complete task
- Chemical compounds or other physical materials

A writer must carefully consider what the reader ought to bring to the table in order to make the process work. Although the list might be compiled before writing the steps of the process, it is advisable for a writer to review the steps after they are written and make sure the list is accurate based on the completed instructions.

Steps. This is the section that the reader is mostly likely to flip to, regardless of the importance of the previous sections. Most of the research and writing energy will go into this section, which can understandably sound daunting at first. The necessary aspects for writing this section are noted below:

- **Prewriting.** After organizing the research, break the process into logical chunks, especially if it is a long process. These chunks will transfer over to the document's organization to help the reader process the information in small, manageable portions. Tackle each chunk one at a time by determining roughly how many steps are in each part of the process. Organize the research to follow the order of the steps. It is not necessary to actually write the steps in order, just as long as the organization is logical by the completion of the document's draft. Consider developing a flowchart of the entire process, much like an outline, to keep the writing on track.

- **Step writing.** As noted earlier, clear, concise, and accurate writing is necessary for instruction writing, especially in this section of the document. Beyond that, there are a few other characteristics to keep in mind when writing this section.

  - Reflect in every step the audience research previously conducted. Whether the content needs to be detailed, or if it needs to be a brief review, is up to the intended reader rather than the writer.
  - Begin each step with an action verb so the reader can clearly follow what needs to be done.
  - Be sure it is clear what the end result should be, not only for the step, but also for the entire process.
  - Use transition words and phrases when moving from one topic to the next (e.g., first, next, furthermore).
  - Try not to mix the action of the step with more conceptual information; make the action clear and separate from in-depth explanations.

- **Extra information.** Some information that may not fall clearly into a specific step still will need to be noted for the reader. Often, it may be important to let the reader know what to do if a step is done incorrectly.

This may take the form of a warning, which should be prominently illustrated by using a bold font, eye-catching graphics, or colored text boxes. It also may take the form of a "tip" or troubleshooting note; these can use a bold font or appear as a sidebar, so as to not interfere with the text of the step.

- **Warnings.** It is important to try and predict what actions may be dangerous to a reader if done incorrectly. It is a writer's duty to advise the reader on potentially hazardous situations so that injury can be prevented. Keep in mind that the reader should be warned when doing a step incorrectly or out of sequence may break the product; for example, "Do not turn on the PC prior to attaching the CPU cooling unit, as this will cause the CPU to overheat and irreparably fail."

- **Graphics.** Users will greatly benefit from relevant graphics, print screens, and depictions of the process or components used in the process. Placement of the graphics should be next to, or very close to, the text relevant to the graphic. Also, the graphic should be labeled for easy reference. If the graphic is complex or not intuitive, a brief caption should be included with the label. The graphics should be simple and clear. When a large graphic is necessary, it can be placed in an appendix at the end of the document, though this will cause the reader to flip back and forth between the text and the appendix. Whenever possible, keep the graphic near the text. For more insight on using graphics refer to chapter 15.

Conclusion. It is important to not just trail off at the end of the set of instructions. A concluding paragraph will add a sense of closure to the process, while summarizing the process and the expected outcome. The conclusion can serve as a means to look beyond the process to show its relevancy to other processes or scenarios. This paragraph also can create a sense of community between readers or empowerment for completing the given task. Essentially, the conclusion should complete the sense of reassurance and confidence that the document conveyed to the reader overall.

Industry Standards

There are standards supported by industry-recognized organizations, including International Standards Organization (ISO), International Electrotechnical Commission (IEC), American National Standards Institute (ANSI), and Occupational Safety & Health Administration (OSHA). Technical writers need to be familiar with these standards as related to the content of the document. Warning colors and signs are examples of standards that writers should adhere to in order to meet the expectations of readers. Red is typically related to a fire hazard; yellow is caution or noting a possible physical injury hazard; orange is for dangerous machinery parts; and purple is for radiation hazards (Hayes 2005).

Optional Sections. Although the sections listed below can be skipped when writing sets of instructions, their inclusion will help further ease the reader's experience in completing the instruction process:

- **Table of contents.** If every heading or section is numbered in the document, then that numbering system should be reflected in a concise table of contents, along with page numbers where the content begins.

- **Glossary of terms.** If the document includes jargon, acronyms, or words only used in a particular industry, a reader may benefit from brief definitions in a glossary at the end of the document.

- **History.** Background information that will help the reader see the process as a whole or part of a larger context can be included. This should not just be filler information; rather, it needs to clearly help the reader complete the process.

- **Troubleshooting.** Not every process will be completed successfully, so a writer must account for variations that will cause the process to go wrong. These variations may not be readily available to the writer, so testing and research should be done with users who are not familiar with the process.

- **Advanced tips.** Some readers may need further information than just what is contained in the basic steps explained in the main part of the document. These tips can be a separate section or text boxes near the relevant step.

- **Checklists.** Providing a basic list of what will be accomplished can be a quick way for readers to assess whether they are on track with the process.

- **Bibliography.** If outside research is used in the document, then the sources need to be accurately cited. This also will provide a list for readers to find more information on the topic.

- **Contacts.** For readers who experience difficulties beyond what can be covered in the document, a list of names, telephone numbers, and email addresses should be provided so the reader can find further help as needed.

Document Design

Although a writer may feel that the text of the steps is the most important part of a set of instructions, in fact, the design of the document is just as important. If the document's design is disorganized or otherwise incomprehensible, the reader will never make it to the text of the steps before discarding the document and taking a chance by doing the process without help.

Numbering. In relation to organizing sections and subsections in a document, there are different numbering methods to choose from, such as Roman numeral (e.g., I) or standard (e.g., 1). Using letters is also an option, though a numbering system for the whole document is likely to be more appropriate than using letters, because numbers lend themselves well to creating a table of contents and being cross-referenced in the text. Also, numbers should be used when the steps need to be followed in a sequential order and if there are several steps to the process. Conversely, bullets should be used only when listing items or setting off explanatory text. Finally, it is important to maintain a consistent numbering system throughout the document. This will help keep the sections organized in the reader's mind.

Numbering Conventions

There are three standard numbering formats for technical documents. One method should be chosen and used for every section and subsection of the document. Within a section, steps can be numbered or lettered normally (e.g., 1, 2, A, B). Following are the three formats:

1. **Traditional outline system.** This follows the pattern Roman numeral, upper-case letter, standard number, and lower-case letter. This format can be confusing for documents with large sections and extensive information.

2. **Century-decade-unit system.** This is also known as the Navy system. The pattern begins with 100 for a main section, and then 110 for a subsection; the next main section would be 200, with a subsection of 210.

3. **Multiple decimal system.** The pattern begins with 1.0, and subsections add on to the decimal place (e.g., 1.1, 1.2, 1.2.1); the next main section begins with 2.0. This method can get confusing if there are several levels of subsections that need to be numbered.

Headings. As with every technical document, headings play a key role in quickly orientating a reader. Headings are of great value with sets of instructions when there are many processes or subprocesses to discuss. Beyond helping readers keep track of where they are in the process, readers also can scan the document looking for headings to find the exact content they need to read immediately. Although the headings should be displayed prominently, such as making them a larger font size or weight, the phrasing of the headings should be carefully considered. Here are a few characteristics to consider:

- **Parallel.** This is a grammatical term for creating words and phrases with similar grammatical structure; this is generally relevant to a series of items, ordered and unordered lists, and headings. In regard to headings, an example of a parallel structure would be:

– **Baiting** [-ing verb] **the** [article] **Hook** [noun]
– **Casting** [-ing verb] **the** [article] **Line** [noun]
– **Catching** [-ing verb] **the** [article] **Fish** [noun]

This can be compared to a nonparallel structure on the same topic:

– **How to Put Bait on the Hook**
– **Casting: The Perfect Process**
– **Fish on a Hook**

The first example maintains a consistent structure in content, grammar, and punctuation to show connections between the sections; whereas the second example uses a variety of heading styles, which is chaotic and jarring for the reader.

• **Specific.** Although it is tempting to put vague and predictable headings on each section, it is best instead to rely on specific wording for headings. For example, rather than use the heading "Background," something more specific would be appropriate, such as "History of Acme Snowboards."

• **Brief.** As noted above, the headings should be specific, but this does not mean that they should be long. Generally, one to four long words, or two to five short words are appropriate. The objective behind headings is to create short bursts of text to catch the reader's attention; long phrases, or sentence-like headings, will not accomplish this.

• **Nonstacked.** Headings should not be back-to-back without explanatory text between the headings. Each heading should denote a section or subsection of the document, and should have explanatory text beneath it. It also is required to have some introductory text prior to jumping into the steps or bulleted list. This helps the reader put the information into context.

Page Layout. The overall layout for a set of instructions ultimately should serve for easy reading by the intended user, but there are several specific factors to consider during the design process:

- **White Space.** Many readers need to take notes as they read or complete instructions. Margins should be set large enough to allow for minimal note taking, or the other option is to leave space at the ends of sections for notes. Either way, the spacing should not be excessive or disruptive, but it should be just enough for some brief hand-written notations by the reader.

- **Binding.** It is important to keep in mind how the document will be bound and distributed; this will impact margin setting, the inclusion of tabs, and how much information to put on each page.

- **Color.** Be sure to determine if color or how many colors are an option, or if the document will be printed or copied in black and white. If a document is designed in color, but printed in black and white, what looks ideal on a color monitor will not translate well upon printing because the colors are turned shades of gray. If a document is to be printed in black and white, then design it using only these colors to see the document exactly how the reader will see it. When color is not an option, headings, tables, and other features will need to be displayed prominently. This can be accomplished using bold typefaces, black boxes with reversed out (white) type, and appropriate white space.

- **Quick access.** Depending on the needs of the audience, the document or part of the document may need to be designed for quick access. If the document is long and thorough, then include some pages with brief overviews and easy to see graphics. Also, consider creating a table of contents and tabs on the side of the pages beginning new sections.

- **Appeal.** On a visual level, the document should appeal to the reader. This can be achieved with the use of color and engaging text, and with unique graphics and a clean layout. Rule lines and borders can help give the document a more professional look, while unique fonts can make a less formal document more fun to read.

- **Boxes and bars.** In an attempt to draw a reader's attention to particular information, or even as a means to not distract the reader from the steps of the process, text boxes and sidebars can be used. The step in the process in which the box needs to support will determine the format of the box; for example, its size, shading, border thickness, and font format will be determined by how much the information needs to stand out to the reader. These boxes are especially effective for explanatory text about a step, tips on how to better complete the step, or warnings about dangers involving the step. Similar to graphics, it is important that these boxes and sidebars appear near the relevant step.

Overall, the layout should be simple, consistent, and easy to follow throughout the document. Refrain from using too much formatting in a document. The reader will be distracted by overuse of colors, lines, graphics, or other features not related to the content. As far as consistency, if text boxes are used for warnings in one section, then every section should use the same format for warnings. The reader should be able to predict the format after a certain point, rather than having to figure everything out again for each section. And, finally, the document should be easy to follow because, as previously noted, the reader is likely to have a low attention span or be aggravated when approaching the document. Do not give the reader an excuse for putting the document down and ignoring it.

Editing and Revising

Once the document is written, the writing process is not over. There are several steps yet to be taken in order to refine and polish the document prior to actual completion. The revision and editing process should include the same steps that are taken with any other document: look for grammar and punctuation mistakes, review overall organization and content, and read the document aloud to hear possible errors.

Beyond these steps and others that writers may employ, sets of instructions need to undergo two other essential revision steps:

1. **Contact experts to review the document for accuracy and completeness.** Those contacted during earlier research are the best options to contact again. Although the writer may be confident in capturing everything correctly, it is worth taking extra time to have the process double-checked by an expert.

2. **Complete the steps as they are actually written in the document.**
Ideally, someone familiar with the process and someone unfamiliar
with the process should review the document in this manner. The
individual familiar with the process will readily know if a step is inaccurate, missed, or in need of more information, such as a warning
or tip. The individual unfamiliar with the process will help point out
where there are gaps in the steps for someone who does not intuitively
know what to do next. See chapter 17 for further details on conducting
and analyzing usability testing.

Even if the deadline for the completed document is nearing, the above
revision steps need to be completed. Otherwise, the target readers will be
the ones who find the errors, and then potentially lose faith in the document
and the writer. Beyond that, an inaccurate document can bring about legal
repercussions, depending on the process and target reader. It is not worth
taking that chance in order to meet an impending deadline.

It is important to remember that the reader is ultimately relying on the
writer to convey accurate information in a detailed, logically organized, and
clear way. The document should bring down the stress level of the reader, not
add to it. This is often a challenging task for a writer, and it might take several
drafts—along with constant testing—to get the instructions perfect.

TECHNICAL SPECIFICATIONS

Technical specifications, also referred to as functional requirements specifications, are detailed descriptions of software, websites, or other consumer products being developed by a company or organization. Although specifications
can be written after the product is developed, it is ideal to write them prior
to beginning the development process. Like blueprints, the specifications will
serve to clearly portray the expectations of everyone involved in creating the
new product, including features, functionality, dimensions, and appearance.
The focus of the specifications is only on the product, not on how to actually
create the product.

Often, the substantial need for taking time to write specifications is overlooked by those who want to get a product on the market quickly. Although
a writer may continually be harassed to complete the specifications quickly,

Life without Technical Specifications

There is a theory in the technology field that technical specifications should not be written because they do not portray what those who proposed the product really want. Individuals will "sign off" on the specifications without really understanding them and how they apply to the development of the product; thus, a company may end up with a final product that followed the specifications, but does not meet their expectations. This is not enough of a compelling argument to do away with technical specifications.

Consider the following dialogue concerning the development of a product without specifications.

"I thought the background of the first screen was going to be blue with a white border," Tim commented while looking at the software prototype.

"No, Sarah said it should be purple with a black background," Greg, the product developer, responded. "Isn't that right, Sarah?"

"Yes, that's what we agreed on," Sarah said.

"No," Tim argued. "I never agreed to that change."

"It isn't a change. It's what we agreed on when we started out," Sarah explained. "It's in the meeting minutes that Rick emailed everyone a while back."

A conversation like the one above can continue for every aspect and feature of the product. People will have to think back to the original concepts and track down various methods of documentation to figure out if the product is what everyone expected it to be upon completion. Well-written specifications are truly a means to overcome the confusion. The writer needs to do thorough research on what the product should look like, and then clearly translate that information into the specifications. It is the responsibility of a technical writer to be sure readers are clear about what is written in the specifications.

it is important to approach the writing methodically so that nothing is missed or underplayed in the final document. Specifications are the foundation that products are created upon, thus flawed or incomprehensible writing will lead ultimately to longer development time and possibly a faulty product. The first step to writing accurate specifications is researching and understanding the product about to go into development.

The majority of the research for specifications will be conducted by interviewing the individuals who proposed the product idea. The writer must understand every facet of the proposed product, because aspects not reflected in the specifications may not end up in the final product. This is not to imply that gathering this information is simple; there may be many individuals with very different ideas about the proposed product. These ideas may only be intangible concepts, and in need of concrete details. Meetings will be conducted, along with email and other communications, as means to ferret out all the information. A writer needs to document all the ideas, sift through them, and accurately portray the proposed product in a way that the developers can clearly understand. It generally is not necessary to interview the individuals who will work on developing the product, unless the writer needs to understand complexities of the product to accurately reflect them in the specifications.

Once the research has been gathered, organized, and agreed upon by those proposing the product's development, the writing can begin. There are some writing conventions for specifications that are best to adhere to. Primarily, the writing should be detailed when possible, so that the developer can clearly picture what must be accomplished. Vague writing often leads to developers having to make decisions about various aspects of the product. Or, if the developers are not comfortable with making decisions, they will contact everyone involved with the initial product proposal. This extra step will add time, and possibly confusion, to the overall project. Do not leave room for interpretation in the specifications—write with detail and accuracy.

Detailed writing has an added benefit when the specifications are sent to international readers for development. Language gaps are filled when the specifications account for every angle of the product. If the text is not explicit about what is needed, a writer cannot assume that the reader will make the same interpretations as a native speaker might. To meet the needs of international readers, a formal writing tone is required. Slang and clichés are unacceptable because the reader may not be familiar with these words used in different contexts. A study presented by William M. Wilson (2007) during a NASA conference explains that using informal, or natural, language in complex specifications causes "ambiguity, inaccuracy and inconsistency". Whether readers are native speakers of English or international readers, it is best to only rely on Standard English to write specifications documents.

Sit and Think

Many writers feel compelled to rush to their computers and begin writing the specifications document after all the research has been gathered. Technical specifications are precise and complex documents that take critical thinking skills to accurately process the information for inclusion in the final version. It is a good idea for writers to take time to reflect on the gathered information and clearly visualize the proposed product in a multidimensional perspective. Creative writers often adopt this approach when verbally creating new worlds for fictional stories; a technical writer is also verbally creating something new in the minds of readers. Thus, sit and think about what should be written so that a clear mental picture is formed before actually beginning to write.

It is tempting for many writers to use future verb tense when writing specifications about a product yet to be developed. For instance, "The top of the table *will be* sierra brown, with gold accents. The four legs *should be* flat black." It seems logical and accurate at that point, but this style weakens the writing and limits the value of the specifications. Instead, write in present tense, where the product already exists in its final and expected form. The revised example from above is now: "The top of the table *is* sierra brown, with gold accents. The four legs *are* flat black." The tone becomes assertive, so that the developer sees there is no question in how the product will look after development. More importantly, though, the specifications easily can be used for the user guide or other documentation written for the product after its development. Even if the information is not reused, the specifications will be an accurate representation of the product for historical purposes. The writer will still need to be conscious of updating the specifications if the information changes during development, because not all projects complete according to plan.

What to include in the specifications is obviously dictated by the needs of the developers and ideas of those proposing the product; however, there is some standard information that should be included in specifications. Begin with an overview of the product, describing the product in general terms. Noting the target clients for the product is useful information for the developer in that it helps put the product and its needs in perspective. Whether it is a niche market or something made widely available, the developer will be able to determine how many resources to invest in certain aspects of the product. Overall, the bulk of the specifications will cover the description of the product from every perspective. Also be sure to note any special restraints, requirements, and features that may push the product's development time out further than estimated. It is important to keep the writing focused, though. Irrelevant information should be excluded or only included as appendixes. Background information, opinions, and comparisons to other products should generally be avoided because they only serve to confuse the developer. Although the writing in specifications is detailed, it needs to be focused on the information that is necessary to build the proposed product.

Other than keeping the writing focused on pertinent information, the design of the document overall can help make for easier reading and comprehension. If a template is available, then it should be used as a means to meet readers' expectations, otherwise there are a few guidelines to consider while developing the document. Begin with a clean layout, which includes using white space between sections, bulleted and numbered lists where appropriate, and tables for extensive numerical data. Developers often only read the specifications related to their particular tasks; create a modular effect in the document by making sections freestanding and highlighted with bold headings that are coordinated with a table of contents at the beginning of the document. Use rule lines between sections if the breaks are not prominent. Most importantly, do not overuse formatting; the reader should not be distracted or confused by the formatting in a specifications document.

Be prepared to revise the specifications, even after they have been signed off on by everyone involved in the project. Whether it is due to unclear writing, previously unexpressed product characteristics, or just the inevitable changes that arise during development, the specifications need to be revised to reflect these changes. A simple method of reflecting these revisions is to have a separate section in the document that notes the change, who requested the change, and the date it was made to the specifications. Those who have access to this document must be vigilant about tracking the changes. As for the actual changes in the body of the specifications document, one method is to alter the text format by changing its color, using strikethrough, or highlighting anything that has been modified. A writer also can use square brackets to cordon off the text that was changed. It is not advisable to just delete the old text and replace it with the changed text. Using this method makes it difficult to see what the original idea looked like prior to development. If the document gets too chaotic with all the changes, a simpler method is to change the document's name when text is deleted and added. For example, if the original document was named "Functional Specifications for Acme Learning Software," then the revised document should be named "Functional Specifications for Acme Learning Software Revised." This is a simplistic naming convention, so a more complex one may need to be adopted if the document is changed several times. Essentially, no matter how the changes are tracked, it is important that anyone who picks up the document can readily see what changes have been made, along with clarification that he or she is reading the most recent version of the specifications.

Figure 10.6 is an example technical specification for educational software. This example includes the major aspects required in most specifications; note that a further elaboration in each section may be necessary in real-world scenarios.

USER GUIDE

A user guide is a document that accompanies a product or service. It is generally written after the product has been developed and tested. This document can be a few pages long or several volumes, depending on the complexity of the product and the expected usage by the reader.

A user guide has similar characteristics as a set of instructions, in that they both often include overviews of a product and step-by-step processes. A user guide, though, will provide more depth than a set of instructions. This depth is primarily due to the reader's need to know about every aspect of the product, which is generally the motivation behind reading a user guide. Obviously, writing a guide is an arduous task that should not be underestimated. A writer needs to map out what content needs to be included and then set up appropriate interviews with product experts. This might include assigning certain writing tasks to those who developed the product, though these sections will need to be edited in order to maintain a common writing style and tone throughout the guide. Beyond mapping out what to include in the guide, audience analysis needs to be completed.

FIGURE 10.6 *Technical Specification*

Product Name	*Blue Bird 1-2-3*
Team Members/ Title	Sharon Smith, Marketing Coordinator; Mark Jones, Content Editor; Ryan Thomas, Content Editor; Delia Brown, Managing Editor; Mary Fox, Artistic Design Coordinator; Robert Johnson, Technical Coordinator
Department	Primary School Educational Software
Specifications Author	Jason White
Specifications Creation Date	November 12, 2007
Date Approved	December 9, 2007
Final Product Deadline	May 3, 2008

PRODUCT OVERVIEW

Purpose: *Blue Bird 1-2-3* educates children on number recognition and progressive counting from one to ten through use of four different games, each having seven progressive levels.

Target Audience: English speaking children, ages 3–7, home-schooled or enrolled in a private/public school.

Benefits: This software is easy to learn by use of repetitive actions for each game and level, so that once a user learns the first level of the first game, the same actions can be used to successfully navigate the subsequent games and levels. The games are brightly colored, relying on primary colors, while the graphics are large and well defined for easy recognition by children. Although very young children will need adult supervision while using the software, older children will be able to navigate the software independently with minimal or no adult supervision; this is due to the clear verbal cues as to what step is next in the game

Scope: This software teaches counting, number recognition, how to follow instructions, and independent learning.

FIGURE 10.6 *Technical Specification (continued)*

USER REQUIREMENTS

Software: Windows 98, Windows Millennium Edition (Windows Me), Windows 2000, Windows XP

Hardware: Acme II processor (300MHz); 32MB RAM; 90MB Hard Drive Space; 8MB SVGA DirectX 9.0-compatible video card; DirectX 9.0-compatible sound card; CD-ROM 8x

Skill Set: Ability to move and right/left click mouse, comprehend basic computer commands to move and click on objects, and understand English

SOFTWARE FUNCTIONALITY

Software is loaded from a CD-ROM. The initial screen displays a menu with options for the users: Play Game, High Scores, Setup, and Internet Features. The Play Game menu will lead to a second menu level, where users can choose one of four games to play. After choosing a game, the user can choose a level (the default setting is Level 1). If a user chooses High Scores from the main menu, all the scores (levels) for previous games played will display; if no scores are available, then the text "No Scores" will appear. The Setup menu selection will allow a user to configure computer components (e.g., speakers, mouse) and game speed/difficulty. If the computer has Internet access, accessing the Internet Features from the main menu will open an Internet browser window that will go directly to the KidEd Software URL: *www.KidEdSoftware.com.*

SOFTWARE FEATURES

- There are four different games, each focusing on different learning outcomes:
  - Birds of the Jungle: counting from 1 to 10 out loud
  - Birds on a Wire: recognizing numbers from 1 to 10
  - Backyard Birds: matching identical number
  - Bye-Bye Birdie: recognizing numbers written out (one to ten)

- Each game has seven levels of difficulty. The user progresses thro level by successfully completing 10 tasks related to numbers/cou

- Users are prompted to complete a task verbally (a female child's voice) and visually (clear, bright numbers/letters).

- Throughout the each game, background music plays to keep the user engaged.

- Users can access more features available on KidEd Software's website.

FIGURE 10.6 *Technical Specification (continued)*

ADD-ONS

This software stands alone; no add-ons, upgrades, or expansion editions are available.

HISTORY

– Changed title of product 12/3/07 (JW)

– Added specific hardware requirements to User Requirements section 12/1/07 (JW)

– Removed proposed upgrade package from Add-ons section 11/19/07 (JW)

– Created 11/12/07 (JW)

Audience Analysis

A good place to start when trying to determine potential readers of the user guide is with the person or group responsible for marketing the product. Contacting these individuals with a set of questions about who they will be selling this product to will help take the guesswork out of the writing process. Beyond contacting marketing, also reach out to the group who worked on developing the product. They will have a good idea of who they designed the product for and what needs these potential readers might have. Furthermore, when possible, contact potential readers directly to interview them on their needs for a user guide and the product. When conducting audience analysis, try to approach it from a variety of angles in order to accurately predict a reader's expectations and needs.

Research

When conducting research for the content of the user guide, the writer should first turn to any previously written documentation on the product. This includes previous versions of the guide, guides written for similar products, marketing material, and technical specifications written during the product's development. The technical specifications can be a critical document in facilitating the writing process because the specifications should detail the criteria used for developing the product. Granted, aspects of the product may have

Questions for Audience Analysis

Consider the following questions when researching potential readers for the user guide:

- Are the readers experts in the field in which the guide is related to?

- Are the readers' expectations high due to the cost or complexity of the product?

- Will the readers potentially read every section of the guide, or only focus on certain sections?

- Will the readers want to access the guide electronically, for example, in an HTML or PDF format?

- Is there any training that will accompany the guide?

- Will the readers already be familiar with potential dangers or hardships when using the product?

- Are there other resources for the readers to access for information on the product?

been altered during development, but those modifications should be reflected in the final version of the specifications. If technical specifications are not available, or if they are severely lacking, then the writer needs to do extensive research about the product.

The developers who worked on creating the product, such as engineers or software designers, should be interviewed by the writer to obtain firsthand knowledge about the product. Try to elicit specific details from the developers because the guide will cover every aspect of the product; furthermore, the writer needs to have a good understanding of the product prior to writing the guide. Obviously, known defects or inadequacies of the product should not be included in the guide, even if the developers pass along this information; rather, this information should help guide the writer as to what aspects of the product may need warnings or extensive troubleshooting explanations.

Firsthand use of the product by the writer is another means to acquire information to use in the guide. If the writer does not have access or authority to use the product, then sitting in on usability testing for the product is also an option. Essentially, the writer must explore various options for research, and not just rely on a single option. Doing so will create a one-dimensional approach to the product, while the reader will benefit most from a multidimensional and detailed approach to the product.

Tone and Writing Style

Two primary writing characteristics for a strong user guide are descriptive text and formal tone. The product needs to be described to the reader from every angle and feature. This description cannot use vague words; instead, precise details should be noted. For example, rather than stating the "LCD screen is small in comparison to the rest of the device," use actual dimensions: "The LCD screen is 3" × 5", as compared to the overall dimensions of the device, 12" × 12"." Verbally portraying the product so that it is easy to visualize will help a reader get a clear understanding of the entire product and its functionality. Beyond description, a user guide should be formal in its tone. Formal writing is clear, because it does not rely on clichés or slang, and is professional sounding. The reader will have confidence in the material presented in the guide, as well as have confidence in the product. A casual or informal tone makes the text ambiguous and less trustworthy in a user guide. Detailed and formal writing are standard characteristics, yet the overall style of the guide is determined by how readers will use the guide.

Determine how to approach the guide and meet the needs of potential readers. Will the readers be focused on completing specific tasks with the product? Or, will the readers want to capitalize on the features of the product? The guide can essentially meet both needs, but not at the same time. Readers new to the product will be task orientated; they will want to quickly get the product up and running in order to perform basic operations. Readers more experienced with the product, or similar products, will want to know about the special features and how to best use them. Writers should be sure not to combine the two orientations in the same section because there is no seamless way to do so. One solution is to split the guide into two distinct parts, where the first half is task orientated and the second half is feature orientated. A second option is to use the document's design to clearly note task versus feature passages, either through color, text boxes, or headings. Without a clear distinction, readers will become frustrated because they cannot readily find the processes they need to effectively use the product.

What to Include

A user guide is a complex document, covering every aspect of a product. Based on expressed requirements for the guide, along with how much time and resources a writer has available to complete the document, there are sections that can be excluded from a guide while still conveying enough information to the reader. At a minimum, the following sections should be included:

- Title
- Table of Contents
- Product Overview
- Materials
- Specific Product Description
- Operating Instructions
- Troubleshooting
- Contact Information

These additional sections will enhance the reader's experience with the product:

- Front Matter
- Configurations (tables/charts)
- Appendixes
- Glossary
- Index

Keep the target reader in mind when deciding on what to include in the guide. If the reader is likely to turn to the guide for answers about dimensions, then the writer needs to include a section detailing all the configurations of the product; however, if that information is not relevant to making the product work effectively, then it should be excluded so as to not make the guide more complex than it already is.

Title. Although it will be clear that the document is a user guide, the writer should create a title that is more descriptive. This may just mean that the title should include the name of the product. The title does not need to be creative or catchy; rather, it should be able to stand on its own without further explanation.

Table of Contents. User guides are often lengthy, yet readers only need certain sections of information at a time. A well-organized table of contents provides a means for readers to access relevant information quickly. Headings used in the guide should clearly match up with the entries in the table of contents.

Product Overview. The section of the guide that introduces the reader to the overall appearance of the product should rely on both verbal explanation and graphics. An example representation is shown in figure 10.7. Describe the basic use of the product, along with key features, but do not go into great detail at this point. The details will be covered extensively later in the document. The description of the product should be accompanied by clear graphics of the product. To further enhance the graphic, use text alongside the graphic to explain aspects of the product.

FIGURE 10.7 *Product Overview Graphic*

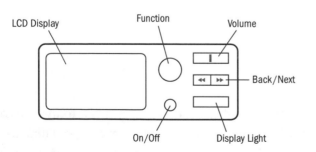

Acme MP3 Player

LCD Display: displays track title, artist, album title, and volume level

Function: choose options to shuffle, repeat, play continuous, play by artist, album, or song list

Volume: adjust up or down

Back/Next: go back to previous track or skip to next

Display Light: increase or decrease the brightness of display (x3)

On/Off: turn player on or off

Materials. Any accessories or parts included with the product should be listed so readers know they have received the product in its entirety. If there are many small or similar looking materials, include detailed graphics of what each looks like along with a clear label. It should also be noted what is not included with the product; explain that the reader will need to acquire these materials prior to using the product. When writing a guide for software, the reader should be made aware of system requirements, such as memory capacity, operating system, and hardware. When possible, provide suggestions of where the reader can obtain the necessary materials if they are uncommon.

Specific Product Description. Audience analysis will dictate if the product description needs to be extremely explicit, such as noting the size of the screws holding the product together. Do not write in explicit detail if it will not benefit the reader. Focus on the details that will help the reader understand the product and how to best use the product and its features. This is another section that benefits from the use of graphics. Unlike the graphics used in the product overview section, these graphics should be cross sections and insets of specific aspects of the product. Each graphic should have coordinating explanatory text and a label. Refer to chapter 15 for information on using graphics in communications.

There are different ways to approach writing a product description. For software, begin by describing the first screen the reader will see and the significance of that screen. Next, progress through all the main screens that will give the reader insights into the product, but don't focus on how to use the software specifically because that information will be covered later in the guide. If the product is an object, the writer can take a simpler approach and describe it from top down, outside to inside, and left to right.

Features of the product also will need to be described, though this information should not necessarily be integrated with the general product description. Keep information about features separate so that the reader is not overwhelmed with information. The features are not key to making the product work initially, so the reader should not be distracted by this extra information.

Operating Instructions. Steps on how to use the product and features should follow the same writing style as sets of instructions, covered previously in this chapter. Each set of instructions should focus on one task or feature; combining multiple tasks and features into a single set could lead to confusion or errors by the reader. More specifically, the reader should have easy access to the steps needed to set up and install the product, even if this means putting these steps in a separate, smaller document. After setup has been detailed, the writer then can present the processes for using the product and its features.

When presenting instructions for use, it is the writer's duty to provide the reader with clear and precise warnings about safety and repercussions of using the product improperly. The warnings should not be hidden or obscure, such as burying the information within a long paragraph of text. Use document formatting, such as color, bold lines/boxes, and increased font size, to draw readers to this information. That said, a reader can be desensitized toward the warnings if there are too many stacked together or too prominent on the page. Structure the information carefully so readers are inclined to see the warnings and cautions.

Troubleshooting. This is often the most vital section of the user guide because readers generally turn to a user guide only when they are having difficulty with the product. The sections describing the product and how to use it are important, but it is unlikely that a reader will experience no complications. Due to these potential circumstances, it is important for the writer to visualize every potential problem a reader may encounter and then write clear and concise solutions. Consider scenarios from setting up the product to using specific features correctly and incorrectly to not having all the required materials available.

Do not simply rely on information from those who developed the product as to what problems might occur when using the product. These individuals have a thorough understanding of the product, whereas the reader may have limited or no knowledge of the product. There are many pitfalls the reader will encounter that developers may not consider. To help predict problems, a writer should consider watching users inexperienced with the product set up and use it with and without the guide on hand. This method will help the writer see problems as they happen, and then be able to write clear and tested solutions to include in the troubleshooting section.

Contact Information. Readers should not feel abandoned after reaching the end of the guide. Providing contact information for customer service, sales representatives, and distribution/repair centers will help build a relationship with the reader. If the information is likely to change often, then only provide general information, such as the company's website, email address, and telephone number. The more information provided, though, the more confident the reader will be in the company and product.

Optional Sections. There are other sections that can be included in a thorough user guide. These sections should be included if they will make the reader's experience with the product easier:

- **Front matter.** At the beginning of the guide, a writer may be required to include information that does not necessarily enhance the reader's experience with the product. This information may include what edition the guide or product is, legal disclaimers about the guide and product usage, warranty information about the product, and copyright information about the guide. Some information is more important, which is why it is included up front. Safety issues and warnings often appear in the front matter so that the reader encounters them prior to beginning to use the product.

- **Configurations.** Although the configurations and dimensions are good details to include about a product, the reader might not need this information, which is why it is optional. This section should be designed with tables and charts if the data is numerical or complex in nature. Be sure to explain the numerical data if it is not inherently clear.

- **Appendixes.** Any information that is not directly relevant to understanding or using the product can be included in an appendix at the end of the guide. Each appendix should be clearly labeled and listed in the table of contents.

- **Glossary.** A user guide may need to continually rely on jargon or acronyms throughout the writing. Even if the words are defined once in the guide, they also should appear in a glossary for easy access by the reader.

- **Index.** Including a listing of all the topics and subtopics covered in the guide is useful if the guide is extensive. Small user guides can rely on the table of contents to help orientate the reader.

Document Design

A user guide contains a lot of dense information about a product, so a writer must design the guide for quick access and easy reading. Clear section headings that coordinate with the table of contents are required. The headings should be bold and in a font larger than what is used for other text on the page. Along with headings, design white space into each page by using lists, text boxes, and graphics; it is also important to not overload each page with information. There are also more practical design issues that a writer needs to consider when creating a guide.

The overall dimensions of the user guide will dictate how much information will be on a page. If the guide is 8" × 11", then the writer can include longer paragraphs and larger graphics on each page. If the guide is limited in size to 6" × 8", then the writer needs to carefully plot out the content and graphics for each page. Another consideration is the use of color. If the graphics will be printed in black and white, then it is generally better to use simple line graphics to make sure they appear clearly on the page. If the graphics will be in color, then be sure the colors used do not distract from the text explaining the graphic.

Editing and Revising

Once the user guide has been completely written, the editing and revising phase is the next test for a writer. During this phase the writer needs to look for more than just typos and grammatical errors. Make sure the content is organized logically and every section is complete in its coverage. If several different writers contributed content, then the entire guide will need to be reviewed to make sure the writing maintains the same style and tone. All graphics should be printed out and checked to ensure they are not blurry or misleading, and that the labels are accurate and numbered sequentially.

As the writer nears the completion point with the guide, it is important that people not familiar with the product review the guide to look for gaps in logic and confusing explanations. The writer and product experts generally cannot see the same content issues as an inexperienced user will when reviewing and using the guide. Chapter 17 explains how to conduct usability testing on communications like user guides. While inexperienced users are reviewing the guide, it also should be submitted to experts to do fact checking. Any inaccurate or misleading content could have serious effects on the reader and the product.

A completed user guide will be dense with information, both about the product and its features. Well-written guides build reliable relationships with readers because they are confident in the product and the company; furthermore, readers are confident in their abilities to successfully use the product and get the most out of the included features.

REFERENCES

Hayes, C. 2005 (September). "Know the codes." *Industrial Safety & Hygiene News,* 39 (9).

Wilson, W. 1997. "Writing effective requirements specifications." NASA Software Assurance Technology Center. 22 November 2007. *http://satc. gsfc.nasa.gov/support/STC_APR97/write/writert.html.*

CHAPTER 11

Proposals and Grant Writing

P roposals vary in format but are written with a common purpose: to present an offer and have the readers accept it. Two common types of proposals include research proposals and grant proposals. *Research proposals* are written to request funding to begin or to continue research on a particular topic or hypothesis. *Grant proposals* are written to request funding of an activity or project. The difference between the two is that research proposals ask for funds to conduct research to establish the credibility or feasibility of an idea, which means that these types of proposals are often associated with academic papers, fellowships, and dissertations. Grant proposals usually do not request time or money to conduct research, but they have a definite plan of action that is being proposed. While the formats for the different types of proposals vary, the purpose is the same: to convince the reader that a project is worth pursuing and being funded.

RESEARCH PROPOSALS

The purpose of a research proposal is to persuade readers that extensive research into a topic, or the ability to conduct research in order to prove a hypothesis, will make a significant contribution to a particular field of study. The bottom line, though, is that a writer has to convince readers to spend their money on a proposed research idea.

Research proposals can be funded by various organizations, both public and private; therefore, the superstructure shown and discussed below is general and should be modified according to both the guidelines of the individual organization that it will be sent to and/or the request for proposal (RFP). For a sample of a full research proposal, see example 1 at the end of the chapter.

Components of a Research Proposal

Submission guidelines vary from organization to organization, so it is imperative to review RFPs carefully. A general superstructure of research proposals is described in detail below.

Abstract. The abstract is the first component of the research proposal. It is usually a 250- to 500-word summary of the entire project that briefly reviews the major elements in the proposal, such as introduction, theoretical framework, statement of the problem, purpose of the study, research methods, and findings. The literature review is not typically included in the abstract. A sample abstract for a research proposal is shown below.

> This multiple-case study provides a description and explanation of educational leaders' perspectives on technology use in the curriculum of general education programs. The theory that guided the study was constructivist leadership. The study employed qualitative data collection techniques of transcribed interviews, observations, researcher field notes, researcher reflective journal, and documents and artifacts. A purposive sample of two deans, two academic technology directors, and two faculty members from two colleges participated in the study. The two colleges were selected because of their extensive use of technology in the undergraduate general education curriculum, accessibility, and participants' willingness to participate in the study.
>
> Participants' attitudes, perceptions, and opinions of technology use in the undergraduate general education curriculum were presented in the findings, which were illustrated through

the use of excerpts from interview responses. The participants discussed the benefits and challenges of technology use. These benefits and challenges were expressed in six sub-themes: 1) faculty resistance, 2) use of technology in the curriculum, 3) distance learning for institutions, 4) accessibility, 5) technology as learning partner, and 6) distance learning for students. Other key findings included the way in which growth and change fostered technology growth and the ways technology transformed the department and curriculum.

Introduction. The purpose of the introduction is to provide readers with background on the research topic or project. The introduction serves the following three functions:

1. It creates interest in the research topic or project by looking at it from the funder's perspective.

2. It establishes significance for the study within the scope of the field.

3. It provides a framework for the research that is involved.

By considering these three things in the introduction, a writer offers vital information and gain readers' attention because a point of view other than the writer's is being considered. Funders may not continue to read the rest of the proposal if the introduction does not indicate significance to them, their mission, or the field. A reader-centered introduction will grab funders' attention and interest and encourage them to continue reading. An example introduction for a research proposal is shown below.

The use of the Internet and other instructional technologies has begun to play an important role in the curriculum of general education programs. Educators have been using instructional technology to enhance student learning for more than 30 years. However, the 21st century has introduced more powerful tools, such as the Internet and multimedia educational software, allowing students new ways of analyzing the world around them. An understanding of the leadership practices employed by educational leaders is essential to utilizing the best possible form of technology for instructional use in the undergraduate general education curriculum. Today, educational leaders need not be asked if they use instructional technology in the curriculum, but in what capacity.

The rapid growth of computers and introduction of the Internet have provided educational leaders with a new means of presenting information. With these resources, educational leaders need to rethink classroom approaches, utilizing the increased capabilities of instructional technologies to develop educational settings that will help broaden the opportunity for student success.

Instructional leaders posed with the task of integrating technology into the curriculum are faced with multiple challenges. They must first seek out faculty members truly interested in the topic and those that see value in this type of teaching approach. Questions that need to be asked include: How will students be assessed? What type of technology should be used? In what manner should technology be integrated into the curriculum? Leaders such as deans and academic technology directors should encourage faculty interested in this topic, but should not force integrating technology in all general education courses. Benefits of this approach need to be explained and suggestions for integrating technology into the curriculum need to be offered.

Educational leaders are charged with determining the most effective means for technology use in the curriculum. There are numerous applications associated with instructional technology ranging from simple word processing to complex educational administrative and support functions. The wide range of applications, and the rapid pace at which new technological media are being introduced, creates challenges for educational leaders in defining instructional technology and evaluating the effectiveness and applicability of technological media.

This study examined the challenges and benefits of technology use in the undergraduate general education curriculum at two urban colleges. In particular, this study will assist deans, academic technology directors, and faculty members of general education programs to understand ways technology is used to enhance the curriculum. I have been inspired to inquire about technology use in the general education curriculum because many institutions talk of technology, but the manner in which it is being used and the effectiveness of technology needs further discussion.

Problem Statement. A problem statement includes the context of the research project and the issues that exist in the current body of literature. It should answer the question, "Why should this topic be researched?" Clearly written problem statements also include the theoretical or conceptual framework in the study. They should be written for an audience of academic sophistication but with presumed limited knowledge on the specific area of research. An example problem statement for a research proposal is shown below.

> It is reasonable to suggest that instructional technology use in the general education curriculum is a topic of interest for many educational leaders. Educational leaders are faced with a number of factors concerning integration of technology into the curriculum.
>
> First, deans, academic technology directors, and faculty members must employ strong leadership skills as well as technological knowledge. The decision to change the curriculum is challenging, and educational leaders must be able to motivate others to see the value of the change. Due to the vast amount of technology and the rapid pace at which technology changes, educational leaders must be open to suggestions from others regarding the appropriate technological medium to be employed into the curriculum. A general knowledge of instructional technology is also needed to guide deans, academic technology directors, and faculty members in choosing and using technology in the general education curriculum.
>
> Second, academic technology directors and faculty members must rethink teaching methods. There have been many attempts expressed in the literature to describe the types of technological

media available. Categorizing the forms is a difficult task given that technology is always changing. Market demands influence the decision as well. Oftentimes, institutions attempt to keep abreast with the competition without reflecting on the needs of the individual institution. In addition, teaching methods must be considered. Instructional technology use in the undergraduate general education curriculum allows for new approaches for students to actively gain knowledge, but also requires instructors to redesign presentation material.

Finally, integrating technology into the undergraduate general education curriculum involves attention to a future vision and establishment of specific policies and procedures. Trends need to be observed and integrated into a long-term technology plan. The institution must be committed to investing in upgrades for technology and training for its leaders and instructors. Educational leaders must also be committed to continual training as new technologies emerge. Use of the Internet for posting syllabi online and distance learning courses raise issues of intellectual property and fair use. Deans, academic technology directors, and faculty members must have a clear understanding of intellectual property law and help maintain fair use. While the world of technology may be rapidly moving, educational leaders need to cautiously develop appropriate policies, but must quickly devise new guidelines regarding technology.

Based on these facts, it is reasonable to assume that deans, technology directors, and faculty members may have a different perspective on integrating technology into the graduate curriculum depending on the institutional resources available and types of technology used. Additionally, educational leaders are challenged with addressing a number of issues associated with integrating technology into the curriculum. The problem presented in this study is to investigate and determine the perspectives of deans, academic technology directors, and faculty members of undergraduate general education programs on integrating instructional technology use in the curriculum.

Purpose of the Study. The purpose of the study section of a research proposal is to provide a synopsis of the main reasons the research needs to be conducted. It is important that the purpose of the study limits the specific area of research. In the purpose of the study section, a detailed account of the entire research project is not presented at this time. The goal is to concisely state the rationale for conducting the study. An example purpose of the study for a research proposal is shown below.

> The purpose of this study was to describe and explain the perspective of selected deans, academic technology directors, and faculty members on instructional technology use in the curriculum of undergraduate general education programs. The results may assist educational leaders in three areas.
>
> First, the findings of the study will inform deans, academic technology directors, and faculty members of the types of technological media available for use in the curriculum. Second, the findings will inform current and future educational leaders of the ways other leaders approach the use of technology in the undergraduate general education curriculum. In addition, the study will provide the basis for greater understanding of the constructivist leadership needed in educational settings that both want and have an interest in employing use of technology into the curriculum.

Questions and/or Hypothesis. The decision to include research questions and/or a hypothesis depends on the nature of the research method selected. A *qualitative* research method, which is the study of a problem or phenomena in a social context, uses questions in the research proposal and written study. A *quantitative* method involves the use of statistical analysis in analyzing a specific research problem. The practice of using a hypothesis is grounded in the scientific method, common to quantitative methods. A research question poses a relationship between two or more variables but phrases the relationship as a question; a hypothesis represents a declarative statement of the relationship between two or more variables (Kerlinger 1979; Krathwohl 1988). The decision to use research questions or a hypothesis depends of the purpose of the study, the nature of the design and methodology, and the intended audience for the research. Example exploratory questions used in a qualitative study are listed below.

Three major exploratory questions guided this study:

1. What elements constitute perspectives on technology use in the undergraduate general education curriculum?

2. What variables influence this perspective on technology use?

3. What beliefs do these educational leaders hold that support or negate this perspective?

To answer the relevant research questions, interviews were conducted with persons who currently serve as undergraduate general education deans, faculty members, and technology directors, had a minimum three years of experience in planning and integrating technology in the curriculum, and currently use instructional technology in the curriculum at their respective institutions. Additionally, participants were selected from two colleges (in an urban setting) based on accessibility, willingness to participate in the study, and the previously mentioned requirements. The data collection strategies used in this study were transcribed interviews, observations, researcher field notes, researcher reflective journals, and documents and artifacts.

Theoretical Framework. Research often falls under a specific theoretical framework, which means that findings of the research study will relate to the theory that guides the study. Use of theoretical framework, theories, or lines of inquiry is dependent upon the methodology selected for the study. Quantitative studies use theory deductively and the theoretical information is placed toward the beginning of the plan for the study. The purpose of the study is to test or verify theory. As the research study progresses, the researcher reflects on whether the theory was confirmed or negated by the results of the study (Creswell 1987). In qualitative studies, theories are used to provide a framework for which findings of the study are grounded. An example of the use of theory and the way the theory frames the study is shown below.

This study was guided by constructivist leadership theory. Lambert (1995) challenges educators to rethink old paradigms regarding leadership and shift toward a new dynamic approach focused on relationships. Lambert (1995) defines constructivist leadership as "the reciprocal processes that enable participants in an educational community to construct meanings that lead toward a common purpose about schooling" (p. 29). Understanding the constructivist approach involves relationships, a reciprocal approach that invites "anyone in the educational community—teachers, administrators, parents, students—[to] engage in leadership actions" (Lambert 1995, p. 29). Thus, the constructivist leader is charged with motivating others and ensuring multiple voices are heard.

Lambert (1995) states that there are patterns to describe leadership or the actions of a leader. The definitions fall into three categories: what the leader does, for whom or with the action is taken, and toward what end the actions are taken (p. 30). This three-dimensional analysis is illustrated in the definition of "leadership" or "leader" by several authors. DuFour and Eaker (1998) postulate that leaders foster individual and organizational renewal (p. 274). This concept reflects the constructivist leadership approach.

Lambert (1995) describes the reciprocal process of leadership as incorporating four elements: evoking potential in a trusting environment, reconstructing old assumptions and myths, focusing on the construction of meaning, and framing actions that embody new behaviors and purposeful intentions. Participants in the reciprocal processes are "all members of the education community, not segregated as leaders and followers. At any given time, roles and behaviors will shift among participants based on interest, expertise, experience, and responsibility" (Lambert

1995, p. 39). The constructivist leader sees the various talents in all members of the educational setting and encourages others to use their talents.

Constructivist leadership theory is relevant to educational leaders who wish to learn more about technology use in the curriculum or those who seek to implement a technology plan for the curriculum. Constructivist educational leaders collaborate with others in a social environment where all are seen as potential leaders. This environment allows multiple voices to be heard. Because the concept and definition of technology is varied and is constantly changing, it is essential to gain feedback from all members of the educational setting. The constructivist leader has the ability to instill a sense of accountability and responsibility in others. To do this, constructivist educational leaders must look beyond self and encourage shared inquiry among all its members. Constructivist leaders listen and evaluate findings from others to resolve decisions on technology decisions.

Clearly the need for understanding constructivist leadership in higher education exists. Therefore, to understand the perspectives of deans, academic technology directors, and faculty members on the use of technology in the undergraduate general education curriculum, interviews, observations, and reflective journal case studies are in order.

Literature Review. The review of the literature section covers pertinent research existing in the field. This section provides readers with an overview of the existing studies closely related to the study being proposed. A comprehensive review of the literature is presented in the completed research paper. For the research proposal, a short review of the major studies is included. For the proposal, only the most pertinent and relevant studies are included.

Methods and Procedures. The methods and procedures section is the heart of the research proposal. The steps in the research process are described in detail. The steps of the methodology are listed and described in this section. The methods and procedures section attempts to answer the questions raised in the questions/hypothesis section. This section includes the sampling (if quantitative methods) or participants' selection (if qualitative methods), data collection techniques, and limitations of the study. Listed below are example sections from a methods section in a research proposal. Note: The example is not inclusive but is a representation of the major elements covered in the proposal.

Qualitative Research

The decision to conduct a qualitative study was influenced by the characteristics of qualitative design discussed by Janesick (1998). She describes research as being alive and active. It is a way of looking at the world and interpreting the world. This study focused on qualitative methods as means to understand the multiple complexities existing in the social world (Janesick 1998). This desire to understand complexities of an existing phenomenon is necessary for the qualitative researcher. Rubin and Rubin (1995) advised that qualitative research is warranted whenever depth of understanding is required.

Research Design

The research design of this study sought to describe and explain selected deans, technology directors, and faculty members' perspectives on instructional technology use in the curriculum of undergraduate general education programs.

Qualitative researchers need to be flexible and adaptable to changes in the social setting. Thus, although the research design is prepared at the beginning of the study, it will continue to change as information is gathered from the participants (Rubin and Rubin 1995). Denzin and Lincoln (2000) also agree that research designs "should always have built-in flexibility to allow for discoveries of new and unexpected empirical materials and growing sophistication" (p. 368). With these thoughts in mind, the researcher understands the interviewing process is a dynamic, not stagnant, process. Openness to change and flexibility are crucial to gain the fullest understanding of the information.

Qualitative research is designed to understand phenomena. In this study, the researcher sought to understand educational leader perspectives on technology use in the undergraduate general education curriculum. Janesick (1998) emphasized that "the heart of our work is understanding the social setting and all that it entails" (p. 68). With these thoughts in mind, the researcher was cognizant of the unexpected when beginning the study.

Participant Selection

Participants were six educational leaders from two separate colleges in a large urban city, and included two deans (John from William Wallace College and Connie from Jane Byrne College), two technology directors (Kathy from William Wallace College and Kate from Jane Byrne College), and two instructors (Julie from William Wallace College and Christine from Jane Byrne College). One college is a four-year private college; the other is a two-year city college offering only the associates' degree.

The six educational leaders from the two colleges were interviewed individually regarding their perspective on instructional technology use in the undergraduate general education curriculum. Following the recommendations of Janesick (1997), the researcher relied "on many possible sources of data and use[d] a variety of methods in the process" (p. 60). Each educational leader was interviewed at least three times for a total of 21 formal and informal interviews. With the exception of Kate, who was audio taped three times, the educational leaders were audio taped two times for a total of 13 taped interviews and eight informal, non-taped interviews. Data were also from six observations, 19 documents and artifacts, and 27 researcher reflective journal entries.

Purposeful Sampling

Following the recommendations of Janesick (1994), in order to answer the relevant research questions, interviews were conducted with persons who were currently serving as undergraduate general education deans, faculty members, and academic technology directors, had a minimum of three years of experience in planning and integrating technology in the curriculum, and currently use technology in the curriculum at their respective institutions. Additionally, participants were selected from two colleges in a major urban city based on accessibility, willingness to participate in the study, and the previously mentioned requirements.

This study sought to describe and explain educational leaders' perspectives on technology use in the undergraduate general education curriculum. As such, the study called for deans, academic technology directors, and faculty members to be currently employed by a college that is using technology in the general education curriculum. Requiring three years of experience ensured that the participants had been actively involved in the implementation process and have a thorough understanding of this process.

Data Collection

Interviews, researcher's reflective journal, observations, researcher's field notes, documents, artifacts, and transcripts were collected. At least two in-depth interviews were conducted with each participant. In an attempt to gather the rich, descriptive information required for qualitative research, semi-structured interviews with open-ended questions were used. Benefits of this procedure are that it required participants to be asked the same questions so that interviewer effects are minimized, allows for cross-case analysis, allows future researchers to see the instrument used, and is a focused method, which improves efficiency (Patton 1990).

Data Analysis. The data analysis section of the research proposal includes the procedures used (or that will be used) for the research project, and it describes the intentions and reasons for the data analysis methods chosen for the study. This will assist readers in evaluating the choices made by the researchers. Also, any analytic tools for the data analysis (such as SPSS for quantitative research; NUDIST for qualitative research) are indicated here. A clearly stated rationale for the decision to use the design, methodology, and analysis selected for the project is included in this section. An example is provided below.

Data analysis, according to Rubin and Rubin (1995) "is exciting because you discover themes and concepts embedded throughout your interviews" (p. 226). Thus, after each round of interviewing, the researcher reviews and analyzes the data for emerging themes and concepts.

Rubin and Rubin (1995) explain, "The purpose of the data analysis is to organize the interviews to present a narrative that explains what happened or provide a description of the norms and values that underlie cultural behavior" (p. 229). The steps of analysis presented by Rubin and Rubin (1995) provide a basis for data analysis:

1. Code data, letting interpretations develop as data is analyzed response by response.

2. Divide data into smaller categories. Reassemble the information into themes or arguments.

3. Figure out the theoretical or policy implications of the data— what broader questions can be answered and what broader insights can be provided.

4. Choose what themes to emphasize in part based on the audience and what they find stimulating, useful, or challenging. (p. 229)

The final stage of analysis suggested by Rubin and Rubin (1995) is the organization of data "in ways that help you formulate themes, refine concepts, and link them together to create a clear description or explanation of a culture or topic" (p. 251). The final stage of analysis also includes "an interpretation of the material . . . in terms of the literature and theories in the researcher's field" (Rubin and Rubin 1995, p. 251). Accordingly, analysis of data for this study began immediately after the first interview and continued through the end of the study.

Significance of the Study. The significance of the study section of the proposal is to describe and explain the ways the research will refine, revise, or expand on existing knowledge in the field of study. Most research proposals will have two audiences: practitioners and professionals in the field. The significance of the study should be written to address the needs and interests of both audiences. When drafting the significance of the study, think about the implications of the study, specifically how the results of the study may affect academic research, theory, practice, educational initiatives, curricula, and policy. The following questions should be kept in mind when thinking about the significance of the study:

- What call for additional research arises from the study?
- What will the findings of the study mean to practitioners?
- Will results of the study contribute to changes in the field?
- Will the findings of the study contribute to the solution of educational or social issues?
- What will be improved or changed as a result of the research?
- Will policies be affected by the findings of the study?
- How will the results be implemented and what innovations will come about?

References. A comprehensive list of references used in the research proposal needs to be included, typically formatted according to APA guidelines; however, an organization might request the use of Modern Language Association (MLA) or Chicago Manual of Style guidelines instead. Only references cited in the proposal are included in the reference list.

Appendixes. Appendixes are useful when additional information is needed to support the research proposal. However, appendixes are not usually provided for a conference proposal. The following material may be appropriate for inclusion in an appendix:

- Complete survey questions given to participants

- Demographic data

- Vita of researcher conducting the study

- Documents or artifacts gathered from the site location, such as meeting agendas, brochures, newsletters, or catalogs

- Verbatim transcripts from interview sessions

- Permissions letter granted to conduct the research

- Informed consent letters from participants

GRANT PROPOSALS

The types of grant proposals a technical communicator may be called on to write vary by funding organization and purpose. The most important factor to bear in mind is that grant writing is part of a process that begins with a funding need. The grant proposal is the written document outlining the project and rationale for funding. However, the grant writing process is a partnership between the organization requesting the funding and the foundations and corporations that can fulfill funding needs. A nonprofit organization may have a program or idea suitable for solving a problem but may lack the financial resources to maintain it or bring it to fruition. A corporation or foundation may have the finances available to support solving the problem but may lack the creativity or other resources needed to carry out the project. This section will focus on the process of writing grant proposals, discussing the components from conception to completion.

Overview of the Grant Writing Process

The grant writing process involves a series of steps, beginning with a concept or idea. An understanding of the grant writing process is needed in crafting an effective proposal. The grant writing process begins with an idea, often a solution to a problem. Establishing a presence, specifically making the organization known to potential funders, and setting funding priorities is the first step. A request for proposal, or RFP, is sent by the potential funder to the foundation that is requesting funding for the project. A comprehensive grant proposal is then written in accordance with the guidelines specified by the funding organization. Proposals are either accepted or rejected. Successful grant proposals may then move forward with the project; unsuccessful proposals must be revised and resubmitted. An overview of the grant writing process is illustrated in figure 11.1. Figure 11.2 shows the steps after a proposal has been submitted.

Cultivating an ongoing relationship with the funding agency is important to receiving additional funding in the future. Required reports need to be filed in a timely manner, and communication needs to occur with the funding agency during the lifecycle of the grant. Research shows that organizations that have received funding in the past are more competitive and more likely to receive funding from the same agency in the future.

What Happens If the Proposal Is Not Accepted?

If a grant proposal is not accepted, the grant writing process begins again. The proposal may need to be revised and submitted to different funders, or it may need to be revised and resubmitted to the original funder for consideration in the next funding cycle. Figure 11.2 illustrates the second phase of the grant writing cycle, beginning with acceptance or rejection of the grant proposal.

Developing a Presence and Setting Funding Priorities

Raising money is essential to every nonprofit organization. At times, there is a misperception that an organization must be working a highly unique or special project prior to requesting money from an outside agency. However, if the organization is already fulfilling a need, the organization is ready to request financing from a corporation or foundation. For example, an existing literacy program may be seeking additional funding to buy computers and literacy software. The problem has been funded by another organization, but a special need has been identified, for example, computers used to enhance literacy skills. In this case, funds would be requested to finance this specific aspect of the project.

FIGURE 11.1 *Overview of the Grant Writing Process*

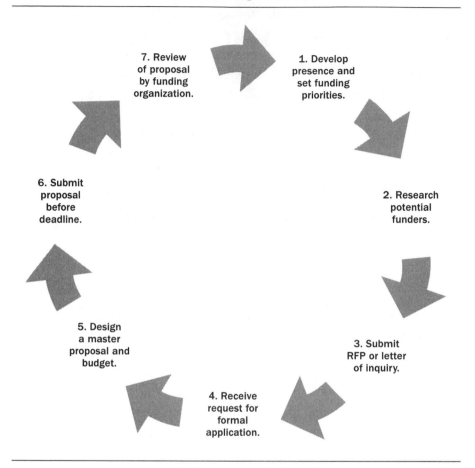

Prior to writing a grant, an organization needs to ensure three key elements are in place: a strong mission statement, nonprofit status, and a credible program or plan to support the mission. For the advanced grant writer, the first step is to identify the focus of the organization and develop a presence in the nonprofit sector. A strong mission statement for the organization needs to be written and committed to by members of the organization. The mission statement is the vision developed by the organization that illustrates what the organization wishes to achieve. The second step for nonprofit organizations is to establish nonprofit status from the federal Internal Revenue Service that permits the organization to receive tax-deductible gifts. This designation is

FIGURE 11.2 *Steps Following Proposal Submission*

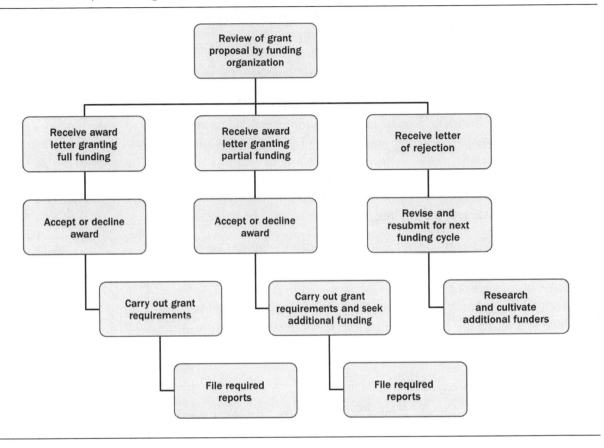

known as 501(c)(3) status, and a lawyer typically handles the filing. The third step is to establish a credible program or services, which can be established in the following ways:

- The organization will alert the funder to how it will fulfill a set need.

- The organization, especially a new organization, will keep the project achievable and include credible individuals to carry out the projects.

- The organization will clearly articulate the means to carry out the proposed project even though funders are tolerant to a certain level of risk with a new organization for an innovative project.

In an attempt to assist with identifying the funding priorities of an organization, the needs of the organization must be established. The following questions serve as a guide for this process:

- Is the organization requesting partial or full funding of a project?

- Is the goal of the project designed to assist an entire group or a single entity? (For example, requesting funding for an individual school arts program versus requesting funding for the arts program in the entire school district.)

- Is the funding request for a large project that will last for several years or is this a short-term funding request?

- Is additional funding actually needed or can the project be completed through readily available resources?

Narrowing the focus of a project will help establish funding priorities as well, and answering the following questions regarding individual projects will assist in this process:

- What is the project? Why is it important?

- What problem is the project attempting to solve? What is the significance?

- Who would benefit from the project?

- After the grant period ends, how can longevity of the project be guaranteed?

Seeking the opinions and input from a committee is an excellent way to establish funding priorities and define the focus of the organization. Managers, employees, volunteers, and other individuals familiar with the organization serve as excellent members of a planning committee. A planning committee discusses the organization needs, current and future funding, and projects that would require funding in the future.

Having a credible organization and clearly understood funding priorities is the baseline for crafting the proposal. Writing a strong proposal is critical to securing funding. Prior to seeking funding for a project or activity, it is important that individuals familiar with the organization establish a presence and set funding priorities. Once these pieces are in place, researching potential funders is the next step in the process.

Finding the Right Funder

Researching and finding the right funder is a time-consuming task. Both corporations and foundations have set priorities for funding nonprofit and for-profit organizations. For example, one foundation may have a focus of funding K–12 science programs only. If an organization is searching for funding for a local high school music program, this would not be a good fit. It is important to fully review the funding objective of the corporation or foundation to ensure that a match is in place.

There are many sources available for locating funding resources, including information on the Internet, local corporations, print and electronic directories, and foundation websites. A list of funding resources is presented in example 2 at the end of the chapter.

When conducting research on potential funders, the goal is to provide a comprehensive list of foundations, corporations, or other funders whose funding interests match the organization's needs. Geographic issues also should be considered. While funding is available from the federal government in many instances, additional local funding sources may be available. Information about local funding can be obtained from researching local news bulletins or newspapers, or attending committee events. Often, this will require talking to members of civic organizations or discussing funding opportunities with local corporations. When compiling a list of potential funders, be as broad as possible with the funding opportunities available. Funds are generally limited and the grant writing field is highly competitive. The more comprehensive the funder lists are, the more options will be available for submitting a grant proposal and receiving funding.

After a comprehensive list of potential funders has been established, it is time to refine the list of potential funders. Carefully review the funding criteria for the compiled list and narrow it down to funders that most likely will provide funding for the organization. As the list is revised, keep in mind the funding objectives and guidelines. Every corporation or foundation has specific funding needs and it is important to know the objectives of the organization and ensure alignment with the specified criteria of the funder.

Once the list of potential funding sources has been narrowed down, it is time to make contact with potential funders. Cultivate a relationship with the funders, if possible. The grant process involves a partnership, and the more knowledge the potential funder has about the organization, the more likely it is that the organization will receive funding. Contact with a potential funder can be made in several ways, including a letter of inquiry or request for proposal, telephone calls, or a face-to face meeting. The tone of the communication needs to focus on requesting guidelines or on clarification of information in the guidelines, *not* on solicitation for funding.

Prior to establishing contact with the funding agencies, prepare what to say about the organization. Time is valuable for foundations or corporations and the message needs to clearly state the goals of the organization and articulate why funding is needed. If contacting by telephone, provide an introduction by giving the name and location of the organization, and the purpose of the call. State that research has been conducted on the funding organization and that there is a strong fit between the organization and the funder. Ask if there are specific guidelines, such as in an RFP, required for submission of a grant proposal. If logistically possible, ask for a time to schedule a meeting. It is useful to meet face-to-face with a funding organization when appropriate. This meeting can provide an opportunity for the funding agency to become familiar with the organization and gain a better understanding of the funding request before the formal grant proposal is submitted.

Prior to submitting a formal proposal, many funding agencies require a letter of inquiry or request for funding before giving the requesting organization the formal grant proposal guidelines. This letter is designed as a screening device for funders, allowing the funding agencies to eliminate proposals that align with the funding interests of the agency. An example letter requesting guidelines, or an RFP, is shown below.

January 1, 2008

Ms. Jane Doe
Director of Foundation Giving
Sample Foundation
1111 Mailing Address
Any city, any state 11111

Dear Ms. Doe,

Any City College has partnered with Sample Elementary School on the city's south side to provide economically disadvantaged kindergarten and first-grade students and their parents with a program designed to enhance reading skills. The program is called Sample Program. The focus is on delivering workshops to parents on methods to stimulate their children's reading and writing skills—the basic skills absolutely necessary for later academic success. By focusing on one skill per session, such as asking questions during and after reading, the program approaches the enormous challenge of gaining reading readiness skills in a measured way. We respectfully **request guidelines** for submission of a full proposal for the continued support of Sample Program.

Research shows that significant differences exist in reading achievement levels in minority students in high-poverty areas. It is also stated that minority students attending school in high-poverty areas have less access to computer technology. Combined, these factors become a basis for unequal participation by minorities in higher education and employment fields requiring strong literacy skills. To remedy these situations, intervention must occur early on in a student's educational experience. Most family literacy programs focus on parents of "emergent" and early readers in kindergarten and first grade, which allows the greatest opportunity for literacy growth. Sample Program supports this research by focusing on improving the literacy skills of kindergarten and first-grade students. Parents are viewed as learning partners and are provided the training and tools needed to assist their children in improving early literacy skills.

Any City College is appropriately qualified to carry out this project because of its experience with and commitment to diverse student populations. The College graduates more minority students at the associate degree level (all disciplines combined) than any other higher education institution in the state; it is also the state's largest grantor of bachelor degrees in Business to minorities. Nationally, it ranks 16th and 28th, respectively, as the leading grantor of bachelor degrees in Business Administration to African Americans and to Hispanic Americans.

The following highlights the core elements of the Sample Program:

- Parents gain greater understanding of their role in the promotion of reading readiness in the home.

- Any City College students serve as interns with the program and, if interested, receive job training to become teachers of the program.

- Parents are trained to become teachers of the program to ensure sustainability.

- Participating teachers and administrators attend the program.

- The curriculum is designed based on guidelines from the Any City's Board of Education.

- The program is an immediate response to the priorities expressed by the mayor and the State Board of Education, and it is hoped that our Sample Program will gain the attention of the public school system to become a model reading readiness program within the city.

I wish to invite you to attend a Sample Program session at Sample Elementary School. Please contact me at (555) 555-1234 if you need additional information. I look forward to hearing from you.

Sincerely,

Director Name
Director of Development
Any City College

Prior to Writing the Grant Proposal

There are 10 general guidelines to keep in mind prior to writing a grant proposal:

1. Begin the process early.

2. Apply early.

3. Include a cover letter that can serve as a stand-alone document.

4. Develop clear objectives for what the project hopes to achieve.

5. Follow all guidelines for the specific grant proposal.

6. Include specific responses.

7. Take a realistic approach to the project.

8. Revise and resubmit, if rejected, during the next funding cycle.

9. Continue to research potential funding sources.

10. Cultivate existing partnerships with funding organizations.

Understanding that grant writing is a process is important when crafting the proposal. Because funding from corporations and foundations is highly competitive, revise and resubmit grant proposals that are not accepted the first time. The following sections will discuss in greater detail the steps of the grant writing process.

In addition to a written format for letters of inquiry or RFPs, funding agencies may have online application forms that serve as a written letter of inquiry. Similar to written letters of inquiry or RFPs, online applications require strict adherence to submission guidelines. Below is the description of the online application process for Heartland Hospice Memorial Fund.

Grant Application Process for Heartland Hospice Memorial Fund:

- Review the grant guidelines. Contact our office to discuss any questions regarding the potential grant application.

- Grant applications must be submitted through the online grant application system.

- Complete the entire grant application prior to submitting it for review. This includes a completion of the Projected Budget and any supporting documentation. An incomplete grant application will be returned to the applicant and will delay the decision-making process.

- Provide detail on the grant application. Include a detailed background and an explanation of need for the request.

- Include a list of other organizations that have been investigated as other sources of funding prior to applying for a grant. Include any funding received from other sources.

- Provide supporting documentation (e.g., statements, invoices, current bills, advertisements of event, etc.) to support the grant application.

- Notification of the status of a grant application will be received within 14 business days. Grant requests for over $1,000 will be reviewed by the Board of Directors and may take an additional 2–3 days for review by the Board.

An additional example of more detailed online application guidelines is found in example 3 at the end of this chapter.

Designing a Master Proposal

After specific guidelines for formal proposals have been received from the requested funding agencies, it is time to design the master proposal. Before beginning the writing process for the proposal, be sure to gather information and documentation for the project or initiative. The Foundation Center (2004) suggests that documentation be gathered in the following three areas: concept, program, and expenses. The *concept* of the project needs to be clearly articulated and support the argument for funding, which should be well-documented. The Foundation Center (2004, p. 8), offers the following checklist of the program information required:

- The nature of the project and how it will be conducted

- The timetable for the project

- The anticipated outcomes and how best to evaluate the results

- The staffing and volunteer needs, including deployment of existing staff and new hires

At this stage, the actual expenses have not been mapped out. A broad estimate of the expenses required to fund the program need to be included. The actual expenses will be written in the budget section of the master proposal. If it seems that the costs, even with grant funding, will be too large for undertaking the project, reduce or adjust project objectives to the most cost-effective means.

Grant proposals are unique documents that must be tailored to funding guidelines established by the funding agency. Because the grant proposal may be the only contact with the funding agency, the proposal must be well-written and self-explanatory. Listed below are some suggestions on writing the master proposal:

- Include clear objectives of the program.

- Do not assume the funder knows the subject area. Avoid jargon and other technical terms that may be confusing to the reader.

- Describe the problem the organization is attempting to resolve in factual and human interest terms.

- Be realistic about the proposed outcomes of the project.

- Discuss the target audience and the ways the audience will benefit from the project.

- Describe the change that will take place with the funding of the project.

- Review and follow guidelines for the specific funding agency. Complete all parts of the proposal as required.

- Eliminate wordiness and keep the proposal clearly written.

Although specific criteria for master proposals vary for individual corporations or foundations, the Foundation Center (2004) suggests some general components of a master proposal, as illustrated in table 11.1.

Proposals vary according to the requirements and guidelines set forth by the funding organizations. The sections that follow provide additional information on developing the various components of a master proposal. An example full grant proposal is provided in example 4 at the end of this chapter.

Executive Summary. When writing the executive summary for the master proposal, keep elements of time in mind. Readers of the proposal have limited time and the first page of the proposal needs to provide a clear synopsis of the project. This section must convince readers that the project is deserving of the requested funding, and that they should continue reading the proposal document. A summary of the elements of an executive summary suggested by the Foundation Center (2004) includes the following:

- **Problem.** This is a brief description of the problem or need the organization has recognized and is prepared to address.

- **Solution.** This is a brief description of the project, including what will take place and how many people will benefit from the program, how and where it will operate, for how long, and who will staff it.

- **Funding requirements.** This provides an explanation of the amount of grant money required and plans that have been made for future funding and the sustainability of the project after the grant cycle.

TABLE 11.1 *Components of a Master Proposal*

Component	Description	Length
Executive Summary	Statement of the case and summary of the entire proposal	1 page
Statement of Need	Why this project is necessary	2 pages
Project Description	Nuts and bolts of how the project will be implemented and evaluated	3 pages
Budget	Financial description of the project plus explanatory notes	1 page
Organization Information	History and governing structure of the nonprofit; its primary activities, its audiences, and its services	1 page
Conclusion	Summary of the proposal's main points	2 paragraphs

- **Organization and its expertise.** This is a description of the organization and its capacity to carry out the proposal.

Below is an example executive summary. This example might not contain every element of an executive summary, because guidelines vary from funder to funder.

> XX University, a predominately minority-serving private higher education institution located in Anytown, is requesting $70,000 from YY Foundation to support a high school to college transition program. XX University has had preliminary well-received discussions with senior officials from Any City College and seeks to partner with select high schools and a specific Hispanic-serving, community-based organization to ease the transition from high school to community college to a four-year university. The initiative will address a pilot cohort of 50 currently enrolled college students.

Program Overview

The program will 1) enhance the transition from community colleges to baccalaureate institutions for students from underrepresented groups, namely first-generation learners, and 2) reduce first-year college attrition among these students, who have had historically lower rates of degree completion, and improve their rates of persistence and degree completion. We expect this program to be a "curricular and social model" that will have as its primary focus the achievement of these goals for other inter-institutional cooperative agreements. As the program continues, and the evaluation analysis proves positive, other students will be asked to be in the process. Also, XX University would seek out corporate and foundation sponsorship. The XX University Project Confidence program will also provide a system of activities for limited-English proficient students. These will include cross-curricular courses and seminars in listening, reading, and writing.

In addition, XX University is actively seeking corporate and foundation sponsorship. Goals of the program include the following:

- Increased access to higher education for minority students.

- Increased student and instructor interest in the Any City College's online instructional component and other educational technology initiatives through effective hands-on, in-person technology training.

- Increased college preparation skills for minority high school students, leading to a greater opportunity for complementary academic programs through counseling, tutoring, peer and leadership mentoring, and access to social and recreational events.

- Immediate response to the technology priorities expressed by the Sample City Public Schools Board and the Sample State Board of Education.

- Improved technology and socialization skills for students, teachers, and community stakeholders.

- Articulation between Any City College and XX University.

- Analysis of the performance of a cohort of 50 currently enrolled Any City College English/communications, pre-law, and business students.

- Access of Any City College and Sample Public School to XX University's e-Learning curriculum design and evaluation methods.

- Promotion of interaction between XX University and Any City College to provide instructional support and guidance in preparing and delivering blended e-Learning initiatives.

- Regular training to Any City College and Sample Public School System faculty on a regular basis.

The XX University Demographic Profile

XX University's mission is to provide relevant, effective, and convenient education, both in liberal arts and in career-related disciplines, with a global, multicultural, and future-oriented perspective for all racial, ethnic, and socioeconomic groups. The University's current student-body population breaks down as follows:

- 95 percent enrolled full-time

- 85 percent African-American and Hispanic

- 93 percent in need of financial aid

- 98 percent from the Cityland area

- 79 percent enrolled in a career-oriented field

- 36 percent from families with an annual income below $15,000

- 90 percent under the age of 30

As can be noted above, roughly only two-thirds of Sample City's high school students graduated. In order to meet the educational needs of students, Sample City's public schools and independent schools need more resources. Currently, they have fewer resources than the average statewide, which is indicated by larger class sizes and more students per staff member/administration. XX University's program assumes that increased support services will increase the quality of education provided.

Statement of the Problem

Research has shown that minority students in high-poverty urban areas have less access to technology and higher education than their affluent counterparts. This problem is growing in magnitude as the minority population is increasing across the nation. Many minority students at open admissions structured colleges, such as XX University, lack the basic skills and exposure to technology and the basic math and English skills that assist in retention and college completion. These skills are also imperative for success in later life. Because many of XX University's students come to XX University without the technological skills needed to make the most out of their education, as they learn to use this technology, they will become more confident and successful. As the population of minority students, in particular those from high-poverty areas, increases, so does the need for services, such as exposure to technology to accommodate students' need for access to higher education.

Statement of Need. The purpose of the statement of need in the master proposal is to build interest in the project or activity by assisting the funder in understanding the problem and the reasons funding is needed to remedy this problem. The statement of need is written in concise, yet persuasive, language. Additional references often are used to develop a stronger case in support of the problem. References may include surveys, needs assessments, research from outside agencies, and demographic studies. Use of credible sources is essential to strengthen the need for proposed funding. Additional means of supporting the actual problem may include quotes and real-life examples. Keep in mind the emphasis is placed on the needs of the population to be served, not the organization requesting funding. An example is shown below.

Research indicates that significant differences continue to exist in reading achievement among elementary school students who are of minority status. Specifically, African-American students consistently perform significantly below their Caucasian peers on standardized assessments of reading achievement. It is also generally true that students attending high-poverty and high-minority schools have less access to computer technology. These differences in achievement and access can become a basis for unequal participation in further education, employment, and literacy levels.

Most family literacy programs focus on parents of "emergent" and early readers in kindergarten and first grade. Sample Program does the same, allowing kindergarten students and their parents the greatest opportunity for literacy growth. There is an urgent need for a family literacy program on Sample City's south side, which has a minority population of 98.8 percent. According to the 2000 census, 39 percent of the residents are 19 years old or younger, compared with 30 percent of the general city population. In addition, poverty is a major concern. Almost all of Sample City's students (97.3 percent) are from low-income families.

According to research, lack of resources, tolerance, and understanding limits the participation of minorities, women, and people with disabilities in higher education. Research explains that these problems begin at the preschool level (or with the parents of preschoolers) and carry into elementary, secondary, and post-secondary education. To remedy these situations, intervention must occur at the K–12 level.

The research shows we are not doing all that we must do to educate our young. We must continue to provide minority students with added exposure to programs focusing on reading readiness to close the gap in their performance in academic activities. The 2001 Sample City Public Schools' Test of Basic Skills scores acutely demonstrate the need for remedy—only 37.8 percent of students in grades third through eight are reading at grade level! Sample City's test scores are even worse. Only 26 percent of all third-graders and 16 percent of all fifth-graders are reading at grade level.

Project Description. The project description section of the proposal serves as a way for the reader to see the value of the project and determine why it is worth funding. It is useful to state in this section that the project may be adjusted according to feedback gained from stakeholders and that it may be adjusted through the implementation phase. The project description section of the proposal includes the following:

- Objectives
- Methods
- Staffing/Administration
- Evaluation
- Sustainability

Objectives. The objectives of the proposal are the measurable outcomes the project is expected to achieve. The objectives need to be specific and measurable as in the below example:

> **Goal:** The peer-mentoring program will assist students in the transition between high school and college.
>
> **Objective:** The peer-mentoring program will assist 25 students in making the transition from high school to college as demonstrated by tracked retention during the freshman year of college.

Methods. The methods section outlines how elements of the project will be carried out. This section includes a restatement of the goals of the project and the ways the project will achieve the set goals. Strategies for implementation of the project are also included in the methods section of the proposal. This section outlines the steps for placing the ideas into practice, as shown in the example below.

> The XX University Project Confidence program will serve as a peer-mentoring program in an attempt to educate the whole student through a one-on-one learning relationship and an emphasis on individual transformation intellectually, socially, and spiritually. The program will do the following: 1) enhance the transition from high school to baccalaureate institutions for students from underrepresented groups, namely first-generation, minority learners, and 2) reduce first-year college attrition among these students who have had historically lower rates of degree completion and improve their rates of persistence and degree completion. As the program continues, and the evaluation analysis proves positive, other students will be asked to join in the process. The XX University Project Confidence program also will provide a system of activities for limited-English proficient students. These will include cross-curricular courses and seminars in listening, reading, and writing.

> **Sample Methods: Strategy for Implementation**
> The Project Confidence program seeks to develop and establish within XX University a collaborative, systemic effort among students, classroom teachers, and administrators to improve students' retention and academic achievement during the first year of college. In addition, the program seeks to ease the transition from high school to college.

> The mission of the Project Confidence program is to promote and develop a peer-mentoring program between first-year students and upper-level students. Peer mentors will serve as role models in the areas of academic achievement (tutoring), counseling, social, co-curricular involvement, and peer and leadership mentoring in a collaborative learning community, thereby increasing retention and college graduation rates. To facilitate

this process, XX University will have a faculty or staff member working with the peer mentors approximately five hours per week, and five student mentors (junior or senior honor students) paired with five to six mentees of the same major. The goal for the initial cohort is 25 first-year students. During the quarter, peer mentors will organize a host of activities, including weekly workshops, social events, poetry readings, and sporting events. Students will meet with their peer mentor and the faculty advisor weekly throughout the quarter.

Importance of Findings to Research and Practice

The Project Confidence program will have an impact on high schools and colleges both locally and nationally. Issues such as retention, access, completion, and competition challenge higher-education institutions. The following are benchmark outcomes Project Confidence seeks to obtain to assist in these challenges:

- Students will work one-on-one with another student to discuss concerns or questions regarding the academic process.

- Students will be provided academic assistance via tutoring in a small-group setting.

- Students will receive additional attention from faculty and counselors in terms of monitoring students' satisfaction and academic achievement and progress throughout the quarter.

The XX University Infrastructure

The recent award of a Title III grant, entitled "Strengthening Academic Programs through the Integration of Technology and the Acquisition of Equipment," from the U.S. Department of Education demonstrates XX University's commitment to educational technological initiatives. The five-year grant averaging $350,000 per year was awarded in October 2001. Its focus was to improve academic programs through upgrading XX University's network technology infrastructure to increase instructional computing facility, training faculty to use technology in instruction, and providing ongoing technical support for faculty to revise syllabi and incorporate new instructional skills. Thereby, XX University already has established the necessary infrastructure needed to support implementation of the Project Confidence program.

Evaluation. Included in the master proposal is a detailed description of the ways the project will be evaluated. The evaluation section is needed to ensure that the objectives of the proposal are met. Include what is to be evaluated as well as the means for evaluating these components, as shown in the example below and in table 11.2.

Evaluation of the Project Confidence program involves both quantitative and qualitative measure. Quantitative assessment tools include conducting a statistical analysis comparing the retention and grade point averages of students in the peer-mentoring program and students not involved in the peer-mentoring program. Qualitative assessment tools for Project Confidence include student interviews. Guiding questions for assessment will involve issues of student satisfaction, recommendations for improvement, effectiveness of the peer-mentor in terms of adjusting

TABLE 11.2 *Preliminary Objectives and Evaluation*

Objectives	Evaluation
1. To inform all first-year students at the school about the program and eligibility criteria via counseling office. 2. To identify, recruit, and select 25 qualified participants each 11-week quarter.	Contacts will be monitored weekly to ensure that students' needs are being met. Weekly meetings with staff and mentors will discuss the status of participation, types of problems, and solutions.
3. To assess the academic, career, personal, and motivational needs of *all* program participants and develop an Individual Educational Plan within 30 days of their acceptance into the program.	Documentation will be maintained on all newly admitted Project Confidence participants through the Individual Educational Plan. The participants' individualized needs will be met by the researcher of the project.

to college, and quality of faculty and administrative support. Additionally, students will be required to keep a reflective journal capturing their experiences throughout the period of the project. Excerpts from student journals will be included in the program evaluation report.

Designing a Budget. The budget section of the proposal is seen as a way to refine the picture of the project in numbers. Depending on the specification of the proposal guidelines, a budget may be as simple as a one-page statement of the projected expenses, as listed in the example budget presented below, or it may be complex and comprise a spreadsheet that includes projected revenue support and a detailed narrative explaining the various items included in the projected budget.

Cost, Year 1		Total
Staffing and Training	5 students@ $8/hour × 6 hours/week = $240/week 11 weeks/quarter = $2,640/quarter total 3 quarters = $7,920 Faculty advisor/researcher = $1,300/quarter × 3 quarters = $3,900	$11,820
Materials	Paper, computer disks, pens, notebooks	$500
Travel/Conference Presentation	Presentation/attendance and peer-mentoring/ retention conferences	$800
Marketing and Publications	Brochures, print flyers used to promote the project	$2,000
Overhead	End of the quarter wrap-up party; beginning of the quarter kick-off; advisory board meeting	$1,880
Grand Total		$17,000

The budget section of the proposal includes a narrative of both the personnel and non-personnel items related to the proposal. For example, include salaries for personnel, if appropriate, as well as the cost for materials, training, and other expenses. It is customary to include operating costs of running the project. If the project is large, it is appropriate to include line items that detail the cost of phone, office supplies, and computer-related expenses. Most budgets also include a line item called "overhead," which allows the project to bear some of the administrative costs, such as an audit, board meeting expenses, and other costs not directly attributable to the project.

The budget section also may include other funding sources for the project. For a large project, multiple funders may be needed because few funders would be willing to be the sole supporter. For example, a project looking for $500,000 worth of funding may be required to submit proposals to several organizations in an attempt to gain this large amount of financing. In this section, gifts-in-kind are also included. *Gifts-in-kind* are contributions of goods or services instead of cash; they can include materials, such as computer equipment or time given by an individual. Often, an individual might offer a "discount" for time given to a project. A business also might offer a discount for services, such as equipment rental or rental of office space. An example of a budget section with gifts-in-kind funding is shown below.

Expenses

Office rental	$5,000
Print marketing materials	$1,000
Web designer (consultant)	$2,000

In-kind contributions

Best Business (office space)	$2,500
Promotional flyers	$500
Susie Smith (Web designer)	$1,000

In this example, Best Business is offering a discount for the use of office space. Promotional flyers will be produced at a reduced cost for the program and Susie Smith is offering her Web design services at a reduced cost. Including any in-kind contributions is important because it helps additional funders see the true cost of the program. If applying for a matching grant, a funder may be willing to fund the additional costs.

If the project is expected to continue into the future, a narrative description of the ways the project will be funded after the initial funding period expires must be included. Funding agencies often look for sustainability of the project. *Sustainability* refers to the ways the project can continue beyond the lifecycle of the rewarded grant. Future funding is important to think about in terms of continuation of the project from the organization's perspective as well as for the benefit of the funder.

After all of the costs of the project have been calculated, the items are summarized in a worksheet. The worksheet is a useful tool when discussing the proposal with potential funders because it clearly outlines the costs for the project and creates a rationale for the specific funds requested.

Organizational Information. In most grant proposals, it is common to place a complete description of the nonprofit organization at the end of the proposal. The rationale for placing this information at the end of the proposal is that the goal is to sell the project first, then discuss the organization. Information can be provided by attaching a brochure, referring the funder to the organization's website, or by including other prepared organizational material. This section is written in two pages or less and includes when the organization began, the mission statement of the organization, discussion of how the proposal fits into the organization's mission, organizational structure, programs, and expertise of staff members.

Conclusion. Grant proposals end with a concluding paragraph or two that summarizes the main aspects of the project. Because this is the last section to be read by potential funders, it is also a place for a final appeal for funding the project. Highlight again what the organization is attempting to accomplish and state reasons why funding is needed. Emotional appeal also might be included in the conclusion section. The following is an example of a conclusion for a grant proposal.

> The significant differences that exist in literacy skills among those of minority status are alarming. It is also true that students

attending high-poverty, high-minority schools have less access to computer technology. Combined, these factors become a basis for unequal participation by minorities in further education and employment. To remedy these situations, intervention must occur early on in a student's educational experience.

The partnership between Any City College and Sample Elementary School to increase reading readiness among African-American students at a young age will have a lasting impact on the community. Our efforts to expose these minority students and their families to this literacy program could not have come at a more critical time because reading scores among students in the Sample Public School System continue to remain low. The goal of Sample Program is to reverse this trend. The program is an immediate response to the priorities expressed by the mayor and the Sample State Board of Education, and it is hoped that Sample Program will gain the attention of the Sample Public School System to become a model reading readiness program within the city.

Sample Program offers a rare opportunity for young African-American students at a critical age and their families to become exposed to a literacy program that will have a tremendous impact on their future academic success and career path. We respectfully request from YY Foundation a grant of $25,000 to provide the kindergarten students and their parents with a much-needed opportunity to become proficient readers. Only then can the current vicious cycle of failing reading scores by the majority of students at Sample Elementary School be broken. This grant will help ensure the best chances for a hopeful future for the young people in Anytown.

Life After the Submission Process

After the grant proposal has been reviewed and edited by various members of the organization, the proposal must be submitted by the deadline. Submitting a grant proposal after the specified deadline is often automatic grounds for disqualification of any funding opportunities. The next step is to wait to see if the grant proposal has been fully accepted, partially funded, or rejected.

If the grant is fully funded, the organization might receive a check and a cover letter outlining status reports that need to be completed throughout the grant cycle. Immediately acknowledge receipt of the funding. For the advanced grant writer, if the funding is large enough to gain media attention, such as invitation to a public event, invite the funder to attend. If there are newspaper articles written on the receipt of funds, send copies to the funder.

If a project is partially funded, a decision must be made to request additional funds from other sources or assess if the project can be accomplished through the partial funds. If it has been determined that the project cannot continue without the additional funds, the check must be returned immediately. Often, corporations or foundations may agree to provide the additional funds needed. However, the proposal must be revised and submitted through the formal grant application process.

If a grant proposal is rejected, it is time to review the guidelines and prepare to reapply during the next grant cycle. Funding for projects is highly competitive; therefore, do not be discouraged. If the organization has the time, it is beneficial to ask the funder the specific reasons the grant proposal was rejected. Often, it simply may be that money is not available. This telephone call should be informative in nature, not used to express anger or disappointment about not receiving the funds. Go back to the drawing board and revise and refine the proposal for future submission to the same organization and other corporations or foundations.

REFERENCES

Anderson, P. V. 2007. *Technical communication: A reader-centered approach.* 6th ed. Boston, MA: Thomson Higher Education.

Creswell, J. W. 1994. *Research design: Qualitative & quantitative approaches.* Thousand Oaks, CA: Sage.

DuFour, R. and R. Eaker. 1998. *Professional learning communities at work: Best practices for enhancing student achievement.* Bloomington, IN: National Educational Service.

Geever, J. C. 2004. *The Foundation Center's guide to proposal writing.* 4th ed. New York, NY: The Foundation Center.

Heartland Hospice Memorial Fund. 2007. *Grant application process.* 19 November 2007. *www.heartlandhospicefund.org/grant_process.htm.*

Janesick, V. J. 1998. *Stretching exercises for qualitative researchers.* Thousand Oaks, CA: Sage.

Kerlinger, F. N. 1979. *Behavioral research: A conceptual approach.* New York, NY: Holt, Rinehart & Winston.

Lambert, L., et al. 1995. *The constructivist leader.* New York, NY: Teachers College Press.

Patton, M. Q. 1990. *Qualitative evaluation and research methods.* Newbury, CA: Sage.

Rubin, H. J., and I. S. Rubin. 1995. *Qualitative interviewing: The art of hearing data.* Thousand Oaks, CA: Sage.

EXAMPLE 1 *Research Proposal for Professional Conference*

Minicourse Proposal Cover Page
Sample Company Professional Development & Training

Proposal Title:
Making sense of qualitative data: Analyzing interview transcripts, observational field notes, researcher reflective journals, and archival documents and photographs

Proposer Name:
Address:
Telephone:
Fax:
Email:

Proposal Statement:
The purpose of this session is to describe and explain strategies for analyzing and interpreting qualitative data, including interview transcripts, observational field notes, researcher reflective journals, and archival documents and photographs, with active participation of audience members.

Audience:
Prospective and active doctoral students, assistant professors, even experienced researchers may wish to participate. Participants are encouraged to bring in transcripts from their own studies, but are requested to bring at least four copies for some small-group activities.

Substantive Area of the Program:
Analyzing mounds of interview transcripts, observational field notes, researcher reflective journal entries, and various documents and photographs can be daunting. But it need not be, given the long and dependable history of qualitative methods, coding, analysis, and interpretation of data techniques already written about through history. Hands-on experience of various types of qualitative data will be the basis for the training session. Practice is a key ingredient of getting to the analysis and interpretation stages of qualitative data analysis.

Format:
The audience will be placed in small groups, changing hourly, and participation will include the following: 1) actual category development of interview transcripts, provided by me, sample observational field notes, researcher reflective journal entries, and archival documents including photographs;

EXAMPLE 1 *Research Proposal for Professional Conference (continued)*

2) direction, feedback, and mini lectures interspersed throughout; 3) model development from the categories created; and 4) narrative writing exercises each hour.

Minicourse Proposed Budget:
Sample Company Professional Development & Training

Proposal Title:
Making sense of qualitative data: Analyzing interview transcripts, observational field notes, researcher reflective journals, and archival documents and photographs

Based on 16 participants

A. Non-personnel Services
    1. Supplies $____0_____
    2. Reproduction $____0_____
    3. Communication $____0_____

B. Do you require audiovisual equipment? NO

Because the meeting is in Sample City, and I am here, there will be no cost to Sample Company for the non-personnel services. Likewise, I have all my materials here that I use to teach both of our qualitative courses, including some best practices examples of field notes, transcripts, category development, models, strategies for coding data, and the like.

In the future, I would consider expanding this to a full day or even a weekend.

MAKING SENSE OF QUALITATIVE DATA: ANALYZING INTERVIEW TRANSCRIPTS, OBSERVATIONAL FIELD NOTES, RESEARCHER REFLECTIVE JOURNALS, AND ARCHIVAL DOCUMENTS AND PHOTOGRAPHS

By: [Presenter names]

ABSTRACT:
In this session, participants will have the opportunity to learn about strategies for coding, developing categories, and analysis and interpretation of interview transcripts, observational field notes, researcher reflective journal entries, and various archival documents, such as photographs. Participants will experience the task of category development and developing working models. Students and practitioners of research will take part in small-group and large-group activities to gain facility with working with large amounts of narrative data. Writing up the narrative representation of the data is a must.

EXAMPLE 1 *Research Proposal for Professional Conference (continued)*

AUDIENCE DESCRIPTION:

The target audience is doctoral students, assistant professors, and educators documenting their own work. I am besieged with emails, letters, and calls from practitioners who wish to know what to do with all those transcripts, documents, and research reflective journal entries. Many texts in the field do not clearly deal with this serious need.

Prerequisite:

Must be genuinely interested in this topic. Participants may bring in their own interview transcripts as long as there are at least four copies of same for small-group work.

PROPOSAL:

The field of qualitative research has a long and dependable history but only in the past 30 years have educational researchers realized that many questions in educational research are suited to the qualitative techniques of interviewing, observational field notes, journal writing, and document analysis. Our field has grown and many texts in the area are available. As a teacher of qualitative research methods for more than 20 years, I find it remarkable that questions posed by learners eventually come down to the following:

- How do I make sense of all these transcripts?
- What do I do with my researcher reflective journal entries?
- How do I handle member checks and my outside reader comments?
- How do I develop a model to accurately portray what occurred in the study?

In a sense, this mini-course grew out of these questions. Thus, the purpose of this session is to describe and explain successful strategies for analysis and interpretation of qualitative data, which are the major issues.

Expected outcomes:

When participants leave this session, they will have had the opportunity to practice some techniques of coding, analysis, and development of models of what occurred in the study in question. They also will receive an annotated bibliography as a take-home resource. In addition, a list of websites, listservs, and other resources will be part of the training packet. I will use exemplars of finished studies complete with the following:

- Part of an interview transcript (no more than eight pages)
- Part of a transcript of field notes (no more than four pages)

EXAMPLE 1 *Research Proposal for Professional Conference (continued)*

- Part of a researcher reflective journal (no more than four pages)
- One sample of an archival document
- Various photographs relevant to the study used as an exemplar

I envision a packet with about 20 pages of documentation, though no more than 25 pages.

Realistically speaking:

Realistically, the four hours will be jammed with information and activity, which I find to be an energizing way to learn. The audience will be an attentive audience because they will be a self-selected group with a keen interest in this area. There is nothing more powerful than someone who wants to learn.

Hour One:

20 minutes: Warm-up activity in which participants will be asked to write a sentence about what they already know about qualitative data and one on what they would like to learn about it:

1. In one sentence, describe something about what you already know about qualitative data analysis.
2. In one sentence, please explain what you would like to learn about qualitative data analysis.

Participants then volunteer to read their responses, and I get a sense of the audience milieu.

40 minutes: Introduction to the materials, break up into first small groups, which would include four groups of four. Two groups will get one set of transcripts, and two groups will get another set.

Task A: Compile a list of frequently occurring words, themes, and ideas that seem to crop up and that may become the categories for analysis.

Task B: After the group compiles the list of initial categories, find the larger theme, which may subsume components of this list.

Task C: Have a spokesperson from each group list three themes from the transcript.

Task D: Share findings with the large group. Look for indices of behavior, recurring behaviors, and points of tension and conflict.

EXAMPLE 1 *Research Proposal for Professional Conference (continued)*

Hour Two:
20 minutes: Task E: Participants are asked: What have you learned from this activity? While we start processing this at this time, the last 30 minutes of the session will be used for overall processing and "lessons learned."

40 minutes: Discuss how to deal with observational field notes, researcher journal entries reflecting on the process throughout the study, and archival materials in print and non-print media.

At this point, I will take a check of the participants to determine if they are able to work in their groups or not. If small groups work, we will continue with the option to join another group. If not, I will ask for a group of five volunteers to self-select for this activity. All other participants will take field notes on the process.

Task A: Participants will be asked to pull out three themes from each of the data sets: field notes, journals, and archval material. Next, they will be asked to make a visual representation or narrative (a model) of what they pulled from the data.

Task B: Participants will be asked to report to the entire group.

Hour Three:
15 minutes: Coffee Break. I am assuming there will be some light refreshment for all of us as in the past?

20 minutes: Task C: Processing what has been learned from this exercise.

Hour Four:
20 minutes: Writing activity following a discussion of these events and what has been accomplished up to this point.

Writing Task: Participants will be asked to write as if they were including a section in their researcher reflective journal. What was learned today? What three techniques did they find helpful in making sense of the data? There will be 20 minutes for writing and 20 minutes for volunteers to report.

Commentary will be interspersed throughout the session as needed. When someone volunteers, I will ask them to identify themselves, where they are from, and why they are here.

Principles and Skills Overriding the Session:
Participants will practice the skills of category development, reflective writing, and developing a model grounded in the data.

EXAMPLE 1 *Research Proposal for Professional Conference (continued)*

PERSONNEL:
List credentials of presenters.

REFERENCES:

Berg, B. 2001. *Qualitative research for the social sciences.* 4th ed. Boston, MA: Allyn and Bacon.

Cole, A., and G. Knowles. 2001. *Lives in context: The art of life history research.* Sherman Oaks, CA: Alta Mira.

Janesick, V. J. 1998, *Stretching exercises for qualitative researchers.* Thousand Oaks, CA: Sage.

Locke, L., W. Spirduso, and S. Silverman. 2000. *Proposals that work.* Thousand Oaks, CA: Sage.

Merriam, S. B. 2001. *Qualitative research and case study applications in education.* San Francisco, CA: Jossey-Bass.

Rubin, H. J., and I. S. Rubin. 1995. *Qualitative interviewing: The art of hearing data.* Thousand Oaks, CA: Sage.

Silverman, D. 2000. *Doing qualitative research.* Thousand Oaks, CA: Sage.

Wolcott, H. 1994. *Transforming qualitative data.* Thousand Oaks, CA: Sage.

EXAMPLE 2 *Resources for Grant Writers: Foundation and Corporate Grant Opportunities*

Management Concepts
Website: *www.managementconcepts.com/grants/glinks.asp*

This site contains lists of grant opportunities and resources for grant writing professionals with links to the following:

- Federal Agency Grants Information
- Laws and Regulations
- Resources for Finding Grants
- Professional Associations
- Audit Resources
- Other Grant-related Sites

The Foundation Center
Website: *http://foundationcenter.org/findfunders/fundingsources/fdo.html*

This site contains information on requesting access to national grant databases.

Minority Grant Funding Source
Website: *http://minorities.grantfundingsource.com/?gclid=CLXMtMCX548CFR JgWAodxinaDQ*

This site includes grant opportunities for minority-based projects.

American Library Association
Website: *www.ala.org/ala/acrl/acrlpubs/crlnews/backissues1999/julyaugust4/ grantresources.cfm*

This site contains useful links to grant proposals on the Web as well as resources for grant writing professionals.

Fundsnet Services Online
Website: *www.fundsnetservices.com/grantwri.htm*

This site includes a fundraising resource section with grant opportunities. Grant opportunities are broken down by geographic location.

eSchool News Online
Website: *www.eschoolnews.com/funding/*

This site includes references for education-specific grants.

EXAMPLE 2 *Resources for Grant Writers: Foundation and Corporate Grant Opportunities (continued)*

AT&T Education
Website: *www.kn.pacbell.com/products/grants/locate.html*

This site includes a comprehensive list of state, local, and government grant opportunities for educationally related grants.

Corporation for National and Community Services
Website: *http://nationalserviceresources.org/resources/grants/index.php*

This site includes resources for grants available in the following categories:

- Citizenship
- Community and Economic Development
- Education
- Environment
- Health
- Media/Telecommunications
- Sciences/Social Sciences
- Social Issues
- Special Populations
- Technology

Unites States National Library of Medicine (NLM)/National Institutes of Health (NIH)
For an overview of grants available and resources for grant writers, see: *www.nlm.nih.gov/ep/*

For information on specific NIH grant programs, see: *http://www.nlm.nih.gov/ep/Grants.html.*

This site provides grant programs for topics relevant to public health and informatics for disaster management.

National Center for the Dissemination of Disability Research
Website: *www.ncddr.org/rr/Grants_and_Foundations.html*

This site includes information on various foundations and grant programs.

EXAMPLE 2 *Resources for Grant Writers: Foundation and Corporate Grant Opportunities (continued)*

AT&T Excelerator Grants and Funding Areas

Website: *http://www.att.com/gen/corporate-citizenship?pid=7745*

AT&T Excelerator helps nonprofit organizations meet their missions by improving technology resources, including hardware, software, and networking tools. AT&T Excelerator grants also help nonprofit organizations put technology tools into the hands of the communities they serve, providing resources such as Internet access, computer training, math and reading programs, and job skills development.

Edutopia: The George Lucas Foundation

Website: *http://www.edutopia.org/grantinfo*

This site includes a listing of several grant opportunities from various funding agencies.

EXAMPLE 3 *Spectra Energy Foundation Online Grant Submission Guidelines*

Introduction

Spectra Energy's mission is to be a good corporate citizen and a neighbor of choice, and we believe this can be accomplished by investing in the communities where we have operations and our employees live. Spectra Energy distributes its charitable contributions through the Spectra Energy Foundation. The criteria that the Spectra Energy Foundation considers when evaluating a grant request are listed below.

Application Process

The Spectra Energy Foundation utilizes an online grant request process to consider funding requests. To begin the process, please carefully read the qualifications and other considerations outlined below. If your organization qualifies, you may click "Online Grant Application" on the left-hand side of the page to begin the application process. The Spectra Energy Foundation's annual budgeting process begins in early summer for the following calendar year. Although requests will be accepted throughout the year, applicants are encouraged to submit requests by June 1 for the following calendar year. Please note that Foundation funds are limited and, unfortunately, we cannot support all requests.

Qualifications for Nonprofit Organizations

In the United States, grant applicants must be organizations with a 501(c)(3) verification from the Internal Revenue Service (IRS) or part of a governmental entity. In Canada, grant applicants must be recognized as a charitable organization registered with the Canadian Customs and Revenue Agency (CCRA).

In addition, all organizations applying for a grant must submit to the Spectra Energy Foundation:

- The completed Online Grant Application;
- A clear reason for making the contribution that relates to our areas of focus; and
- Regular reports on the measurable results of the project.

Other Considerations for Applicant Organizations

In keeping with Spectra Energy's community relations mission, Spectra Energy has developed focus areas to ensure that our contributions are strategic and have maximum benefit on our communities. Spectra Energy Foundation will consider grant requests from qualified organizations that promote the following areas of focus.

EXAMPLE 3 *Spectra Energy Foundation Online Grant Submission Guidelines (continued)*

Educational Attainment	• Programs that help ensure at least a high school education or equivalency for at-risk students • Pre-K through 12 education that meets the company/community's professional needs, including math, science, technology, and business acumen
Community Vitality	• Health and human services, through federated campaigns (e.g., United Way) • Environmental conservation, education, and research • Community leadership development • Targeted arts giving
Competitive Workforce	• Job entry skills for the new economy • Retraining of unemployed and underemployed workers • Research needed to retool industries and create opportunities that fit the potential of each community's workforce skill pool • Higher education that meets the company's professional needs

Inclusiveness/diversity initiatives underpin all three areas of focus.

Other Restrictions for Applicant Organizations

The Spectra Energy Foundation will not consider funding grants to or for:

- Organizations that discriminate by race, creed, gender, age, or national origin
- Political activities and organizations
- Individual agencies of the United Way, because contributions to health and human service organizations are made through significant support of the United Way by Spectra Energy and its employees.
- Capital campaigns, endowments or multi-year commitments
- Multi-year gifts, commitments, or pledges
- Individuals
- Athletics, including individual sports teams and all-star teams
- Underwriting of films, video, and television productions

EXAMPLE 3 *Spectra Energy Foundation Online Grant Submission Guidelines (continued)*

- Sectarian or religious organizations
- Conferences, trips, or tours
- Fraternal, veteran, or labor groups serving only their members
- Advertising
- Membership fees or association fees, either personal or corporate
- Dinners or tables at fund-raising events (rarely considered)
- Family foundations
- Trips or tours
- Reducing the cost of utility service (prohibited by law)

Source:
*https://secure2.easymatch.com/SPECTRAGRANTS/Content/help/help.asp?Topic
_T_1=GrantGuidelines*

EXAMPLE 4 *Grant Proposal*

A BRIEF HISTORY AND ACHIEVEMENTS OF SAMPLE COLLEGE

Sample College's long and proud history can be traced back to 1913 and the founding of the XX School, a premier post-secondary independent business school. In 1975, the XX School merged with Sample College. Today, the College has the distinction of pioneering innovative approaches to higher education that have enabled students throughout the city of Sample City and the state of Sample State to rapidly achieve academic success and successfully enter the workforce in high-demand fields. Moreover, this private, not-for-profit college has instilled in a new generation of students the awareness that learning is a lifelong journey that can enable them to adapt to economic change and realize new dreams. The mission is dedicated to providing students from diverse socioeconomic and academic backgrounds the foundation necessary to meet the expectations of business and society.

This distinct formula for success is demonstrated in the following achievements:

Activities & Accreditation:

Sample College today is accredited by the Sample Association of Colleges and Schools and authorized by the Sample State Board of Higher Education to award the following degrees:

- Bachelor of Business Administration
- Bachelor of Applied Science in Graphic Design
- Bachelor of Applied Science in Computer Studies
- Associate in Applied Science

Timeline:

Sample College offers an accelerated, step-by-step approach to earning a college degree that has turned daunting, long-term objectives into a series of attainable, short-term successes. After 10 months of study, it is possible for a Sample College student to obtain a professional diploma in one of 16 high-demand specialties in technology, health care, business, or the arts. With this first achievement in hand, students can choose to enter the workforce immediately—but most do not. The College's curriculum and culture strongly encourage them to build on their initial success and stay on for the broader coursework needed to earn an associate's or bachelor's degree. Students who continue their studies at Sample College can earn an associate's degree in 15 months (from start to finish) or a bachelor's degree in a total of 3 years.

EXAMPLE 4 *Grant Proposal (continued)*

Facilities:

Sample College is committed to providing quality facilities, equipment, and furnishings on a timely basis. Sample College is composed of several campuses in Sample State, including the main campus in Sample City and five branch campuses [name the branches].

Staffing:

Sample College employs faculty, full- and part-time, who have earned at least a master's degree from an accredited institution. To be credited to teach a course, the faculty member must have at least 18 semester hours of graduate coursework in the discipline; the Dean of each academic division is responsible for verification of faculty credentials. Currently, 18 percent of Sample College's full-time faculty hold a doctorate degree; considering both full- and part-time faculty, 20 percent of the courses offered each quarter are taught by doctoral faculty.

PROGRAM SUMMARY

Sample Program, the reading enrichment program at Sample College, has partnered with Sample Elementary School on the city's south side and is designed to work with parents and their kindergarten-age students to improve literacy skills. The focus is on delivering workshops to parents on how to stimulate reading and writing—the basic skills absolutely necessary for later academic success. The workshops are two-part: The first session is for parent training, the second part is for both parent/caregiver and student. By focusing on one skill per session, such as asking questions during and after reading, the program approaches the challenges of gaining greater reading readiness skills in a measured way. The program is in its first year of operation, and currently two kindergarten classes and the students' parents are enrolled in the program. Our plans for the future include a program expansion to include additional underserved communities in Sample City. We are currently working with public school representatives hoping that our Sample Program will become a model reading readiness program within the city.

The majority of the workshops are geared toward educating parents on methods for promoting and increasing reading skills in the home. However, the overall emphasis is on creating a learning community that involves parents, students, classroom teachers, and members of the community with reading enrichment. Thus, workshops have incorporated student/parents/classroom teachers in reading activities. The workshops are coordinated with classroom teachers to enhance reading skills being taught in the classroom, as well as aligning workshop goals with the public schools' curriculum guide.

EXAMPLE 4 *Grant Proposal (continued)*

Benchmark Outcomes:

The following are benchmark goals for Sample Program:

- Parents will gain greater understanding of their role in the promotion of reading readiness in the home.
- Parents will understand the role of the family portfolio and its purpose for recording reading readiness activities used in the home.
- Parents will be provided with techniques for increasing reading comprehension and fostering critical thought through questioning of a story.
- Parents, students, and teachers will increase understanding of ways computer software can enhance reading skills and become familiar with a basic knowledge of computer and Internet usage.
- Parents will discover ways to improve vocabulary skills as well as gain insight into ways phonics can enhance reading readiness.
- Parents, students, and teachers will gain increased awareness of reading materials and technology available in their community.
- Parents will gain greater understanding of the role reading plays in academic achievement and the social and emotional development of children.
- Parents will discuss the effectiveness of the family portfolio and share their work.
- Students will display improved classroom achievement.
- Student test scores will increase.

Why the Problems to Be Addressed Were Selected:

Research indicates that significant differences continue to exist in reading achievement among elementary school students who are of minority status. Specifically, African-American students consistently perform significantly below their Caucasian peers on standardized assessments of reading achievement. It is also generally true that students attending high-poverty and high-minority schools have less access to computer technology. These differences in achievement and access can become a basis for unequal participation in further education, employment, and literacy levels.

Most family literacy programs focus on parents of "emergent" and early readers in kindergarten and first grade. Sample Program does the same, allowing kindergarten students and their parents the greatest opportunity for literacy growth. There is an urgent need for a family literacy program on Sample City's south side, with a minority population of 98.8 percent.

EXAMPLE 4 *Grant Proposal (continued)*

According to the 2000 census, 39 percent of the residents are 19 years old or younger, compared with 30 percent of the general city population. In addition, poverty is a major concern. Almost all Sample students (97.3 percent) are from low-income families.

According to research, lack of resources, tolerance, and understanding limits the participation of minorities, women, and people with disabilities in higher education. These problems begin at the preschool level (or with the parents of preschoolers) and carry into elementary, secondary, and post-secondary education. To remedy these situations, intervention must occur at the K–12 level.

The research shows we are not doing all that we must do to educate our young. We must continue to provide minority students with added exposure to programs focusing on reading readiness to close the gap in their performance in academic activities. The 2001 Sample City Public Schools' Test of Basic Skills scores acutely demonstrate the need for remedy—only 37.8 percent of students in grades third through eight are reading at grade level! Sample City's test scores are even worse. Only 26 percent of all third-graders and 16 percent of all fifth-graders are reading at grade level.

PROGRAM DEVELOPMENT

The program originally began as a vision from Sample College's president, who participates in the public school's "Principal for a Day" program at the school. He saw a great need to improve the students' literacy skills. From this idea the Sample Program was developed. Working with the public school curriculum, a program was designed to offer kindergarten-age children and their parents the opportunity to attend reading enrichment workshops. Planning for the workshops involved collaboration with the school's principal, project coordinator, and two kindergarten classroom teachers.

The program began offering bimonthly workshops in October 2001, and has been well-received by Sample administrators, classroom teachers, parents, and children.

PROGRAM GOALS AND OBJECTIVES

The project involves all (approximately 75) Sample kindergarten students and their parents. The student profile for the school is predominantly minority and economically disadvantaged:

School	%Black	%Hispanic	%Asian & Other	%White	%Low Income
Sample	100%	N/A	N/A	N/A	97.3%

EXAMPLE 4 *Grant Proposal (continued)*

At the end of the first program year, we have the following expectations:

a. That 100 percent of the participants in the enrichment/supplemental program will demonstrate a higher level of mastery of reading readiness.

b. That participation by teachers at the participating elementary school(s) in the staff development activities will be encouraged and supported by their administrators.

1. Objectives

a. Provide kindergarten students and their parents a learning environment designed to improve the children's reading skills by incorporating a supplemental reading curriculum that integrates community resources.

b. Acclimate students to the school climate by improving their reading readiness.

c. Provide parents with a greater understanding of their role in the promotion of reading readiness in the home.

d. Increase African-Americans' access, representation, and participation in higher education.

2. Activities

a. Hold orientation for participants, their parents, and teachers/administrators from the participating school(s) and community centers.

b. Conduct workshops and activities focusing on enhancing literacy skills.

c. Provide "discovery" opportunities for participants through field trips, guest speakers, and technology.

d. Assess participant's mastery of reading as well as changes in their interests and achievement levels.

e. Present staff development workshops for elementary school teachers from the participating school focused on teaching methodologies to increase students' reading skills.

3. Persons to be served by the project (first year of program):

- Currently 27 families of the Sample School kindergarten classes are participating.
- Teachers from the participating elementary school

4. Number of underrepresented persons/students to be served (by ethnic category):

- 100 percent of the students are African-American

EXAMPLE 4 *Grant Proposal (continued)*

5. Performance measures to be used as evidence of results and desired changes:

   a. Workshop assessment techniques, subjective evaluation of project activities, and the perceived value of the program by participants, parents, and school personnel

   b. Longitudinal follow-up study of participants to determine the residual effect on their educational progress and plans

The long-term objectives of the project focus on the impact that can be made on the educational achievement/persistence and career choices of minority students. It is planned that by the second year of the program, an additional school located in the neighborhood of ZZ, will be added to the program. Additional schools will be added as funding becomes available. Sample College hopes to make a systemwide difference on the Sample City public school system, creating a model program that can be copied in various communities in the Cityland area. The involvement of 27 plus families in the first year of the program, which is expected to grow to include an additional 20 families after one year of operation, at a critical intervention point, will have a lasting significance now and for the future.

To accomplish this, Sample College is committed to do the following:

1. Provide highly qualified faculty to deliver the enrichment program's instruction and supportive activities.

2. Promote sharing of ideas and methodologies through staff development activities for the elementary school participating teachers and the college/university instructors and staff for the project.

3. Integrate motivational activities in conjunction with features and resources of the collegiate learning environment to stimulate young minority students' self-esteem and their enthusiasm about learning.

4. Act as partners with the participating elementary school(s) and community organizations in their efforts to improve student performance and retention.

STAFFING AND QUALIFICATIONS OF PERSONNEL

The Sample College Literacy Coordinator and faculty will organize and deliver each session in coordination with Sample teachers. Sample College students will serve their internships with the program.

1. Administrative: [Name], Project Coordinator

   Qualifications: [List qualifications]

EXAMPLE 4 *Grant Proposal (continued)*

2. Instructional: [Name], Workshop planner and instructor

   Qualifications: [List qualifications]

Skills Required:

Knowledge of public schools and Sample State's guidelines for reading instruction and delivery, and experience working with primary children in Sample City's public school system are required skills. Additional experience with multiple forms of assessment, including authentic assessment, reading instruction, and curriculum design at the elementary school level for under-served diverse populations is also necessary. In addition, the ability to design and create reading materials for workshops is required.

PROGRAM EVALUATION AND ASSESSMENT

Data will be gathered from parents surveyed at three points in the program: 1) at the beginning to gather ideas, 2) at the end of the first semester to solicit strengths/weaknesses of the program, and 3) at the end of the academic school year to assess the overall program. A frequency distribution will be conducted that will also include parent participation rates. A qualitative analysis will be conducted using interviews from parents, children, and instructors and via the family portfolio. Because standardized testing begins in the third grade, long-term assessment may include student scoring on these standardized tests. A database will be set up to track unit tests and parent and student participation in the literacy workshops, and to record responses to qualitative inquiries. The database must include the public school number, student name, parents names, type of activity, length of activity, and amount of time parents spent on using the methods discussed in the sessions at home.

Parents are encouraged to complete a family portfolio. Research has shown that portfolios are a successful alternative to standardized testing for assessing the effectiveness of a program. Specifically, instructors, parents, and children can agree on format. Most common are file folders, notebooks, albums, photos, videotapes, audio tapes, computer disks, or some combination. Questions designed to guide parents on self-reflection of the program will be designed and discussed with parents monthly. At the end of the year, the families can enter their portfolios in a composition and exhibition at a location to be determined. Both parents and Sample teachers and administrators have expressed positive feedback about the program.

Workshop Methodology:

The majority of the workshops will be geared toward educating parents on methods for promoting and increasing reading skills in the home. However,

EXAMPLE 4 *Grant Proposal (continued)*

the overall emphasis is on creating a learning community that involves parents, students, classroom teachers, and members of the community with reading enrichment. Thus, the majority of the workshops have incorporated student/parents in reading activities. At least 12 sessions, delivered twice per month, will each have a theme, such as "Reading Aloud" or "The Importance of Talking and Listening to Children." At each session, parents will learn skills that will encourage literacy. Also included in the workshops are computer training and field trips. After every session, children's books and other reading materials will be donated to the students and their families to assist them in creating a reading-friendly environment to practice the skills reviewed.

Technology:

Research has shown that use of computers can improve a child's vocabulary skills, enhance reading skills, and promote enjoyment of reading. A technology component using reading software is used to integrate learning styles with the appropriate technological medium. Parents also will benefit from learning to use the computer. The workshops include sessions on computer usage for parents, such as using the Internet, resources online for parents and reading, general applications use (needed to assist children in writing their own books), and software demonstrations. A Web page is currently being designed for Sample City's Sample Program. The page will include a parent page produced by the program coordinator, an academic calendar, and a listing of community events related to literacy. It also will provide email access to parents, allow classroom instructors to post weekly lesson plans, and link to parent and reading pages. Through the donation of computers and printers from Sample Corporation, a Parent Resource Room with technology access has been established at Sample enabling parents to practice their new computer skills.

SUSTAINABILITY

In the short time since its inception, we have seen the need for and the importance of Sample Program by communicating with the administrators of Sample College and community leaders. Sample College is committed to offering this program on an ongoing basis. With Sample Program, we intend to secure a base of funding from corporations and foundations with a known and demonstrated interest in funding education programs serving minority and/or economically disadvantaged youth. We will maintain an ongoing systemic and consistent approach to potential funders.

EXAMPLE 4 *Grant Proposal (continued)*

BUDGET

Cost, Year 1		Total
Staffing	18 sessions @ 2 hours each × 2 groups of 20 parents = 36 hours total × $100/hour = $3,600 Additional training costs for Sample College faculty = $2,000 Salary, Coordinator: $16,000 Babysitting staffing: 48 hours × 2 staff × $7/hour = $672	$22,272
Technology	Disks: $100 Software: $1,000 Videotapes: $100	$1,200 (est.)
Literacy Materials	Paper: Pencils: Flashcards:	
Books	Other: phonics books, blocks, videos	$15,000
PR Materials:	Flyers, brochures, press kits, film/developing costs	$2,000
Misc:	T-shirts for participants, food for sessions, holiday/end of year party, gift certificates for parents attending 80% of sessions	$2,500
Transportation	Bus for field trips 2 × $85	$170
Grand Total		**$43,142**

Budget and Personnel Justification:

The budget includes an explanation of each category and how each entry was calculated. Only direct costs have been requested for grant funding.

Qualifications for faculty at Sample College require a minimum of a master's degree in the discipline or a closely related one with accompanying professional qualifications. Because the mission of Sample College is wholly devoted to instruction, faculty must have a true love for teaching and helping students succeed. The instructional team will comprise of Sample College faculty members, elementary school teachers, a technology instructor, and

EXAMPLE 4 *Grant Proposal (continued)*

Sample College student interns to facilitate hands-on experiments and pro-mote student self-efficacy.

A Sample College program coordinator, who has the appropriate education and skills to work as a liaison with elementary schools, will oversee the project. Coordination activities among the participating school(s)' princi-pals, "cooperating" teachers, and faculty for the enrichment classes is the project coordinator's highest priority followed by a longitudinal follow-up study of the previous participants and general assessment activities for project development.

CONCLUSION

The significant differences that exist in literacy skills among those of minority status are alarming. It is also true that students attending high-poverty and high-minority schools have less access to computer technology. Combined, these factors become a basis for unequal participation by minorities in further education and employment. To remedy these situations, intervention must occur early on in a student's educational experience.

The partnership between Sample College and Sample City to increase reading readiness among African-American students at a young age will have a lasting impact on the community. Our efforts to expose these minority students and their families to this literacy program could not have come at a more criti-cal time because reading scores among students in the Sample City public school system continue to remain low. The goal of Sample Program is to reverse this trend. The program is an immediate response to the priorities expressed by the mayor and the Sample State State Board of Education, and it is hoped that our Sample Program will gain the attention of the public school system to become a model reading readiness program within the city.

Sample Program offers a rare opportunity for young African-American stu-dents at a critical age and their families to become exposed to a literacy program that will have a tremendous impact on their future academic success and career path. We respectfully request from the Sample Foundation a grant of $25,000 to provide the Sample kindergarten students and their parents with a much-needed opportunity to become proficient readers. Only then can the current vicious cycle of failing reading scores by the majority of students at Sample be broken. This grant will help ensure the best chances for a hope-ful future for the young people on Sample City's south side.

CHAPTER 12

Writing and Designing Training Materials

Learning new information can be difficult, but add the anxiety of learning a new task at work and it becomes nerve-racking and difficult. Solid, well-structured training documents can help with this, however. Regardless of how a company or organization decides to train individuals, each new staff employee, volunteer, board member, and manager will require training on at least one task. Training documents may be their introduction to the tasks they are to perform and the documents that the company produces.

TRAINING DOCUMENTS

Training documents, as a group, convey information that will qualify a reader to do or take part in an action, process, or task. However, these documents may have additional purposes, such as evaluating a reader's knowledge of specific information or acting as an introduction to material and later as a reference to that information. Also, training documents often combine many of the elements of other technical documents. For instance, these materials may contain instructions, a list of policies and procedures, or organizational history and specifications.

As with all other types of technical documents, the writer must follow a number of in-house or company-approved guidelines and work with specific information, purposes, and audiences. Sometimes these will be dictated by company standards, compliance to other documents or company style guides, or how the document will be distributed. Training documents can be delivered as hard copy, via email, or posted on the Web as manuals, Web links and resources, or course-like curriculum requiring trainee interaction. Because of the variety of delivery methods, the writer must consider this when designing the document and organizing information. Above all, because this document often will include the basic information an employee must know to begin or progress in a position, it should be clear, concise, complete, and accurate.

Writing training documentation follows the same process as writing other documents, including researching, organizing, drafting, and revising the documents. In addition, some training programs require test phases to ensure that the training goals are adequately covered and that evaluation processes work to assess these goals (see chapter 17).

Training documents are unique in the realm of technical communication in that they combine a number of other forms of writing. For instance, a policy and procedure manual may be a part of a training program (see chapter 10). Also, instructions are common finds in training documentation (see chapters 3 and 10).

Purpose

As with anything a technical communicator creates, before making any other decisions, the purpose of the document needs to be determined. Knowing why the information is important to the reader helps the writer make it relevant. While the information may not be interesting, making it relevant to the readers and their positions can make it easier for them to retain. Also, knowing the reason the trainees need the information gives a clearer vision of the purpose behind the document. Finally, it is important to gauge how much the reader already will know prior to reading the training material. If the reader knows little about the topic, then the purpose of the training material is to thoroughly cover every aspect of the process; whereas, if the reader has some knowledge about the topic, the material's purpose may be to break bad habits or reinforce the correct way to do the process.

Using Evaluations and Surveys

When revising training programs that are already in use, consider implementing a trainee evaluation of the program in order to determine its usefulness. This evaluation should be anonymously submitted and allow for comment on materials, instructors, usability, comprehension, and accuracy. Take into account the results when looking at what works, needs to be expanded on, should be added, and can be deleted from the training program. Also, collecting evaluations on the program after its revision is a good idea in order to measure the effectiveness of the changes and to gather information for future revisions.

When developing a new training program, consider surveying employees who already hold the position for which the training pertains. This allows for firsthand comments about what should be included in the training program, how information should be prioritized, and how much time should be allotted to specific tasks. Considering the opinions of veteran employees is a way of consulting subject matter experts and allows employees a hand in developing the training of their colleagues. There is additional information about creating surveys in chapter 14.

There are generally three purposes behind training documentation:

1. To teach tasks that will be performed on the job

2. To inform of policies regarding employee action, interaction, and expectations

3. To familiarize with procedures that will not be performed, but with which the reader may need a working knowledge

The documents should be designed and written to fit the purpose, including all of the needed information, and be formatted in accordance with the task. For instance, when designing an employee training manual for a newly hired receptionist, the document might require a job description, a checklist of duties to be performed upon the opening of the office, information on operating the company switchboard, instructions for some of the commonly used office equipment, such as the fax machine and copier, and the training module that each employee must pass in regard to sexual harassment. Some of this information, however, would not be needed in the training of other employees. The purpose of the document determines what needs to be included.

Audience

Determining who will use the training material is the next step in document design. This decision will influence how the training is written, including the words and sentence structure chosen, how it is presented or formatted, and the type of materials used to convey the information. Writers must consider who will be trained. Will the materials be used by entry-level or senior employees? The answer to this question alone can help writers elect the information the training must contain, whether it should be set up in volumes, and how it should be distributed. Knowing who will read the information helps determine how it will be used, coupling audience with purpose.

Audience Analysis

When conducting an audience analysis, surveys can be helpful formal tools. While an examination of the audience can be done without their participation, involving them can provide a clearer understanding of what will be helpful to them. By creating and distributing a survey that determines what the audience already knows, feels they need to know, and wants to know, a writer can help meet the readers' needs. Also, surveying those who are already trained, if possible, can be helpful to determine what trainees must know and what might be worth knowing, but can be gained elsewhere, such as while working with a mentor.

A complete audience analysis should be conducted (see chapter 2) to determine the best possible document type(s) to convey the information appropriately. Considering the audience means more than thinking of who will use the training. A complete analysis considers whether the participants will receive additional information from other sources and the knowledge they have coming into the program.

Working with Adult Students

Extensive research has been done regarding *andragogy,* which is the science of educating adults, and many theories work to explain working with adult students and their particular needs. Malcolm Knowles (1984) took the idea of andragogy the furthest in educational theory by developing a number of tenets explaining the characteristics of adult students:

1. Adults have a developed self-concept that allows for the advancement of independence.

2. Adults have personal experiences that influence how they interpret new experiences and information and become learning resources.

3. Adults' readiness to learn is connected to the task or information being acquired and the need for such information.

4. Adults are more likely to learn information they can put to immediate use and are more problem-centered than subject-centered.

5. Adults have internal motivation to learn that can be based on a number of wants and priorities including an interest in or a need to know the information.

Considering these characteristics outlining adult students, a writer should be able to develop materials that work for those using them.

Adults need a reason to know the information they are being taught and for which they are held accountable. Explaining how the information will be used, how it is relevant to the readers and then becomes an important part of making it a significant piece of their training. If information is pertinent, it is easier for the trainee to devote time and attention to it. Of course, this implies a responsibility for the writer to include only information in the training program that is necessary. Training is a not a place for "busy work" or inundating new employees with historical or background information that they do not have an immediate need for or that does not clarify their role in the company. However, making this information available or pointing out its location for later use is appropriate and ensures thoroughness. For example, referencing that the company's policy and procedure manual includes the dress code, appropriate conduct policies, and an organizational chart in a training program ensures the trainees know how to locate that information, but it does not make them immediately responsible for it while they learn a new task.

Educating Adults

Educating adults is not the same as educating children. Adults, after all, are not traditionally students. As adults, people typically use their past education at work. This means adults will have a lifetime of prior learning experiences that bias how they feel about new tasks and information. This can make the audience analysis that much more important. It also means that a writer needs to consider any biases or sensitivities the audience may have to particular experiences, information, or tasks. Consider this when creating examples and choosing material to include.

Another consideration for working with adults is time constraints. The audience of a training program is generally learning while on the job. This may indicate a large amount of time that can be devoted to training, such as the first days or weeks of employment. However, it also might suggest training that needs to be done in smaller chunks of time, such as an hour a day over a few weeks. Ongoing training is also an option and works well to break down information and present it over time. This strategy allows for material to build on itself in a progressive manner or to focus trainees on disjointed material by presenting it at different times. Also, training designers must consider what material is immediately necessary when working on organization. For instance, a company may feel that immediate knowledge of the sexual harassment policy is essential to ensure immediate compliance. This means that the writer must make the presentation of this material a priority.

Objectives

Unlike some other technical documents, training requires that individuals learn something and retain that information for real-life use. These objectives should act as the goals of the training programs, even if they are not tested on at the end of the training. Without these clear objectives, evaluation is not possible, because a trainee should not be tested on retaining material that has not been delivered. The development of objectives may not be solely the role of the technical writer; others may be involved in this process. This requires collaboration, as does any writing project involving an expert who is not the writer.

To create objectives, training developers must first determine what is to be learned during training. Consulting subject matter experts allows for technical data and a brief training for the document developer. Also, experts can key into the most important tasks and information that need to be conveyed.

Objectives give the training materials a focus. If trainees are informed of the objectives of their training, they are being told what it is they will be learning and for what they will be held accountable. They are also more prepared, and often more comfortable, with any assessment after training. For example, if trainees are told to read a general training manual, but they are unaware what information pertains to them or for which they will be responsible, they can easily become lost in the text. However, given objectives, or a list of things they will learn in the material, they are better prepared to identify the most important information.

Using Objectives

Objectives allow a writer to guide trainees through their training programs; objectives act as a road map, giving key points to look for along the journey. They offer insight to the purpose of the program, offering claims that can be tested and assessed.

Goals versus Objectives. While a writer may substitute the terms *goal* and *objective*, they are two distinctly different items. *Goal* refers to a general intention, while *objective* communicates a distinct and specific claim. Goals are broad in scope and cannot be evaluated or validated as they are. They do not measure the readers' ability or understanding, as noted in the example goal statement below:

Sample Goal Statement: Readers will learn about personal websites.

Objectives are narrow, can be assessed, and offer tangible undertakings. They are measurable if written correctly, such as the one below:

Sample Objective Statement: After thoroughly reading this document, readers will be able to create a personal website.

Because this statement declares that the readers will be able to complete a task, the objective can be assessed by testing the readers' ability to successfully create the site.

Writing Objectives. The intent of objectives is to determine and communicate the purpose of the training. To write them, the audience must be considered, as well as the material they will be trained on, how the training will be conducted, and why they are being trained.

Training objectives should convey a summary of specific tasks and information trainees will be expected to know and understand. Also, how well readers should know the information and what is to be done with it becomes important, as noted in the following example:

Training Objectives: At the end of this training module, the reader will be able to do the following:

- Write reader-friendly, interactive content for a personal website.
- Use basic design principles to design a personal website.
- Organize content and graphics for a multiple page personal website.
- Select appropriate graphic content for a personal website.
- Publish the completed website.

Bloom's Domains of Learning

Benjamin Bloom, an educational psychologist, worked with a group in 1956 to classify three types of learning: cognitive, affective, and psychomotor. The cognitive domain focuses on the retention of knowledge, while the affective emphasizes emotional knowledge and learning, and the psychomotor is concerned with motor skills, both basic and complex. The group decided that what instructors wanted learners to know could be put into a hierarchy of complexity. Within the cognitive domain, basic knowledge is the lowest level of the categorization and evaluation is the highest. The affective domain ranges from receiving phenomena to internalizing values, and the psychomotor domain begins with perception and builds to origination.

Training materials focus mostly on the cognitive domain because its goal is to retain knowledge and use that information to create new ideas and theories. However, the psychomotor domain holds a place in training because many programs include hands-on sections that require the completion of tasks while on the job.

Using action verbs makes the objective observable. Discernible behaviors allow for measurement of the objective. Bloom's Taxonomy (1956) offers a number of education-focused action verbs, such as *describes, differentiates, distinguishes, identifies,* and *compares.* Key words help evaluate the level of intellectual behavior that Bloom determined were important to learning. He discerned three domains of learning—cognitive, affective, and psychomotor—and assigned tasks to each that ranged from the basic to the most complex. The complex terms within each domain, those listed last, require mastery of the previous levels. Figure 12.1 shows Bloom's verb examples for level of mastery.

These terms relate to a specific type of learning. A writer can determine what type of learning is needed and use the coordinating words to promote the completion of that task.

Accuracy

Because training information often assists employees in learning their job and covers information they are required to know, these documents must be accurate. Content errors cannot be overlooked because they can interfere with the

FIGURE 12.1 *Bloom's Taxonomy Verb Examples*

Domain	Evaluation Level	Key Verb
Cognitive	Knowledge	Arrange, define, duplicate, label, list, memorize, name, order, recognize, relate, recall, repeat, reproduce, state
	Comprehension	Classify, describe, discuss, explain, express, identify, indicate, locate, recognize, report, restate, review, select, translate
	Application	Apply, choose, demonstrate, dramatize, employ, illustrate, interpret, operate, practice, schedule, solve, use, write
	Analysis	Analyze, appraise, calculate, categorize, compare, contrast, criticize, differentiate, discriminate, distinguish, examine, experiment, question, test
	Synthesis	Arrange, assemble, collect, compose, construct, create, design, develop, formulate, manage, organize, plan, prepare, propose, set up, write
	Evaluation	Appraise, argue, assess, attach, choose, compare, defend, estimate, evaluate, judge, predict, rate, select, support, value
Affective	Receiving Phenomena	Ask, choose, describe, follow, give, identify, locate, name, select, reply, use
	Responding to Phenomena	Answer, conform, discuss, greet, label, perform, practice, present, read, recite, report, select, write
	Valuing	Complete, demonstrate, differentiate, explain, follow, initiate, justify, propose, read, report, select, share, study, work
	Organization	Adhere, alter, arrange, combine, compare, complete, explain, formulate, generalize, identify, integrate, modify, organize, prepare, relate, synthesize
	Internalizing Values	Act, discriminate, display, influence, listen, modify, perform, practice, propose, qualify, question, revise, serve, solve, verify
Psychomotor	Perception	Choose, describe, detect, differentiate, distinguish, identify, isolate, relate, select
	Set	Display, explain, move, proceed, react, show, state, volunteer
	Guided Response	Copy, follow, react, reproduce, respond
	Mechanism	Assemble, calibrate, construct, dismantle, display, fasten, fix, manipulate, measure, organize, sketch
	Complex Overt Response	Assemble, calibrate, construct, dismantle, display, fasten, fix, manipulate, measure, organize, sketches NOTE: The key verbs here are the same as for Mechanism, but should be qualified with adverbs or adjectives to indicate that the tasks are completed in a more productive manner.
	Adaptation	Adapt, alter, change, rearrange, reorganize, revise
	Origination	Arrange, build, combine, compose, construct, create, design, initiate, make, originate

knowledge needed to correctly perform a task on the job. Also, as with other technical documents, the cost to redistribute materials due to content errors can be costly, while the price for not correcting the mistakes can be much higher.

Subject matter experts should be involved when the document creators do not have this knowledge. Collaboration in this scenario offers additional technical information and feedback from someone who completes the necessary tasks. These individuals also should be included in any post-draft testing. This type of testing allows for an analysis of material accuracy and how well the program meets the determined objectives.

Uniformity

Ensuring that training documents are uniform across departments and components may be one reason to make them the product of a technical communicator. By creating documents that share a format, organization, and tone, trainees can move easily from one document to another. Also, a company can use its training documentation as a chance to continue any branding efforts, so that all of its produced documents appear similar and ensuring they are identified with the company.

Uniformity does not merely refer to format and visual similarity. The issue of company style or format also should be considered to guarantee wording choices, titles, and other information, such as organizational flow charts and information used in a number of departments, are identical. When using multiple document types or training methods, a writer must create a sense of uniformity and reconcilability between all pieces of the set.

Document Types

While determining the purpose and audience of the training documents should assist a writer in deciding the best suited document type, there are additional deciding factors involved, too. As with other projects, budget constraints play a part, as do timelines, distribution concerns, and the frequency of updates. Considering this information, along with purpose and audience, directs the product design and allows the writer to choose from the various training document types. These documents can be used alone or combined to develop training programs discussed later in the chapter.

Manuals. Training manuals are often delivered as hard-copy documents, and can be given to employees when newly hired, upon position changes, or when new equipment or procedures are in use. Occasionally, training manuals are the first and only information employees receive on a process or task, but more often companies offer training courses or periods that culminate with an evaluation of knowledge. Printed manuals can be a part of these training programs as well, but they are complemented by live or online interactive training tutorials.

When producing documents that will only be distributed as hard copy, a writer must consider the time and cost it will take to update the document as the procedures and training processes change. These considerations can determine how the manual is organized—in chapters, tasks, or even by piece of equipment used. For example, if the company replaces its equipment or database program often, the writer might consider including this information in one section that is either distributed separately from the rest of the material or can be easily taken out of the original manual and replaced.

Manuals can be mass-produced in-house or by an outside printing company, and binding options are nearly endless. Many organizations favor bindings that allow for the inclusion of additional information as it becomes available, such as three-ring binders, a number of section- or task-specific manuals, or files kept in a shared directory on a server and that can be readily updated and distributed via email.

Websites. Websites designed for training purposes may be posted on secure sites, giving access only to those individuals within the company and assigned to use the information. These sites can be interactive or static displays of information, but either way, they are often easier to update than hard-copy manuals, while production and distribution costs are greatly reduced compared to printing and binding. The material covered in printed manuals also can be covered in websites, but a website has the additional advantage of allowing for trainee interactivity and the use of multimedia. For instance, quizzes to evaluate the knowledge gained or to pre-assess the knowledge of the trainee can be used, as can audio and video clips allowing trainees to see a procedure or to hear the audio queues a piece of equipment may give. Trainees can link directly to further information on a given topic as needed, yet the extra information will not distract the flow of training for those who are already familiar with the topic. Be sure to understand the capacity of the technology available for training purposes; for instance, consider file size constraints or access to software that can run movie clips.

Another aspect of website training that a writer needs to understand prior to developing the material is the intended trainees comfort level with technology. Posting training on a website for individuals who have limited knowledge about computers will intimidate the trainees before they even begin the actual training. Furthermore, the trainees who are technologically savvy will expect the training to use the latest software to provide interactive and stimulating training; posting a Portable Document Format (PDF) version of the training manual will disappoint and possibly frustrate them.

Supplementary Materials. Training materials often contain a number of supplementary documents to ensure the needed information is presented as succinctly as possible. These documents allow for quick reference or further explanation, making the information accessible to the trainees in a number of different formats. These materials might include checklists, glossaries, Frequently Asked Questions (FAQ) sheets, quick-reference guides, forms, templates, troubleshooting documents, and sample documents.

Checklists work well to ensure readers have documentation of specific tasks that must be accomplished. Activities that need to be completed daily, weekly, monthly, or annually work well on checklists. The tasks can be checked off as they are completed and the lists create reminders for the readers. The time frame for the listed tasks should be clear, as should the person responsibile for each task. Below is an example checklist.

Manager: Opening Tasks
As the opening manager, the following tasks need to be completed upon your arrival:

☐ Ensure employee entrance doors are unlocked by 8:30 AM.

☐ Unlock lobby doors and ensure lights are on by 9:00 AM.

☐ Transfer office phone from voice mail.

☐ Turn on front office copy and fax machines.

☐ Run *Daily Production Report* and distribute to management team via email.

Glossaries are short lexicons offering readers definitions of key terms. They can be listed within the training material or created as their own documents and should offer definitions of company or task-related jargon, and words that relate to specific activities, groups, or professions. Occasionally, a glossary will be combined with an index, offering definitions and page numbers where the word is referenced within the text. If a glossary worth of words is not needed, a writer might choose to define the words in the training documents using sidebars, note boxes, or contextual definitions. Each of these options is viable, but suits a different purpose. The readers' needs should be considered when the decision of how to present this information is made.

Frequently Asked Questions sheets list a number of questions that are common during the training program and their answers. A survey of trainees prior to their completion of the program can determine which questions to add to the FAQ sheet. These questions should be general enough to be asked by any trainee using the program and not require overly detailed answers. An example FAQ sheet is shown below.

Frequently Asked Questions: Benefits

Please read through this list of frequent questions and answers regarding the benefits offered to you by Taylor Fundamental, Inc.

1. When am I eligible to enroll in medical and dental insurance programs?
A. You will be able to make your benefit selections at any time during your probationary period, but your insurance benefits will not become active until after that period or two weeks after your selection, whichever is later.

2. When am I able to change my benefit elections?
A. During your initial enrollment period, the 90 days correlating to your probationary period, you can change

your benefit elections as needed. However, after your enrollment becomes active, changes to your elections can be made during the month of October for the following calendar year. Also, any time there has been a life change, including a marriage, divorce, birth, or adoption, you may elect to change your benefit choices.

3. Who do I contact to report a life change?
A. Your local human resources department can work with you to record a life change and change your benefit elections. You may also call the HR toll-free number at 1-800-555-H-E-L-P, or log on to the company's HR site at *www.TaylorInternational.com/HR/benefits.* You will be able to log into the site using the same username and password you use for web mail access.

Quick-reference guides offer readers a fast way to obtain information they might need. These documents are generally task-oriented and tell the readers how to complete a specific task, such as running a report, logging in to web mail, or setting up personalized voice mail. While these tasks may not be joined in purpose, the guides are generally stand-alone documents that are much shorter than training or policy and procedure manuals and may include checklists, glossaries, FAQ sheets, and other supplementary materials.

Forms include any blank forms that may need to be used repeatedly or possibly samples of forms that have been filled out correctly. When forms are incorporated as supplementary material, explanations of when they are to be used, how to fill them out, and who they need to be submitted to should also be included. Forms that may be worth distributing include time sheets, vacation/sick leave requests, schedules, direct deposit forms, and other general use forms that might not be available on a company intranet or website.

Templates are useful additions to training material that can be accessed on the Internet or sent via email because templates are generally computer generated. Documents that require specific formatting, such as schedules that are turned in as spreadsheets, should have templates that allow trainees to re-create them repeatedly. They can be developed in most word processing, spreadsheet, and database programs, and offer efficiency when dealing with items that require content but not format changes.

While most *troubleshooting documents* are of a technical nature, explaining how to fix a problem in a computer program, for example, they can be used for any number of issues. These documents explain a potential solution by walking users through a number of questions or symptoms until the final issue is determined. An example troubleshooting document is shown below.

Troubleshooting: Voice Mail

Section I

Retrieving Voice Mail:

If you are having a problem accessing your voice mail, there are a number of issues that could be the cause. Work through the following set of problems to determine the probable cause and solution.

1. Is the red light on the phone flashing, signifying there is voice mail to retrieve?
   A. Yes. Go to question 2.
   B. No. There are no voice-mail messages to receive. If you think this is an error, turn to section II, Deleted Messages.

2. Is there an audible dial tone when you lift the receiver?
   A. Yes. Go to question 4.
   B. No. Go to question 3.

3. Is there an audible dial tone when you put the phone on speaker?
   A. Yes. Put the phone on speaker and go to question 4.
   B. No. Go to section III, Dial Tone Issues.

4. Do you have a personal password for the voice-mail account?
   A. Yes. Go to question 5.
   B. No. Call your HR representative or 1-800-555-H-E-L-P to obtain a password.

5. When you dial *575, does it ask for your password?
   A. Yes. Go to question 6.
   B. No. Your voice mailbox is not set up to use your password. Go to section IV, Setting Up Voice Mail.

6. Is your password accepted and voice mail accessible after entering *7 and your password?
   A. Yes. Retrieve messages.
   B. No. You need to reset your password in order to retrieve messages. Go to section X, Voice-mail Reset.

Sample documents offer examples of documents the readers might have to create during or after their training. The documents included here should not contain any factual personal data. For example, samples of letters sent to clients in default should not include actual client names, addresses, account numbers, or the like. This keeps any confidential or privacy protected information from being unduly distributed.

Program Types

Training programs generally combine document types including manuals, handouts, presentations, and hands-on and online training modules. The delivery of the information and evaluation of participation also can include a combination of program elements.

Blended Learning. Training courses or tutorials can be live sessions led by a qualified trainer or online interactive modules allowing for the use of multimedia. Regardless of how these programs are distributed, they normally contain more than one module or session and have an assessment process included. With the development of these programs, the writer must first determine the objectives to be evaluated and assessed at the end of the program. These objectives should be developed first to ensure they are all covered within the training material and that the assessment material works with the covered objectives.

A tutorial might ask a trainee to read information and then put it into practice by completing the task in real time or online, or it might test trainees after information has been delivered. Often, to successfully complete the training, trainees are required to pass final evaluations with a minimum score.

Many training programs combine numerous document types. For instance, there may be a computer tutorial that trainees work through while reading their policy manual. However, their hands-on training may come in a face-to-face practicum format with assessments done online and in person. The combination of materials allows for the creation of unique programs that meet the specific needs of those being trained.

Interest and Expectations

Keeping trainees interested in the material they need to work with can be difficult because many writers do not have the ability to write in an informal tone or add exciting examples. However, if training designers can make the information relevant to the trainees, explaining why they need to know it and how it will be pertinent to their positions, it may be easier for them to prioritize their participation in the programs.

The use of end-of-program assessments also might encourage active participation in the programs. By letting trainees know the minimum level of participation or the score they must earn on their final assessment in order to progress, training designers set clear expectations and encourage trainees to meet those expectations.

Computer-Based Training (CBT). CBT modules offer training tutorials and information online without direct instructor evaluation. These components deliver training material, including assessments and virtual "labs," while combining text, audio, and video to create a curriculum. The training programs are all-encompassing and any assistance trainees require must come from the program designer or technical support. These training programs normally reach the trainees using software applications on intranets, hard drives, or CD-/DVD-ROMs.

Web-based training (WBT) is a type of CBT that is accessed via the Internet. Also called e-Learning, the information is delivered by way of a website that requires a user name and password to designate which trainee is logged in and record assessment scores into a database. Internet connection speeds can drastically affect a trainee's experience with this medium, and should be considered when developing complex WBT material.

Assessments used in CBT and WBT programs are self-grading and completed using the computer. True/False and multiple-choice questions are the most common forms of assessment; however, because they are conducted using computers, they can involve audio and video capabilities along with text on which to base the questions. For example, a videotaped scenario might be included and questions created regarding the actions and interactions of the characters. This example would be useful in a management training session.

The benefits of these programs are that they can be used easily when participants are in various geographic locations, work different hours or shifts, and can work independently. A weakness, though, is there are often equipment requirements for trainees accessing these programs.

When writing material that will be used in a CBT or WBT program, the writer must be sure not to overwhelm the user. Because this material typically is read, although it can be delivered via audio and video as well, consider the guidelines associated with writing for the Web. Grouping information and keeping the documents clear and wording concise can assist in comprehension. Adding graphic elements, such as color, illustrations, and charts or graphs that refer to the material, helps break up large sections of text and further convey information.

The organization of the material is another concern. It should be clear how the material progresses from point to point because there will be no one there to facilitate or explain how the information is related. If the information has no relation to the other material, the order in which it is presented remains important and needs to be considered. For instance, if there is no relation between pieces, alphabetical organization may be the easiest way to organize. This allows readers to know where they are in the midst of the training and helps ensure they will not miss points.

Virtual, Instructor-Led Web-Based Training. WBT courses that include a facilitator or instructor often contain discussion elements. These discussions can be synchronous, requiring trainees and trainers to meet online at a specific time, but most rely on asynchronous participation. Regardless of the type of participation, these courses give trainees a chance to interact with each other and seek guidance from a trainer and their peers. Immediate, real-time communication can take place as well.

The decision to use this type of program allows for differences in location for both asynchronous and synchronous programs and time when asynchronous discussion is used, but there are equipment and facilitator training requirements. Complex theories and procedures can be more fully defined with the help of a facilitator, however, as this type of WBT allows for interaction.

Web-Based Platforms

Virtual courses that allow for instructor interaction require specific Web-based platforms for their presentation. There are a number of platforms available, all with varying costs, technical requirements, and abilities. If a technical writer is charged with choosing a platform, budget, time, and technology constraints, as well as how user-friendly the system is, should be considered.

Designing the training program prior to knowing how it will be presented is often counterproductive because these platforms vary in how materials are most commonly presented. Some require information to be written in the system while others allow for uploads of previously written information. Some require material to be presented in html as well.

Some common WBT platforms include WebCT, eCollege, Blackboard, and Angel.

Information delivered by instructors in virtual training courses should be multifaceted and require the assistance of a facilitator. The instructor also should have access to any explanations or assistance in the manner of instructor manuals or notes. When writing this information, ensuring the facilitator will have access to the information prior to becoming responsible for teaching it is important, as is thorough training in the method of delivery.

Face-to-Face, Instructor-Led. These courses are held synchronously and require a facility, equipment, texts, and time. Participants are required to meet with the trainer at a set time and place, sometimes requiring travel and schedule changes.

Instructor-led, face-to-face courses are well used when the material is highly advanced or technical in nature, although these courses often take up more time than CBT or WBT sessions. Also, class size is limited not only by the trainer's abilities, but also by the facility's size and availability.

Benefits to this type of training include the ability for immediate feedback and more complex assessments, including practicums and presentations. Also, instructor-led training courses, be they virtual or traditional and in-person, offer trainees the opportunity to connect with the facilitator and make contact with other trainees, which can increase a sense of identity and community with the company.

While some of the information presented in this type of program may be chosen or written by the instructor, the training designer should write and distribute program objectives in order to ensure trainers are focusing their efforts on conveying the needed information. This information, because there is an instructor available for explanation and questioning, can be more complex and less defined than in other program types. However, instructors will require training and supplementary materials in order to effectively deliver the information in the course.

Self-directed. In self-directed training, trainees work through coursework on their own, without the benefit of computer technology. These courses can include real-world training sessions on the job or live lab-like experiences coupled with information delivered via hard-copy document or video.

Occasionally, self-directed study will offer instructor support, making a trainer available for questions and feedback on assessments. Even with facilitator availability, these courses allow trainees to work at their own speed, completing tasks at their own pace and chosen times.

A weakness of these training programs is that, while the material delivered is controlled, how it is used is not. Also, the courses are difficult to customize for individual trainees and often assessment materials are not strictly monitored.

Material delivered via this type of program should not overwhelm trainees as they attempt to work through it. It may be presented in volumes, organized progressively, to allow learners to go from one volume to another as each is completed. This will keep them from having too much information on hand at once. However, the material needs to be thoroughly explained to compensate for the lack of personal explanation.

Mentoring. This training program involves the relay of information from a mentor to one or two trainees. It allows for a unique teaching relationship that takes place during on-the-job training and creates a more intense and longer lasting relationship than instructor-led courses. In this program, the mentor is considered an expert and works to share information regarding the tasks, equipment, and policies, as well as social and cultural expectations.

The inefficiency of this training type generally limits its use, although it can be used as a final step in the training process. Also, the content delivered to the trainees may or may not be monitored or standardized.

In a mentoring program, the training designer might do little other than distribute the training objectives. These programs are generally mentor-led, although supplementary materials may be helpful.

Assessment

Assessment documents allow for an evaluation of the trainees' retention or understanding of the training materials and need to be based on the objectives of the training program. Objectives must be determined prior to developing the assessment to ensure that the assessments test for the predicted behaviors. Assessments should focus on Bloom's taxonomy key terms used in the training objectives, as previously noted.

Exercise/Case Study. Trainees complete a written exercise with this assessment type and turn it in for evaluation and feedback from a facilitator.

The exercise focuses on the retention of the information or allows for analysis of a given scenario, a case study, and asks about the appropriate responsive behavior.

A case study gives trainees a chance to put themselves into a hypothetical situation and decide on their response including their course of action, communication they would send, and policies to which they would refer. This is an in-depth opportunity to educate trainees as to possible incidences and to evaluate their predicted behavior.

A writer tasked with designing this type of assessment must decide if the scenario will be presented via audio, video, or text. Regardless, this may be written as a script, allowing for dialog between characters within the exercise. However, it is often easier for a writer who is not familiar with this type of writing to begin with a basic story. Once the scenario is created, it can be broken down into dialog, giving characters roles and lines within the scene. If this is then converted to audio or video, a writer will most likely be responsible for the overall production, including casting and recording of the scenario. This, too, should be considered when determining the cost and timeline of the training program's creation.

Testing. Tests can be focused on successful understanding or progressive knowledge. Either way, tests are the most common form of training program assessment. They can be directly correlated to the determined objectives and either self-scored with CBT or by a facilitator. Facilitator-graded tests allow for open-ended questions, scenario use, and short-answer personalized statements. These tests, along with those used in CBT, also can contain multiple-choice, fill in the blank, matching, and true/false questions.

Progressive knowledge tests ensure that trainees have a minimum competency on specific information or exercises before moving on to additional information. These tests may come at the end of training phases and must be passed with a minimum grade to allow successful completion of that module. Progressive testing works well when theory is introduced prior to hands-on use of the task or when material builds on that presented previously. This allows a training designer to break tasks into pieces that build upon each other and then test on each skill or piece. Therefore, each progressive test would ultimately cover the material learned in that section and, by default, the material covered earlier.

The tests, regardless of whether they are progressive, should focus on the measurable objectives of the program. Determining the specific tasks or information covered in the test might require consultation with those who currently hold the position. A survey might be applicable, as would interviews and reviews of previous tests.

Pre-test/Post-test. A specific testing scenario, the use of pre- and post-tests shows how much knowledge existed before training and allows for a comparison to what was garnered from training. Two identical tests are administered, one at the beginning of and one at the culmination of training or the module of concern. The results are compared and can be used to evaluate the training program as well as the trainees' retention. Like the other testing strategies, the questions on the pre-/post-tests need to be directly related to the training objectives.

Self-evaluation. While not considered a test, self-evaluation allows trainees to contemplate their own participation and performance in the training program. These evaluations can be done at any point in the program and focus on the trainees' view of their own knowledge and retention. This self-reflection can give trainees a chance to focus on and voice their concerns or questions. Interspersing these assessments throughout the program allows for multiple reflections and chances for facilitator feedback based on the assessments.

Feedback and Revision

When developing training programs, experts should be consulted to determine the accuracy and completeness of the information. Having these experts participate in a training session allows for quality control testing and an analysis of the objectives, strategies, techniques, and materials used. After participating, experts should contribute formal evaluations of the program and revisions should be made accordingly. Once revisions are made, the material should be retested.

Resources for Future Consideration

Due to the complexity of the subject of developing e-Learning modules, which whole books are written on and cannot possibly be covered here, consider the following resources for further information:

Ashburn, E. A., and R. E. Floden. 2006. *Meaningful learning using technology: What educators need to know and do. TEC Series.* New York, NY: New York Teachers College Press.

Monolescu, D., C. Schifter, and L. Greenwood. 2004. *The distance education evolution: Issues and case studies.* Hershey, PA: Information Science Publications.

Palloff, R. M., and K. Pratt. 2001. *Lessons from the cyberspace classroom: The realities of online teaching.* San Francisco, CA: Jossey-Bass.

Rudestam, K. E., and J. Schoenholtz-Read. 2002. *Handbook of online learning: Innovations in higher education and corporate training.* Thousand Oaks, CA: Sage Publications.

Trainees also should evaluate the training program after completing it. These evaluations should discuss the quality of the information, teaching strategies used, personal actions of any instructors, equipment function, and ease of use. Like scales, surveys that offer a 1–5 value and give participants a chance to agree or disagree with statements (1 strongly disagree, 2 disagree, 3 neutral, 4 agree, 5 strongly agree) offer numeric criteria for evaluation. When creating this survey, each statement must work to cover only one point. Also, allowing open-ended questions or the ability to freely comment may give the training designer additional information. An example evaluation form is shown in figure 12.2.

If the training program is divided into multiple phases, evaluations should be given after each phase. Also, a revision plan should be designed and include information as to the frequency with which the training designer will review the evaluations and make changes. Making changes after each

FIGURE 12.2 *Evaluation Form*

New Hire Training: Company Policies and History

Please fill out completely the following evaluation form pertaining to the training you have received regarding the policies and history of Taylor Fundamental, Inc. These evaluations will be anonymous and will not affect your final assessment in the program or your position at the company. Your candor and honesty are appreciated.

Mark the following statements by placing an X in the box that signifies your level of agreement with the statement. Please select one box for each statement.

New Hire Training: Company Policies and History

Statement	1 Strongly Disagree	2 Disagree	3 Neutral	4 Agree	5 Strongly Disagree
1. The information presented was necessary for me to feel comfortable doing my job.					
2. The information was presented in an interesting manner.					
3. The trainer was engaging and enthusiastic.					
4. The information was clearly presented.					
5. I had access to the technology required to complete the WBT portion of the training.					
6. This training session was worthy of my time and energy.					
7. The training session required too much time to complete.					

Please answer each of the questions below, being as specific as possible.

1. What was the most important information presented during this training session?

2. Was there anything you would remove from the training material? If so, what?

3. How much time did you devote to the training program?

4. What changes would you suggest be made to the materials or presentation methods?

training session is not practical if sessions run continuously. However, revision of annual training programs can be made yearly, especially because the information delivered most likely will be in need of updating.

REFERENCES

Bloom, B. S. 1956. *Taxonomy of educational objectives, handbook 1: The cognitive domain.* New York, NY: David McKay Co. Inc.

Knowles, M. S., et al. 1984. *Andragogy in action. Applying modern principles of adult education.* San Francisco, CA: Jossey Bass.

CHAPTER 13

Writing in Digital Environments

W riting for a digital environment is challenging in the sense that the writer must develop interactive content for readers. Interactive content allows readers to take an active role in obtaining desired information. This information can be obtained through hyperlinks, audio files, or video clips. Thus, digital information is conveyed to readers through multimedia, which means there is more than one way to communicate.

Writing for a digital environment involves using multiple techniques, including writing to be read (journalism, poetry, copywriting); writing to be heard (radio, narration); writing to be seen (presentations, film, video); plus writing for the special requirements of the computer screen (Garrand 2006). For the purpose of this chapter, writing for the digital environment will focus on writing and designing for the Web. Writing for other forms in the digital environment, such as blogs, video, audio, and e-Learning solutions, are briefly discussed at the end of the chapter.

WRITING IN A DIGITAL ENVIRONMENT

When writing for a digital environment, the writer must compose for an interactive audience. Computer-mediated material, such as content delivered through text, video, or audio, allows users to have some control over the format for obtaining information. Interactive media is present in many formats. For example, think of a website for a department store. The user is able to view photographs of a product, such as an item of clothing, or listen to a sample audio recording of a song. The format creates a sense of interactivity, allowing the user to gain as much information as desired in multiple formats. Additionally, multimedia reaches beyond the Internet to include portable games, interactive television services, phones, CD-ROMs, and DVDs, to name a few.

A technical communicator may create various documents for a multi-media project including proposals, outlines, site maps, design documents, scripts, and text. The interactivity of multimedia makes presenting ideas to future clients difficult because of the complexity. A writer can present ideas in a written format first in order to visualize the interactive elements of the content. The format for presenting these ideas depends on the individual project (e.g., website, audio, video, or a combination). Example formats for writing for a digital environment are listed below. Discussion on writing site maps is included later in the chapter.

Proposal

Unlike research and grant proposals discussed in chapter 11, the term "proposal" is used to refer to the format for an informational design document written so that the reader may visualize the project. The following elements are standard to a design document proposal:

- **Design objective.** This is a description of what the project hopes to accomplish. The length may be a paragraph or slightly longer, but it is important to grab the attention of the reader.

- **Creative treatment.** This section is a detailed description of the entire project. Included is a written narrative that describes the purpose of the project as well as a description of the multimedia to be incorporated.

- **Navigation.** This section describes the interface and the ways the user will navigate through the program or website. A flowchart is often included in this section.

- **Production and marketing.** Design documents often include a project schedule or marketing ideas. Suggestions for marketing the project to the public are included in this section.

Outline

It is useful to write an outline for a website or another project that contains text-heavy information, such as an online course. A content outline that includes the major elements of the project as well as a flowchart to explain this content and navigation are included. The outline format should be adjusted to meet the needs of a specific project. Below are common elements to all outlines:

- **Title.** The title page, which includes the same elements listed on the flowchart.

- **Images.** Describe potential images or graphics to be used on the page. Animation, video, or audio also should be included.

- **Text.** Describe the text that will appear on screen.

- **Links.** Includes links on the page both from the navigation bar as well as those embedded in the text.

- **Navigation.** List and describe the buttons that will have to be created for the navigation bar or menu.

- **Functionality.** Describe what the user can do on the Web page besides click and read. For example, on a stress management website, describe the self-analysis test on managing stress.

- **Scripts.** Scripts are written to describe what the user will see on the screen. In addition to text only, a description of the multimedia elements is included.

Presentation

All text is not created equal. When writing for a digital environment, it is important to keep in mind some differences in the format. In print documents, the reader is focused on the entire document. For example, a reader of a print newspaper article often will read the entire article, even if it means turning pages to reach the end of the article. Writing for the Web involves creating shorter groups of texts and inserting hyperlinks that allow readers to have the option to read additional information on the subject.

Readers of the Web typically skim sites searching for pertinent information. Web users usually read slower on the screen than in printed material. As such, writing for the digital environment involves presenting information in about half of the word count used for print. Online readers also do not like to scroll through large blocks of text. If possible, present important information within the size of the screen. Use hyperlinks to direct readers to background or additional information about the topic. Keep in mind the objective of writing for a digital environment: to provide concise information in a format that allows readers to quickly find the desired information.

Because readers skim the information quickly, use metaphor and humor carefully (especially in headings) because readers may take the information literally. Also, keep in mind that information on the Web is available for both national and international audiences. What might be a common phrase in the United States may be ambiguous to an international reader.

The Web is a fluid medium and information needs to be current. Unlike print formats, which take time to update, information presented in a digital environment needs to be current. Credibility of the individual writer or the organization can suffer if information is outdated. Update websites frequently to reflect current events, statistics, and examples. If information, such as copies of old newsletters, is important to house on the website as historical references, place older issues in an archived folder. Readers will be able to view the current newsletter and read updated material and they also will have the option to refer back to older issues.

Provide current, reusable, quality content. Outdated information takes away from both the credibility of the writer as well as the organization it represents. If the Web page contains time-sensitive material, such as the news, it needs to be updated on a daily basis in order to attract new readers and encourage regular visitors to continue using the site. Readers typically scan sites for specific information, and outdated material may discourage them from visiting the site again. For example, a page that announces an event that occurred last month illustrates that the site is not regularly maintained and cannot be relied on for current information.

RSS Feeds

RSS, Really Simple Syndication, is sometimes called a Web feed. This is the format used when a writer wants to syndicate news and other Web content. *Syndication* refers to when one party creates the content and distributes it to many places. RSS feeds are frequently used for the following:

- Recent news
- Feeds from local or national newspapers
- Product news for an organization
- Job vacancies within an organization

WRITING FOR THE WEB

Effective writing for the Web involves more than writing insightful text. Elements of interactivity need to be considered. The role of graphics, color, audio, video, and animation are all part of this. The goal of the Web writer is to make the copy attractive to readers, drawing attention first to the "look and feel" of the site, followed by text that makes readers want to read further. Below are the elements essential to writing successful Web copy:

- **Write clearly.** The majority of readers use the Web to gather information on a topic. To accommodate this search-and-find behavior, text should be written in a simple format, avoiding large blocks of text. Text should be concise and avoid extraneous detail while still getting the main points across to the reader. The tone of the writing should be conversational, written in a format that is communicating *with* the reader, not *to* the reader.

- **Make important points stand out.** Similar to print newspapers, readers of the Web are attracted to headlines. Place important information up front because many readers will quickly skim through Web copy. A well-written headline will grab the reader's attention when surfing through numerous sites. The headline should include main points of the writing using a minimum amount of words. The goal is to grab the reader's attention as early as possible, and encourage the reader to want to read more.

- **Provide ease of accessibility.** Unlike traditional forms of reading text from the beginning, writing effectively for the Web involves allowing readers to begin anywhere and yet gain access to desired information. Random access allows readers to easily find information no matter where they begin. Writing for the Web differs from creative writing in the sense that it is more technical in its orientation, because a Web writer needs to structure and plan text based on the ways it is expected readers will access and use the information.

- **Proofread carefully.** Similar to any form of writing, careful proofreading is needed for establishing credibility of a website and the writer. If a word is not spelled correctly, it can affect the number of hits on a search engine. When correct grammar and spelling is not used, it can give the perception that the business or organization is not concerned with details. Remember that spell check does not catch every grammatical error. It is important to have Web copy read more than once by several individuals. Some writers find it useful to print out text and proofread on hard copy.

- **Maintain consistency.** Because writing for the Web involves thinking beyond the written narrative, a writer might find it useful to review copy after the draft has been completed. Leave the copy aside for a while and then carefully review it for inconsistencies in style, definitions, punctuation, and grammar. Being consistent in writing will give the text a more professional and credible appearance.

In addition to formatting text, a Web writer must keep the concept of interactivity in mind. Make hyperlinks embedded in text concise and easy to follow, as in the following example:

There are many websites that provide information on **local universities.**

is more specific than:

There are many websites that provide information on **colleges.**

Because hyperlinks involve underlining to indicate a link, avoid using underlining text in the Web copy to prevent any confusion. If the reader sees underlined text, there is a perception that it is a link to additional information. When including buttons for additional information, be as specific as possible about the content of the links. For example, a button titled "Mission Statement" is more precise than "Background Information."

Planning

Writing for the Web includes planning, drafting, and revising. Designing a website begins with determining the objective of the communication. For instance, if designing a website for an organization, the purpose of the writing and design should be geared toward the goals of the institution. This can be seen in the design of educational websites that provide information about the university that is of interest to prospective students, provides resources for current students, and caters to other audiences, such as alumni and potential funders. Government sites offer official forms, information about policy, and current events. Defining audience and purpose will help identify objectives, and the following are essential questions to ask:

- Is this an update to an existing site?

- Does a new page need to be created?

- Is the project designed to develop a new website?

In addition to defining the audience for the site, usability needs to be taken into consideration. For example, when designing an educational website, the goal for an elementary school might be to provide information for current students. Elements that would be included are the academic calendar, location of the school, current state test results, special events, and extra curricular activities. Readers need to be able to quickly locate the desired information through easy navigation of various links.

Site Maps. Designing a site map assists in the process of organizing information. The site map is structured through creating a diagram, such as the one shown in figure 13.1.

Site maps also can follow an outline format listing the major headings of topics with the subtopics listed below. For complex websites, the home page might include a site map within the main navigation bar as shown in figure 13.2 of the U.S. Department of Commerce's website. An example of a site map using an outline format is shown in figure 13.3.

Usability Testing. When planning the design of a website, be willing to change the design based on the reader's interests. Usability testing is one way

FIGURE 13.1 *Site Map for a Restaurant Website*

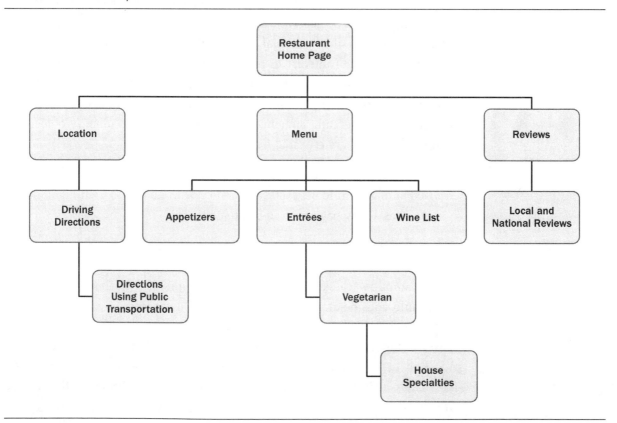

FIGURE 13.2 *U.S. Department of Commerce Home Page with Site Map*

A: Site Map is included on the home page to provide readers with opportunities to view the organization of this complex website.

Source: *www.commerce.gov/*

to gain additional information about the needs of readers. Based on feedback gained from a sample audience, the site map should be revised to meet the objectives of the intended audience. It is common for a site map to undergo several drafts before reaching a final design.

Using Research in Web Pages

Using research to write for the Web follows guidelines similar to writing for print publications. Begin by assessing the readers' needs and questions about the information presented on the site. Investigate credible sources for gathering information such as background material, statistics, quotes, and examples. Evaluate the credibility of sources; be sure to follow the ethics set forth by intellectual property law. Anderson (2007) describes the broad areas that govern intellectual property right law:

- **Patent law.** Governs such things as inventions and novel manufacturing processes.

- **Trademark law.** Pertains to such things as company and product names (e.g., Microsoft™, Pentium™), slogans ("We bring good things to life"), and symbols (the Nike™ "swoosh").

FIGURE 13.3 *Site Map for U.S. Department of Commerce*

Site Map

Help & Information
- About Commerce
  - U.S. Commerce Department Officials
  - Milestones
  - Secretaries of Commerce
- Contact Us
- FAQ
- Commerce Services & Offices Near You
- Biography of Secretary Gutierrez
- Career Opportunities
  - Presidential Appointments

Office of the Secretary
- Office of Business Liaison
- Center for Faith Based and Community Initiatives
- Office of the Chief Financial Officer and Assistant Secretary for Administration
- Office of the Chief Information Officer
- Office of General Counsel
- Office of Inspector General
- Office of Legislative and Intergovernmental Affairs
- Office of Policy and Strategic Planning
- Office of Public Affairs

Commerce Bureaus
- Bureau of Industry and Security
- Economics and Statistics Administration
  - Bureau of the Census
  - Bureau of Economic Analysis

- Economic Development Administration
- International Trade Administration
- Minority Business Development Agency
- National Institute of Standards and Technology
- National Oceanic & Atmospheric Administration
- National Technical Information Service
- National Telecommunications and Information Administration
- Patent and Trademark Office

Newsroom
- Top News
- Press Releases & Fact Sheets
- Secretary's Speeches
- Deputy Secretary's Speeches
- Secretarial Trips
- Photo Gallery
- Media Contacts
- Historical Press Releases: 2001–2004

Contracting, Trade & Grants Opportunities
- Contracting Opportunities
- Trade Opportunities
- E-Commerce Highlights
- Grants

- **Copyright laws.** Deal with such things as written works, images, performances, and computer software. (p. 158)

Drafting a Web Page

An effective Web page needs to focus on the goals and objectives of the organization, department, or purpose of the site. The following checklist provides suggestions for achieving the objectives of an effective Web page:

- Develop a strong online presence for the organization through a number of innovative vehicles, such as audio, video, simulations, and other multimedia tools.

- Include additional information and resources in hyperlinked sections.

- Allow visitors to the site the opportunity to contact the organization for additional information through an email link, forum, or blog specific to the organization.

- Provide information suited to a variety of audiences.

- Use the website as a tool for marketing the organization.

It is useful to create a flexible, detached structure. This means that the Web page should be written in modules for easy reassembling, restructuring, and expansion. Often, technical communicators will write the script or narrative portion of the content for the Web page. This script is then given to a Web designer who will write the HTML code for the Web page. When writing the design script for the Web page, create a simple, yet effective, practical, flexible design. The website should align with the needs of the organization as well as create a unique "look and feel" within the design elements. After the narrative script has been written for the Web page, the Web designer will then incorporate all multimedia elements into the creation of the Web page.

An effective Web page needs to be reliable and exhibit reusable functionality. This is ultimately what the entire site is about. Reliable functionality is reached through well-designed, planned, and tested development processes. Website features, such as graphics, color, and design, are reused to reduce loading time, to improve site reaction speed, and to reduce developer's coding time that allows fast-cycle development. Functionality is the core component of the website and its future development. The main goal of the site is to provide functionalities that reach business goals via the technology of the Internet. The goals of the website relate back to the objectives of the organization and the purpose for creating the site. For example, is the goal of the website to provide information on a product? Is it to offer the opportunity for an online catalog where readers can purchase items directly from the website? The objectives as well as the intended audience for viewing of the site are important factors to keep in mind during the design phase.

During the drafting phase, prepare for efficient, well-planned maintenance. Reports should be collected regularly and automatically about user profiles, site performance, and user interactivity as a resource of off-service and as a base for new site development strategy. A backup system needs to be in place with content, codes, and graphics well maintained and updated.

Navigation Design Tips

To increase ease of navigation, it is advisable not to use a splash page, or an introductory page, to the main home page of the website, such as a Flash movie. Users will not find a Web page easily through a Google search if it does not have the headings and other key words for Google to locate the Web page. Additionally, Flash may take time to download depending on the operating system and computer capabilities of the user. While the Flash is taking time to download, the user may move on to another site.

Navigation is an important aspect of functionality. This begins the moment that a user types the organization's Internet address into a browser. It continues with swift browsing to find exactly what a reader has come to see. The experience culminates with a true enjoyment of the services provided. Readers want to easily obtain information, but also benefit from the experience of viewing the design and features of the site.

Consider including multimedia with Flash movies, creative slide shows, digitized edited videos with audio, and links to dedicated resources and virtual tours. Multimedia tools can grab the attention of the average "surfer" to explore the site in more detail. When planning for multimedia use, consider the functionality of the multimedia tools. For example, if the introduction to the site contains a Flash movie, allow the option of skipping this section and directing the user to the main site. It is important to consider download speeds that users will encounter when a website is filled with multimedia content. If it takes too long to download, the user is likely to move on to a different website rather than wait for the content to completely load.

Page Design

When working on page design, create easy to use, visually stimulating, interactive communication. Layout is critical to gaining and keeping readers' attention. Most Web pages use a grid design, similar to that of written pages. Figures 13.4 and 13.5 illustrate two commonly used grids for page design.

Illustrated in figure 13.6 is an example web page that uses the three-column grid design. The designer of this website aligned similar items against the same vertical or horizontal grid line to offer readers a visual cue to items that are related. There is also effective use of white space between the various items on the content section, providing readers with an easy way to search for the specific item of interest. The left navigation bar includes a drop-down menu offering readers the option to view more information on a various topic. Because there are many options on this site, the drop-down menu creates a cleaner, less cluttered navigation bar by streamlining the number of options. If a reader would like additional information on a specific topic, the option is there through the drop-down menu.

Using a grid pattern is effective when designing multiple pages because the designer can get the same look and feel for various pages or an entire site. For example, on the U.S. Department of Education pages, the home page, as shown in figure 13.7, uses the three-column grid design. Unity is created in the multiple pages by including the U.S. Department of Education banner, which covers the entire width through the various pages. The "No Child Left Behind" element is featured in the right column. While the

FIGURE 13.4 *Two-column Grid Design with Banner*

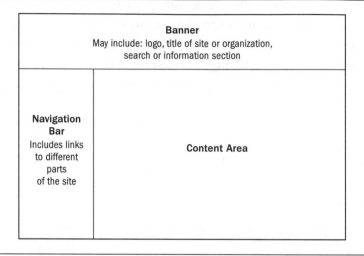

Banner
May include: logo, title of site or organization,
search or information section

Navigation Bar
Includes links to different parts of the site

Content Area

FIGURE 13.5 *Three-column Grid Design with Banner*

Banner

Navigation Bar

Content Area

Highlights Column
May include: special features, advertisements

graphic is the same, the content changes depending on the topic of the various pages. The left side navigation is also consistent with the home page, using the same typeface and format.

FIGURE 13.6 *Web Page Using Three-column Grid Design*

A: Effective use of color: dark typeface on a light background.

B: Effective use of white space. Space and a small dividing line separate topics.

C: Use of the drop-down menu allows readers access to additional information without creating a cluttered navigation bar.

Source: *www.usda.gov/wps/portal/usdahome*

A Web page is effective only if readers can easily read the material. When viewing a draft of the Web page online, remember that information on a computer screen is much more difficult to read than printed material. The following guidelines can help overcome these challenges:

- Ensure that the typefaces are easy to read on the screen.

- Avoid using light colored letters on a light background.

- Select darker colors, such as navy blue or black, to illustrate contrast on a light background.

- Text should be large enough for readers to easily view the information.

- Avoid using italics because this typeface is difficult to read on a screen.

357

Unity and Consistency in Web Design

Creating unity and consistency across the pages improves the usability for readers. The various pages may be different in content, but should follow the same style as the home page. Replication can assist in this process. Repeating the same design as the original grid creates a similar flow throughout the page. Figure 13.7 illustrates examples of a website that is unified. Notice how the pages have the following similar characteristics:

- The banner is placed at the top part of the grid and is repeated throughout the pages.
- The document colors are the same.
- Typeface is the same throughout the various pages.
- Despite the language difference, the Spanish page follows the same design format.
- The left navigation bar is divided into two groups.
- The right navigation column includes the same format with the "No Child Left Behind" section.
- Menu items are clearly labeled.
- An advanced search option is available in the right-hand corner of every page.

Navigation aids assist in the ultimate purpose of the website and provide readers with the information they want in an easy-to-retrieve format. Readers need to be able to locate information quickly. Navigation aids, such as those listed in the sidebar, help achieve this process.

Special Considerations

An effective website is one that can be used by all individuals wishing to gain information. Special considerations, listed below, need to be made for individuals with disabilities as well as for international readers.

FIGURE 13.7 *Pages Demonstrating Unity*

Home Page

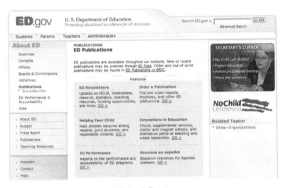

Linked Page

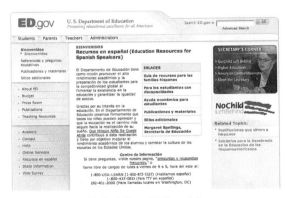

Linked Page in Spanish

Source: *www.ed.gov*

According to Roach (2002), in 2001, the U.S. Government instituted a regulation that mandates all federal agencies and federally affiliated institutions (including most U.S. colleges and universities) to make the organization's website and other electronic information technology accessible to persons with disabilities. Some important guidelines for addressing the needs of persons with disabilities are listed below:

- **Limited-mobility individuals.** Some readers have limited hand mobility and have difficulties moving a mouse. Make navigation areas that involve clicking the mouse as large as possible.

- **Hearing-impaired individuals.** A website that includes audio or video needs to include a volume control option, as well as captions. Movies or other multimedia tools involving sound should include captions in the event the individual is unable to hear the audio or video. For sections that include a verbal message, such as "Hello," the message needs to be typed out. This includes pop-up windows that sometimes appear in the site.

- **Visually impaired individuals.** To increase readability for the visually impaired, the relative size of the fonts should be consistent. Allowing the text to be consistent will allow visually impaired readers to adjust browser settings to view the text. Screen readers are commonly used devices that allow visually impaired individuals to read text on the screen. When designing the site, include an < alt > tag with all images. The tag provides a way for the text to be converted to speech by the screen reader. When designing hyperlinks, highlight descriptive words rather than using a phrase such as "click here." Instead, write: "You can learn more information about the organization." Color blindness may also be a challenge to some readers. When using a color to highlight the meaning of text, include the written words as well. For example, if the color red is used to indicate "caution," type out the word "Caution" instead of only using the color. In other words, avoid using only color to indicate a meaning of a word.

Design for the Visually Impaired

For additional information on designing websites for the visually impaired, see: *www.lighthouse.org/accessibility/effective-color-contrast/*

Because the Internet is available to readers on a global level, there should be special considerations for international audiences. Some websites, such as in the example of the U.S. Department of Education discussed earlier, include versions of the website in both English and Spanish. While it is obvious that a website cannot capture all languages, the following suggestions can increase readability for international audiences:

- **Write simple text.** Avoid slang, metaphors, and colloquial expressions. Check the readability of the site with individuals knowledgeable about the targeted culture.

- **Ensure accurate interpretation of images, colors, and photographs.** These have different meanings for different cultures. Enlist someone with knowledge about the targeted audience to review the material and ensure an accurate interpretation is presented.

- **Design plans in a simple format.** If the site will be re-created by another culture, remember that translation of some English words may be longer in the second language. If the site is expected to be translated into another language, keep the space concepts in mind when designing images, graphics, and text.

Revising

Before allowing the site to go live, have a number individuals review the website to ensure the information is accurate, all elements on the page load quickly, and access to information is easy. Conduct a usability test to make certain the site is available for use with different browsers and previous versions of browsers. Browsers, such as Firefox or Internet Explorer, handle Web files very differently. Additionally, test the site on various screen configurations and monitor sizes, and with different operating systems.

Writing for Multimedia

In addition to writing for the Web, a technical communicator might write blogs, audio, video, or e-Learning platforms. Each communication needs to consider the medium and the ways the information will be interpreted by the reader. There are similarities across all mediums, which include writing in a simple, conversational style. Some common forms of multimedia writing are briefly discussed below.

Blogs may be formal or informal in nature. A *blog* is a website that often allows commentary on a particular topic, allowing posts from various audiences within the Web community. The term "blog" is taken from the words "Web log." "Blog" also can be used as a verb to mean to add content to an existing blog. Often, an organization may use a blog as an opportunity for a manager to provide information for viewing by both employees as well as individuals outside the organization. In an informal sense, blogs may be written casually by customers or employees about general information. A formal blog, such as in the example of a manger conveying public relations materials, should be written in a clear, direct manner with a conversational tone. Often, formal blogs will end in a question in an effort to gain additional reader response.

It is common for blogs to include text, images, and links to other blogs, websites, and other forms of multimedia. Blogs are highly interactive and encourage visitors of the site to post narrative comments as well as multimedia links. Some blogs include a high level of multimedia and it is common for these highly interactive blogs to include the following:

- Art (artlogs)
- Photographs (photoblog)
- Drawings (sketchblog)
- Videos (vlog)
- Music (MP3 blog)
- Audio (podcasting)

As a social networking tool, blogs allow the sharing of both information and personal commentary on topics. Interactive by nature, blogs provide a format for virtual collaboration with readers across the Web.

Audio is used much more frequently because it costs less to produce. The popularity of podcasts has also increased the use of audio files for obtaining information. When writing an audio script, write in a visual manner. Well-written audio scripts allow listeners to see the information. This can be achieved by using descriptive words, metaphors or other comparisons, sound effects, and different vocal qualities. During the revising process, read the text out loud to ensure proper pacing and flow. It is also useful to have someone else read the text back to a small group of reviewers.

Writing for video allows the viewer to both see and hear the information. Write in a way that demonstrates showing, not telling the reader the information. Video images can create a powerful representation that does not need a lengthy verbal explanation. For example, a video showing devastation of a forest fire can use the images to inform the viewer and include a brief audio explanation. The concept of interactivity and chunking needs to be considered during video development. A longer video clip should be broken into smaller segments for the viewer, because viewers may not need all the information at once. This goes back to the concept of Web design and interactivity, which allows viewers to obtain easy access to desired information.

When writing for e-Learning solutions, such as an online course, include images or graphics to help enhance the presentation of the learning material. For example, in a health sciences class that discusses the structure of the human skeleton, pictures of the bones help clarify new or complicated terms. It is also useful to provide readers with additional information through links or other resources. For more information on e-learning, see chapter 12.

REFERENCES

Anderson, P. V. 2007. *Technical communication: A reader-centered approach.* 6th ed. Boston, MA: Thomson Higher Education.

Garrand, T. 2006. *Writing for multimedia and the Web.* 3d ed. Oxford, UK: Focal Press.

Jordan, K. 2007. *Defining multimedia.* 28 July 2007. *www.noemalab.org.*

Roach, R. 2002. "Making websites accessible to the disabled." *Black Issues in Higher Education,* 16, 32.

CHAPTER 14

Research in
Professional Contexts

R esearch in a professional setting has some similarities to research experienced in an academic environment; however, there are some important differences, which are seen mostly in the artifacts used. In academic settings, research typically is used to help establish background for a report, support an argument, or inform the writer and reader about the subject. In the workplace, research more often is used for historical reference on a project, to add credibility to a claim or hypothesis, or to cross-reference material. What many will notice when moving from an academic setting to a professional environment is that the first place to look for research will probably not be the library. Instead government documents, company correspondence or documentation, meeting minutes, email, letters, or contemporary news sources, such as newspapers, are more typical research sources in the workplace; and these are usually found online or in company files. Additionally, a writer may have to gather primary research by conducting face-to-face interviews with subject matter experts or collecting data from custom-made surveys. One obstacle many working writers run into that they may not have experienced in an academic setting is the use of documentation that now has copyright attached to it. This chapter will cover how to gather and appropriately handle all of these research artifacts when used in writing and presentations.

GOVERNMENT DOCUMENTS

Although most libraries have a section dedicated to U.S. Government documents, a workplace writer tends to use the Internet to retrieve government information and publications. For the sake of credibility, only official government websites should be used to gather this information. Furthermore, when using a particular office or agency, only hyperlinks from official websites should be used. For instance, to get to the National Institute of Standards and Technology (NIST), a writer should begin at an official website, such as *www.usa.gov,* and then search for NIST on that website.

Government websites offer incredible resources now. In addition to basic information about an office or agency, these sites also have databases of news releases, publications, resources such as job postings, fact sheets, products and services links, and information and forms about programs, grants, requests for proposals (RFPs), and other funding opportunities. Most sites also customize their information for specific audiences, such as on the NIST site (*www.nist.gov*), where in addition to all of the links mentioned above, they also have portals for industry, researchers, news media, the general public, and children.

Using Government Documents in Written Communication

Many think that government documents are part of what is called the public domain. *Public domain* means information or documents that have no copyright or cannot be copyrighted. To some extent, this does include government information, such as information about an office or agency, but it does not include the publications and resources that are found on or linked to official government sites. When searching the NIST site, the link General Information tells readers what NIST is, what programs it has, where its locations are, what they do, and other organizational information. This information is intended to be shared with the public, and therefore can be considered public domain. Conversely, when clicking on the link Publications under Products and Services, any documents retrieved from the database may be the property of individual authors, corporations, or other agencies, and, therefore, have to be cited when used in written communications or presentations. Guidelines for how to cite common types of government sources can be found in appendix B.

Helpful Government Websites

When looking for general government publications but are not certain what office or agency would have the documents needed, one alternative is to use the official U.S. Government Printing Office (GPO) site at *www.gpo.gov* or *www.gpoaccess.gov*. The GPO is the official clearinghouse for all government documentation, which is indeed part of the public domain and can be used without any restrictions (except where noted).

For local government resources, *www.usa.gov* has a page with links to official state government websites, such as *www.usa.gov/Agencies/State_ and_Territories.shtml;* however, this is not the only website that lists the official links for state and local governments. Additionally, for information about countries around the world, the U.S. Department of State has helpful information at *www.state.gov/countries*. It is a good idea to build a folder of bookmarks to official government sites that are used most often in one's line of work (see sidebar for other options).

Tagging the Internet

Internet technology is evolving and along with that is the ability to save or "tag" information. Tagging on the Internet is a way for ordinary users to organize Web content or label websites. Tagging involves marking keywords in content versus bookmarking entire websites. Furthermore, tagging allows users to create their own system for organizing content. One unique aspect of tagging is that tags can be accessed from any computer because they are stored on the Internet and not on individual computers like browser bookmarks are. There are several sites to get more information on tagging. One such site is *http://del.icio.us/about/*.

COMPANY DOCUMENTATION

Company correspondence and documentation often are used in workplace writing as research sources. This is usually the case when documents intended for company-wide distribution are being created, when there is a confidential matter being written up, or when outside research sources are not relevant. For example, to write an employee handbook, also known as a policy and procedure manual, official company policies documented in separate reports, memos, letters, or emails may have to be referenced to show continuity of the policy from one document to another or to avoid having to rewrite an entire policy or procedure.

Due to cross-referencing like this, many companies use a document numbering system and an archiving process. Without this type of tracking system, it is difficult to organize and maintain accurate files. Document numbering can be as simple as 07-0001, where each subsequent document put out in the year 2007 will be assigned a new document number, such as 0002, 0003, etc. Document numbering, however, is generally reserved for official documentation, such as anything that states company policy or gives a company's position. So while most memos will not have a document number attached to them, there are a few that would, such as a memo stating an update to the company dress code. On the other hand, business letters routinely sent to clients would not have a document number. The numbering system is helpful in that official documentation can be tracked in a database and filed according to number instead of by memo subject line, document title, or date and subject of a business letter, which would be confusing.

Email also can be used as a source for written communication, and this often happens when confidential matters are being documented, or once again, when an official policy or position is distributed via company email. Email can be used for reports, such as a feasibility or progress report. Sometimes decisions will be made via email and, to document that decision in the official report, it is necessary to reference the email.

Meeting minutes are other records that find their way into reports. In meetings, decisions are made, tasks are assigned, or progress is reported. Any of this information might be pertinent to a document and might have to be referenced. Project progress reports often refer to meeting minutes to document developments on a job.

Sometimes readers want to see these shorter pieces of correspondence or documentation as part of the larger document, and in most cases, copies can be provided, but usually this is done as an appendix so that they do not interfere with the flow of the report.

Contemporary resources often are used in workplace writing to illustrate the timeliness of an issue. In this case, writers might have to reference newspapers or other weekly publications, such as news magazines. Guidelines for citing company correspondence, newspapers, and magazines are shown in appendix B.

COPYRIGHT

Copyright is a legal protection given to writing, music, drama, dance, pictures, graphics, sculptures, movies, and architectural drawings. The reason someone would copyright is for purposes of credibility. Original work should be credited to the originator; thus, copyright protects artists and professionals from others claiming certain works are theirs. This is especially important today with the Internet, where outright plagiarism and other forms of stealing are pervasive.

Like plagiarism, it is of no concern to those prosecuting others who infringed on a copyright whether or not it was intentional. It is important to know that in the United States, no notice has to be given that a work is copyrighted, so just because there is no official note stating a work is protected under copyright law does not mean it is not, and it does not make stealing the work any less punishable.

Technical communicators who choose to use information that is copyrighted have several options before using the work. One is to determine if the use falls under the "fair use" doctrine, and the other is to request permission to use the work.

Fair Use

Fair use is a doctrine, not a law, that says that, in some circumstances, reproducing another person's work without asking is permissible. It is a mistake to believe that any use for educational purposes or where no personal or financial gain is made is considered "fair use." According to the U.S. Copyright Office, "The distinction between "fair use" and infringement may be unclear and not easily defined. There is no specific number of words, lines, or notes that may safely be taken without permission. Acknowledging the source of the copyrighted material does not substitute for obtaining permission." In other words, "fair use" should not be taken for granted, and it is considered on a case-by-case basis. The U.S. Copyright Office also is not as liberal with its definition of what constitutes works in the public domain as may be found on other websites. The official website of the U.S. Copyright Office at *www.copyright.gov* gives examples of when "fair use" may be considered, but makes it clear that it will not determine "fair use" of any work. Unless a writer has a clear understanding of how "fair use" applies to what is being taken from someone else's work, then it is best to ask for permission before using it.

Obtaining Permission

The best way to ensure there is no infringement on someone else's copyrighted work is to ask for permission. This can be done several ways:

- Ask the person directly if such information is provided on the work, such as in the back of a book. Some websites contain information at the very bottom of a home page about how to request permission to use information presented on the site.

- Ask the publisher or company representing the work to provide the author's information so a request can be made.

- Search the U.S. Copyright Office records. According to the official website of the U.S. Copyright Office, records from 1978 to present are searchable online; however, anything prior to 1978 requires a manual search and includes a fee.

Obtaining permission can be a lengthy process, so it is advisable to identify at the start of a project any works that may need permission and have those in process while continuing other work on the project. Information that authors and artists may want to know before granting permission is the purpose, scope, and audience of the project or report in which their work will be used. In addition, they may also want to know the context in which their work will be used, and to what extent the work will be copied, both in the text and how many copies of the report or document will be made.

INTERVIEWING

One of the chief ways a writer in the workplace obtains information is from interviewing subject matter experts or other personnel. Interviewing is actually an art; therefore, preparation is key to conducting a meaningful interview that will yield the results hoped for. Interviewing is not just a matter of thinking of a few questions and then sitting down with the person being interviewed. This section provides guidance on how to appropriately prepare for and conduct a professional interview for the purpose of gathering data.

An *interview* is an exchange between two or more individuals who use a question/answer format for the purpose of gathering information. Interviews happen every day in various situations, such as teacher–parent conferences, physician–patient consults, employers bringing in candidates for a job, lawyer–client consultations, and journalistic interviews. Likewise, a technical writer interviews engineers, information technology personnel, software developers, scientists, and other coworkers for the purpose of obtaining information for various documents, such as technical reports, proposals, or user guides.

An interview should be planned, which means an interviewer must do some homework before meeting up with the interviewee.

Homework

Before taking up another person's time, an interviewer should have a solid idea about the subject of the report, including the scope of the project. The type of document that is to be produced and the purpose also should be well established before bringing someone else into the matter to obtain information. Most interviewees will want to know why they are being interviewed and might request information about the subject, scope, purpose of the document, and intended audience. In other words, interviewees need a context for what they will report to the interviewer during the meeting. To get to this point is similar to preparing a research report. The interviewer should have the subject narrowed down to a working thesis with a list of research questions that have to be answered.

The next task is to identify personnel to interview. There is more to this job than simply naming the person. Interviewees usually want to know why they have been chosen to be interviewed. To answer this, an interviewer should know as much as possible about the interviewee before meeting. It is a good idea for the interviewer to answer the following questions before meeting an interviewee:

- What is the interviewee's background?
- What is the interviewee's area of expertise?
- How has the interviewee been associated with the project?
- What contribution can the interviewee make to the project?

An interviewer who approaches an interviewee without knowing anything about the person is seen as amateur or rude; therefore, it is important to know as much as possible about the person to be interviewed before even setting up the time and place.

Preparing Questions

Questions are what interviewers count on to obtain information from an interviewee, especially for interviewees who are not forthcoming with information. So, plenty of thought and preparation should go into formulating the exact wording, structure, and sequence of the questions to be used.

There are two basic types of questions, and each one is developed to elicit different information from interviewees. Of course, depending on the wording, there are also varying degrees of these basic types of questions:

1. **Open-ended questions.** These are designed to allow interviewees freedom to answer the question with as much or as little information as they want to divulge. Examples of open-ended questions include the following:

   - Tell me about yourself.
   - What is your background in the field of engineering?
   - Is there anything else you can add?

2. **Close-ended questions.** These are designed to narrow answers down to specific information, such as yes/no, or choosing from a list of options, such as multiple-choice questions. Close-ended questions are meant to get only one answer from the interviewees. Examples of close-ended questions include the following:

   – Did you conduct these experiments yourself?
   – How would you rank this product on a scale of 1–10, with 10 being the highest?
   – What is your position title?

Depending on the time allotted, open-ended questions are a good way to begin interviews because they allow the individuals involved in the meeting to warm up to each other; however, some interviewees might prefer to begin the interview with pointed (close-ended) questions and then allow for elaboration toward the end of the meeting. The interviewer needs to gauge the situation, either before the interview or as the interview begins, to determine which set of questions to begin with.

The next thing to consider is the sequence of questions. This, again, often is determined by time. If short on time, it might be a good idea to begin the interview with close-ended questions that will hopefully provide needed information, in which case the open-ended questions will be left for the latter part of the interview, if time allows. If time is not a concern, a mix of open- and close-ended questions can be used. No matter what types of questions are being asked, the sequence should show progression of some sort, such as going from general to specific or vice versa. Take care to order the questions so that interviewees do not have to provide long, detailed explanations to answer a question or jump back to a previous question and re-explain that answer. Question preparation is a key reason why it is so important to have working knowledge of the project before asking another person to devote time to providing you with information. An interviewer who does not know enough about a project to know how to sequence questions should ask for help from those more knowledgeable about the potential content.

Basic Questions to Get Started

If one is at a loss for questions to ask during an interview, a good place to start is with the six basic journalism questions. From here, other more complex or detailed questions may emerge. Below are the six basic journalism questions:

1. **Who?** Who am I interviewing? What is this person's background or connection with the subject material or project? Who will use the information from this project?
2. **What?** What is this person's expertise? What does it have to do with the project? What is the significance of this project?
3. **When?** When did this person begin his or her work on this subject? When did this project begin? When will it end?
4. **Where?** Where will the work on this project take place? Is there some significance to this place? Where will the results be published?
5. **Why?** Why is this project so important? Why would someone want to know the information that results from this work?
6. **How?** How will the information from this project be used?

Conducting the Interview

Once an interviewer has a grasp of the subject, scope of the project, a working thesis, background information about interviewees, and a well-thought-out and planned list of questions, the next thing to do is conduct the interview. Always ask for permission to record an interview. Never pull out a recorder and then ask, because it is likely to make the interviewee insecure or suspicious. Whether a recorder can be used should be established at the time the interview is scheduled. Other important considerations during the actual meeting include the following:

- **Arrive on time and dress appropriately.** Because someone else is taking time out of the day to help with a project, it is only courteous and professional to arrive on time, or even a few minutes early. When conducting an interview in someone else's office or building, it is only courteous and professional to dress according to that environment, so be sure to find out what it is prior to the meeting.

- **Be prepared.** An interviewer should arrive completely equipped for conducting the interview. This means have the list of questions documented and in a format that is easy to keep track of the notes related to each question. Have something to write with and write on because sometimes interviews may be conducted while walking or touring a facility. Even if recording the interview, take notes as best as possible to supplement the audio version. An interviewer should be prepared for just about any scenario because the opportunity to meet with the interviewee at another time might not be possible.

- **Structure the interview.** An interview can be thought of as a verbal report. It should have an introduction, middle, and ending. Begin an interview by thanking the person for taking time to meet. An interviewer also should allow a few minutes to explain the purpose of the project and why the interviewee has been asked to do an interview. The middle is where the list of prepared questions is asked. An experienced interviewer knows that there are times when not every question will be asked, because sometimes they become irrelevant once the interviewee begins explaining answers to other questions. Sometimes, questions may have to be rephrased on the spot as well. Interviewers should be so familiar with their list of questions that this can be done instantaneously. The ending to an interview is where interviewers wrap up the meeting, just as a conclusion wraps up a report. Further details about how to end an interview are discussed below.

- **Maintain eye contact.** One action that a novice interviewer might do and not be aware of is to become so preoccupied with taking notes that little to no eye contact is made with the interviewee. This can make an interviewee feel uncomfortable, and thus, have some impact on the outcome of the meeting. To avoid this common mistake, on the sheet that contains the questions, provide space between questions with visual guides to help keep certain information together, such as blank bullets. When taking notes, jot down key words or phrases. If a quote is particularly intriguing, ask permission to quote. In this way, the interviewee understands that extra time is being taken to ensure the quote is recorded accurately. This, however, should be a rare occurrence during an interview. This type of interruption is okay if used sparingly, but can be distracting if used too often. Immediately after the interview, either outside of the interviewee's office or in the parking lot, take time to fill in spaces with details of the interview that were not able to be captured during the meeting itself. It is important not to wait too long because information may be lost or misconstrued as more time elapses between the meeting and actually using information from the interview.

- **Pace the interview.** Nervousness can be experienced on both sides of the interview; however, it is up to the interviewer to set the pace of the meeting so that as many of the questions prepared can be answered as completely as possible in the time allotted. Pacing an interview means considering the sequence and structure of the questions. Close-ended questions generally create a fast-paced interaction, whereas predominantly open-ended questions may make the interviewee feel there is plenty of time to cover the information or that only a few questions will be asked. If there is a tremendous amount of information that has to be covered, then close-ended questions are usually best. This can become tedious for the interviewee, however, and the interviewee may get the feeling that it is not appropriate to elaborate on any of the questions when indeed further explanation may be exactly what is needed in some instances. In this case, the interviewer may consider adding an open-ended question after every few close-ended questions, which will give the interviewee a chance to expand on any of the previous answers. Something as simple as saying "Do you want to add anything?" or "Is further information needed to fully understand the concepts from these last few questions?" can be asked every now and then during the series of close-ended questions. Most interviewees will not mind an interview that does not take up the whole period asked for; however, if the interview moves too quickly and only close-ended questions are asked, the interviewee may feel like the experience was not helpful or that the interviewer did not really know what to ask or have time to conduct a thorough interview. Conversely, an interview that drags on into a 20-minute response for one question may compromise the whole meeting because most of the other questions may have to be left out, which would then make the interview incomplete. In this case, interviewers have to be prepared to convert open-ended questions into close-ended questions to pick up the pace of the interview.

- **Ending the interview.** Interviewers should have a watch to keep track of the time during the interview. This helps with pacing, but it also helps to be respectful of the interviewee's time and end the meeting as scheduled. An interview does not end with simply the last question on the list. The last one or two questions should be more open-ended to allow the interviewee to correct or go back and expand on previous questions, and the last question should be one that asks the interviewee for any information that was not covered during the interview. After establishing that the meeting has indeed come to an end, thank the interviewee and ask about follow-up. Ask the interviewee if it would be okay to call, email, or possibly meet a second time if other questions arise as the material is being written up.

Using Recording Devices in Interviews

If wishing to use a recording device during an interview, ask at the time the appointment is made whether a recorder can be used. Before going to the interview, test the recording device for proper functioning. Bring along extra batteries and conduct a mini-test again at the interview site.

Avoiding Problems during the Interview

Even if an interviewer has appropriately prepared for the interview, things still can go wrong, which influences the outcome of the interview and information obtained. Following are certain problems that an interviewer can prepare for to ensure a smooth interaction during the meeting:

- **Cultural differences.** With today's global society, it is not uncommon to have regular contact with people from other countries. Every culture has its level of comfort when it comes to face-to-face meetings. This is where having background information about the interviewee is helpful. Some cultures do not maintain eye contact and consider it rude for certain people to make an effort to do so. Some cultures are not comfortable with the direct approach that many Americans are accustomed to when it comes to asking questions, especially for journalistic endeavors. Knowing the cultural background of the person being interviewed, along with his or her professional experience, will help an interviewer avoid potentially embarrassing or damaging interactions during a meeting.

- **Setting.** To some extent, the interviewer may be able to control the setting in which an interview takes place. Conducting an interview in a coffee shop or other crowded place is not a good idea for several reasons. First, there may be difficulty hearing each other, especially when recording the interview, in which case either party could become confused or frustrated, or the wrong information could result from the meeting. In addition, an interviewee may feel uncomfortable talking about certain topics in public and, as a result, might not be truthful or willing to share pertinent details. When it is up to the interviewer to set the time and place for the meeting, a location that is convenient for the interviewee should be chosen. It also should allow for some privacy and not be too noisy. When it is not up to the interviewer, if the interviewee suggests a public, noisy place, it is not out of line to ask for something quieter, using noise as the reason and not necessarily privacy. Or, if the interviewee wants to meet in a restaurant, suggest a less busy time when not as many people are around. In the end, when it is not up to the interviewer, it is customary to choose a location that is best for the interviewee, however, be prepared to deal with certain issues and to minimize any problems, such as choosing a corner table away from other customers in a noisy café.

- **Nonverbal language.** Body language makes a difference in how people interact with one another. For Americans, someone who will not look at another person in the eye is usually thought of as having something to hide or just plain rude. This can be especially disastrous when that person is the interviewer. Also, for Americans, an up-and-down nodding head implies understanding or agreement. Some people may do this out of habit or because they are nervous, and one should be especially conscious of this when asking for technical information during an interview, particularly if the explanations are complex or confusing. When an interviewer nods his or her head, the other person is not going to stop until there is body language to indicate otherwise. An interviewer should be conscious of other nervous ticks, such as laughing inappropriately, nail biting, finger tapping on the table, or excessive touching of one's face or hair. It would not hurt to film oneself conducting a mock interview just to watch for body language.

- **Losing control of the interview.** An interviewer is the one who is supposed to be in control of the meeting. This means that the pace and questions asked should be up to the interviewer; however, this is not always the case. Sometimes, an interviewer will run into someone who does one of two things that can throw off an interview or completely render it useless. The first is that the interviewee could be talkative and want to answer every question with a story, even close-ended questions. What usually happens in situations like these is that the interviewee talks about only what he or she wants to talk about or considers important, which could be rather useless information in the end. The other situation is when the interviewee cuts off the interviewer or tells the interviewer that the questions asked are not valid, fair, or useful, and again, the person gives no practical information and instead talks about only what he or she considers important. In either situation, it can be difficult to maintain a courteous and professional demeanor; however, something has to be done.

  As mentioned earlier, there are varying degrees of open- and close-ended questions. In the case of the talkative interviewee, an interviewer has to be prepared to restate questions in an extreme close-ended format, such as asking simple yes/no responses or other one-word answers. While it is not polite to interrupt, a skilled interviewer learns how to interject pointed questions during the storyteller's pauses.

Another tactic is to remind the person about the limited time available during the meeting and that there are vital questions that need to be answered.

For the opposite problem of an interviewee who does not want to share any information, an interviewer has to be prepared to open up the questions somewhat. An interviewee who does not want to give a lot information usually has a reason for doing so. To help open up this type of interview, rephrase questions and ask what the interviewee considers important regarding a certain issue. Additionally, if the interviewee tells the interviewer that the questions make no sense or are the wrong ones to ask, then remind the interviewee about the purpose and goal of the interview. Ask the interviewee how to reword the question in order to elicit the needed information. Most people are willing to offer their advice and, in turn, will be more willing to share other information.

Either situation is difficult to deal with, and in both situations, the integrity or credibility of the information is altered somewhat from the original intent. This has to be taken into consideration when using the information in a report. Sometimes, these types of interviews are so unsuccessful that an interviewer has to go back to the drawing board and find someone else to interview.

- **Interviewees who demand sign-off.** Especially in journalistic interviews, some interviewees may demand the "right" to read and approve whatever is written regarding them or the interview. It is not a good idea to indulge interviewees in this practice for many reasons, the worst of which could be to never get the person's approval; thus, the whole story or project is compromised. Instead, the best way to deal with this is to assure the person that he or she can review the final document and provide feedback (as long as sensitive information is not included); however, the "right" to sign-off on the final document may not be granted. Some companies actually have a form they use to tell the interviewee about this process before conducting the interview. Depending on the purpose of the interview and rapport the company has with the individual, this may or may not be necessary.

Phone and Email Interviews

Face-to-face interviews are preferable when two people do not know each other well. The reason is obvious in that most people feel comfortable about being interviewed when they can see who is asking the questions and vice versa. Sometimes, this is not possible due to distance or the logistics and time involved. In these cases, phone or email interviews may be substituted. Even though these are alternatives, no less preparation should go into these interviews. Interviewers still have to do their homework and be prepared.

In phone interviews, a good way to begin is to establish a friendly working rapport with the interviewee by allowing the first 5 or 10 minutes for personal and professional introductions. Just like in face-to-face interviews, be prepared to tell the person background information about the project and reasons for conducting the interview with him or her specifically. Because body language is not part of a phone interview, it is essential to be an active listener who knows when the interviewee is finished with an explanation or is simply pausing or thinking. Do not be afraid to allow reasonable moments of silence. Filling every silent moment with a comment or other question may distract the interviewee from thinking through an answer completely. One way to make sure the interviewee is not cut off prematurely is to ask, "Is there more you would like to add to this before we move on to the next question?" Structuring and pacing the interview still apply to phone interviews, as do the other problem areas mentioned in the section above.

An email interview is probably the easiest to work with because the answers are written out for the writer, but as with the other types of interviews, they are no less work to set up. Again, research on the project and background of the individual still has to be conducted. While everything for face-to-face and phone interviews still apply, email interviewers have the disadvantage of not being able to reword questions on an as-needed basis. This is where knowing as much as possible about the individual is crucial. If only online interactions have taken place, look back over past emails to get the feel for the openness of the individual. How wordy or direct is he or she in previous emails? How willing to conduct this interview has he or she been? Close-ended questions are probably best for non-willing participants because they lessen the amount of content returned in the email interview.

Open-ended questions will most likely be welcome if the participant is a good writer and/or excited about being part of the project or being interviewed.

The email itself should contain an introduction that offers a basic explanation of the project and reasons for interviewing the recipient. Then, a transition into the list of questions should be provided, such as "The following is a list of questions deemed necessary for the project at this time, so please feel free to elaborate as much as needed or add additional information you consider important if it is not included in this list." As in a face-to-face interview, an interviewer usually concludes with the open-ended question, "Is there anything else you would like to add that we have not covered?" This transition serves as an open invitation to add information as the interviewee answers each question. Email interviews should also end with a thankful closing, contact information, and a request for follow-up should it be necessary.

Follow Up to the Interview

Besides attending to interview notes immediately following the meeting, it is also important to thank interviewees in writing for their time and contribution to the story or project. This can be a simple thank-you business letter, thank-you card, or even an email, the latter being the least formal and appropriate only when the two parties know each other well. This additional thank you tells the interviewee that his or her time and information is valuable, and it shows courteous and professional behavior. A thank you can be simple and short as in the following example:

> Thank you for taking the time to meet with me today to discuss the eye retina scan project. Your knowledge of the specialized equipment needed to make this project successful is valued highly among all team members. If I have any further questions or need to clarify information, I will be sure to call on you. Thank you again for your time and contribution.

Using the Interview Data

Assuring interviewees that nothing said during the interview will be taken out of context or misused is not only a reassurance for them, it is good writing practice. Another important consideration is that an interviewee's information should not always be taken as fact. When it comes time in a report to use information obtained during an interview, a writer has to know the difference between opinion, inference, and fact. Using the interview notes, or when going through an interview transcription, sort facts from opinions and decide how certain facts can be verified. Opinions and inferences from the interviewee can be used, but only if the writing that directly precedes or follows such statements is clear about what they really are. Facts should be presented as facts, and opinions can be used, as long as they are labeled as such in the report.

In technical writing, information from an interview is not generally presented in question/answer format, but instead integrated into the report appropriately so it flows with the rest of the writing, as in the following example:

> The American Medical Association has strong financial ties with pharmaceutical companies, and basically American health care is big business, plain and simple. Some doctors maintain that they do not recommend alternative treatments to patients because there is no research to support the claims of natural remedies (Appadurai 2006); but, the interesting question is why are there no studies when about 62 percent of American adults use some form of alternative therapy (Arias 2004)? One possible answer is that there is no money in prescribing chicken soup for a cold. Mark Smith, MD, a practicing family practice medical doctor of 25 years, agrees, and says that, in his opinion, patients are often viewed as consumers, and their treatment is what drives this nation's medical consumerism (personal communication, April 18, 2002).

In the above example, information from the interview is part of the discussion in the paragraph and flows smoothly with the rest of the text, while the doctor's opinion is clearly presented as such.

SURVEYS OR QUESTIONNAIRES

Sometimes it may be necessary to poll a group of people in order to obtain primary information. This can be part of the process for justifying the development of a new software tool, or possibly when company policy is being challenged continuously. These are times when it is necessary to poll a target population to obtain information before any other decisions are made.

Surveys poll a group of people for the purpose of collecting data. The data is obtained by a set of questions, also called a *questionnaire*. So, essentially, questionnaires are the question portions of surveys. Developing a survey is not a simple task, and a great deal of work goes into creating the questions and forms. In fact, this is probably one of the most time-consuming research methods discussed in this chapter. The process of creating a survey involves many steps, which are explained below.

Identify Purpose and Goal of the Research

The first thing to do when developing a survey is to identify why the survey has to be conducted, and what is hoped to be the end result of such research, as in the example that follows:

> Company dress policy is being challenged every day by at least one individual in the warehouse. Employees are being sent home due to inappropriate dress, which means money is being lost by employees, time is being lost by the company, and production rates are down; however, it is of concern to the company how outside clients perceive the workers. Warehouse employees state they fall into a different category than office personnel and should not be held to the same dress code because they work under much different conditions. For example, all employees reprimanded have been wearing jeans or t-shirts. What is different about the working conditions of the warehouse and office environments, and why do the warehouse personnel need a separate dress code? How can a new dress code also ensure visitors will consider workers are appropriately dressed, which has been linked to their confidence in company products?

Target Population

In the example above, the target population is warehouse personnel. Office personnel are not challenging the dress code, so only warehouse personnel need to be polled. Bringing in too many participants can confuse the results,

What Is an IRB?

An Institutional Review Board (IRB) is a committee in most universities and within certain professions that is concerned with the welfare of human participants in studies and surveys. These committees have several ways of operating depending on the institution. In some instances, researchers may need to complete training and certification before they are able to conduct experiments or surveys, and in other cases, the board oversees and monitors experiments. Usually, approval is needed by such boards before an experiment can begin. Not following the guidelines of an IRB may result in termination of the experiment, personnel, or even legal action.

Institutional Review Boards are mandated by federal law and serve as a way to ensure ethical and safe behavior when dealing with human subjects. The need for such boards resulted from unethical experiments that even caused death, such as the famous Tuskegee experiment where low-income African-American men were diagnosed with syphilis and then studied for decades to watch the progression of the disease. These men were not offered treatment for their condition nor were they even told they were part of a study. Some of the men died from the disease ("What is an IRB?" 2007).

For more information on the Tuskegee experiment, visit *www.npr.org/programs/morning/features/2002/jul/tuskegee/* or *www.npr.org/programs/morning/features/2002/jul/tuskegee/.*

so it is important to narrow the target population. Likewise, polling too few people or not the right population also will render the results of the survey useless. It is not only a matter of deciding who is directly affected by a certain issue or action, but also determining ripple effects as well when deciding whom to allow to participate in a survey.

When determining the target population, make sure the selected population is fair to all groups involved. For example, polling employees who have been working for the warehouse for more than 12 months is unfair to the new employees who should have an equal opportunity to express their opinions on the matter. Every affected group needs to be able to respond to the poll, no matter what their demographics are.

Questions and Results

Qualitative data is information that usually is derived from open-ended questions. Open-ended questions are helpful to identify issues or obtain information that cannot be extracted from numerical data. They allow participants to answer questions in their own words and add as much or as little information as they want. Open-ended questions are usually used when smaller groups are polled because of the time it takes to read each response and extract needed information. Examples of open-ended survey questions are as follows:

- What is your position in this company?
- What is your marital status?

Quantitative data is information that can be put in terms of numbers, such as "10 percent of warehouse personnel are women." This kind of data is usually achieved through close-ended questions where the choices for how to answer questions are limited, such as in multiple-choice, yes/no, or true/false. These questions are used when larger groups of people are polled because responses can be run through programs and the end result is only a number for each question. Usually, close-ended questions can be validated or proven, such as with the following examples:

What is your gender?
☐ Male
☐ Female

What is your age range?
☐ 18–24
☐ 25–33
☐ 34–45
☐ 46 or older

Those taking the survey can choose only one answer and there is no room to explain anything or provide additional information they may think is necessary.

No matter whether one wants qualitative or quantitative data, all questions should be reviewed continuously to make sure they match research objectives and are fair and unbiased.

Another consideration when developing questions is to decide if a scale is wanted or needed. This is sometimes substituted for an open-ended opinion question, such as with the following question:

The dress code for the company is appropriate and fair for all employees.

☐ Strongly agree

☐ Agree

☐ Neutral

☐ Disagree

☐ Strongly disagree

It is also important to decide if participants can "opt out" of a question by allowing them a choice of "don't know" or "not applicable." Forcing participants to answer a question by not providing such an option has its benefits in that they have to make a decision, but this could backfire because maybe the options in the answer are not representative of the truth of a situation.

Choosing the right language is essential when developing survey questions. It is often more effective to choose friendly, conversational language rather than strictly formal and possibly confusing wording when writing survey questions. A good way to gauge the effectiveness of the language as well as the types of questions is to test the survey on a sample of the target population to get their reactions and feedback.

There are several reasons why surveys fail to meet objectives, including the following:

- **The purpose of the survey is not explained clearly.** People want to know why they are being asked to give information to sometimes complete strangers. If a clear explanation about the purpose is not provided, many people may choose not to participate, or if they do, they may not take the survey seriously and so intentionally answer erroneously.

- **Directions are not provided or are not clearly stated.** What seems common sense or self-explanatory to one may not be to another, so it is essential to include clear directions about how to complete the survey.

For instance, is only one answer per question allowed or can as many as apply to a participant's situation be chosen?

- **Participants do not know if the information is confidential.** State clearly if the information is confidential or will remain anonymous. This may influence how much information participants are willing to provide, especially in personal matters or issues that might affect their position in the company.

- **Surveys are not turned in on time.** A closing date should be clearly indicated at the top of the survey with the directions. If surveys are not being returned, it may be helpful to send out reminders about the impending closing date.

- **Questions are too long and participants lose interest or become confused.** Word questions clearly and concisely. Test surveys on a sample of the target population to get further feedback on this aspect of the survey.

- **There is no motivation to participate.** Response rate to surveys are usually fairly low unless there is some motivator behind taking the survey. If the response rate is too low, then the results can be deemed inconclusive and the survey will have to be developed all over again. It is best to consider motivating factors before sending out a survey so that the response rate will be high enough the first time around.

ANNOTATED BIBLIOGRAPHIES

Research, as seen from the many sources from which it can be obtained, can be complicated. It is easy to get confused about what information came from what source, whether or not it is credible information, how or where it should be used in a report, and if permission is required to use it. One of the best ways to organize research is to create a working annotated bibliography right from the start.

An annotated bibliography contains bibliographic information and an annotation. *Bibliographic information* is a complete citation of a source written according to a formal style guide. An *annotation* is a short summary of the material being used from that source. Annotations can have different information in them depending on what is most useful to the writer; however, the most common type of annotation is the summary. Annotations also can include an assessment of the credibility of the source, as well as a determination about whether the research is applicable to the report, and if so, how it will be used. The anatomy of an entry on an annotated bibliography is as follows:

A: Bibliographic information: Complete source information is formatted according to a style guide. In this case, the style is APA.

Ⓐ Tagg, J. (2003). *The Learning Paradigm College.* Bolton: Anker Publishing Company, Inc., 4–11.

B: Summary of the pages noted in the bibliographic information above.

Ⓑ Tagg asks administrators, teachers, and other college staff, "What are colleges for?" This question is what many schools are finding to be the most challenging because it is often ignored. It is ignored because people become accustomed to their environment. Despite changes to programs, curriculum, assessment, and even operations, Tagg challenges readers to consider how well colleges are educating their students.

C: This small paragraph is an assessment paragraph that determines the author's and source's credibility.

Ⓒ Tagg is a respected author, speaker, and educator, and his credentials are cross-referenced to other sources. The book is thoroughly researched and well cited; therefore, the information is considered credible for purposes of this report.

D: This short statement reminds the writer where this information can be used in the report that is being written.

Ⓓ The first chapter of this book is important to the report because it will help establish the seriousness of why teachers need to regularly reflect on their teaching practices.

While it may seem like a lot of work to put together an annotated bibliography of all working research sources, the time is actually minimal, and the payoff tremendous; information is organized and the short summary paragraphs remind a writer about the overall message of the source, as well as how it may relate to the document under construction.

REFERENCES

Tagg, J. 2003. *The learning paradigm college.* Bolton, MA: Anker Publishing Company, Inc.

"What is an IRB? 2007." *Banner Health.* 9 December 2007. *www.bannerhealth. com/Research/For + Research + Investigators/ What + is + IRB.htm.*

CHAPTER 15

Professional Document and Page Design

C reating professional documents involves both effective writing and page design. In chapter 6, an introduction to effective page design and use of visuals was presented. Because technical documents often include complex information, use of visuals and clear page design are needed to increase the reader's understanding of the material. This chapter will address the preparation of professional documentation including the use of visuals and elements of page design. In a more advanced fashion, the topics related to page design, such as using visuals to increase the clarity of technical documents, appropriate font selection, and placement of visuals, will be covered.

DESIGN FORMATS

There are differences between page design and information design in a technical document. *Page design* is concerned primarily with the visual appeal of graphics, color, illustrations, and other elements on a page. When designing for the layout of print information, issues such as typography, page layout, flow of text, and word choice are considered *information design*.

The differences between print and electronic mediums need to be considered as well. Print design involves a two-dimensional approach with a high level of attention paid to layout. Readers can turn the pages of a newspaper or magazine, but it is a fixed format, with little interactivity.

Web pages simultaneously appear one-dimensional and n-dimensional. When used in the design of Web pages, *n-dimensional,* which stems from a mathematical term, refers to hypertext navigation throughout the site. A Web page does not lay out like a printed, two-dimensional magazine or newspaper. Instead, it is a scrolling experience. Readers can scroll through multiple screens and are not bound to information contained on an individual page.

VISUALS

The purpose of using visuals in technical documents is to clarify information for the readers. Before discussing the type of visuals often included in technical documents, an overview of the types and purposes of visuals is in order. Visuals can be used to represent the following components in technical documents:

- **Numbers.** A narrative description of complex data can be confusing to readers. It is useful to present this same data in a table or chart.

- **Objects.** A document that includes the description of an object, such as an airplane engine, should include a visual to show readers what the object looks like, the location of various parts, and the like. Pictures, drawings, diagrams, and schematics show information about objects.

- **Words.** Visuals may be used to represent or highlight text. A sidebar is an example of using a basic visual to break up large portions of text and emphasize related or additional information. Highlighting and color can be used as part of the page design process to draw a reader's attention to key points.

- **Ideas or concepts.** A document that compares one concept to the next might be depicted through organizational charts or flow charts, which show the hierarchy and relationship between the concepts.

Visuals should be used when it is necessary to provide complex information in a format that is easy to read or understand. However, when using visuals in a technical document, place text discussions near the visual. Confusion can occur if a visual appears without a description of the information it represents. The following guidelines should be kept in mind when using and designing visuals:

- Ensure the visual is appropriate to the audience. Be sure a visual is not too complicated as to cause confusion.

- Use titles, numbered titles, and keys or legends to explain information.

- Document sources for any information borrowed from outside references. This includes data, text, illustrations, charts, and graphs.

- Keep the visual within the standard margins of the document. If the visual does not fit, enlarge or reduce the visual. At least two line spaces should be placed above and below the visual.

- Place visuals near their description in the text. However, if a visual does not fit on the page, it should be placed on the following page. Do not split graphs or charts between pages.

- Cross-reference all visuals to the appropriate text. In the cross-reference, provide the figure number, indicate the subject matter of the visual, and provide additional information, if needed.

Cultural Considerations

When designing a technical document, it is important to remember that visual language, like spoken and written language, varies among cultures. For example, individuals from Western countries typically read graphics from left to right; the Japanese read from right to left (Stevenson 1983). Some technical symbols are used worldwide; however, not all technical symbols are the same across cultures.

When designing objects or pictures, cultural considerations come into play as well. Hand gestures, dress, and even where individuals sit in certain business situations have different meanings in different cultures. Colors also have different meanings across cultures. For example, the United States typically views yellow as a sign of caution or cowardice. However, the color yellow

Working with the Gestalt Principles

The Gestalt Principles are the theories of visualization researched by a team of psychologists in the 1920s. These principles explain how individuals see graphic elements. They are explained by five basic ideas and shown in figure 15.1.

- Similarity explains that individuals interpret pieces as a whole if they are similar in color, shape, or size. This allows for designers to create emphasis by breaking a pattern and changing one of these elements. This anomaly allows the item to sit apart from the rest without changing its physical location on a page.

- Continuation describes the ability of an item to direct a viewer's attention to another item or to see units as a whole based on the design. Curved lines or directional symbols such as arrows allow for the flow of visual information from one graphic element to the next.

- Closure clarifies the ability of viewers to see an item as complete regardless of the empty space and unfinished image. Positive and negative space work together and are seen as one item rather than separate pieces.

- Proximity refers to the location of pieces in a whole and how they are viewed as a group because they are close together. Uniform distance between pieces allows for them to be perceived as a whole.

- Figure and ground offer a view of elements on two different plains in an image. The figure is the graphic image while ground refers to the background on which the figure rests.

suggests prosperity in Egypt, grace in Japan, and femininity in other parts of the world (Thorell and Smith 1990).

In an effort to avoid confusion across cultures, it is important to review graphics with someone familiar with the customs of that country.

Tables

Tables may be used to help readers find information quickly. In a narrative description involving numerical data, it may take readers time to process the numbers and then analyze what the data mean. Common forms of tables include informal tables, which flow into the body of the text, tables with

FIGURE 15.1 *Gestalt Principle Images*

Similarity:
Despite the difference in shape, the figure is seen as one item because each piece is the same color.

Continuation:
The line segments are seen as one rather than four distinct pieces going in opposite directions due to the continuation through a center point.

Closure:
Even though the main shape is not finished, it is clear that it is a circle.

Proximity:
The five diamonds are seen as one item due to the location of each. They are close together, uniform distance apart, and create a pattern or entire object.

Figure and ground:
The white square sits on a black background, delineating that the two are in separate fields.

numerical data and text, and tables with text only. Selection of the type of table depends on the information the writer would like to present to the reader. Examples of the various types of tables are shown in tables 15.1–15.3.

An informal table is included directly in the body of the text. The information presented in the table is easily understood with the preceding sentence describing what the table is about. An example informal table is shown in Table 15.1

Using a table with text can present information to readers in a format that is easier to read than paragraphs.

TABLE 15.1 *Informal Table*

Average housing prices in the Midwest region have shown a steady increase in the past four years.

2004	$150,000
2005	$152,000
2006	$158,000
2007	$160,000

TABLE 15.2 *Table with Numerical Data and Text*

Table 34 Ⓐ
Quarterly Sales Report for Divisions Ⓑ

Thousands of Dollars Ⓒ

Product	North Ⓔ	South	Central
Laptops	$250.05	$340.54	$609.83
Printers Ⓓ	450.54	321.98	439.00
Ink	123.00	876.11 Ⓕ	512.76
Desktops	719.67	854.00	748.43
Monitors	527.34	621.67	763.32

Source: Annual report Ⓖ

A: Table number

B: Title: Be short and specific

C: Units of measurement

D: Headings: Use clear and precise wording

E: Column headings: Use clear and precise wording

F: Data: Align right or on decimal point

G: Source: Identify source of information unless it is obvious to readers

TABLE 15.3 *Text-Only Table*

Employee Name	Position
Jill Snow	Marketing Manager
Mike Cross Ⓐ	Acccountant
Lisa Stevens	Art Designer

A: Alignment: Align text on the left or center within the column

Graphs and Charts

Graphs and charts are visuals used to display relationships between two or more variables, or to show trends. When creating charts or graphs, keep in mind the following:

- **Keys.** Bar graphs, pie charts, and line graphs often use color, shading, or line style to distinguish one variable from the other. To avoid confusion define the information in a key or legend (a text box near the visual).

- **Axis labels.** Graphs and charts need to include a description of what the x-axis (horizontal) and y-axis (vertical) mean. For example, one axis might indicate the amount of sales in one year; the other axis might indicate the type of product sold.

- **Titles.** Titles should be included above or below graphs and charts so that the reader can easily identify the context of the information. If more than one chart or graph is to be used in the document, include a number title as well.

- **Sources.** Information that is used from an outside source needs to be documented at the end of the graph or chart. Sources need to be included for any borrowed information regardless of whether the graph or chart was created by the writer, photocopied and pasted into the document, or drawn freehand.

Graphs may be simple in design, as in an example of showing data points only; or complex, as in the example of showing interaction among variables. These examples are shown in figures 15.2 through 15.6. When deciding on the type of graph to use to represent information or data, reflect on the purpose of using the graph. Review options for graph style and decide which format would represent the information clearly and accurately. The following examples illustrate a series of graph styles, all representing the same data: growth of an example account across four quarters.

The scatter graph may be used to show individual data points rather than graphed lines. This simple design allows readers to see easily the

FIGURE 15.2 *Scatter Graph*

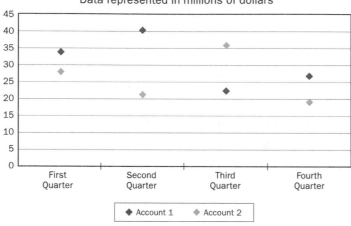

Account Growth across Four Quarters
Source: Sample Company's 2008 Annual Report
Data represented in millions of dollars

◆ Account 1   ◆ Account 2

FIGURE 15.3 *Line Graph*

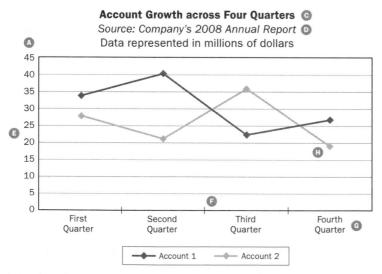

Figure 1 Ⓑ

Account Growth across Four Quarters ⒸFigure
Source: Company's 2008 Annual Report ⒹData
Data represented in millions of dollars

◆ Account 1   ◆ Account 2

A: Axis length: Make the y-axis slightly longer than the highest value on the graphed line

B: Figure number

C: Title: Be clear and concise

D: Source: Provide a source for referenced material

E: Labels for y-axis: Be clear and concise; avoid vague abbreviations

F: Tick marks: Provide tick marks to show units

G: Labels for x-axis: Be clear and concise in naming

H: Data points: Points that introduce a new piece of data

Resources for Using Graphics

The University of Texas at Austin's Writing Center provides a handout on integrating visual aids into text. *http://projects.uwc.utexas.edu/handouts/?q=node/28*

Mississippi State Agricultural Information Science and Education's page provides information on using graphics, charts, and graphs. *www.ais.msstate.edu/AEE/Tutorial/graphs.html*

comparison between two or more variables. In a graph illustrating trends or growth, one data point would be marked on the graph, allowing the reader to view the trends across a specific period of time.

Line graphs serve the same purpose as scatter graphs, but the difference lies in the visual effect. Instead of only marking data points, you would include lines to connect the information. Deciding between these two types of graphs is dependent on the look of the visual the writer wishes to create.

Bar or column graphs are used most effectively to compare quantities and view trends easily. Multiple bars are used to show a trend over a period of time. In the example of account growth across four quarters, two bars are used to assist readers in seeing the comparison between the two accounts. When designing a bar or column graph, try to begin the bars at zero to avoid misleading the reader. Use color, if possible, to highlight individual bars. Various colors will help readers easily see the differences between the variables. This is especially important when using graphs with multiple bars. Figures 15.4 and 15.5 show the comparison of the data in two different formats.

An area graph is used to compare two or more variables. Instead of showing only lines and data points, the percentage of the area is colored or shaded. This type of graph allows for an easy comparison between the variables. Figure 15.6 is an area graph using the extended example of account growth across four quarters.

FIGURE 15.4 *Bar Graph*

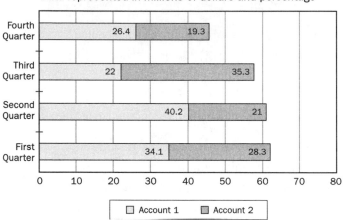

Account Growth across Four Quarters

Source: Company's 2008 Annual Report
Data represented in millions of dollars and percentage

FIGURE 15.5 *Column Graph*

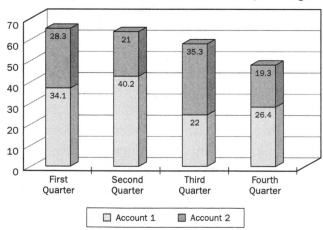

Account Growth across Four Quarters

Source: Company's 2008 Annual Report
Data represented in millions of dollars and percentage

FIGURE 15.6 *Area Graph*

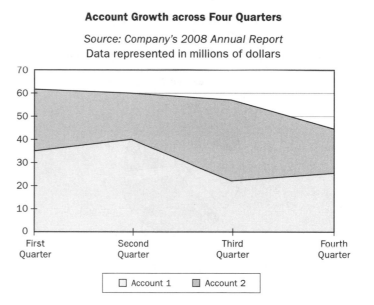

Account Growth across Four Quarters

Source: Company's 2008 Annual Report
Data represented in millions of dollars

Charts

A pie chart is used to compare parts to a whole in numerical data or text. When designing pie charts, it is important to ensure that all parts of the pie chart add up to 100 percent. Plus, in an effort to create a clear and concise visual, use fewer than eight wedges. Eight or more wedges reduce the visibility of data, and the comparison between the parts is not seen easily. If there are several similar categories that can be grouped together, create an "Other" category. This category can capture the data without causing clutter on the pie chart by having too many smaller categories. In the narrative portion of the written document, be sure to define what items are captured in the "Other" category.

If a particular wedge needs to be emphasized more than another, a contrasting color should be used. Use of contrasting color that is much lighter or darker than the other colors in the pie chart will draw the readers to that particular wedge. Another technique to draw attention to a particular section of the pie chart is to pull out the wedge, as illustrated in figure 15.7.

FIGURE 15.7 *Pie Chart*

Account Growth across Four Quarters

Source: Company's 2008 Annual Report
Data represented in millions of dollars and percentage

Account 1

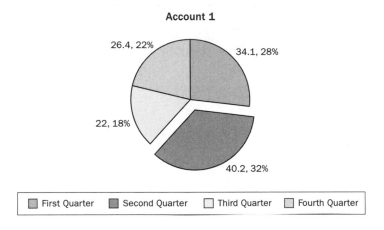

First Quarter   Second Quarter   Third Quarter   Fourth Quarter

Although there are several different styles of pie charts available, it is important not to create visual distortion among the data. Often, three-dimensional pie charts can give the illusion that one section looks larger than the other. Therefore, two-dimensional pie charts are recommended to avoid this potential distortion. Graphics, like words, can be misleading. When using visuals in professional documents, writers have an ethical obligation to avoid leading readers to the wrong conclusion. Examples of two- and three-dimensional pie charts are shown in figures 15.8 and 15.9. In the three-dimensional pie chart in figure 15.9, notice the way the percentages look distorted based on the view of the pie wedge.

Flowcharts and organizational charts are also common in professional documents. A flowchart helps readers follow a process or see options in decision making. An organizational chart is used to show hierarchy among members of an organization or hierarchy in a process. An example flowchart illustrating the process for the literature review in a dissertation is shown in figure 15.10. An example of the ways charts can provide a comparison of roles of relationships in an organization is shown in figure 15.11.

FIGURE 15.8 *Two-dimensional Pie Chart*

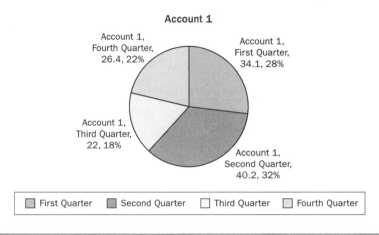

Account Growth across Four Quarters

Source: Company's 2008 Annual Report
Data represented in millions of dollars and percentage

Account 1

Account 1,
Fourth Quarter,
26.4, 22%

Account 1,
First Quarter,
34.1, 28%

Account 1,
Third Quarter,
22, 18%

Account 1,
Second Quarter,
40.2, 32%

☐ First Quarter   ☐ Second Quarter   ☐ Third Quarter   ☐ Fourth Quarter

FIGURE 15.9 *Three-dimensional Pie Chart of Account Growth across Four Quarters*

Account Growth across Four Quarters

Source: Company's 2008 Annual Report
Data represented in millions of dollars and percentage

A: Visual distortion: The 22% wedge looks significantly larger than the 18% wedge. This distortion occurs because the reader sees both the top and the side of the pie wedge.

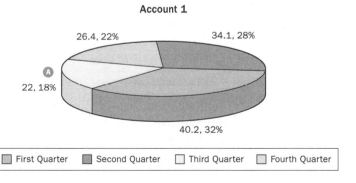

Account 1

26.4, 22%   34.1, 28%

22, 18%

40.2, 32%

☐ First Quarter   ☐ Second Quarter   ☐ Third Quarter   ☐ Fourth Quarter

FIGURE 15.10 *Schema for Review of the Literature for A Case Study on Educational Leader Perspectives*

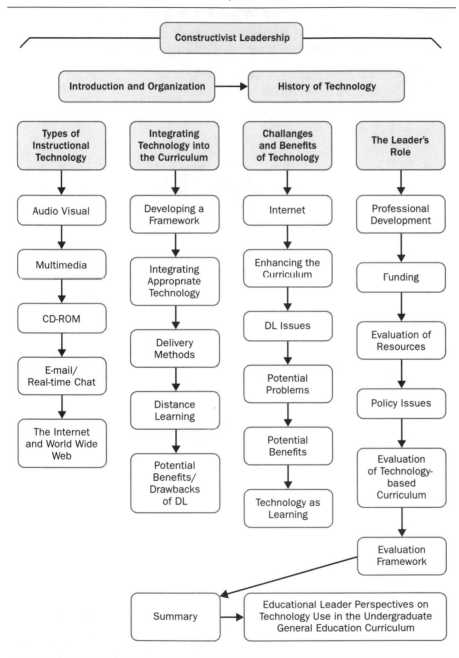

FIGURE 15.11 *Model of Participant Leadership Styles*

Participant Name	Position	College	Leadership Style	Example Illustrating Leadership Style
John	Dean	William Wallace	Visionary	Looks for ways to improve curricula; interested in new technologies for improving the way things are done. Discussed future growth of the college and the department.
Kate	Vice President of Information Services	William Wallace	Visionary	Looks for future uses of technology in the college and curriculum.
Julie	Director of Faculty Development, Faculty Member	William Wallace	Constructivist	Works in collaboration with others to bring about use of Prometheus at an institutional level. Holds workshops and "brown bag" lunches to promote collaboration of ideas among every member of the learning community.
Connie	Dean	Jane Byrne	Participatory	Oversees and administers changes for departmental growth in technology use, such as the integration of BlackBoard into the distance learning courses.
Kathy	Assistant Dean	Jane Byrne	Transformational	"Fix it" mentality; describes herself as a "change person"; enjoys new challenges and once "things are fixed, stalls a bit."
Christine	Faculty Member	Jane Byrne	Roving	Participates when needed; steps back once the initial challenge has been met. Wants to initiate a new project but does not want to administer it.

Pictures

Pictures or photographs make effective visuals when used to do the following:

- Assist readers in understanding material
- Locate an object
- See how something looks

Photographs also can help readers see the condition of an object. When using photographs and pictures, include only information readers will find helpful. Crop any information that takes away from the purpose of the photograph or picture. Photographs are most often used in feasibility, recommendation, and evaluation reports, and in user guides and instruction sets. Figure 15.12 is a sample photograph of water lilies. Using a photograph in addition to text can help readers visualize how something looks in greater detail than narrative text can provice.

FIGURE 15.12 *Photograph*

Using Pictures in Documents and Email

Photographs or pictures can help emphasize main points or present a visual concept more effectively than text alone. The following tips can assist in adding photographs or pictures to Microsoft documents or email.

Inserting pictures into Word, Excel, or PowerPoint files:

Once a picture is saved on the computer, there are different ways to place the image into the document or email, as outlined below:

- Click on the Insert Picture icon (shown below on the Drawing toolbar in Word, Excel, or Power-Point) to browse to and select the desired pictured to be added to the file. The option to insert a picture from a file is also available on the Insert menu in each program. If the Drawing toolbar does not automatically appear at the bottom of the screen in Word, Excel, or PowerPoint, go to the View menu, select Toolbar, and then click on Drawing.

- Pictures or graphics may be copied and pasted in Word, Excel, or PowerPoint instead of inserting them. On the Edit menu, click Paste Special to open a dialog box. Select from available picture formats to find the best resolution of the image.

- To add pictures or images to an email message, the images can be either inserted or copied, and pasted into the body of the email. Compressing the file in a zip or JPEG format will avoid sending large files.

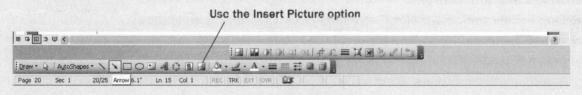

Use the Insert Picture option

Compressing Pictures and Photographs

Programs such as Microsoft Word feature the ability to control the image size of photographs and pictures. One of the drawbacks is that there is little control over the resolution of the images. The images can be cropped to a smaller size, but Word stores the entire image with the file, creating large file sizes that make documents difficult to share via email and that consume a considerable amount of hard drive space.

Word does offer a "Compress Pictures" feature, which is a button on the Pictures toolbar. While this feature does not allow much control over the editing of photographs or pictures, it does assist in managing the size of the files. To use the "Compress Pictures" feature, follow these steps:

1. Click on a picture in the document.

2. On the **Picture** toolbar, click the **Compress Pictures** button (it is the button with arrows at all four corners).

3. Open the **Compress Pictures** dialog box.

4. To apply changes to all the pictures in the document, click on the button beside **All Pictures** in the document in the **Apply** to section.

5. Under **Options,** there is a feature to compress picture(s) and/or to delete the cropped areas of the picture(s) by selecting the appropriate box.

6. Once all changes have been made, click **OK.**

Creating JPEG files is another way to compress files. JPEG files need to be created prior to placing the images into the document.

Drawings and Illustrations

Drawing and illustrations are effective visual choices when attempting to show objects, or the relationships between people and places. Drawings and illustrations may range from simple sketches to detailed drawings. Figure 15.13 shows a simple drawing of a scanner and CD drive that may be appropriate for use in an instruction set. Listed below are some guidelines for using drawings and illustrations in professional documents:

- Use simple drawings or illustrations in user manuals or instruction sets. By keeping the visuals simple, readers can focus on the details of complex information.

- Use detailed drawings when describing a situation or objects. Detail may involve color, shading, or highlighting parts on the drawing or illustration.

FIGURE 15.13 *Simple Drawings of Scanner and CD Drive Appropriate for Use in an Instruction Set*

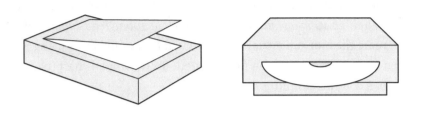

- Include labels, with words or phrases, about the points being described.

- Indicate details in a key if color, shading, or highlighting is used. Readers will need to know the meaning of the details.

- Include a title in a drawing or illustration to cross-reference within the text.

- Place drawings and illustrations within the typical margins of the page.

- Create drawings and illustrations within the level of technical detail understood by readers. The purpose of using drawings and illustrations is to simplify information for readers, not cause confusion.

Converting Word Documents into PDF Files

Converting files into PDF files allows readers to view a document, regardless of the software package being used. If users are using an incompatible software package, they will not be able to open the file. Most computers come with Adobe Reader as standard software. Adobe Reader allows users to open any Adobe document that has the file extension .pdf, which stands for Portable Document Format. Although the file is sent as a read-only format, users can open and view the file. This is especially useful when files are being sent via email. When files are not compressed in an email document, the images are often too large to view. Additionally, without compressing files, it takes a considerable amount of time to send images as attachments or in the body of the email message.

To convert documents, such as Microsoft Office documents, into PDF files, you can use Adobe Acrobat software. This is available for purchase wherever computers are sold or can be downloaded from Adobe's website. To download Adobe Reader, go to *www.adobe.com/products/acrobat/readstep2.html.*

To create files for the visually impaired and for individuals using a screen reader, a plug-in must also be downloaded. To download the plug-in, go to *www.adobe.com/accessibility/index.html*

Using Color

Working with more than one color in a document allows a designer to emphasize material, add visual interest, and organize information. However, adding color also tends to increase production costs. Depending on the document's audience, purpose, and production budget, color may be a viable option, but it should not be used without a purpose.

Color is often used to emphasize a point, make things more visually stimulating, or highlight transitions. For example, key terms may be put in color within text to draw the readers' attention. Color also might be used on specific pages of a document, such as section or title pages, to differentiate between them and other pages. And, of course, color can be used to enhance visuals in a document, allowing for more visibly discernable graphs, charts, and diagrams.

However, color does not always refer to the traditional concept of white paper, black text, and added colors throughout. Sometimes using color means working with shades of one color, the use of negative space, or colored backgrounds and papers. When production costs are a concern, using shades of one color is a less expensive way to add visual interest. Also, in many production facilities, black ink and colored ink are priced the same. This means that using blue, red, or green text would be the same price as black text and allow for shadings in that color rather than gray.

Choosing Colors. When choosing colors for a document, consider the colors associated with the company or department where the document will be used. An obvious color choice often can be made by looking at the company letterhead or logo. The company color scheme can be seen in these areas most often, or in additional documents produced by the company.

Various color models are used to create colors on computers. The RYB color model refers to the primary colors red, yellow, and blue, and offers variations of the traditional color wheel including red, yellow, blue, orange, green, and violet. The RGB mode, red, green, and blue, adds colors together in different degrees to create hundreds of computer-recognized hues. Also, the CMYK color model works to create various colors using cyan, magenta, yellow, and black. The color model used depends on the printer and/or software used to create the documents.

Contrast may be sought when choosing colors; however, appealing color combinations should be the goal of the designer. Basic color knowledge is all a designer needs in order to choose an attractive palette. This knowledge would include the primary colors, what they create when combined, and the idea of contrasting colors. The three primary colors are red, blue, and yellow. When combined, red and blue make purple, red and yellow make orange, and yellow and blue make green, the three secondary colors. Contrasting colors are found opposite each other on the color wheel containing both primary and secondary colors: red and green, blue and orange, and yellow and purple. These color combinations are high contrast. However, these combinations may not be the best choice for your situation, and none of these blends includes the traditional black, white, or gray.

TEXT AND LAYOUT

Video games, movies, and other audio-video productions have made words on a page boring to some audiences. However, page and document design can pull readers in to the information, helping them work from one point to the next, guiding them and offering visual cues. How the text is placed on a page and its organization, along with the use of color and visuals, make up the *layout* of the document, and offers readers a way to relate to the information. Creating visual elements by dividing and placing text also shows readers what information should be considered related, and offers a piece of design even if color and graphics are absent.

Organizing information is a large part of writing and document design. While a technical communicator may be assigned only one of these tasks, it is beneficial and necessary to know how to organize text, how to display it on a page, and how these things influence readers. Chapter 5 sheds light on a number of information organization strategies, giving insight as to how different approaches guide readers through information.

Similar to other aspects of technical communication, text layout depends on a number of things, but none more than audience and purpose. Determining the purpose and audience of the document allows for layout designs, such as which information should be grouped, what the size of the text should be, and which visuals should be used.

Chunking

Chunking text refers to breaking it into pieces that make it easier for the audience to read. Chunking can be basic, such as forming paragraphs, or drastic, such as grouping lines of text and placing them carefully on a page. Regardless of the complexity, chunking groups information for display and comprehension.

Designers and writers should avoid presenting solid blocks of text. They are difficult to read through, and readers can be lost in the midst of them. Instead, offering smaller blocks of text helps readers focus visually. This also keeps pieces of related information together, thereby aiding in comprehension.

Chunking can be found on most websites because reading online documents requires staring at a screen and scrolling, two things aided by separating text effectively. Readers trying to skim through information in order to find the needed material will have an easier time when reading short lumps of related text that are separated from other information. Examples of text before it was chunked and after are shown below:

Text before Chunking

Employees' attire should be professional and meet all company guidelines. Clothing should fit well and be position-appropriate. Failure to meet dress code guidelines will result in suspension for the day without pay and will continue until the employee complies with dress policy. Those working in the field are expected to dress for the climate, wear steel-toed work shoes and work site appropriate head gear (e.g., hard hats for construction zones), and have clothing free of rips, holes, or cuts. Cut-offs or homemade shorts, tank tops, or sleeveless shirts should not be worn. Office employees are expected to dress in business attire Monday–Thursday, but may wear business casual dress Friday and Saturday. Shorts, sandals, capris, tank tops, and sleeveless shirts should not be worn. Jeans may be worn on business casual days only.

Chunked Text

Employees' attire should be professional and meet all company guidelines. Clothing should fit well and be position-appropriate. Failure to meet dress code guidelines will result in suspension for the day without pay and will continue until the employee complies with dress policy.

Those working in the field are expected to dress for the climate, wear steel-toed work shoes and work site appropriate head gear (e.g., hard hats for construction zones), and have clothing free of rips, holes, or cuts. Cut-offs or homemade shorts, tank tops, or sleeveless shirts should not be worn.

Office employees are expected to dress in business attire Monday–Thursday, but may wear business casual dress Friday and Saturday. Shorts, sandals, capris, mini skirts, tank tops, and sleeveless shirts should not be worn. Jeans may be worn on business casual days only.

Dividing the information offers visual queues as to which information is related. However, it requires that material be written in self-contained topics. Unlike paragraphs, chunks must be able to stand by themselves as topics because readers might not read every block of information. Chunks are often separated by additional white space, discussed later in the chapter, and they give readers shorter pieces to focus on.

By chunking material, a writer increases the readers' ability to find, read, and remember the information. Reading page-long blocks of text can be tedious; chunks limit strain when reading and encourage readers to access pieces of information rather than the whole document. Because of this reaction, chunking may not be appropriate for every document. For instance, if the intent is that the audience access all of the information in a document, using headings and paragraphs should be enough to encourage that type of comprehension. Chunking may deter them from reading the document from cover-to-cover, and is best used in documents such as quick reference guides and manuals where readers can choose the blocks of information that relate to their particular needs.

When chunking text, authors should remember the following:

- Keep related pieces of information together.

- Write material as self-contained topics that can stand alone.

- Label chunks to offer additional information to the reader.

- Divide large topics into smaller pieces. Outlines can help with this task.

Reading Text on a Page. Depending on the culture, readers approach the text on a page differently. For instance, in the Asian culture, text is read from right to left from the top of the page down. However, Western societies read from left to right, top to bottom. This not only changes how words are placed on a page, but how they relate to text as well.

Most readers in Western societies prescribe to the zigzag pattern of reading, approaching a page left to right across the top, diagonally from top right to bottom left, and from left to right across the bottom, creating a "Z" as they scan the page, regardless of whether it is a left or right page (see figure 15.14). This is important to remember when including text on a page, and especially when combining text and graphic elements. Because of this reading pattern, it is important to focus design elements in particular spots, such as the top and bottom lines and to the bottom left or upper right. These positions have been shown to be key points of entrance for readers. For instance, if readers see a graphic in the top-right corner, they generally begin there. This works well unless there is important information that leads to the graphic that is overlooked. Placing information in the "Z" path gives readers spots to focus on while reading, but it should not overshadow other information or cut it off from the rest of the page.

This pattern increases the importance of page headings or headlines, as they offer key information about the document or page in the key spot, the top line of the page. Also, including graphics along the middle axis of the "Z"

FIGURE 15.14 *Zigzag Reading Pattern*

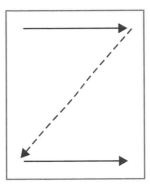

on one side or the other guides the reader down the page. In print documents, special consideration needs to be given to motion on a page. Readers' eyes will actually follow the motion indicated in a visual, such as a golfer's swing. Since it is shown that readers move across the top of the page from left to right, diagonally down the page, and then across the bottom also from left to right, as shown in figure 15.14, motion shown in a visual should follow this pattern. This way, the motion of the visual does not take a reader's eyes off of the page (see figure 15.15). Instead, the motion can be used to draw readers' eyes to a product name, brand name, or other important element on the page (see figure 15.16). For electronic documents, if animation is used, the motion should also be contained on the page. In the example of the golfer, the animation should allow the reader to see the full swing of the golfer, avoiding a portion of the image from being cut off and placed on to another page.

USING WHITE SPACE WITH TEXT

White space is the space found between items on a page. Also called negative space, white space allows for items to be separated, offering an additional design element to a page. Readers may not consider white space as important as the text and graphics on the page; however, the empty space on a page is not wasted. This space, while containing nothing, offers the reader a chance to roam the page and can be created a number of ways with text. It is further discussed in chapter 6.

FIGURE 15.15 *Motion Takes Readers' Eyes Off the Page and Away from the Text*

FIGURE 15.16 *Motion Keeps Readers' Eyes On the Page and Moves Them Toward the Text*

Spacing Lines and Kerning. White space can be controlled by breaking large blocks of text into smaller chunks, but changing the spacing between lines and the kerning of a font, which is the space between letters in a line, also contribute to the effective use of white space. Examples of line spacing and kerning are offered below:

Single line-spacing with normal kerning:

Employees are entitled to a one-hour meal break and two 15-minute breaks per eight hour shift. Employee lunch breaks should be taken according to the posted schedule in order to ensure proper coverage of the sales floor. Short breaks may be taken at any time authorized by the floor manager, but may not be taken in conjunction with any other break.

One-and-a-half line-spacing with kerning expanded by two points:

Employees are entitled to a one-hour meal break and two 15-minute breaks per eight hour shift. Employee lunch breaks should be taken according to the posted schedule in order to ensure proper coverage of the sales floor. Short breaks may be taken at any time authorized by the floor manager, but may not be taken in conjunction with any other break.

Double line-spacing with kerning condensed by one point:

Employees are entitled to a one-hour meal break and two 15-minute breaks per eight hour shift. Employee lunch breaks should be taken according to the posted schedule in order to ensure proper coverage of the sales floor. Short breaks may be taken at any time authorized by the floor manager, but may not be taken in conjunction with any other break.

Leading and Line Length. White space, while associated with the placement of text or the use of graphics, also can be increased or decreased using leading and line length variations. *Leading* refers to the additional space put between lines of text. Unlike line spacing, leading is based on font size and can be controlled in most word processing programs. *Line length* needs little explanation, as it controls the length of individual lines of text.

Changes in leading add space between lines, allowing for additional white space and the spreading out of text. While line spacing offers the options of single, double, and one-and-a-half line height, leading gives writers and designers the option to change the space between the lines based on font points or sizes. For instance, when a document is written in Times New Roman font, a double-spaced document has the same amount of space between lines as a double-spaced document in Arial font. With leading, the line spacing is determined by the font style and the size selected by the writer. Changing the leading allows for different amounts of text to be included in a space and changes in the readability of document, and it alters the overall visual image created by the text. Some examples follow:

Text in 12 point font with 12 point leading:

Employees are entitled to a one-hour meal break and two 15-minute breaks per eight hour shift. Employee lunch breaks should be taken according to the posted schedule in order to ensure proper coverage of the sales floor. Short breaks may be taken at any time authorized by the floor manager, but may not be taken in conjunction with any other break.

Text in 12 point font with 16 point leading:

Employees are entitled to a one-hour meal break and two 15-minute breaks per eight hour shift. Employee lunch breaks should be taken according to the posted schedule in order to ensure proper coverage of the sales floor. Short breaks may be taken at any time authorized by the floor manager, but may not be taken in conjunction with any other break.

Text in 12 point font with 24 point leading:

Employees are entitled to a one-hour meal break and two 15-minute breaks per eight hour shift. Employee lunch breaks should be taken according to the posted schedule in order to ensure proper coverage of the sales floor. Short breaks may be taken at any time authorized by the floor manager, but may not be taken in conjunction with any other break.

Changes to line length also allow for changes in white space. Creating documents that use additional indentation to create blocks or changes in line length allows for visual variations within a document. Sometimes lines will be cut short due to the insertion of elements such as charts, graphs, or pictures. This forced change can be replicated with the use of tabs, indentations, and margins.

Justifying and Aligning Text. While white space is often determined by the line spacing and kerning of the text, *justification* and *alignment* also work to free space on a page. How the text appears on the page and how it lines up with other text or within blocks contributes to where white space is found on a page and how the reader looks at and takes in the information.

Text alignment and justification can be confused, but they are two separate issues. Alignment is the spot on the page where information is lined up, left, center, or right. The most common type alignment is left, with all characters at the beginning of left lines starting at the left margin. This creates a straight line down the left side and a ragged line on the right, which is considered a formal display of information. Sometimes this alignment is also called ragged right because the right side of the text does not align completely but returns to the next line rather than alter the character spacing. This is often used in documents because readers are able to determine the beginning of each line of text with little difficulty, and is shown below:

Left-aligned text:
Employees are entitled to a one-hour meal break and two 15-minute breaks per eight hour shift. Employee lunch breaks should be taken according to the posted schedule in order to ensure proper coverage of the sales floor. Short breaks may be taken at any time authorized by the floor manager, but may not be taken in conjunction with any other break.

Centered text queues text with the center of the margined page, leaving the right and left sides ragged. When margins are changed for the page or text box, centering shifts accordingly, and sometimes it will look as though the text is off to one side due to this fact. Centered text works well with headings or on displayed documents where white space is ultimately needed because it creates the greatest amount around the text, putting space at the beginning and end of each line. However, documents with large portions of text should not be centered as this can be difficult to read, although some websites might use this alignment to separate portions of text from the numerous menu bars included on the site. An example is shown below:

Centered text:

Employees are entitled to a one-hour meal break and two
15-minute breaks per eight hour shift. Employee lunch breaks
should be taken according to the posted schedule in order to
ensure proper coverage of the sales floor. Short breaks may be
taken at any time authorized by the floor manager, but may not
be taken in conjunction with any other break.

Right-aligned text allows a straight line of text at the right margin and creates a jagged beginning to each line. Because of this, it may be more difficult to read right-aligned text that is not adequately spaced between lines. Right-aligned text is also considered a means of informal presentation and can be found in advertisements, brochures, websites, and pamphlets. It allows for white space or graphics to lead into the text and gives readers a visual element with the text because it is generally novel to the eye after reading left-aligned documents. This is shown below:

Right-aligned text:

Employees are entitled to a one-hour meal break and two
15-minute breaks per eight hour shift. Employee lunch breaks
should be taken according to the posted schedule in order to
ensure proper coverage of the sales floor. Short breaks may be
taken at any time authorized by the floor manager, but may not
be taken in conjunction with any other break.

Justified text creates a straight text line on both the right and left sides. In order to do this, the word processing software automatically adjusts the kerning between the characters in each line to create a block of text. While this can sometimes cause awkward spacing, increasing it across the entire line and forcing space between characters, it is a rather formal way to align text in a document and is used in business letters, memos, and legal documents. However, because this alignment creates additional white space within lines, it takes from the white space at the end of the lines as the margins become rigid barriers to the text. These blocks of text, shown below, work well in documents that utilize chunked text or allow for a large amount of white space:

Justified text:

Employees are entitled to a one-hour meal break and two 15-minute breaks per eight hour shift. Employee lunch breaks should be taken according to the posted schedule in order to ensure proper coverage of the sales floor. Short breaks may be taken at any time authorized by the floor manager, but may not be taken in conjunction with any other break.

Using Columns and Text Boxes on a Page. Page design enables writers to turn text into graphical elements with the use of chunks of texts in *boxes* or *columns*. Text boxes give the page designer or writer the ability to set information off to the side, shade it, or put a border around it to create emphasis. These blocks keep chunked portions of text together and give additional freedom for placement of the text as well, especially when working in word processing programs rather than page design programs.

Columns are long blocks of text on a page. There may be multiple columns on one page, and they may or may not go the entire length of the page. Columns can be changed on a page and can work to separate pieces of information. For instance, newspaper layouts might use three columns for one story, and then use the same size block for another but use two columns. This helps create emphasis and avoids the merging of pieces of information. However, in this example, it is important to note that each set of columns is then separated by a headline and sometimes additional graphic elements such as lines.

Regardless of which is chosen, boxes and columns should be used with clear purpose. While columns can allow for more text to be included on a page than regular margin-to-margin layouts, too many or too narrow columns are difficult to read. Also, text boxes, because they become graphic elements, need to be formatted uniformly throughout a document. Boxes may be shaded or bordered to increase their visibility, but the color usage guidelines should then be considered.

Placement of both columns and boxes should follow the zigzag design. While columns are read left to right and down the column before beginning with the next column to the right, when interrupting them with boxes, graphics, or other visual elements, the zigzag design allows for effective placement.

Working with Widows and Orphans

Society easily defines *widows* and *orphans,* but the writing and layout world has far less stringent definitions. However, each refers to information, be it a phrase or word, left alone in a column. The issue comes when the beginning or ending of a sentence is left alone on a page, or a single word is left without its partnering sentence on a line. Abandoned by the rest of the information in the sentence, widows and orphans sit alone and are often forgotten by readers.

Orphans generally refer to the lines of a column or page that represent the first or last portion of a sentence. When these phrases are left alone on a page, the beginning of a sentence on the bottom of one page or column with the remainder on or in the next for example, the result is information that does not flow. A reader could easily forget the beginning of the sentence after turning the page and continuing with the remainder of it, as shown in figure 15.17.

Widows, not unlike orphans, are abandoned pieces of text and shown in figure 15.18. However, widows represent single words that are left alone on a line. These words can be easily overlooked or forgotten, thereby making their accompanying sentences incomplete. A definition issue comes with this concept, though; that is, are all solitary words on a line widows? Some say yes, others say no. For instance, if a two-letter word is left on a line, it would be a widow. But if a 10-letter word is alone on a line, some might consider that to be in fine form. Writers must then consider the word itself and determine if it holds enough weight to anchor a line of text. A general rule to adhere to is six characters plus the final punctuation, making seven characters, as allowable on a line within in a column. However, when dealing with a full page layout, the word should be longer than the standard paragraph indent (half an inch in most circumstances) and must not be the second portion of a hyphenated word in order to stand alone.

FIGURE 15.17 *Orphaned Line*

Employees are entitled to a one-hour meal break and two 15-minute breaks per eight hour shift. Employee lunch breaks should be taken according to the posted schedule in order to ensure proper coverage of the sales floor. However, short

breaks may be taken at any time authorized by the floor manager, but may not be taken in conjunction with any other break.

Employees must follow the company dress code at all company- related functions, not merely during business hours.

In the above illustration the highlighted phrase is considered an orphan because it is a short section of a sentence that ends a column and does not contain enough substantial information to determine the meaning of the sentence.

FIGURE 15.18 *Widowed Word*

Employees are entitled to a one-hour meal break and two 15-minute breaks per eight hour shift. Employee lunch breaks should be taken according to the posted schedule in order to ensure proper coverage of the sales floor. However, short breaks may be taken at any time authorized by the floor manager,

but may not be taken in conjunction with any other break.

Employees must follow the company dress code at all company-related functions, not merely during business hours. These functions include company meetings, parties, conventions, etc.

In the above illustration the highlighted word is considered a widow because it is alone on a line and shorter than seven characters or a paragraph indent.

Avoiding Orphans and Widows. Knowing what widows and orphans are allows writers to create more readable text, but first they must now how to fix these issues. One way to avoid these problems is to revise sentences. If a sentence can be changed to allow for more than one word on a line, that is one fix. However, this can be a difficult fix which can further shift additional lines and re-create the problem elsewhere.

At this point, some writers resort to slight changes in margins or spacing. These work well, especially in the case of widows, as a change to a top or bottom margin one-tenth of an inch can shift lines to different pages. When dealing with columns, the width may be adjusted, as can the kerning. Occasionally inserting page or section breaks will assist with this as well. The problem here is that if the document is changed at all, these forced breaks may interfere with the presentation of the information, creating blank pages in a document, for instance.

Also, numerous word processing programs have options that allow for control over widows and orphans. Searching for widow/orphan control in the Help portion of the program will tell users how to automatically account for these issues. The programs then force returns or shift lines, keeping the beginnings of sentences and paragraphs together, and not allowing single words to inhabit a line within the document.

REFERENCES

Stevenson, D. W. 1983. Audience analysis across cultures. *Journal of Technical Communication*, 13, 319–330.

Using computer color effectively: An illustrated reference. Englewood Cliffs, NJ: Prentice Hall.

CHAPTER 16

Professional Review Processes

R esearch, draft, edit, revise, repeat, such is the life of the writer. However, after this process has been repeated enough to create a final product, outside editors often are brought to the project. During this process there are rounds of editing and revision that take place, as each type of editor comes to the document at a different phase. But before the document can be edited, it must be drafted. And before this can begin, the document proposal must first be accepted.

PROFESSIONAL REVIEW PROCESSES

Technical communicators constantly work to publish documents, often allowing them the opportunity to utilize the professional review process. Before anything can be published, it must first be proposed, drafted, revised, edited, and proofread. All of this takes place in addition to the writer's research and the steps that go into the initial draft, which also includes phases of revision, editing, and proofreading. The professional review process generally involves additional support for the project including editors, design teams, and printers. While this allows for complementary ideas and information, collaboration also can add time and discussion to the process. Determining the extent to which the professional review process will be applicable is important when determining the timeline of the project. as well as the available funds and production type to be used to publish the documents.

Steps in Professional Review

The professional review process takes steps beyond the revision process that each document should undergo with the authors. The process includes the following phases: proposal, drafting, revision, editing, proofreading, and publication. However, not all the steps may be necessary for every project. For instance, the proposal phase will not be needed if a writer is told to begin a project, as it is obvious that the undertaking is supported by the company. Regardless of which phases are included in the overall production of the project, each one adds time and steps to the task and needs to be carefully considered and planned for.

Initial Proposal

The *initial proposal,* also known as a business case, has one aim: to show why it should be allotted time, energy, and funds. The proposal is the introduction to the project and generally begins with those who first conceived of the idea. However, a technical communicator might write a proposal that is for a project undertaken by another department. For instance, the department staff charged with programming new software may approach a technical communication department seeking assistance in creating a proposal that will enable them to create a new program. The technical communication staff would be the team to assist in this endeavor because their experience with analyzing audiences, creating proposal documents, and overall writing skills come together to offer the best chance for the acceptance of the new project.

During the initial proposal, the writer is working to identify the audience and purpose for those who can approve the new project. This is sometimes called a market analysis in a proposal that introduces a product, but all initial proposals also need to identify how the project differs from others, what benefits it will bring to the company, and why it should be allotted funds, time, and labor.

Audience Analysis. The audience of the initial proposal will be those who have the authority to approve the project. Because of this, the proposal writer needs to consider this group when writing the proposal, but the proposal also needs to discuss the audience of the intended project.

Determining who will read the proposal is the first step in the proposal's creation. Once this is decided, the writer can focus on the information the audience requires. To clarify the audience, referencing other proposals or office organizational charts may be necessary. If the product will not come from the technical communication department, working with the subject matter expert can offer this information. It is also appropriate to set the tone for the proposal or project now and ensure that the specifics are communicated effectively, allowing those who will consent to the venture to know as many details as possible in order to make a decision.

Purpose. Initial proposals have a single purpose: to receive authorization for a project or product to be started. They generally require a breakdown of what the project or product will be, including a time line and cost analysis. Often, determining this information will require assistance from others, especially when the project will not be created by the proposal writer. Statements of the project's purpose, scope, or details can provide differentiation from other projects done at the company. Also, explanations of how the project will influence the company offer additional details that are of consequence to any project up for endorsement. The more information that can be determined at this time, the better informed decision makers will be. For instance, explaining the time frame in which the new software will be developed, the cost of creation and testing, and how soon it will be marketable gives an overall prospectus of the project. Also, discussing the audience to which the product will be marketed is important in that it can determine the success rate of the project. A small, niche market may allow for a higher sales price, but for fewer sold items overall.

Once again, the more specifics that can be offered up at this phase, the more the reader has to make a decision in favor of the proposal. However, any predictions that are made in the proposal should be clearly identified. Promises should not be made in a proposal if they can not be substantially backed up with research and information. Chapter 11 contains additional information regarding formal proposals and what should be included.

Elements of a Proposal

While the purpose of all initial proposals is to have an idea accepted or a project authorized, the information each proposal contains depends on the research conducted and data available. However, as many of the following seven elements as possible should be included:

1. **Format of the project/product** (e.g., website, manual, training program, new product to be developed by another department)
2. **Input from subject matter experts.** Experts should weigh in on how the project should be carried out.
3. **Project goals and parameters.** These need to be explained thoroughly in order to effectively communicate the purpose.
4. **Initial estimated time frame.** Knowing how long a project will take allows decision makers to consider the length of time employees will be tied up with the task, and how long it can be expected before a profit will be made or efficiency will be increased.
5. **Comparison to the competition.** It is important to provide insight as to how this product will compare to similar products already available, including their pricing, features, and popularity in the marketplace.
6. **Defined budget.** Guidelines as to the necessary labor and funds should be included, as well as a breakdown of where the funds may come from with specifics as to the departments involved.
7. **Team list.** A comprehensive list of team members should be included in order to determine a division of labor, time, and projected participation.

Revision and Editing. While each document created should go through a formal revision process that separates revision from editing, professional review is more in-depth than a writer's review. This process involves additional people and offers a number of review types. When writers conduct reviews, they should look for information that can be added, removed, moved, or substituted for other information. Writers then determine if there are content-based issues that need to be dealt with. After content is considered, editing takes place, making revision and editing two distinct phases of the writing process.

In writer reviews, editing focuses on format and mechanics, such as punctuation, capitalization, verb usage, and sentence structure. These things are not meant to influence the content of the document, but rather to polish its presentation and make it as clear and readable as possible. However, in professional review, there are levels of editing that often combine the ideas of revision and editing.

Technical Communicators as Editors

There are a number of editing roles throughout the writing process. While each role has its own tasks associated with it, a technical communicator could be called upon to act in any or all of these editing positions. Even if documents are written by those outside the technical communication field or department, the best choice for an editor is generally a technical writer due to the task-specific skills and experience associated with the job.

Developmental Editing. Developmental editing, or content editing, looks at the product as a whole to see where it fits into existing document sets and to ensure that the initial project plan was followed in the production. This type of editing does not require a completed draft. Instead, developmental edits can be done as the draft sections are completed so that the editor can work to ensure that the format decided on is being used and all style decisions followed through. If there is a problem during this phase, catching it early allows future material to be written with the comments from the review in mind. Waiting until the project is complete to find these inaccuracies could add editing work that could otherwise be avoided. Working from an early prototype edit, one that shows general errors that could easily be carried throughout the remainder of the document, gives writers a chance to revise their style or formatting before completing the remainder of the document.

Do-It-Yourself Developmental Editing

Ask questions while editing in order to offer concrete suggestions to authors. Consider the following eight areas of concern:

1. Does the proposed document type meet the needs of the audience?
2. Does the document type fit the purpose?
3. Are the headings and subheadings adequate? Do large sections need to be broken down further; are other areas broken down too specifically?
4. Is/are the table of contents and/or table of figures complete?
5. Are there format, citation, table, or graph errors?
6. Are all sections on the table of contents included in the draft?
7. Is the word choice appropriate?
8. Do the style and tone match those of other company documents?

To complete a developmental edit, the writer should provide the editor with the pre-draft outline or plan and any appropriate style manuals in hand. Without these documents, adherence to format and original project concepts cannot be determined. The reviewer also might require contact information for subject matter experts in order to approach them with any technical questions. Other documents that would be of benefit during this type of edit include a working table of contents and at least one completed section or chapter of the project in order to review the tone, citations, and format.

A technical communicator may be asked to take on this position because it is often the task that involves quality control at the beginning of the project. When taking on the role of developmental editor, the editor needs to work closely with those writing or proposing the document. It is essential that the editor, whether he or she is the writer, an editor from outside the writing team, or a department's technical writing liaison, have pre-draft outlines or proposals in hand. This ensures the editor is able to compare the plan to the actual work produced. Without these initial plans, the editor cannot adequately judge the work for tone, inclusion, uniformity, completeness, or accuracy.

In the developmental stages, the editor must have all pre-draft materials in hand, including proposed outlines, table of contents, and preface (if applicable). A writer and editor should expect differences between the proposed documents and the final product, but any changes should be accompanied with logical explanations, as the proposed documents were those initially authorized.

If the editor is working with a document that is further along than merely the initial steps, considering how the audience is addressed is also important. Looking at the writer's target audience and how the author describes practices, processes, and definitions can allow an editor to determine if the tone, diction, and structure of the document match the determined needs of the audience.

Common errors caught during a developmental edit include writing tone that is inappropriate for the target audience, headings and chapter titles that do not match the table of contents or project plan, too many headings, incorrect format, and missing tables or figures.

Technical Editing. Technical edits focus on the accuracy of the more complex information in a document. Often this is done by subject matter experts, or at least someone with a background or experience in the field. These editors are tasked with finding any information of a technical or scientific nature that could become a legal or safety issue if incorrect. Not every document will require a technical editor; however, having a subject matter expert look over the information is a way of conducting a technical edit.

Common errors found during this type of editing include missing or unclear steps in process descriptions or instructions, inadequate explanations of complex information, oversimplification of information, and incorrect information.

Substantive Editing. Also known as structural editing, substantive editing is heavy, revision-type editing that deals with content and mechanics to ensure the document is as clear as possible to read. This type of editing focuses on how the information is presented, as well as whether it is comprehensive and fulfills the proposed plan. A substantive editor will rewrite or reorder pieces of the document for clarity and offers "fix notes" for the writer to consider and expand upon. These notes may signify sections that require additional information, research, examples, or clarification.

Do-It-Yourself Technical Editing

In the role of technical editor, the editor must work to ensure the accuracy of the information in the document and should consider the following seven questions:

1. Will the intended audience understand the technical aspects as explained?
2. Are all steps included in processes and sets of instructions?
3. Are all sources cited correctly?
4. Were technical experts consulted and credited as needed?
5. Are there issues that are overly simplified or inadequately defined?
6. Is the information technically, logically, and/or scientifically sound?
7. Is the information conveyed ethically and legally correct?

The editor will use much the same process a writer would use when working to revise a draft, but a fresh set of eyes able to look at the document as a first-time audience member is able to offer a different perspective. While it is suggested that a writer take a break from writing before revising, having the document edited by a substantive editor ensures that someone who does not have the background or familiarity of the writer looks at the information.

The organization of the document is also evaluated at this point. If content seems out of order or missing, now is the time to correct it and the editor will make suggestions. Nontextual elements also will be considered during this phase, including graphic elements, layout, design, format, and aspects such as social considerations. Considerations of sentence structure, use of passive voice, parallelism, and wordiness are reviewed as well.

Common errors at this point are those that include organization, content, grammar, mechanics, and format. Citations that are incorrect or missing often are caught during this phase.

Copyediting. Copyeditors and proofreaders are titles often used interchangeably. However, while copyeditors may read proofs, they are not proofreaders.

Do-It-Yourself Substantive Editing

Working as a substantive editor is a complex task that requires content knowledge and the ability to identify issues in others' writing. The following seven ideas and issues should be considered:

1. Are there transitions from point to point to ease the reader through the document?
2. Do headings and subheadings fit with the content in the sections?
3. Is the layout adequate to meet the audiences' needs and the purpose of the document?
4. Are all necessary citations included and complete?
5. Is sexist, prejudicial, or inappropriate language avoided?
6. Are the included graphic elements complete and accurate?
7. Are all sentences complete and readable? If not, how should they be corrected?

Proofreaders, by definition, merely read over material that has already been typeset. They compare the typeset document to the last version for accuracy. Copyeditors look for and correct grammatical and mechanical errors prior to the document being typeset.

Copyediting becomes the last line of defense against errors before publication; it should be done only after a substantive edit and the associated revisions have been completed. These editors work to check for mechanical and grammatical errors, ultimately reading the document and making needed changes. Errors often found at this phase are punctuation, capitalization, typos, and misspellings. Format errors also can be found here and fixed before the information prints. For example, a copyeditor may notice and fix a heading that should be bold and is not. No major changes should be found at this phase, but if a copyeditor finds one and is able to correct it without changing the intent or content of the piece, it is often encouraged; occasionally a writer cannot think of a way to change the information or has missed the error entirely.

Do-It-Yourself Copyediting

Copyeditors work to ensure the final products are mistake-free. To do this, all other editorial roles combine and others are added. In order to offer a complete copyedit, the editor should consider the following seven questions:

1. Do the sections and chapters listed in the table of contents match those of the document?
2. Are pages numbers on the table of contents correct?
3. Are there content errors in the piece? If so, how should the writer fix this error?
4. Are all sentences complete and without structural errors?
5. Are necessary citations included and complete?
6. Can grammatical or punctuation errors be found?
7. Are there mechanical errors found, including spelling, typographical, punctuation, and capitalization errors?

Copyeditors are encouraged not only to read through the finished document, but also to verify the list of tables and figures is correct and ensure that all formatting styles were carried throughout the document.

Track Changes

Word processing programs have evolved to meet the needs of a writer in a number of roles. However, the Track Changes option or tool is purely for editing and inputting comments on documents, making it ideal for any editor or collaborative group. This tool allows a second writer, the reviewer, to add or delete material and insert comments. While this also can be done by changing the color of the font on the document, the Track Changes tool records all changes made to the document. A reviewer, or more than one, is able to comment on the document directly by inserting comments in small balloons that appear in the margin of the document or in a reading pane at the bottom of the screen. Also, this tool records the changes, showing the reader or writer what information was removed or added. Figure 16.1 illustrates how Track Changes works.

FIGURE 16.1 *Track Changes Document*

> Employee manuals should include a number of necessary documents. The purpose of the manual is to offer readers, often new employees, policies, procedures, contacts, and other information. This should be information that they are required to have and know, steps to processes they may need (such as how to read their pay statements), and occasionally job-specific information that assists them in their training. Often there are lists of contacts for the company including main numbers for all departments or any representatives specifically assigned to the employee.

| Deleted: ' |
| Deleted: be |
| Deleted: |

| Deleted: |
| Deleted: S |

| Deleted: in general |

The Track Changes option is especially convenient when revisions are made by someone who is not the original author or when multiple reviewers/authors are working together on a document. Multiple reviewers can be assigned different colors to show their changes and comments, and each reviewer is able to see the changes made by others. The drawback to using this tool is that changes can be made to the document without being considered because many programs offer an "acccept all changes" or "refuse all changes" option. Also, this can be done only on electronic documents, although the change marks can be printed.

Hard-copy Editing

Editing on paper, hard-copy editing, is the tried-and-true method of editing and the one many envision when they think of editors. However, while the typewriter has been replaced by the keyboard, many believe there is no replacement for the red pen of traditional editors. Hard-copy editing can offer the same comments and close reading as on-screen editing, but it offers the additional benefit of allowing reviewers the ability to "see" a number of errors. For instance, font, margin, and format errors are often easier to spot on hard copies because they are visual items. Also, reading hard copies sometimes offers more convenience for the reviewer because it can be done anywhere and requires no special equipment.

There are drawbacks to hard-copy editing, however. For instance, unless copies are made of the editing document, it is all too easy to misplace the edits, wasting time and efforts. Also, hard copies that have been edited are difficult to edit in the hands of a subsequent reviewer. The marks of the first reviewer may make portions of the copy illegible or obscure what was originally written. Also, reading the comments can be difficult because they are handwritten and follow a number of editing marks that must also be understood by those making the final revisions.

Editing Marks

While each editor working on a hard-copy document will include personalized comments, he or she will also include formatted editing marks. The reader, the one responsible for making the changes to the document and incorporating comments, must understand the marks. Commonly used editing marks and their meanings are shown in figure 16.2.

Editors and proofreaders often mark up print copies in two different ways. Editors typically insert symbols in the actual text of the document, which is why they prefer manuscripts to be double-spaced. Proofreaders will mark in the text, and then make a corresponding mark in the margin (both right and left margins). See figure 16.2 for a list of the symbols/marks used by editors and proofreaders; figure 16.3 for a list of abbreviations used by editors and proofreaders. Note that these lists are not all-inclusive, but rather a representation of the most frequently used symbols and abbreviations. See figure 16.4 for an example of a marked up text with proofreader marks and the corrected version of the marked up text.

FIGURE 16.2 *Common Editor and Proofreader Symbols and Their Meanings*

Symbol	Meaning	Symbol	Meaning
ℓ	Delete	ⓣⓡ	Transpose letters or words
◡	Remove space; print as one word	⊡	Indent (one em)
ℰ	Delete and close up space	⸗	Insert hyphen
#	Add space	M̲	Insert em dash
∧	Insert punctuation (comma, apostrophe, quote, etc.) or word; or make subscript	N̲	Insert en dash
∨	Insert punctuation (comma, apostrophe, quote, etc.) or word; or make superscript	⊙	Insert period
¶	New paragraph	/	Used to separate several marginal symbols/abbreviations

FIGURE 16.3 *Common Editor and Proofreader Words and Their Meanings*

Abbreviation	Meaning	Abbreviation	Meaning
abbr	Incorrect abbreviation	sc	Small capitals
agr	Agreement, subject/verb or pronoun/antecedent	slash	Slash (insert)
awk	Awkward, unclear wording	sp	Spell out the word
bf	Boldface	sub	Subscript
cap	Capitalize, upper-case letter(s)	supe	Superscript
cs	Comma splice	tr	Transpose
dm	Dangling modifier	trans	Transition needed
fl	Flush left	w or wdy	Wordy
fr	Flush right	wf	Wrong font
frag	Fragment, incomplete sentence	ww	Wrong word
ital	Italics	eq #	Equal space between word or line
lc	Lowercase letter	hr #	Hair space
ls	Letterspace (insert)	em	"m" space
rom	Roman (not italics)	en	"n" space

FIGURE 16.4 *Document with Editor Marks*

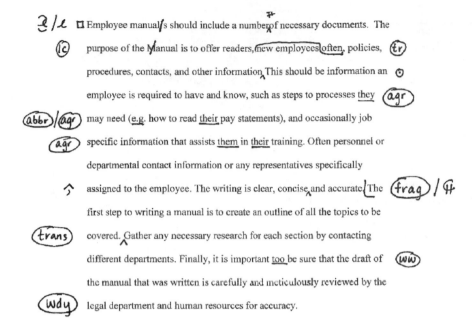

Document Corrected

Employee manuals should include a number of necessary documents. The purpose of the manual is to offer readers, often new employees, policies, procedures, contacts, and other information. This should be information an employee is required to have and know, such as steps to processes he or she may need (e.g. how to read his or her pay statements), and occasionally job specific information that assists him or her in his or her training. Often personnel or departmental contact information or any representatives specifically assigned to the employee is included. The writing is clear, concise, and accurate.

The first step to writing a manual is to create an outline of all the topics to be covered. Next, gather any necessary research for each section by contacting different departments. Finally, it is important to be sure that the draft of the manual is reviewed by the legal department and human resources for accuracy.

CHAPTER 17

Testing and Usability Issues

U pon writing and revising a technical document, there is another step in the process that needs to be completed: *usability testing.* Effective writing cannot happen in a vacuum. Much like having a document reviewed by peers, usability testing is a means to obtaining feedback and often empirical evidence on the strengths and weaknesses of a document based on readers' actual usage. Usability is defined by the Usability Professionals' Association as "the degree to which something—software, hardware, or anything else—is easy to use and a good fit for the people who use it" (n.d.). No matter how complex communication is, it must meet the needs of the intended audience. These usability needs should include five characteristics, as defined by Whitney Quesenbery (2001):

1. **Effective**—accuracy, especially when completing tasks
2. **Efficient**—speed, typically coupled with accuracy
3. **Engaging**—appeal, primarily visual design aspects
4. **Error tolerant**—reliable, reduced user-error potential
5. **Easy to learn**—intuitive, user quickly assimilates necessary skills and knowledge

Usability versus Accessibility

The concepts of usability and accessibility are not interchangeable in the realm of technical communications. *Usability* refers to a communication's ability to meet the needs and goals of specific users, as they are defined in the audience analysis. *Accessibility* is a communication's ability to reach all readers or users, no matter who they are or how they approach the communication; for instance, users with disabilities should be able to benefit from the communication as well as users without disabilities. Section 508 of the U.S. Rehabilitation Act focuses on guidelines to create information technology that is accessible by people with disabilities (*www.section508.gov*). Also, the World Wide Web Consortium (W3C) provides guidelines for web developers who are designing for accessibility at *www.w3.org/TR/WAI-WEBCONTENT.*

The focus of usability testing is to assess how successful a document is at displaying the five above-named characteristics, and at meeting the expectations of those who proposed the creation of the communication.

Testing a technical document can assess a variety of issues, including aspects that are confusing, inconsistencies in the tone or format, places that need more or less elaboration, and tables or graphics that are unclear. This usability information needs to be gathered prior to releasing the document to the entire target audience. Whether this document is in the form of a printed manual, interactive online training module, or annual report PowerPoint presentation, usability testing is not a step to be overlooked.

The writing process for creating a technical communication is often hectic and compressed into a small time frame, and can result in the cutting out of the usability testing phase. Even if usability testing is not formally included in the document's project plan, it still will be done to a certain extent. Target readers will obtain the document, begin using it, and either call customer service with complaints about the document or simply toss it aside and find another means of getting the same information. It is not likely that the writer will receive feedback on the ineffectiveness of the document or that the feedback will get to the writer in a disconnected fashion. Creating a controlled usability testing phase is the best means to evaluate a technical document and its effect, thus giving the writer time to make appropriate changes before the communication is officially released to the entire target audience.

Controlled testing should be done at three points in the process. The first round of testing should be done before the writing even begins. Testers will evaluate the effectiveness of similar documents already created; through this review the writer will learn what works and what does not so that the new document can be adapted appropriately. For instance, when writing content for a company's website, usability testing can be done on competitors' websites; knowing what works and does not work for users on a competitor's website gives a writer a baseline for where to begin developing a more comprehensive and intuitive website. The second round of testing should be done midway through the writing process, as a way to determine if the document is going in the right direction. The results of this round should not completely derail the writing project; rather, they should serve as guidance for the latter half of the project and the revision phase. The final round of testing should be completed prior to releasing the communication to the entire target audience. The results from this final round will need to be analyzed so that only relevant feedback is used to make any changes to the document. It is ideal to do all three rounds of testing, but if pressed for time, then minimally the last round should be done.

The number and selection of usability testers depends on how much time is allotted for testing and the availability of people to dedicate time to the testing process. Common in the usability testing industry, "heuristic evaluations—sometimes called strategic evaluations, documentation audits, or expert reviews—consist of trained evaluators reviewing documentation or product information" (Smart 2002). These trained evaluators will use their past experiences to focus on making sure the document meets the set standards. When these types of testers are not available, instead look to in-house peers or actual target readers. Some other options that a writer should explore include customer service representatives, trainers, external focus groups, and content experts. Remember, though, every person recruited for testing will need to

Audience Analysis

Although audience analysis is not directly tied to actual usability testing, having accurate audience analysis prior to writing the document will help make the testing process easier. The audience analysis will help the writer know the needs of the target reader, thus enabling the writer to create a usable document to begin with. Also, the analysis can be used when choosing potential participants for usability testing. For instance, if the analysis reveals that the target readers are between the ages 55 and 70, then those doing the usability testing should fall into that age range. This analysis is especially helpful if users with disabilities need to be identified; usability and accessibility will need to be tested in these cases. If participants cannot be found to match the characteristics of the target audience, then the audience analysis should be given to those doing the testing so they can try to evaluate the communication from the perspective of the target reader. See chapter 2 for more information on audience analysis.

dedicate his or her undivided attention to the testing, which often results in work hours lost if the testers are in-house. Testers may expect some sort of compensation for their time. After the testers are selected, to forego any legal ramifications of using human subjects to test the usability of a document, it is advised that every participant sign an *Informed Consent Form,* shown in the example below, prior to beginning the process. Participants should feel entirely comfortable with the testing process and with giving their honest feedback about the document.

If it is within the project's budget, consider hiring corporations and universities that specialize in conducting usability tests. They will set up the test and report their findings back to the writer. Although it is ideal to have usability testing experts conduct the testing, it generally is not realistic for many companies and organizations. Thus, the writer or someone from the writer's group may be charged with developing and running the tests. Note that it is not ideal to have the individual responsible for creating the document to facilitate the test because it can be stressful to watch users struggle with the document during the testing process.

Informed Consent Form

I, _____, hereby consent to participating in usability testing for the *X3M User Guide.* I accept that this testing will be digitally recorded; the testing will also be monitored by an Acme Company representative. All results from this testing period will be for internal use only, and will not be made publicly available at any time. I understand that I can quit the usability testing process at any point.

Printed Name: _____

Signature: _____

Date: _____

There is a variety of methods by which to conduct usability testing, so it is important to consider the ramifications and desired results of adopting a particular method. These methods include the following:

- **Controlled environment.** Putting users in a location where all the elements dictated by the person conducting the test will reduce unpredictable variables from interfering with the test results. For example, noise, lighting, workspace, computer speed, and user comfort are the same for every tester in the room. Although this will provide solid results from each tester, it is unlikely that the target reader will actually be using the document in such a strictly controlled environment, so the results may be slightly skewed in that sense.

- **Field study.** Conducting usability testing in the same environment that the target reader will actually use the document will provide realistic results, though these results may be difficult to assess because each situation may differ depending on the user and environment. If the user is interrupted by several telephone calls during the test, assessing his or her comprehension of a section of the document will be misleading.

- **Survey.** A questionnaire given to users after they have reviewed the document is a means to gather specific documented evidence of usability; a questionnaire also should be administered prior to reviewing the document in order to set a baseline of user's knowledge. A survey with open-ended questions allows a user to describe issues in his or her own words, whereas close-ended questions provide answers for the user to choose from.

- **Interview.** Directly contacting a user by telephone or teleconference with a set of predetermined questions after he or she has had time to assess the document allows for more analysis based on the user's responses and inflections in his or her voice.

- **Informal testing.** Giving the draft document to a few colleagues and reading their responses, either written on a printed copy of the communication or via email, is a popular approach to usability testing for projects with limited resources and time. It is difficult to quickly organize the results from informal testing.

A writer can rely on a single approach or a combination of several approaches, but knowing what exactly needs to be tested may further influence which approach is chosen.

Creating a Documentation Usability Team

If many technical communications need to undergo usability testing, it is worthwhile to create a specific group of people to organize and conduct the training for every communication. As proposed in the journal, *Technical Communications,* this team will create standards for the testing process and maintain a database of the results from all usability testing for future reference (Postava-Davingnon 2004).

As with most experiments or tests, results can be quantitative or qualitative. *Quantitative* results are tangible numbers, such as statistics. *Qualitative* results are less tangible because they focus on the motivations behind users' actions. Managers often prefer quantitative results because they can see quickly how well the communication was received by the users. For example, 73 percent of the users completed required tasks in less than five minutes. Anyone looking at those results can see that the document is efficient. But this quick analysis has its drawbacks, as explained by Jakob Nielsen: "It's a dangerous mistake to believe that statistical research is somehow more scientific or credible than insight-based observational [qualitative] research. In fact, most statistical research is *less* credible than qualitative studies" (2004). Statistics can be skewed or misleading if the person gathering the results is not steadfast about presenting the numbers clearly and accurately. Quantitative results do not always take into account variables that are recorded by qualitative results. For example, if 73 percent of the users completed the tasks in under five minutes, yet some were already familiar with the tasks before reading the document, then that variable is not seen in the quantitative results. Qualitative results are often time consuming to gather and analyze, but they are insightful when building a document that can meet the needs of the target audience. To get the most out of usability testing, consider using testing methods that record both quantitative and qualitative results.

It is not practical to try and test every aspect of a document's usability. Carefully take into account which aspects will most influence the success of the document in the eyes of the target readers. Focus the testing on those specific aspects, such as the following:

- **Time.** How long does it take a user to read a passage? How long does it take a user to complete a task as explained in the document? Testing for time relies on using a stopwatch or another timing device, to track when the user begins and completes the task.

- **Accuracy.** When testing a user on how long it takes to complete a task after reading a passage, it is also important to track accuracy. Did the user complete the task quickly, but not follow the directions in the document? Did the user take a while to complete the task, but completed it correctly?

- **Comprehension.** Although a user can view a document quickly, how much will he or she remember? Administering a questionnaire after the user views the document will help pinpoint which sections are easy to recall. Keep in mind, though, the questionnaire should be directed toward assessing the document and not the user.

The results of testing for time, accuracy, and comprehension provide strong empirical evidence of a document's usability. A writer will be able to see clearly what parts of the document held a user back or led the user astray; thus, the communication can be changed accordingly.

If there are set criteria that the document needs to meet, then usability testing can focus on those aspects. As noted earlier in this chapter, this type of testing is called heuristic evaluation and is conducted by usability professionals. Carefully consider the list of criteria for the evaluators to review; some example questions to consider are listed below:

- Does the user need to find the document visually appealing?

- Is the document's tone appropriate for the topic?

- Is the document considered "user friendly"?

- If the users are experts or well experienced in the field, do they find the document to be accurate?

When testing for a variety of characteristics, provide users with a checklist of what they specifically should be looking at in the document. The results obtained from this type of testing will obviously be limited in their scope, but they also will not overwhelm the writer with feedback not clearly relevant to improving the document.

"Talk it out" or "thinking aloud" is a usability testing method in which the user verbalizes his or her thought processes while evaluating the document. This method gives a writer insight into how a user cognitively processes a document, along with any emotional or intellectual response and analysis of the information viewed. For example, a user reads a small passage from a policy and procedure manual, and then verbalizes confusion about the wording and must read the passage aloud several times to understand the content. The writer then knows to go back and rewrite that passage to be more intuitive for the reader. If the talk-it-out method is employed, then audio recording individual user sessions is ideal. Overall, obtaining reliable results for any aspect of a document will ultimately depend on how the person conducting the tests interacts with the users.

The usability tester needs to be unbiased while designing, implementing, and analyzing results of usability testing. The test should be designed in a way that does not give the user an impression about what response is wanted. This is especially relevant to surveys and interviews. For instance, the following question may imply to the user that a negative response is appropriate: "Was step three understandable, or did you find yourself confused about which box to click and why that action was necessary?" The question leads the reader to view step three from a point of view defined by the person who wrote the question. Furthermore, the user is likely to be very sensitive toward everything the person conducting the test says and does. Be mindful of the following actions that may jade the users' responses:

- The person conducting the test should not be overbearing, especially while users are actually testing the communication. Overbearing actions include jumping in and providing cues to the users to help them understand the document better. Assistance can be provided when the user is unclear about the testing process, but confusion about the document is a result of the testing that should be noted.

- The body language and voice inflections of the person conducting the test should not reveal biases toward the document being tested. For example, if the leader rolls her eyes when pointing out a feature of the document that she does not find of value, the users involved in the testing will pick up on this cue and possibly alter their responses to that aspect of the communication.

- Disclaimers or insights about the content of the document should not be provided, unless they are vital to a user's understanding. Telling the user that the second section of the manual was written by an engineer new to the company will make the user biased toward the content of that section. Another example is telling the user that the manual is incomplete due to time constraints.

- Interruptions with further explanations or asides once the testing has begun may negatively impact the results, particularly if testing for comprehension. Some interruptions may be unavoidable, especially when conducting testing in the field, but the interruptions should be limited if possible. Unnecessary interruptions will distract the user's attention from the document, thus lessening the strength of the provided feedback.

Depending on the testing environment and aspects of the document tested, observations by both the users and the person facilitating the test need to be noted. Writing notes in margins or on paper during testing is not the most effective manner of documenting results. The most cost-effective means is to create a form for the observer and users prior to beginning the testing. Figure 17.1 is an example of a form completed by someone observing users testing documentation on using database software. Prior to the test beginning, only the "Process Step" and "Estimated Time" columns are filled in by the individual who wrote the document being tested; the other three columns are filled in as the test progresses.

The "Process Step" column does not have to be word for word from the original document; instead, it can be a summary of the step and substeps that need to be completed, as long as the observer is clear on what is being tested in each row. The "Estimated Time" column is the writer's guess as to how long it should realistically take to complete the task. Although the example in figure 17.1 is for a set of instructions, this form can be used for any type of document where it is important to track how long it takes the user to read or view the document and perhaps complete a given task. Rather than give the same form to the user, there are other forms that are more ideal for a user to complete while testing a document.

Based on the form in figure 17.1, a similar form can be given to the user in order to assess how easy or complicated a section is to understand in a document. Figure 17.2 provides an example of Red/Yellow/Green usability documentation given to users testing database software.

FIGURE 17.1 *Usability Observation Form*

Process Step	Estimated Time	Begin Time	End Time	Comments
1. Open database	0:10	0:00	0:25	User had trouble finding database icon.
2. Enter password	0:07	0:30	0:45	User misspelled password first time.
3. Select "New" from main screen menu	0:03	0:50	1:15	User read entire main screen before clicking on "New."
4. Create column heads	5:30	1:16	12:07	User was confused by directions; she had to look under several menus before finding the "Add Headers" option. User also did not inherently know to tab from one cell to the next after entering text for a header.

FIGURE 17.2 *Usability Red/Yellow/Green Response Form*

Process Step	Red	Yellow	Green	Comments
1. Open database		X		I couldn't find the database icon; there wasn't a screenshot to guide me in this step.
2. Enter password			X	
3. Select "New" from main screen menu			X	
4. Create column heads	X			The directions weren't clear on where to find the Add Headers function in the menu. I also didn't know how to move from one cell to the next after I put in the header text.

Again, the "Process Step" column can be completed by the writer of the document being tested as long as the writer is not interested in testing if a user will intuitively know how to navigate the document without prompting, such as in the case of websites or software. The other columns of the example are to be completed by the user during testing, though a clear explanation of expectations should be provided to the user, such as the following:

- *Red* indicates that the section or step is very unclear or troublesome.

- *Yellow* means that the section or step is a little unclear or vague.

- *Green* means that there is not a problem with understanding the section or step as it is written.

Rather than colors, numbers can be used to describe the degree of confusion or ineffectiveness; for example, 5 indicates the section is unclear while 1 indicates the section is perfectly clear. Providing a "Comments" column allows the user to further explain any difficulties encountered with the document.

If the writer needs only specific characteristics of the document tested by users, providing a checklist of those characteristics is an effective way of noting users' findings. Figure 17.3 provides an example of a checklist of specific aspects a user should focus on.

The list of characteristics in the first column should be provided by the writer of the document, while the other three columns are left to be completed by the user during testing.

FIGURE 17.3 *Usability Checklist Form*

Characteristic	Yes	No	Comments
Headers/footers are clear.	X		
Slang or clichés are used.		X	
Tables are clear.		X	The font for all the tables is too small to read easily.
Graphics are appropriate.		X	The graphic on page 2 doesn't relate to the text above or below it.
Headings are specific.	X		

Creating a questionnaire for users to respond to after viewing the document being tested will provide usability results on comprehension, which is generally influenced by the clarity and consistency of a document. To obtain credible results from this method, users should be surveyed prior to reviewing the document to set a baseline of their existing knowledge. If the communication is extensive and takes a while for users to review, consider quizzing users after they review major sections of the document and then again at the end of the usability testing session. There are two weaknesses to this documentation method to consider. First, many users may be intimidated by being forced to take a quiz and "prove their intelligence." It is important that the person facilitating the testing make it clear that the focus is on the document's content, not on the user's level of education or overall intelligence. Second, each question needs to be carefully designed to elicit an honest response based on viewing the document. In other words, the user should not be able to determine what answer is being sought based on the wording of the question.

Eye Tracking

Technology allows usability testing to document where a person looks when viewing a monitor or document. Although most Americans will read from left to right, top to bottom, eye tracking usability testing will measure if that is truly the case. This technique also will document how long a user looks in the same direction, which is helpful in determining the readability of passages. Knowing where users look and for what length of time is particularly important with software and websites, where a user's attention may be pulled in several directions because of nonlinear designs.

When multimedia resources are available, usability testing can be recorded with video, software, or audio technology. It is important to have the users' consent if recording the sessions in any manner, though the user may be more apprehensive during testing knowing he or she is being recorded. Explaining that the recording is for in-house evaluation only, while stressing the evaluation will focus on the document and not the user, may help alleviate some apprehension. Also, when setting up the recording device, try to make it less obvious so as to not constantly draw a user's attention.

Although sessions are recorded, the person observing or listening to the recordings still will need to document the results of users' actions. Documented results from a recording are easier to compile and review by the writer who needs to make changes to the document.

After testing, the person who conducted the usability testing will compile the results, often in the form of a formal report. For a writer, it is not practical to make all the changes reported during testing; focus instead on patterns in the usability testing results. Developing an affinity diagram will help visually depict the relationships between similar results. The diagram can be organized by section of the communication and then by feedback specifics, as shown in figure 17.4.

Consider the different formats of affinity diagrams, including index cards on a flat surface (often called Card Sorting) or sticky notes on a wall, to see the results in a larger context.

Evaluate results that do not fall into a pattern, and analyze whether if the suggested changes are needed in order to strengthen the communication, or if the user's feedback was based on a personal preference that does not fit with the overall goal of the communication. Both large and small changes need to undergo this scrutiny before implementing the change. With any feedback for a writer, it is important not to take the results as personal attacks, even if all the feedback is negative; the results are simply insights into the thought processes of target readers as they view the communication. After the changes are complete, it is conceivable that regression testing will need to be done to ensure the changes did not have a negative impact anywhere else in the communication. At a certain point, though, the testing will need to be cut off and the document released to the entire target audience; do not get caught up in constantly tweaking the details of a document. Finally, be sure to store the testing results so that they can be consulted when writing similar documents.

The results of usability testing are crucial to producing a document that positively influences the target audience, so the approach to testing should be as methodical as the approach to writing the actual document. Create a

FIGURE 17.4 *Affinity Diagram Usability Testing Results and Recommendations*

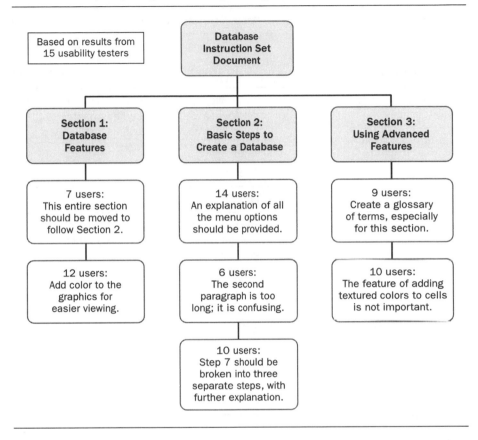

plan for how the testing will be designed, implemented, and documented. Figure 17.5 details an example usability testing plan for a policy and procedure manual. Plans will vary depending on which characteristics in the document need testing and what types of resources are available, though they should all detail every aspect of the testing process.

There are three primary Internet resources for technical writers conducting usability testing, listed below. These resources will provide insights into various aspects of usability.

1. Society of Technical Communications Special Interest Group
   www.stcsig.org/usability/

453

FIGURE 17.5 *Usability Testing Plan*

Title	Acme Software Co Policy and Procedure Manual
Writer	Michelle Yang
Document Summary	
Overview	This policy and procedure manual contains 15 essential policies for employees and 12 procedures related to the policies. Also included is basic information on benefits, with a step-by-step procedure on how to access further information.
Length	125 pages
Format	Print, 8.5 × 11, comb-bound
Audience Analysis	The manual is for both new and established employees of the company; the age range is generally from 20 to 57 years old. There will not be international readers.
Usability Testers	
Characteristics	There should be an even number of new employees (with the company less than six months) and established employees (preferably more than five years).
Minimum Number	10
Maximum Number	30
Compensation	$20 gift certificate
Test	
Objective	Test readability and comprehension of all policies; readability and time to complete procedures; and whether or not the user feels satisfied with the amount of information provided in the benefits section of the manual.
Test Dates	November 5–8
Session Length	3 hours each day
Facilitator	Brad Smith
Location	Conference Room B, 2nd floor
Recording Method	Administer questionnaire to users at the beginning of the first session and at the end of all four sessions. Also, users will complete red/yellow/green form while reading the manual.

2. Usability Professionals' Association, *www.upassoc.org/*

3. Jakob Nielsen, a recognized expert in the field of usability *www.useit.com/*

For specific communication types or testing methods, there are several peer-reviewed journals that contain results from specific research topics. Although these results may not precisely translate to every communication type, the journal articles will provide insight on what does and does not work when conducting usability testing:

- *Journal of Usability Studies*

- *Technical Communications*

- *Journal of Technical Writing and Communication*

- *Journal of Business and Technical Communication*

- *IEEE Transactions on Professional Communication*

REFERENCES

Nielsen, J. "Risks of quantitative studies." *http://www.useit.com/alertbox/20040301.html.*

Postava-Davington, C., et al. 2004. "Incorporating usability testing into the documentation process." *Technical Communication,* 51 no. 1: 35–44.

Quesenbery, W. 2001. "What does usability mean: Looking beyond "ease of use." Paper presented at the 48th annual conference, Society for Technical Communication, Chicago, IL.

Smart, K. 2002. "Quality and the customer experience: Methods of collecting data." *Intercom,* April.

Usability Professionals' Association. "About usability." *http://www.upassoc.org/usability_resources/about_usability/index.htm*

CHAPTER 18

Oral Presentations

Delivering an effective oral presentation plays an important role in the field of technical communications. At times, a technical communicator may be called upon to present information from written documents in a professional presentation to a client, employer, organization, or potential funder. Through the spoken word, an oral presentation adds another dimension to the written text by providing an interactive opportunity for both the presenter and audience members. The presenter can highlight information from the written document, and audience members have the opportunity to ask clarifying questions or provide feedback on the topic. This chapter will provide information on writing the speech, creating effective visuals aids, delivering the presentation, and engaging the audience. Pacing, nonverbal communication, and answering questions from the audience will be addressed also.

DEVELOPING THE PRESENTATION

Identifying the purpose of the presentation is an important step when planning a professional presentation. Prior to writing the speech, the audience and purpose must be decided on. A technical communicator may be called upon to deliver a speech for a variety of purposes, including the following:

- To persuade current or future clients that a project or the technical communicator's services are needed. The speech needs to draw the audience's attention to the product or service and clarify a need.

- To present a proposal for an idea, product, or procedure. The speech needs to include a problem–solution format, with specific recommendations for resolving the problem.

- To present a progress report on development updates for an ongoing project. The speech needs to highlight progress made during a specific period of time, the amount of time and type of activities completed by individuals, and the estimated time needed to finalize the tasks needed to complete the project.

Writing the Outline

An effective presentation begins with organization and planning. A planned presentation will allow time for not only writing the speech, but also for practicing it. To begin the process, develop a specific purpose or goal of the speech. For example:

> **Specific Purpose:** To explain to the audience the importance of building a recycling center in the downtown area.

Next, develop a central idea or key points to be made in the speech, such as:

> **Central Idea:** Environmental concerns and the growing support for "going green" have increased residents' interest in recycling; however, a recycling center is not currently available in the downtown area.

Main points with supporting examples are then developed for the speech. Typically, a speech will highlight main ideas of the written document. Due to the time constraints of most presentations, limit the amount of detail, thus allowing adequate time for presenting key aspects of the written document to the audience.

Presenting in Teams

Presentations may involve small groups of individuals responsible for dividing the tasks of preparing and delivering the information. Unlike individual presentations that involve one person, a team presentation involves shared responsibilities among members. In order for a team presentation to be effective, each member must complete assigned tasks and responsibilities in enough time to allow for a mock presentation before the real version is delivered. To facilitate this process, team members should be assigned roles, such as the following:

- The team leader is responsible for motivating individuals and keeping group members on task.

- The opening of the presentation needs to be delivered by a credible individual who can draw the audience into the presentation with effective speaking skills.

- The conclusion of the presentation also should be delivered by a strong speaker.

Because this is the last piece of information the audience will receive, it is important to leave the audience with a positive, memorable impression of the presentation.

- The middle portion of the speech can be delivered by less experienced speakers. While this information is important, the audience will remember the opening and conclusion of the presentation more vividly.

- An individual should be assigned to handle presentation aids, such as turning a flip chart, moving PowerPoint slides, or replacing transparencies. This same individual should be responsible for testing any visual aids prior to the presentation.

- An individual confident with public speaking and the topic should oversee the question-and-answer period. This individual should have strong listening skills, which are needed to respond effectively to the audience.

Main points of the speech may be organized according to several patterns: topical, chronological, spatial, causal, and problem–solution, as explained below:

- **Topical.** Main points of the speech are organized into major categories. For example, a speech on the feasibility of building a community center could be divided into categories such as need, cost, and benefit to the community.

- **Chronological.** Main points of the speech are organized in a time sequence. For example, a speech on the process of performing CPR would break down the steps in terms of what to do first, second, third, etc.

- **Spatial.** Main points of the speech are organized according to the way the items relate to one another in physical space. For example, a fire evacuation plan would show exits in relation to various parts of the building.

- **Causal.** Main points of the speech are organized in a cause–effect relationship. For example, some residents refuse to recycle (effect) because a recycling center is not downtown (cause).

- **Problem–solution.** Main points are divided into two categories: the problem and solution. For example, the absence of a recycling center creates a large amount of garbage in the downtown area (problem). Providing a recycling center would allow residents to drop off recyclable items rather than rely on city pick-up (solution).

Writing an outline of the main points with supporting examples helps to organize the speech logically, no matter which organization pattern is chosen for the overall speech. Main points presented in the speech need supporting material to be effective. Supporting material may be in the form of examples, statistics, survey results, testimonials, or anecdotes. Create a balance with supporting examples by providing enough supporting research to strengthen the main points without becoming repetitious in the process.

Transitional words should be included to show logical connections between ideas. In an outline of the speech, place transitions in parentheses. These signals, which are designed to show the presenter's train of thought, will help audience members to follow the flow of the speech. The following is a list of but a few transitional words:

- *To show addition:* and, also, furthermore, moreover, in addition
- *To show time:* soon, then, later afterward, meanwhile

- *To show contrast:* however, yet, but, instead
- *To show examples:* for example, for instance, to illustrate
- *To show conclusions:* in summary, therefore, as a result

Abrupt changes in topic or direction may jar audience members, because they are not able to make the cognitive leap from one topic to the next. Transition words and phrases will clearly point out the shift in topic.

Avoiding Plagiarism

As in writing, sources for an oral presentation need to be documented. In speeches, references need to be included for any thought, idea, or expression that is not the speaker's own. Supporting material, such as examples, statistics, and short stories, is often used to enhance a presentation. It is important to verbally state your source if any of this information is not original. Plagiarism can be avoided by stating the source of the information.

Introductions and Conclusions

Introductions and conclusions set the tone for the success of a presentation. Like writing an essay, the introduction prepares the audience for the information that will follow in the body of the presentation. A strong conclusion ensures the audience will remember the key elements of the presentation.

Gaining the attention of the audience is important to the overall success of the presentation. Like a text introduction, a presentation's introduction needs to catch the audience's interest. A strong introduction does the following:

- Provides an overview of the main points of the presentation, perhaps in the form of an agenda
- Grabs the audience's attention through the use of brief quotations, statistics, rhetorical questions, or an anecdote
- Clarifies the relevance of the topic

An example introduction using rhetorical questions follows:

> Are you tired of driving 15 miles to drop off recyclable items? Do you find yourself constantly picking up paper from your apartment courtyard? If the answer is yes, you will want to learn more about the proposal presented today. The proposal for a new recycling center may assist in lessening these environmental issues.

While humor is sometimes used to begin a presentation, caution should be exercised. Humor can help ease the tension of a presentation when it is appropriate to the speaking occasion and it is certain the audience will understand the humor. When presenting in front of a culturally diverse audience, however, humor should be avoided because it may seem inappropriate, unclear, or offensive. Humor that insults others, such as topics related to gender, ethnicity, religion, or ability, should be avoided at all times. If humor is used as an introduction for a presentation, be sure to practice the introduction before a representative group of individuals to ensure that the humor is funny and appropriate to the context of the speaking occasion.

A well-developed and well-delivered conclusion will leave audience members with a memorable impression of the presentation. The purpose of a conclusion in a presentation is to provide closure for the audience. It is also a time for the presenter to stress the main points and purpose of the presentation. A strong conclusion will do the following:

- Summarize the main points and goals of the presentation.
- Encourage the audience to respond to the material presented.
- Provide a sense of closure to the presentation.
- Restate the central idea of the presentation.

Use of transitional words or phrases, such as *in summary, finally,* or *in closing,* alert the audience that the presentation is coming to a close. The conclusion should be relatively brief in comparison to the main points of the presentation. An audience can grow irritated if the words *in closing* are used and the presentation continues on for an extended period of time.

In addition to providing a summary of the main points of the presentation, leaving a memorable impression on the audience is critical to an effective conclusion. A conclusion can be made memorable in the following ways:

- Use a quotation.

- Pose a call to action.

- Link back to the introduction.

- Use an anecdote that applies to the presentation's central idea.

Creating Effective Visual Aids

When it comes time to choose a presentation aid, ask this question: How will the visual aid add to the desired outcomes of the presentation? There are several types of visual aids available and it is important to analyze how visuals will enhance the presentation. Visual aids commonly used for professional presentations include models, objects, handouts, flip charts, posters, marker boards, photographs, slides, transparencies, and electronic/multimedia presentations. PowerPoint is commonly used to create computer-generated visual aids and carries with it both benefits and challenges (see chapter 8 for additional tips on using PowerPoint).

Objects are a three-dimensional representation of an idea that will be communicated. According to Verderber and Verderber (2008), objects make good visual aids if they are large enough to be seen by all members in the audience and small enough to be carried to the location of the presentation. For example, a cell phone with video recording capabilities may be acceptable to use as an object to introduce the audience to the look of the item. However, a cell phone may be an ineffective model to demonstrate how to create a video because the screen is too small for the audience to see.

Models are three-dimensional, smaller versions of large objects. Models may be effective when the real object is too large to bring into the presentation setting. For example, a replica of the Sears Tower would serve as an effective model to describe the design of the building to the audience.

Handouts benefit the audience by reducing the amount of time and attention needed for taking notes. A major drawback does exist when handouts are provided at the start of the presentation because audiences have a tendency to focus on the handout rather than on the presentation. One option is to distribute handouts at the end of the presentation to ensure the audience's attention is on the speaker. Instead of distributing the entire packet of handouts at the start of the presentation, a one-page agenda may be used to guide the audience. A sample agenda is shown in figure 18.1.

Marker boards or chalkboards may be used to highlight key elements of presentations. While material or drawings placed on the marker board or chalkboard can create a visual image for the audience, there are several drawbacks to consider before using these types of visual aids. Because material cannot be prepared ahead of time, the presenter must be organized and skilled at both writing and speaking at the same time. There is a tendency to view presentations involving marker boards or chalkboards as less professional. If a decision is made to use these visual aids, practice is required. The presenter must ensure that the drawing or text is clear and readable by all members of

FIGURE 18.1 *Agenda for Use as a One-page Handout*

Status Meeting

**Starting a Local Chapter of the Association
for Women in Communications**

1. Welcome and Introductions
2. Mission of the Organization
3. Benefits to Students
4. Beginning the Application Process:
   a. Letter of intent
   b. University support
   c. Eight committed students
   d. Faculty advisor chosen
5. Application Process: Phase Two
   a. Creation of bylaws
   b. Election of officers
   c. Kick-off meeting
   d. National dues

the audience. Time cannot be lost by waiting for information to be placed on the marker board or chalkboard. The presenter must practice speaking and writing (or drawing) at the same time. In terms of readability of text, Hamilton (2008) suggests that a capital letter be three inches high, and basic text at least 1 ½ inches high. Colors should be bold and pastels avoided.

Flip charts are large pieces of paper mounted on an easel and may serve as an effective visual aid in the event that technology is not available or desirable. The size of the flip chart can be adjusted to fit the audience. For example, for small presentations involving four or five people, a desktop flip chart is adequate. For a large audience, a 30-foot by 40-foot flip chart is needed to ensure that all audience members can view the information.

The benefit of a flip chart is that information can be prepared prior to the presentation so that the presenter has time to effectively organize material and rehearse. Colorful markers may be used to draw attention to important points. Drawings, photographs, or other art may be included within flip charts to enhance the visual experience of the presentation.

Verderber and Verderber (2008) state that for flip charts to be effective, information that is handwritten or drawn must be neat and appropriate in size. Unorganized or sloppy flip charts can actually take away from the credibility of the presenter. Flip charts can effectively be used for smaller audiences (fewer than 10 people), but they are not effective for larger audiences. For flip charts to be used effectively as a presentation aid, it is important that the information is written large enough to be seen by the entire audience.

Poster boards are another visual aid that may be used for smaller audiences (fewer than 10 people). Charts, maps, and drawings can be secured to a poster board and placed on an easel. Similar to flip charts, information presented on a poster board must be large enough for the entire audience to see. This is especially true when labeling charts. If the audience cannot view the information clearly, confusion can occur, taking away from the credibility of the presenter.

Photographs can enhance a presentation by creating visual pictures for the audience. For example, when writing a grant proposal for a potential funder, using actual photographs to show the deterioration of schools provides a powerful, persuasive visual for the need to provide funding to build a new school. Still photographs may be included in computer-generated or electronic presentations as well. Photographs also may be enlarged for the entire audience to view. When using photographs, detail must be visible by all audience members. If an audience member has to strain to view the image, credibility is lost.

Slides and transparencies were common visual aids prior to the advent of computer-generated presentations. Although not as commonly used as in the past, slides and transparencies should be considered as another option for a visual aid. Slides are effective because information can be projected to the entire audience. Still photographs can be transformed into 35 mm slides. The disadvantage of using slides is that the presentation room must be darkened to view the slides. Bring along a pencil flashlight so that notes can be viewed in a darkened room. Practice the slide presentation to ensure slides are in the correct order and presentation format. Having slides appear upside down not only distracts the audience and consumes valuable time, but it also sends a message that the presenter is unorganized.

The benefit of transparencies over slides is that transparencies can be viewed under normal lighting conditions. Eye contact still can be kept with the audience. The presenter has the capability to use markers to further add to the printed transparency. Transparencies also can be easily converted into PowerPoint presentations. If transparencies are used, it is important to avoid reading the text. Key points should be included on transparencies and complete sentences avoided. The goal of transparencies is to capture the key points of the presentation rather than represent a word-for-word narrative of a written document.

Electronic or multimedia presentations are the most common form of presentation aid used in today's workplace. Microsoft's PowerPoint is a common electronic presentation aid. When using computer-generated visual aids, remember the following:

- **Enhance the content of the information for the audience.** Having too many slides, colors, sounds, video, or audio takes away from the value of presenting key points to the audience.

- **Create clear visuals.** Including a distorted image takes away from the value of the presentation and causes confusion in audience members. Be sure that all labels on charts and graphs can be seen.

- **Use standard slide transitions.** PowerPoint includes many bells and whistles in slide transitions. Text and graphics can spin, creep in slowly, or fly across the page complete with sound affects. Effective presentations avoid including these effects altogether. Not only do the special effects use up valuable time (for example, by having text creep across the screen), but they also create distractions for the audience. Using distracting slide transitions and sounds takes away from the presentation outcomes. Ultimately, though, whichever transition is chosen, be sure to use it throughout, and not a variety or random effects.

- **Ensure visuals and presenter can be seen.** If a room is too dark, the presenter cannot be seen. Audience members may be interested in taking notes and it is critical that light is available. Ensure that visuals can be seen by all audience members. For a small presentation (one to five people), a computer screen is appropriate for presenting information. For a larger audience, a projector must be used.

- **Keep audio and video clips short.** If video or audio clips are used in the presentation, they should be kept short. Hamilton (2008) suggests that 15–30 seconds is adequate. If there is sound, test it on the actual equipment being used for the presentation prior to the formal presentation. Also, ensure that the video or audio tape is cued to the right location. Providing video or audio in an incorrect location can create confusion and cause distractions.

- **Prepare for technology failure.** Bring a hard copy of the outline and slides to the presentation. In the event that technology is not in working order, the presentation can continue. Practice using both a hard copy of the slides as well as the computer-generated presentation prior to the event.

Delivering the Presentation

Oral presentations and written text are different in several ways. In written text, a reader can go back and review material for clarification on what the writer intended to say. In oral presentations, audience members have only one opportunity to get the message and understand key points. Therefore, effective oral presentations require clear use of language. Oral presentations should use simple sentences, familiar words, repetition, and transitions. Use of clear language and strong organization of the presentation will assist the audience in focusing on the main points of the presentation. Unclear wording or inappropriately complex words will confuse the audience. One of the benefits of an oral presentation is that the speaker can adjust his or her presentation style to the needs of the audience. For example, if the audience members look confused, additional examples may be given to clarify information to the audience.

Avoid Buzzwords

Effective presentations gain and keep the attention of the audience. Avoid using buzzwords and idiomatic expressions because these may bore the members in the audience. Buzzwords are words, often technical in nature, used in an attempt to impress audience members. Also, diverse audience members whose first language may not be English will be confused by these broad terms. Because there is often a strict time limit for presentations, be as concrete and direct as possible. Sample buzzwords to avoid include the following:

- User-friendly
- Seamless
- Customer-centered
- Game plan
- Empowerment
- Value-added
- Win-win
- Best practice
- Paradigm shift
- Outside the box

Instead of using these types of broad expressions, explain the concept. Strong presentations are about clearly communicating the message.

The following checklist can be used as a guide for effective oral presentation style:

☐ Use personal pronouns, such as *we* or *us,* to personalize the presentation and create a sense of inclusion for the audience members.

☐ Avoid unnecessary jargon.

☐ Choose simple, clear words for description.

☐ Use repetition and transitions.

Controlling Nervousness

When called upon to deliver an oral presentation, many people feel nervous about speaking in front of a group. This real or perceived feeling of apprehension can be controlled by understanding the cause of communication apprehension and ways to build speaker confidence.

The body has a way of reacting to stress in a chemical and physiological manner. Adrenaline increases, breathing quickens, and a sense of "fight or flight" sets in. These reactions are similar to other stressful situations. Physiological changes may include increased perspiration and sweating, blushing, shaking, dizziness, numbness in extremities, or "butterflies in the stomach." Although individual responses vary from person to person, it is common for all speakers to experience one or more of these symptoms. Even the most confident speaker may have a sense of stress when anticipating delivering a presentation.

The goal of growing in confidence as a speaker lies in controlling nervousness, not eliminating it completely. In fact, some level of stress can cause increased performance in public speaking. This "positive stress" may take nervous energy and channel it into energy for delivering an engaging presentation. For example, instead of moving from foot to foot, this energy can be channeled into focused movement during the presentation. Walking into the audience not only releases some of the physical tension, but also gives the audience the impression that the speaker is engaging them.

Identifying ways that an individual's body reacts to stress can help manage it effectively. Techniques for reducing stress, such as relaxation exercises, can be engaged prior to giving the presentation. For easing tension, roll the head from side to side, clench and unclench the fists, and take deep, slow breaths. If there is a fear that the audience will not be receptive to the information in the presentation, a speaker should locate a friendly face in the audience and speak to this person initially, while being sure to make eye contact with the rest of the audience as soon as the speaker is more comfortable. Assessing public speaking strengths and weaknesses can assist in developing effective oral presentation skills. While weaknesses may never go away, understanding personal strengths and weaknesses allows the presenter to prepare a speech that focuses on individual strengths. Grice and Skinner (2004) suggest the following guidelines for building speaker confidence:

- Know the ways an individual reacts to stress.
- Understand public speaking strengths and weakness.
- Know speech principles.
- Believe in the topic.
- View speech making positively.
- Visualize success.
- Project confidence.
- Test the message.
- Practice.
- Learn from experience.

Delivery Methods

An effective oral presentation is one that appears to have a natural flow and delivery style. One way to achieve this effect is to think of the oral presentation as a formal conversation. Allow individual style to show through a natural, not dramatic, performance. Showing enthusiasm for the topic will engage the audience. If the speaker is interested and enthusiastic about the topic of the presentation, the audience is likely to be enthused and interested as well. Presenters should speak about the key elements of the proposal or project that they are passionate about.

There are four types of ways to deliver a speech: impromptu (without preparation), from memory, from a manuscript, or extemporaneously (from notes or with support of a visual aid). Speaking from a manuscript or speaking extemporaneously are the best delivery choices for a professional oral presentation. These methods allow the speaker to be organized and prepared, and to present in a natural manner.

Impromptu speaking occurs in daily conversation. For example, when an employer asks casually, "How is the project going?" the individuals engage in impromptu speaking. However, this format is too risky to use for a formal presentation. An unprepared speech can give the audience the impression that the speaker does not care about the presentation or topic and also takes away from the credibility of the speaker.

Speaking from memory is appropriate for professional presentations on rare occasions. Memorizing a speech word-for-word takes a great deal of time. Delivering a speech in a memorized format involves a great deal of concentration. The speaker may be concerned about forgetting a portion of the speech and this may result in a mechanical, robotic presentation. Also, if a section of the speech is forgotten, the speaker can become nervous and have to take time out of the delivery to gather thoughts. Memorized speeches are best used for very brief presentations, such as introducing a speaker or accepting an award.

Speaking from a manuscript ensures that the speaker is well prepared and that the contents of the speech will not be forgotten. A manuscript is a document that is prepared prior to the presentation and is a word-for-word text of the speech. Delivering a speech from a manuscript can increase confidence because the speaker does not have to be concerned with omitting details of the speech. The manuscript should be written in a conversational style—as if there is a conversation between the presenter and the audience. While a manuscript does take a great deal of time to write, edit, revise, and practice, the end result is that a complete speech is prepared. When delivering a speech from a manuscript, it is important to make and maintain eye contact with the audience and not to just read from the manuscript. The presentation needs to flow in a natural, conversational style, with well-placed pauses and emphasis.

Sample Speeches

It is useful to view sample speeches to assess effective delivery methods and speaking style. The History Channel's website at *www.History channel.com/speeches/index.html* provides an index of more than 100 speeches and verbal messages. Access the speeches by clicking on "Speech Archive" for a complex listing of presentations. Also, Toastmasters International, at *www.toastmasters.org/,* is an organization that assists individuals in cultivating communication and leadership skills through live meetings to present speeches. These speeches are positively critiqued by the organization's members, allowing for personal growth and confidence in public speaking.

Speaking extemporaneously, or speaking from prepared notes, is the most effective method for delivering a professional presentation. This delivery method involves preparation and practice. Materials should be organized and the speech practiced prior to delivery. Visual aids, such as PowerPoint slides, can serve as effective notes for guiding the speaker through the presentation. Following are some of the benefits of speaking extemporaneously:

- The speaker does not have to worry about forgetting information because key points are highlighted in prepared notes or the visual aid.

- The language of the speaker is more natural and conversational because the information is not written out word-for-word.

- The speaker and the audience can interact more freely.

- If the audience does not understand something said in the presentation, the speaker can expand on it using additional impromptu examples and explanations, or phrase it in a different manner.

Delivering a speech extemporaneously involves practice. Prior to the formal presentation, practice from notes and be aware of eye contact. The more a speech is practiced, the greater the confidence of the speaker. If using notecards, clearly number each one. Ensure the proper order of the notecards prior to the presentation. Special attention should be given to the conclusion; because the conclusion leaves a memorable mark on the audience, it should be delivered with emphasis and enthusiasm. Taking time to organize notes or reading directly from notecards takes away from the dynamics of the conclusion. Avoid distractions, such as letting the mind wander, focusing on an audience member's appearance, or thinking about the noise from the next room, and reinforce the message of the presentation through body language, voice, and gestures.

Vocal Delivery

Delivering an effective speech involves vocal elements as well as a delivery method. Even the most organized, prepared speech may fall short of its intention if effective use of vocal delivery is not applied. Improving the vocal quality of presentations involves practice and identification of areas that need improvement. Vocal delivery consists of rate and pause, volume, pitch and inflection, voice quality, and articulation and pronunciation. Mastering these elements will provide a speech that is engaging and informative to the audience.

Appropriate rate of speech is important to gaining and keeping the attention of the audience. A speech that is delivered too fast may prove difficult for the audience to follow and process what is being said. There is also an impression that a fast rate of speech is a sign of hiding something or that the speaker is nervous or unprepared. On the other hand, a speech that is delivered at a rate of speech that is too slow may seem boring to the audience. The audience may perceive that the speaker is not interested in the topic or in giving the presentation. The appropriate rate of speech for a professional oral presentation is one that is neither too fast nor too slow. Rate of speech should also be varied in the presentation. When presenting details or complicated information, the speaker should slow down the rate of speech. Speaking slightly faster in some situations may increase the persuasive nature of the presentation by sending the message to the audience that the speaker knows exactly what to say.

Pauses, defined as intentional or unintentional periods of silence during a presentation, provide emphasis or transitions in the presentation. A slight pause may allow the audience to reflect on what the speaker just said or create suspense for the words to follow. For pauses to be used effectively in a presentation, they must be intentional. If a presentation includes too many pauses or "ums" or "you know," the audience members will be distracted. Prepare intentional pauses in the presentation by practicing the speech out loud.

Volume is the relative loudness or softness in a speaker's voice. An effective professional presentation needs to include an appropriate level of volume. Extreme loudness can cause the audience members to view the speaker as boisterous or belligerent. A speaker who delivers a presentation in too quiet of a manner may be perceived as being timid or weak. Additionally, if a presentation cannot be heard, the audience becomes frustrated because the message and meaning of the presentation are lost. The size of the room also can impact the level of volume needed for effective delivery. If possible, view the room in which the presentation will occur to understand the acoustic setup (e.g., a high ceiling may cause an echo effect). Practice the speech and adjust volume accordingly. If a microphone needs to be used for a presentation to a large group, practice beforehand to become comfortable with the sound of amplified voice. The speaker also needs to be aware of external distractions, such as the sound of construction, an air conditioner unit, talking in the next room, and the like. Adjustments in volume may need to be made to overcome these distractions.

Pitch and inflection also play a major role in the effective vocal delivery of a presentation. *Pitch* refers to the highness or lowness of a speaker's voice. *Inflection* refers to the patterns of change in a speaker's pitch level while talking. The ideal pitch for a speaker's voice is the level at which comfort in speaking is achieved. This will vary from individual to individual. Inflection can assist the speaker in creating an interesting, enthusiastic speech. A presentation delivered without inflection results in a flat, monotone, boring speech. Listening to inflection during the practice period of the presentation allows the speaker time to adjust inflection accordingly.

Voice quality refers to the unique characteristics of an individual's voice. This is the least flexible element of vocal delivery because it is difficult to change the characteristics of a person's voice without the assistance of a trained speech therapist.

Articulation and pronunciation are two ways of forming the sounds necessary for communication. *Articulation* refers to the process of forming sounds necessary to communicate in a particular language. *Pronunciation* refers to how the sounds of a word are to be said and which parts of the word need to be stressed. Basically, pronunciation is how the letters of a word will sound and where the stress falls in spoken words. It is important to the credibility of the speaker to pronounce words, especially names of people, correctly. To check the pronunciation of a word, a dictionary may be used.

Engaging the Audience

An effective oral presentation is one that not only provides the audience with information, but one that engages the listeners in the presentation. Showing a level of enthusiasm through appropriate gestures and vocal qualities causes audience members to pay closer attention to the speaker. Enthusiasm is indeed contagious and can carry over into the audience. If the speaker is excited by the presentation, the audience can see and feel this level of enthusiasm.

Confident speakers engage the audience members in the presentation. When a speaker focuses on the intended message and delivers the message with confidence, the audience pays closer attention to the presentation. When the message of the presentation is delivered directly to the audience, the listener focuses on the meaning and not on the behavior of the speaker.

Effectively engaging the audience involves establishing a connection between the speaker and the audience members. The speaker must develop a sense of caring for the audience and their reasons for listening to the presentation. This can be accomplished by ensuring the message is relevant and interesting to the audience members, and by showing interest and concern for the audience in the delivery of the information. Being direct is an effective way to demonstrate interest and concern for the audience and involves doing the following:

- Maintain eye contact with audience members.
- Use a friendly, conversational tone of voice.

- Use animated facial expressions, especially smiling, when appropriate.
- Present in close proximity to the audience members.

Nonverbal Communication

In the case of professional presentations, actions can speak louder than words. In addition to the vocal and visual components of a professional presentation, nonverbal communication needs to be considered. In a broad sense, nonverbal communication is commonly used to describe all human communication events that transcend spoken or written words (Knapp and Hall 2006). Nonverbal actions are typically those that follow a verbal expression. The behaviors often are interpreted as intentional and have agreed-upon interpretations in a particular culture (Burgoon and Hoobler 2002). Effective use of nonverbal communication can add credibility to the speaker. Use of eye contact and posture can show speaker interest and enthusiasm in the topic. Being mindful of the impact of nonverbal communication can greatly enhance a professional presentation.

Unlike verbal communication, which is planned and intentional, nonverbal communication is continuous and may be unintentional. For example, an individual can plan what to say in a speech; however, some nonverbal responses such as a smile or a frown cannot always be planned or controlled by the speaker. The meaning of nonverbal communications can be ambiguous, because nonverbal communication can be interpreted differently by different members of the audience. Understanding the various types of nonverbal communication, such as those listed below, can assist in alleviating some of this ambiguity that may occur among audience members:

- Eye contact
- Movement
- Gestures
- Facial expression
- Appearance
- Movement
- Posture

Eye contact can be defined as the visual contact that the speaker maintains with the audience members. Making direct eye contact with the audience is a sign of the trustworthiness of the speaker. Eye contact also can be a sign of confidence, concern, sincerity, interest, and enthusiasm. Lack of adequate eye contact can signal deceit, disinterest, or insecurity (Grice and Skinner 2004). Facial features play an important role in the nonverbal communication used in a presentation and the eyes carry the most amount of information. There is a difference between eye contact and staring at an individual audience member. Staring intensely at an individual creates an uncomfortable feeling. A speaker should give the impression that he or she is looking at all members of the audience, without staring at individuals. Making eye contact with a variety of audience members can help give this impression.

Gestures can assist the speaker in emphasizing main points of the presentation, as well as help to clarify meanings of the words in a presentation. Gestures also can help fill a gap between words, providing clarification in a presentation. For example, to show the size of a microchip, a presenter may hold two fingers slightly apart. The key element to using effective gesturing in presentations is to find a natural flow. Because gestures reflect individual personality, do not force a gesture that is unnatural. Additional guidelines for using effective gestures in a professional presentation include the following:

- Practice gestures prior to the presentation.

- Know individual weaknesses in presentation style. Videotaping a speech can help show annoying or distracting mannerisms.

- Use gestures that are appropriate to the topic and the audience.

- Use natural, not forced, gestures. Avoid being too dramatic because this will distract the audience from the meaning of the message.

- Do not use antagonistic gestures. Pointing toward the audience or shaking a fist will have a negative effect on the audience; try a less antagonistic gesture, such as the forefinger curved around the top of the thumb, which is a common gesture for politicians.

By definition, Verderber and Verderber (2008) define *facial expression* as "the arrangement of facial muscles to communicate emotional states or reactions to messages" (p. 81). Facial expressions are important in demonstrating the emotional side of the message. While individuals can attempt to mask emotions, facial expressions are sometimes out of the control of the speaker because they occur naturally. Wrinkled eyebrows, for example, may be an unconscious gesture based on deep concern. During a professional presentation, audience members will observe the speaker and will notice the role facial expressions play in the consistency of the message. If the speaker smiles while talking about the benefits of building a community center, the audience is likely to believe the speaker finds this project a benefit to the community.

Although individuals attempt to keep an open mind about the appearance of others, judgments are made about the presenter based on the way he or she looks. While it is difficult for an individual to alter body physique, there are elements of physical appearance that can be controlled by the presenter. Clothing and grooming communicate a personal message about a person. When giving a professional presentation, dress the part. Jeans and a t-shirt is a casual style of dress for an informal situation. However, this casual style is likely not appropriate when presenting a proposal to a CEO. The speaker should be mindful of the message sent with clothing and grooming. It is better to err on the side of being conservative, than be misinterpreted by casual dress. For a formal presentation, men should do the following:

- Wear a dark colored suit of jacket and pants. Colors should be navy, black, or gray.

- Ensure facial hair, such as beards or moustaches, are well groomed.

- Ensure hair is combed.

- Avoid heavy use of fragrance or cologne.

- Straighten necktie, if worn.

- Avoid large pieces of jewelry and earrings.

For a formal presentation, women should do the following:

- Wear conservative colors such as navy, black, or gray. Avoid loud or bright colors.

- Select conservative styles of skirts and pants.

- Avoid trendy styles in pants, such as flared legs, tight pant legs, etc.

- Wear small pieces of jewelry. Wearing large pieces of jewelry will distract from the speaker and the message of the presentation.

- Keep hairstyles conservative.

- Avoid heavy use of perfume.

Movement during the presentation can assist both the speaker and the audience members. As noted earlier, when a speaker moves from place to place, nervous energy can be released; however, frantic pacing does not constitute effective use of movement, but is seen as a sign of nervousness by the speaker. Movement, chosen with a purpose, can help the audience members to pay closer attention to the presentation. For example, movement can signal transitions or emphasize main points.

Podiums can cause a barrier between the speaker and the audience. Moving away from the podium reduces this barrier. This is especially useful during the concluding portion of the speech. To bring a presentation to a powerful close, moving slightly toward the audience creates a sense of physiological closeness and draws attention to this important part of the presentation.

Good posture is a sign of confidence. Posture, which may be defined as the position of the body when an individual sits or stands, is a form of nonverbal communication that is easily seen by the audience members. The correct posture to use in a professional presentation involves standing up straight with feet slightly apart. Avoid slouching over or shifting weight back and forth too frequently, which can be perceived as a sign of uneasiness by the presenter, because the audience may become distracted by the movements. If a podium is used during the presentation, be careful not to lean on it. Avoid rocking back and forth while holding on to the podium because this type of movement is distracting and adds an informal feeling to a professional presentation. Professional presentations also should be given while standing. Sitting with the audience creates an informal feeling to the presentation, and reduces visibility of the presenter. While sitting with the audience members may be appropriate for a roundtable discussion, standing is appropriate when the goal of the presenter is to inform or persuade the audience.

Diversity in Nonverbal Communication

Gender and culture impact nonverbal communication. Knowing the demographics of the audience can assist in ensuring the proper nonverbal messages are conveyed in a presentation. Western cultures view eye contact as a sign of confidence and trustworthiness. Direct eye contact is not seen the same way across different cultures. For example, Verderber and Verderber (2008) explain that in Japan, direct, prolonged eye contact is considered "rude, disrespectful, and threatening" (p. 89). Individuals from Latin America, Caribbean cultures, and Africa often avoid eye contact as a sign of respect (Verderber and Verderber 2008).

Women in the United States have more frequent eye contact in conversations than men (Cegala and Sellars 1989). Women also have a tendency to hold eye contact longer than men, regardless of the gender of the person to whom the woman is speaking (Wood 2007). These differences are important to note so that the speaker may adjust eye contact according to the demographics of the audience members.

Research shows that there are many similarities in facial expressions across cultures. For example, a slight raising of the eyebrow to communicate recognition, or wriggling of the nose and a disgusted facial look to show social repulsion (Martin and Nakayama 2000). However, many nonverbal gestures carry very different meanings across cultures. For example, the forming of the "OK" sign in the Unites States means "worthless" in France, is a symbol for money in Japan, and is a vulgar gesture in Germany and Brazil (Axtell 1999).

Responding to Questions

When planning a professional presentation, include a question-and-answer period at the end. This is an important time when the audience can ask for clarification or additional information on points made during the presentation. This section of the presentation is impromptu in nature and should have a set time limit. Stay within the time frame for the question-and-answer period. Use a transitional phrase, such as "There will be time to address one more question," to signal that the presentation time is drawing to a close. If there are still hands raised at the end of the allotted time, the presenter may suggest talking to the individuals at a later time, outside the presentation format, by saying, for example, "The project team members would be happy to address additional questions via phone or email. Business cards have been left on the podium. Feel free to contact us at a later time and we can address additional questions." If the allotted time is not followed, the presentation may continue on past a time frame suitable for both the audience members and/or the speaker. Additionally, speaking in an impromptu situation for an extended amount of time can be stressful for the presenter.

At the start of the presentation, it is a good idea to announce to the audience that a question-and-answer session will be held for (set) number of minutes at the end of the presentation and to please hold questions or comments until after the end of the presentation. An exception can occur in the case of a technical presentation where the audience must have an understanding of the foundations of the technical material before moving to the next phase; in these situations, the presenter may have to pause every 15 minutes or so to see if there are any questions. Informing the audience up front that a question-and-answer period will be held at the end of the presentation will avoid having audience members ask questions during the presentation. Interruptions during the presentation may cause the speaker to lose focus or distract from the flow of the presentation. Also, addressing questions in the middle of the presentation may be redundant if the information will be presented at a later time.

Question-and-answer sessions are common in most technical presentations. However, confirm with the person planning the program that there will be time for such a session. Because time is often limited in professional presentations, specifically schedule in a block of time at the end of the presentation to address questions. During the practice stage of the presentation, carefully time the presentation and make necessary adjustments in time if a question-and-answer period will occur. Following are additional suggestions for planning a question-and-answer session:

- View the question-and-answer session as a positive experience. Although it may be stressful for a presenter to respond quickly to questions, this is a good opportunity to clarify information from the presentation. Valuable feedback can be gained from audience members if comments, as well as questions, are entertained.

- During the planning stage of the presentation, think of potential questions that the audience may ask. Write down potential questions and answers on notecards and rehearse the responses. If possible, ask an individual familiar with the topic to listen to the presentation and write down questions. Practice responding to the questions asked by a colleague.

- Prior to the presentation, decide if both questions and comments will be entertained from audience members. If time is limited, it is a good idea to limit the question-and-answer period to questions only. Some comments can take up a considerable amount of time, which can take away valuable time that could be spent clarifying questions from other audience members.

- Although there is no way to predict the exact questions or reactions by the audience members, try to anticipate ways of controlling the session so that one person does not dominate the conversation. At times, one person may attempt to ask a string of questions, preventing others from asking questions.

At the start of the question-and-answer period, allow the audience members a brief amount of time (10 seconds is a good standard) to think of questions to ask. If there are no questions from the audience, state, "If there are no questions, this concludes the presentation." This statement will bring necessary closure to the presentation. In some settings, it may be appropriate to raise questions to the audience if feedback is wanted on the presentation.

For example, a presenter may ask, "What challenges do you foresee with building a community center in the downtown area?" This may engage the audience members in a discussion that will provide valuable information for the presenter. However, this type of audience questioning should be used only if the presenter wishes to gain feedback and information. In a situation where time is restricted, stay focused and limit questions. Other suggestions for fielding questions include the following:

- Look directly at the person asking the question. The presenter should demonstrate active listening by maintaining eye contact with the person asking the question.

- Respond to the question by looking at all of the audience members, not only the person who asked the question. Responding to all audience members will ensure that everyone feels included in the response.

- Respond loudly and clearly to questions so that all audience members may hear the response. It is useful to repeat the question asked to ensure that everyone has a clear understanding of the question. If the audience members cannot hear the question, the response might be confused and result in more questions.

- Be consistent with giving responders' compliments such as, "Thank you for asking that question." If praise is given only to a limited number of questions, the audience members may feel that their question was not valuable. A presenter should attempt to connect and engage with the audience members at all times and avoid alienating individual members, especially at the concluding portion of the presentation.

- Be honest in responding to questions. If an audience member raises a question that the presenter does not know the answer to, it is important to say so; the presenter should not attempt to make up a response. This situation can be handled by asking other members of the project team to respond (if appropriate) or by saying that this specific answer is not known at the moment. The presenter can then exchange information stating that the answer will be researched and a response will be given at a later time.

Even with the best planning, problems may occur in the question-and-answer period. There may be an audience member who is argumentative or challenging. The presenter should attempt not to become defensive. If the comments from the audience member are accurate, respond in a conciliatory manner by stating that additional research will be conducted or statistics updated, and offering appreciation for bringing up the point. This approach builds good will with the audience members, as errors may occur in a presentation.

At times, an inappropriate question may be asked by an audience member. If a response is personal or involves a long, detailed explanation not appropriate for all audience members, it is best to inform the person asking the question that the response will be given privately. This situation may occur in a technical presentation with mixed levels of expertise by the audience members. Someone unfamiliar with the technical material may ask for information that may be common knowledge to the other audience members. In this case, a long explanation would bore the other audience members. The presenter may inform the person asking the question that a one-on-one meeting could be arranged to address the question in greater detail.

REFERENCES

Burgoon, J. K., and M. Burgoon. 2002. "Nonverbal signals." In: R. F. Verderber and K. S. Verderber, eds. *Communicate!* Belmont, CA: Thomson Wadsworth.

Cegala, D. J. and A. L. Sillars. 1989. "Further examination of nonverbal manifestations of interaction involvement." In: R. F. Verderber and K. S. Verderber, eds. *Communicate!* Belmont, CA: Thomson Wadsworth.

Grice, G. L., and J. F. Skinner. 2004. *Mastering public speaking.* 5th ed. Boston, MA: Pearson.

Hamilton, C. 2008. *Communicating for results: A guide for business and the professions.* 8th ed. Belmont, CA: Thompson Higher Education.

Knapp, M. L., and J. A. Hall. 2006. "Nonverbal communication in human interaction." 5th ed. In: R. F. Verderber and K. S. Verderber, eds. *Communicate!* Belmont, CA: Thomson Wadsworth.

Martin, J. N., and T. K. Nakayama. 2000. "Intercultural communication in contexts." 2d ed. In: R. F. Verderber and K. S. Verderber, eds. *Communicate!* Belmont, CA: Thomson Wadsworth.

Neuleip, J. W. 2006. "Intercultural communication: A contextual approach." 3d ed. In: R. F. Verderber and K. S. Verderber, eds. *Communicate!* Belmont, CA: Thomson Wadsworth.

CHAPTER 19

Writing in Other Professions

Technical communication is a career that applies to every profession. Even if a job title does not specifically say "technical communicator," all companies need writers on staff. In some fields, specialized certifications or degrees are required, but this is not always the case. Some companies actually want to train their writers themselves. There are basic skills most technical communicators are expected to possess, such as the ability to communicate appropriately to a specific audience; meet deadlines; write for various mediums, such as print, broadcast, video, or Internet or other electronic formats; and have an excellent command of the English language. Along with the more common forms and formats of writing that have been covered in this book so far, medical, science, legal, business, and information technology all have specialized genres and required skills, which is what this chapter discusses.

Audience, ethical concerns, and other considerations cannot be covered in a comprehensive manner because every profession spans the entire spectrum of issues and concerns for each of these factors in writing; therefore, only a few of the most common aspects about each is covered in the following sections.

MEDICAL WRITING

Medical writing serves various purposes, such as educating or informing patients and the general public, instructing patients before or after a procedure, providing outreach services, advertising, and such highly technical purposes as reporting research. Skills range from note taking to researching and composing full-length medical reports or scholarly articles. A medical writer may be required to have certification or an advanced degree in the sciences, medicine, or pharmacy, but some companies prefer a communications, journalism, or English degree and maybe a few years of experience writing medical documentation of some kind. In this particular field, medical transcription may be a requirement as well. Medical writers have to feel comfortable interviewing physicians and researchers, and in order to prepare for such tasks, they have to be able to research, read, and comprehend medical, scientific, and statistical data.

There is a wide gap in the audiences one may address in the medical field. Audiences range from children and the general public to expert researchers and medical practitioners with many years of experience.

Ethical concerns for a writer in this field include presenting statistical data accurately, using correct terminology, writing comprehensible and usable instructions, and paying attention to the smallest detail because someone's life may be at stake. Keeping up to date with current research and trends in the field is also critical.

Opportunities for medical writers exist in medical research and development organizations, health insurance and pharmaceutical companies, individual medical offices, and on medical publications staff.

Genres Associated with Medical Writing

Forms of writing in the medical field include broadcast, video, websites, and print, which encompasses journal or scholarly articles, press releases, and marketing and informational materials, such as handbooks, brochures, pamphlets, and newsletters. Due to the nature of this field, marketing is often presented in creative formats that remind people to take their medicine, consider a new medication, or schedule an appointment for a procedure. These formats include bookmarks, calendars, magnets, and pocket guides or instructions. While some may consider medical writing only for those who have a more

TABLE 19.1 *Short Forms of Medical Documentation*

Short/Form Document Types	Explanation
Patient charting	Records data regarding patients and often includes observations, history, information from physical exams, or admittance information.
Procedural reports	Documents what has taken place during a procedure or the care required afterward.
Progress notes	Data sheets record the progress of a patient.
Instruction sheets	Lists steps to be followed by patients before or after a procedure.
Discharge summaries	Provides patients with expectations and instructions for home care and continued treatment upon release from a hospital.

practical and factual approach to their writing, creativity is also highly valued. A brief description of some of the most common forms of medical writing are shown in tables 19.1 and 19.2.

Resources for Medical Writers

A medical writer might find the following references helpful:

- *Gray's Anatomy of the Human Body*
- Medical dictionaries and style guides
- Pharmaceutical guides
- *Physicians' Desk Reference*

Listed below are professional organizations that offer online resources for writers in the medical field:

- **American Medical Association (AMA).** The AMA is a national physicians group concerned with promoting national health standards. *www.ama-assn.org*

TABLE 19.2 *Longer, More Complex Medical Documents*

Longer/Complex Document Types	Explanation
Instruction sheets	These provide patients with self-care instructions or how to administer a procedure themselves; or, they are instructions to health care providers about how to administer a particular procedure. Depending on the procedure, instruction sets can also be long and complex.
Clinical studies, trials, or protocols	Scientific reports that inform how a medicine or treatment works.
Discharge summaries	Depending on the patient's individual case, discharge summaries (as described in the previous table) can be long and complex.
Presentations for conferences	Medical writers may be asked to prepare research proposals, papers, or presentations for conferences. Sometimes, medical writers are asked to travel to conferences and report on the proceedings.
Journal publications	Medical writers may be asked to research or write up complete articles for journal or scholarly publications. Interviewing or working with expert medical staff is part of this process.
Fundraising materials	These may include writing individual campaign materials for private funding for a hospital to searching for public funds for research activities.
Advertisements for drugs or treatments	These may include handbooks, brochures, or pamphlets for specific drugs, treatments, or procedures. These may also be informational in nature describing signs, symptoms, and treatment for diseases or other health-related conditions.
Proposals	Medical writers may write full-length research or grant proposals to government agencies or private funding organizations.
Websites	Medical websites can range from an individual medical practice's website that provides physician background, specialty, and services provided to larger organizational medical sites that contain databases of articles and comprehensive medical information, such as lists of physicians and other medical experts, and interactive functions (*www.webmd.com*). These sites are geared for the general public to look up signs, symptoms, and recommended treatments; find local physicians; chat with nurses or other medical personnel; and perform certain activities on a site, such as inputting data to determine one's body mass index or where one falls on a chart for weight and height. Other interactive components include providing insurance information or updating one's personal data.

- **American Medical Writers Association (AMWA).** The AMWA was founded in 1940 to help medical writers improve their writing skills. *www.amwa.org*

- **Board of Editors in the Life Sciences.** Created in 1991, this board is dedicated to establishing proficiency among editors in the life sciences. *www.bels.org*

- **European Medical Writers Association (EMWA).** The EMWA is a support for medical writers and editors in European countries. It offers information on training, jobs, conferences, and other resources for medical writers. *www.emwa.org*

- **National Association of Medical Communicators (NAMC).** The NAMC is a national association for those involved with medical newscasting or medical public relations. *www.namc.info*

SCIENCE WRITING

Technical writing first became a career in the 1940s when many science disciplines found a need for someone to be able to communicate technical information to general and expert audiences. For those with an interest in science, but who wish to continue working as a writer, there is always the option of working as a science writer. Whether it is engineering, geology, meteorology, anthropology, national defense, aerodynamics, chemistry, biology, or any other science discipline, there is a need for writers. A technical communicator can find fulfilling employment writing research and technical reports, marketing materials, government documentation, specifications, proposals, presentations, speeches—the list is as varied as the many facets of society that have anything to do with science. Generally, science writing is meant to educate or inform the general public or create an interest in a particular subject among experts; therefore, oftentimes, a science degree or experience within a particular field is required.

Audiences that a science writer might address run the entire spectrum, just like in medicine, from children and the general public for educational purposes to expert scientists, engineers, or other technical personnel, such as when reporting research results.

Ethical concerns for a science writer include accurately representing data and statistics, ensuring there is no bias when reporting results, and communicating at an appropriate level for the intended audience. Although the focus of ethics in science is generally on the actual experimental procedures, a writer also is bound to the same code of ethics. Inaccurately reporting results or construing them in a manner that confuses the reader will undermine the principles set by distinguished scientists in the field.

Opportunities for those interested in science writing can be found in local, state, and federal agencies, such as the Bureau of Land Management, U.S. Geological Survey, Department of Defense, Department of Agriculture, and other science and technology agencies, which can be found at *www.usa.gov/ Citizen/Topics/Science/Agencies.shtml.* Private companies and universities also hire science writers in the same capacity as government agencies.

Genres Associated with Science Writing

A science writer composes materials for print, broadcast, video, websites, and other electronic formats. A science writer may write or edit educational material for children from kindergarten to high school, such as textbooks, magazines (such as *Kids Discover* or *National Geographic Kids*), documentaries, science activities, and general information guides, such as guides to the stars or field guides for the life sciences. In addition, a science writer might write and edit college materials and informational web materials intended for the public (some of which can be found at *www.worldbestwebsites.com/ science.htm*). On the other end of the spectrum, a science writer may be deeply entrenched in writing white papers, research papers, or laboratory reports, or preparing technical and scientific presentations for clients or conferences. Furthermore, proposal writing is big business in the sciences because funding is competitive. A science writer may be hired solely to research funding opportunities by looking through volumes of requests for proposals (RFPs) and to write research and grant proposals to government agencies or private organizations. Marketing material is also a part of science writing, and will include the usual brochures, pamphlets, and Internet advertisements.

Forms of writing associated with science include empirical research reports and other technical reports as mentioned previously in this book. Other forms include those shown in table 19.3.

TABLE 19.3 *Forms of Science Writing*

Document Type	Explanation
Laboratory reports	Technical reports that allow scientists to communicate research results.
Standard Operating Procedures (SOP)	Provides step-by-step instructions associated with materials, methods, study details, precautions, and other pertinent information. They often deal with federal regulations or other mandated scientific guidelines.
Press releases	Announces or describes projects under research or results from completed research projects.
White papers	Provides overviews of technology, a product, or research topic. White papers can precede or follow conference papers or presentations, proposals, or technical reports.
RFP analysis	Science writers are often hired to search for funding opportunities. They have to know where to look for RFPs, read them regularly, understand them for relevance to the subject or project they are working on, and evaluate success potential. This is often part of a proposal writer's job.
Technical definitions, descriptions, specifications	These can be stand-alone documents or part of other larger document sets. For instance, in many sciences, technical definitions or descriptions may be separate handouts. See chapter 10 for details about these documents.
Marketing/advertising materials	These materials publicize products and include brochures, newsletters, commercials, documentaries, Internet content, or other materials used to market or advertise a product, program, agency, etc.
Education materials from kindergarten-level on up	Writers may be asked to write or edit textbooks, experiments, handouts, magazines, videos, science shows, or documentaries.
Journal or scholarly articles/conference papers and presentations	Science writers may help researchers by assisting with research for journal or scholarly articles or conference papers and presentations, or they may have to research and compose entire articles, in which case interviewing scientists and other technical personnel is required.
Websites	Websites may include an organization's site with a mission statement, background information, and resources for others associated with that particular branch of science. Some science websites may be for children or teachers and include educational materials presented in entertaining and interactive formats, such as shown at *http://kids.discovery.com.*

Resources for Science Writers

An online list of science references can be found at *www.refdesk.com/ science.html* or *www.ipl.org.*

Listed below are professional organizations that offer online resources for writers in the sciences:

- **Council of Science Editors.** This council serves as a support for professionals in the sciences as well as those who work in publishing in the sciences. *www.councilscienceeditors.org*

- **IEEE.** This organization covers a multitude of disciplines, not just engineering. *www.ieee.org*

- **International Science Writers Association (ISWA).** The ISWA is a professional organization for science journalists. *http://international sciencewriters.org*

- **National Association of Science Writers (NASW).** Chartered in 1955, this society is dedicated to "promote good science writing." Includes information for freelancers as well as those working in established companies. *www.nasw.org*

- **New England Science Writers.** This is a support and network organization for freelancers and other professionals working in the sciences mostly in the New England region of the United States. *www.nasw.org/ users/nesw/home.html*

LEGAL WRITING

In the legal field, writers and editors are needed as legal research assistants, as well as overseers of contracts, intellectual property, and copyright material. A technical communicator may also find opportunities for transcribing legal information into documents that can be understood and used by clients or the general public. In addition, criminal investigative reporting, forensics, and other specialized fields are open to those who are skilled writers with a background in criminal justice, science, or medicine.

Legal writing relies on precedence and persuasion. Source documentation and citation are key to this type of writing. Legal writers have to possess deep analytical skills because they are required to scrutinize data, check facts, interpret the data and facts, and then apply them correctly to a given situation.

Audiences for a legal writer range from the general public, such as where contracts are concerned, to lawyers and other legal professionals.

Ethical concerns for this type of writing relate to whether or not the language used fits the intended audience. It is unethical for a company or individual to execute a legal document where the language is beyond what the reader can reasonably understand, especially when it comes to using legal jargon. In other words, it is disreputable to hide information through convoluted text that the intended audience cannot reasonably comprehend. Clear and precise writing are mandatory writing characteristics. Citation and credibility of sources are also concerns because so much of legal writing depends on where information originated from.

A technical communicator can find writing opportunities in the legal field as a paralegal or research assistant, a contract specialist in corporations, a patent or trademark researcher, or a compliance and regulation officer in insurance and health organizations or scientific companies and agencies.

Genres of Legal Writing

Legal documentation and forms vary according to the type of law practiced, such as criminal, real estate, intellectual property, family, bankruptcy, civil rights, corporate, general practice, personal injury, and many others. A legal writer may also write in other formats, such as those presented in table 19.4.

Resources for Legal Writers

For citation, a profession standard is *The Bluebook: A Uniform System of Citation* published by the Harvard Law Review Association.

Listed below are professional organizations that offer online resources for legal writers:

- **American Association for Paralegal Education (AAPE).** The AAPE is a support for paralegals and those who provide education to paralegals. *www.aafpe.org*

TABLE 19.4 *Forms of Legal Writing*

Document Type	Explanation
Legal documentation	This can range from forms most commonly used in the legal field to summaries of laws and lawsuits.
Scholarly articles	Articles bound for publication in professional and scholarly journals.
Customer correspondence	Client letters and email are usual forms of correspondence that are considered customer correspondence.
Office correspondence	Memos and other employee materials, such as policies and procedures from a human resources office, qualify as office correspondence.
Contracts	Includes legally binding agreements.
Case briefs	These summarize the facts and legal issues of a court decision for research or legal delivery.
Web development	Includes website content that may be for an individual practice or a comprehensive legal website with databases of legal documentation, forms, directories of lawyers, and interactive features, such as chat rooms and blogs.

- **American Bar Association (ABA).** The ABA is a resource site for lawyers and others working in the legal field. *www.abanet.org*

- **Association of Corporate Council (ACC).** This council serves attorneys who work in corporate or other private sector situations worldwide. *www.acc.com*

- **Association of Legal Administrators (ALA).** The ALA is an organization dedicated to improving legal management in law firms and other legal organizations. *www.alanet.org/default.aspx*

- **Association of Legal Writing Directors (ALWD).** This is an association for those working as legal writing directors at law schools. *www.alwd.org*

- **Legal Writing Institute.** This is a non-profit organization for legal writers. Includes information on writing and research in the legal field. *www.lwionline.org*

- **National Association of Legal Assistants (NALA).** The NALA is an association that supports legal assistants in education and professional development endeavors. *www.nala.org*

- **National Court Reporters Association.** This is an association specifically for court reporters. Includes information on education and professional expertise. *www.ncraonline.org*

- **National Federation of Paralegal Associations (NFPA).** The NFPA is an association for paralegals with information on news, positions, legal resources, and more. *www.paralegals.org*

- **Scribes—The American Society of Legal Writers.** Established in 1953, this organization is dedicated to improving writing in the legal field. *www.scribes.org*

BUSINESS WRITING

Writing in a business environment is probably one of the most collaborative of all of the fields discussed in this chapter. Furthermore, the persuasive element in business writing is probably just as important as it is in legal writing. Generally, a writer in a corporate environment is expected to have additional skills other than excellent writing ability, such as customer relations, presentation, collaborative, analytical, and even leadership skills.

Business writing is often coupled with other job responsibilities, such as business analysis or project management. In this highly collaborative environment, a business writer may write sales proposals and also deliver sales pitches to clients; he or she may write product documentation, testing procedures, and product training materials, and may even conduct the product tests and deliver the product training. Other common responsibilities include managing interoffice documentation, such as writing policies and procedures and other human resources related material; working with marketing to write and design product information and advertising kits; and writing, designing, and managing all website content. A business writer often is responsible for managing an entire company's documentation, including Web content, and is expected to know about knowledge management tools (programs that help a company organize, manage, and store internal and external communication) and content management systems (tools used to manage content of a website so that material can be easily created, modified, organized, and removed).

In business writing, audiences range from the general public, when trying to sell a product, to interoffice personnel to external customers and potential clients.

Ethical issues for a business writer are mostly concerned with the heavily persuasive aspect of business writing. Has the information been presented accurately or is it implying or promising something beyond its potential? Have statistics and testing data been presented accurately and completely? As mentioned in chapter 4 on research, are independent studies conducted under ethical conditions and are the results of those studies being presented in a true light? It is easy to get carried away with strategies and techniques that can persuade the public and clients, but is that persuasion ethical? These are questions around which a business writer must constantly monitor his or her work, or risk ruining a company's image in the eyes of customers.

Business writing opportunities exist in every corporation or company that cares about its image as portrayed through written documentation. A business writer can find a position as part of the human resources department, marketing and sales staff, information technology staff, or as a proposal writer, documentation specialist, copyeditor, or desktop publisher. The positions available for technical communicators in the corporate world are as varied as the businesses that exist.

Genres of Business Writing

A business writer may find the document types listed in table 19.5 to be typical forms of writing expected on the job.

TABLE 19.5 *Forms of Business Writing*

Document Type	Explanation
Interoffice communication	Includes emails, memos, technical reports, human resource documentation and job descriptions.
Process documentation	Usually refers to policy and procedure manuals.
Sales proposals	Includes documents designed to sell a product or service to a customer or potential client.
Business proposals	Documents that propose a new business or project within a business.
Presentations	Includes product or sales information to customers or potential clients.
Marketing materials	Includes brochures, commercials, Internet content, newsletters.
Training materials	Human resource or client training documentation.
Business plans	Documents that provide operating plans or procedures for a company.
Product test plans	Test plans and procedures for company products.
Web content	Includes writing content for websites that may be for a single company that lists what the company is, what it produces, and information about its products, or websites that may be more comprehensive and include databases and interactive components.

Resources for Business Writers

For business writers who are involved in interoffice, human resource, or process documentation, having handbooks, dictionaries, and grammar books within arm's reach can be helpful. Other reference books include the following:

- *The Chicago Manual of Style*
- *The Gregg Reference Manual*
- *Publication Manual of the American Psychological Association*

For a business writer involved in proposal writing, the Foundation Center lists websites and a recommended book section at *http://foundationcenter. org/getstarted/guides/proposal.html.*

Listed below are professional organizations that offer online resources for business writers:

- **International Association of Business Communicators (IABC).** The IABC provides products, services, activities and networking opportunities to help people and organizations achieve excellence in public relations, employee communication, marketing communication, public affairs, and other forms of communication. *www.iabc.com*

- **International Women's Writing Guild.** The Guild was established in 1976 and provides support for women in writing professions regardless of the discipline. *www.iwwg.com*

- **Public Relations Society of America (PRSA).** Provides professional development, job opportunities, and resources for professionals in public relations positions. *www.prsa.org*

- **Society of American Business Editors and Writers.** This is a non-profit organization for journalists in business. *www.sabew.com/news/home.htm*

WRITING FOR INFORMATION TECHNOLOGY (IT)

Technology is part of everyone's life regardless of age, culture, or economic status. For a technical communicator, this field is rich in opportunity to write and also branch off into other specializations within the profession. Employment prospects for a technical communicator in an IT company include documenting manuals and software specifications, creating architecture and security programs/plans, writing policies and procedures, maintaining websites, and programming. Writing opportunities in IT are as varied as the technology associated with it.

Audiences for documentation in IT range from general use, such as manuals that accompany products meant for the general public, to professional software developers and architecture specialists. One of the main concerns for writers in IT is that they be familiar with the technology that is being written about and understand the technology from the developers', architects', and users' perspectives. Oftentimes, complex and new information needs to be translated to readers who may not be technically savvy.

Ethical concerns for a writer in the IT field include issues related to usability and accuracy. *Usability* refers to how well documentation can be employed, drawn on, or applied by a consumer. *Accuracy* means that when instructions are given for a process, that the steps are correct and will produce the desired outcome. It is advisable for a company to test IT documentation on representative audiences before sending it out en masse, because its reputation and continued sales rest on how well the documentation is received. Guidelines for writing user manuals and technical instructions can be found in chapter 10, and testing and usability issues are discussed in chapter 17.

A writer who is interested in working in IT can find work in most companies that use computers or computer technology. This includes corporations, universities, science laboratories, and medical facilities.

Genres Associated with IT

When writing IT documents, a writer has to have the background and knowledge to be able to interview software developers or other technical subject matter experts. Document design and graphic design are sometimes a big part of an IT writer's responsibilities, so familiarity with graphics software, such as Photoshop, is helpful. Understanding procedures associated with designing, developing, and rolling out a software program, for instance, is also critical to someone who wants to work with software developers. Additionally, a writer may have to know certain programming languages. Typical documents associated with writing in the IT field are listed in table 19.6.

Resources for IT Writers

For a writer in the IT field, various books on programming languages that are used by the software developers are helpful to have as a desk reference. Books on writing and designing for the Web or other electronic formats are essential as well.

A professional organization that offers online resources for professionals in IT is the Association of Information Technology Professionals at *www.aitp.org/index.jsp.* Other resources for technical writers in the IT field include the following:

- **American Chemical Society (ACS).** There are 34 ACS divisions, representing a wide range of disciplines for chemists, chemical engineers, and technicians. *www.acs.org*

- **American National Standards Institute (ANSI).** The ANSI has served in its capacity as administrator and coordinator of the United States private sector voluntary standardization system for 80 years. *www.ansi.org*

- **American Society for Information Science (ASIS).** The ASIS is a society for information professionals that searches for new and better theories, techniques, and technologies to improve access to information. *www.asis.org*

TABLE 19.6 *Forms for IT Writing*

Document Type	Explanation
Technical instructions	See chapter 10.
User guides	See chapter 10.
Architecture plans	These are blueprints of a company's IT elements, how they are connected, and how they work together.
Security plans or programs	Descriptions of how a company's IT elements are secured from internal and external sabotage.
Operating procedures	Process documentation which describes how to conduct certain processes or procedures.
Online help guides	Online help should not simply be transferred from hard copy to an online environment; they have to be reworked according to the principles for Web writing and design.
Technical definitions and descriptions/ specifications	See chapter 10.
Client training materials	Instructions for using a product, service, or certain technology; they may be administered through face-to-face presentations, in hard copy, or online.
Software test plans	Detailed procedures that outline how a software program will be tested for usability and accuracy.

- **Association for Computing Machinery (ACM).** The ACM serves a membership of more than 80,000 computing professionals in more than 100 countries in all areas of industry, academia, and government. *www.acm.org*

- **HTML Writers Guild (HWG).** The HWG is the world's largest international organization of Web authors with more than 85,000 members in more than 130 nations worldwide. *www.hwg.org*

- **IEEE Professional Communication Society (PCS).** The primary mission of the IEEE PCS is to help engineers and technical communicators develop skills in written and oral presentation. *http://ewh.ieee.org/soc/pcs*

- **Internet Society (ISOC).** The ISOC is a nonprofit, nongovernmental, international, professional membership organization. It focuses on standards, education, and policy issues. *www.isoc.org*

- **National Writers Union (NWU): Technical Writers Code.** To promote fair standards and encourage professional working relationships, the Technical Writers Trade Group of the NWU presents a Code of Professional Practice for technical writers in the hardware and software industry. *www.nwu.org/nwu*

- **The Web Standards Project.** The Web Standards Project is a coalition of Web developers and users. The project's mission is to stop the fragmentation of the Web by persuading browser makers that standards are in everyone's best interest. *www.webstandards.org*

- **Usability Professionals' Association (UPA).** Recognizing the need for a practical-oriented organization dedicated to enhancing the skills and professional success of usability professionals, Janice James created the UPA in 1991. *www.usability professionals.org*

- **World Wide Web Consortium (W3C).** The W3C was founded in October 1994 to lead the World Wide Web to its full potential by developing common protocols which promote its evolution and ensure its interoperability. *www.w3.org*

SALARIES FOR TECHNICAL WRITERS

Salaries for technical communicators depend on the years of experience, location, and degree of technical knowledge required for the job. Salaries can be found on several Internet sites, as well as through the *Society for Technical Communicators* (*www.stc.org*) for members. Listed below are additional Internet sites that give salaries for technical communicators:

- Payscale.com, *www.payscale.com/research/US/Job = Technical_ Writer/Salary*

- Tech-Writer.net, *www.tech-writer.net/hourlyratesandsalaries.html*

According to *STC's 2003 Salary Survey,* the mean salary for entry-level technical writers/editors in the United States was $43,260. For these professionals in Canada, it was $41,030.

Job Market

The U.S. Bureau of Labor Statistics' *Occupation Outlook Handbook* (2004–5 edition) predicts that, among the different areas of writing, opportunities will be best over the next several years for technical communicators and writers with specialized training. It goes on to say:

> *Demand for technical writers and writers with expertise in specialty areas, such as law, medicine, or economics is expected to increase because of the continuing expansion of scientific and technical information and the need to communicate it to others.*

The full entry can be found at *www.bls.gov/oco/ocos089.htm* (scroll to the section "Job Outlook").

Salaries for Communication Majors

Communication majors work in a variety of media-related jobs in areas such as television, newspapers, radio, and online. Recent graduates earn an average annual salary of $29,962, according to a fall 2005 survey by the National Association of Colleges and Employers (NACE) in Bethlehem, Pennsylvania, while communication majors earn $31,879.

News assistants at television-news organizations earn an average annual salary of $25,000, according to a 2005 survey from the Radio-Television News Directors Association in Washington, D.C. Sports reporters at radio-news organizations earn $21,400 in average annual salary.

The average annual base salaries (weighted by newspapers) for entry-level reporters and copyeditors are $28,234 and $30,687, respectively, according to a 2005 survey of 519 daily newspapers by the Inland Press Association, a trade group in Des Plaines, Illinois.

Annual salaries for Web-content writers with one to five years of experience range from $33,500 to $47,500, according to a 2005 report from the Creative Group, a staffing firm in Menlo Park, California.

Junior-level business publication editors, including assistant editors, editorial assistants, and copyeditors, earn $30,000 in median annual salary including bonus, according to a 2004 survey from the American Society of Business Professional Editors in Naperville, Illinois.

Graduates in 2004 who majored in communications received a median annual salary of $27,800, according to a survey from the Grady College of Journalism and Mass Communication at the University of Georgia in Athens. They received the following in median annual salary according to the type of media organization they joined:

- Daily newspapers: $26,000

- Weekly newspapers: $24,000

- Radio: $23,000

- Television: $23,500

- Cable television: $30,000

- Advertising: $28,000

- Public relations: $28,500

- Consumer magazines: $27,000

- Newsletters, trade publications: $28,000

- Websites: $32,000

Publishing

Publishing employees, including college graduates and experienced professionals, earn the following in total median annual compensation, including base salary and bonus, according to a 2005 report from Abbott, Langer & Associates Inc., a Crete, Illinois-based human resources consulting firm:

- Production editor: $36,184
- Marketing specialist: $35,699
- Copyeditor: $30,668
- Writer, editorial: $32,580
- Reporter/correspondent: $26,873

Film and Television

Broadcast-journalism majors earn an average annual starting salary of $26,339, according to NACE. Communication majors earn $29,763.

News assistants at television-news organizations earn an average annual salary of $25,000, according to a 2005 survey from the Radio-Television News Directors Association in Washington, D.C.

The average weekly salary for an editorial apprentice is $1,039, according to a 2004–2005 report by the Motion Picture Editors Guild in Hollywood, California.

CHAPTER 20

Jobs in Technical Communication

As seen in the previous chapter, there is a tremendous need for writers who can target specific audiences and convey information accurately and clearly. While there is incredible choice in the field of technical communication, one key to finding the right job is to be happy by doing what is interesting now and promising for the future.

This chapter covers how to prepare materials for finding the right job in technical communication, such as writing and designing an effective résumé, cover letters, and portfolios. It also discusses how to prepare for and do well in a job interview.

FINDING THE RIGHT JOB IN TECHNICAL COMMUNICATION

Finding the right job is not as difficult as some may think. The right job does not have to be the result of years of hard work at the "wrong" job; it can simply be a matter of knowing one's interests, getting actively involved in professional activities, and being prepared.

To begin with, it is important to know what employers want. This means going beyond the job title and learning what skills and responsibilities are required for certain positions. This information is also valuable to help a writer decide if this is the type of work that will sustain their interest, and if so, determine if he or she is truly prepared. There are several ways to investigate the requirements for certain positions, such as browsing job advertisements, talking with a company directly, or querying others who work in a similar position.

The Language of Job Advertisements

The first thing to note is that many professions require technical communicators even if they are not titled as such or even established within that particular career field. When searching for a job, the keyword "technical writer" most likely will result in thousands of jobs nationwide; however, listed below are other keywords that mean the same as technical writer, and in some cases may even help narrow the results of a search:

Communications specialist	Marketing specialist
Copyeditor	Media specialist
Copywriter	Medical, legal, or business writer
Documentation specialist	Project manager
Editor	Proposal writer
Grant writer	Publications coordinator
Internet content developer	Staff writer

Narrowing the search is only the beginning to finding a job that is meaningful, rewarding, and lasting. The newspaper is still a valid resource for employment information, but there is also the convenience of searching online employment databases as well. Online job searches have several benefits in that most advertisements provide brief background information about the company and even an Internet address, which is really an invitation. Companies want prospective job candidates to search their websites and learn as much about them before putting in an application. One reason for this is that a company wants potential employees to know who they will be working for and determine if the company is a good fit for them. This is actually a key bit of information because the company a person works for is probably more important than the actual job. Learning about a company means checking out its website for the following:

- Image

- Rhetoric used on the site (i.e., formal or informal tone); this can give a feeling for the atmosphere of the company

- Design of the site (e.g., professional, amateur, jazzy and driven by popular culture, traditional, or practical)

- Links, which show what they consider to be important to customers as well as employees

- Background and history (e.g., how long the company has been in business)

- Customer base (most will brag about big name customers)

- Contact information (it is not out of the question to call the company and ask for more details about the posted job or speak directly to the hiring contact)

Companies want potential employees to do their homework before applying. This cuts down on the number of applications from those who do not know what they want, or what the company wants. A person who does not do his or her homework regarding a company is really looking for just a job and not a career. This can be disastrous for both the employee and the company.

After researching the company, the next thing to look at in the advertisement is what the job entails. When looking through the advertisement for job responsibilities, read the whole advertisement carefully, and don't just browse for certain keywords. Reading the advertisement slowly and in its entirety is important because there may be additional clues that tell the writer what his or her experience might be in that position. For instance, there is a big difference between an advertisement that says:

> Work with product managers, developers, and client services
> to continually improve printed and online user guides.

and one that says:

> Write regular updates to printed and online user guides.

While each example can imply several scenarios, the first example seems to suggest that updating materials is more of a collaborative effort between the writer, product managers, developers, and client services personnel. The second example implies that updating materials will be the responsibility of the writer alone and something that should be monitored and done regularly. For someone who likes to work with others, the first example is probably more appealing; for someone who works well independently, the second example might be preferred. When looking at a job advertisement, ask not, "Can I do that?" but rather, "Would I like doing that?" And, read scrupulously to determine what is being conveyed by the particular language used in the advertisement.

Other factors to take into consideration are the skill sets and the knowledge of technology wanted by employers. For careers in communication, writing skill sets will be rather general, such as, "Excellent writing skills, ability to convey technical information to non-technical audiences, ability to work independently and quickly learn new software applications." More specialized skill sets are something to pay particular attention to, such as, "Familiarity with health care clinical and/or billing systems. Prior end-user training or implementation experience a plus." If one's interest is more along the lines of corporate writing, such as in a marketing department, and this job came up in the list of results, then the keywords used for this job search are probably not narrowed down enough, and this job is not right, even if all of the requirements can be met. Again, looking for interesting and intriguing work should be a major goal during a job search.

If, however, the job seems to fit at this point in the search, then the next thing to examine is the technological skills required. Usually, advertisements will list a series of software programs the company expects the writer to know how to use. While a potential applicant may not be familiar with all of the software programs listed as "preferred," it would be appropriate to apply for this job if he or she has knowledge of or experience with similar programs. Usually, what employers want to discern is whether the person knows the principles behind certain programs and has enough experience to pick up new applications quickly. In a case where the wording is more direct as to what is "required" on the job, then having experience with certain applications is more serious. For instance, if an advertisement says "Mac OS X Server and server technologies, Windows, and UNIX experience needed," then it implies that the applicant has to already have this experience; there probably is no time for learning these programs. Of course, all of this is up to the employer, and if there is any question, it would not hurt to contact the employer and ask questions about the position so that no one's time is wasted.

An applicant's needs are just as important as an employer's needs. If insurance benefits or a retirement plan are needed, then those are things to look for in an advertisement or search for on the company's website. When it comes to salary, most times this is negotiable depending on experience, unless firmly stated in the advertisement. If, however, the salary is quite low and one is still very interested in the job, then it might be advantageous to contact the employer directly. This is not to say you should ask the employer about the salary right away; instead, discuss the job responsibilities. They may not be what they appear to be in the advertisement, which could explain why the salary is lower than expected. Sometimes, though, the salary is just that low depending on the area of the country or the company. A low salary may be supplemented with other benefits, such as tuition reimbursement, on-site child care, flexible hours, or a casual atmosphere. If an applicant is not bound by monetary needs, then a position with a low salary can still be appealing.

Once a fit has been established after reading the advertisement carefully and researching the company website, then the next step is to prepare a résumé and cover letter, as well as ask for letters of recommendation, if required.

Résumés

A résumé gives potential employers a snapshot of an applicant's recent experience and accomplishments. It is not a generic document though; one format and set of content does not fit all situations. In fact, it is wise to have several versions saved because a résumé will change depending on the emphasis of a job. For instance, a person who has a background as a technical communicator and as a college instructor would have several versions of a résumé. One would be formatted for times when the writer is looking for editorial work, one for freelance work, one for technical writing jobs, and one for jobs in education. Format, in this case, means both the way the information is presented on the page as well as the information provided on the résumé. There is no one right way to write and format a résumé because it is such a dynamic document; however, there are ways to write a résumé that are more effective than others. Listed and discussed below are parts of a résumé and ways to write them effectively. All sections should be written and designed for easy reading and browsing. The sequence of each of these sections is not set either because that also depends on what is emphasized in the job description.

Name and Contact Information. Generally, this information is provided at the top of the page. Most times it is centered for easy reading, but it does not have to be. Usually, the name of the applicant is in a larger font size than the rest of the contact information and even other text on the page. Bolding the name will highlight who the résumé belongs to. Some individuals may have logos associated with their names, which also can appear at the top of the document.

Employment Objective. The employment objective is a brief statement that tells readers what the applicant has in mind as far as what position he or she would like. An employment objective can range anywhere from one very concise sentence about what the applicant wants in the near-term to a short paragraph that includes future goals as well, as in the example below:

> I am interested in working as a developmental editor, mentoring authors through the book writing process and editing their work for adherence to established guidelines and contract specifications. I am also open to cross-training or assisting in other editorial areas as, eventually, I would like to expand my career and work as a production or acquisitions editor.

Some employers and résumé-writing books will insist that every résumé must include an employment objective. This is actually debatable. In some cases, an employment objective is necessary and quite appropriate, such as when applying with a large corporation for a job that was listed on a general employment website such as monster.com, and especially when the job title is rather generic, such as "editor" or "writer." When the job title and job description are generic or broad in scope or description, then an employment objective helps employers distinguish serious applicants from those who are simply sending out generic résumés to multiple companies. On the other hand, when applying for a specific position, and the title and description are explicit, then it may not be necessary to include an employment objective. Examples of this type of situation can include teaching positions or executive jobs. Generally, the more senior the position within a company or the more experience it requires, the less the employment objective is necessary.

Education. For those who have already obtained degrees, information to include under this heading would be the title of one's degree, the name of the institution, and the year the degree was granted, as in the following example:

> Master of Science in Technical Communication, Michigan Technical University, 2007

> Bachelor of Science in Communication, Kaplan University, 2005

Any continuing education classes can be listed either in this section or in a later professional development section. Education generally follows the employment objective, if one is included, because most professional jobs have educational requirements.

If a college degree is in progress, then the applicant can list the intended degree, name of the institution, anticipated date of graduation, and classes that are relevant to the job, as in the following example:

> Bachelor of Science in Communication, Kaplan University. Anticipated date of graduation: May 2007

> Relevant coursework:
>
> - Introduction to technical communication
> - Advanced technical communication

- Interviewing skills for technical writers

- Writing for the Web

- Software applications (covers Microsoft Office, Adobe products, and other publishing programs)

- Writing for the workplace

- Mass communications

What this list of courses shows employers is that the student, while not yet graduated, is taking classes that pertain to the job. The anticipated date of graduation gives an employer an idea of when the person will be finished with school and can then commit to full-time employment. Both the list of classes and anticipated date of graduation help an employer determine if this person can be considered for the position.

Professional Work History. Employers are looking for several things when browsing someone's work history. They are looking for who the person has worked for, how long, in what capacity, and keywords that match keywords in the job advertisement. They also are looking to make sure the applicant has had steady employment.

Conciseness is paramount when it comes to writing job responsibilities on a résumé. Some employers do not even mind phrases, but this is usually not a good idea because phrases can be interpreted in different ways or can limit the context. It is better to use complete sentences, but make sure they are direct and include keywords from the job advertisement, if possible. Below is an example entry for this section:

Technical Writer, Northrop Grumman Mission Systems, Crystal City, VA, July 2003 to July 2005

Managed all project documentation. Responsibilities included technical editing, managing online collaborative writing projects, synthesizing information into one comprehensive document, reviewing all documentation for correctness in language, format, and standards. Aided in the design and implementation of an electronic document management system, and managed the collection and indexing of all project documentation; transferred information onto various media, and distributed to customers. Other duties included serving as member of Change Control Board, a committee designed to track and document changes to computer laboratory baseline. Composed process documentation to achieve CMMI Level III. Contributed to Northrop Grumman's Missile Defense Division Newsletter *Expressions.*

Work history can be ordered in one of two ways: chronologically starting with the most recent job first or according to position. If an applicant has experience in two different professions, then ordering the work history according to type of position makes more sense. If an employer sees that the applicant's most recent job is in another field, and it is the first thing listed under professional work history, then he or she might be thrown off and not continue looking through the rest of the work history section. Another way to deal with this situation is to have a professional work summary that categorizes the work history according to profession, listing the most relevant jobs first. Then the details of the applicant's job history can follow a chronological order so that employers can see the that person has been employed continuously.

Skills. A skills section is relevant for a technical communicator so that all of the software programs and other technology experience relevant to the job being applied for can be listed. Obviously, these same programs would be part of the job responsibilities described in the professional work history section, but a separate section like this gives employers a supplemental and comprehensive list for easier reading.

Professional Organizations. Belonging to professional organizations has many benefits for a technical writer. To show an affiliation with a professional organization implies that the applicant is most likely someone who keeps up to date with the latest trends and issues in the field. The advantages of membership in a professional organization are discussed in depth in chapter 21.

Submitting Résumés Online

Many companies now have websites where applicants can submit their résumés online. One thing to note about online submittals is that all document formatting is stripped when the text is pasted into the program boxes. If a document is not formatted for this kind of stripping, the end result could be completely illegible at the other end. It is advisable to have a formatted résumé for times when an attachment can be sent, but one should also have an unformatted résumé for the purposes of copy-and-paste.

The unformatted version has no bold, italics, bullets, indentation, or tabs. Instead, it is simply plain text, left justified, and formatted using only line spaces. An example unformatted résumé is shown at the end of this chapter.

It also should be noted that when submitting a résumé online, the review of the electronic file is not conducted by actual people. Instead, information is electronically reviewed using keywords associated with the job description.

Professional Development. Several things can fall under the professional development section of a résumé, such as the following:

- Continuing education courses
- Conference attendance and/or presentations
- Special committee membership
- Other activities associated with career development or career contribution

Publications. A list of publications enhances a technical communicator's résumé because it shows active engagement in the field and experience with professional writing. Choose an appropriate style guide from which to cite one's publications and list the most recent first.

As with any professional document, the guidelines for effective page design apply to a résumé. Leave plenty of white space, chunk information, bullet certain items, and use headings and subheadings appropriately. An example résumé is shown at the end of this chapter.

Cover Letters

The cover letter, also called a letter of application, may be more important than a résumé, especially in the field of communications. After all, the cover letter is the first piece of writing a potential employer will read. An effective cover letter will demonstrate clear, concise, and engaging writing. Steps to create a letter of application which meet all of these requirements are discussed below. An example cover letter is shown at the end of this chapter.

State the Purpose. For American companies, the first sentence of the opening paragraph should state the purpose of the letter and accompanying résumé. In this sentence, include the exact title of the job position (and position number if one is given in the advertisement), as well as where the advertisement was found. Following is an example of how to do this:

> I am applying for the editor position (ID# 1234) at McGraw-Hill Education, as advertised on monster.com.

Follow this sentence with a quick background statement and brief explanation about why this job is of interest, as in the following example:

> My experience encompasses over 15 years working as a developmental, production, and acquisitions editor in the K–12 market. I am particularly interested in this position because I noticed in the advertisement, and on your website, the innovative steps that McGraw-Hill is taking toward putting educational resources in electronic format. Technology used for educational purposes is something I have kept current with throughout the years.

This opening may catch a reader's eye because it focuses on the writer's interest in technology related to publishing and education. Because this was mentioned in the advertisement, it most likely is a major consideration for the person chosen for this position.

Illustrate Experience. In school, writing teachers often use the "show, don't tell" phrase to get students to add detail and appropriate description to their writing. This same rule applies to cover letters. It is not enough to say, "I have excellent writing skills." Instead, show or illustrate one's excellent writing skills through the writing contained in the cover letter (discussed below) and when describing the details of one's experience. Show the reader why the information is significant enough to be included in the cover letter, as in the following example:

> Improving workflow processes is a part of every editorial position I have held. In addition to analyzing processes for efficiency and effectiveness, I am always searching for technology that can make collaborative efforts more organized and resourceful. For example, in my present position where I am responsible for synthesizing information from seven authors into one final report, I introduced the team to Microsoft Word's master document feature. By using this resource, all seven authors were able to work on their own chapters independently and simultaneously, without having to pass files around and run the risk of sending out wrong versions. The result was less time spent in development and in the final editing stage because there were no file version mishaps to work through, thus saving the company money.

In this example, great lengths were taken to describe an instance of where the writer demonstrated effective workflow improvement. No matter how much information you want to include in the letter of application, make sure to describe how you met certain major requirements.

Use Keywords. Analyze the advertisement and company's website to locate keywords and insert them into the cover letter. *Keywords* are words that can be unique to a particular company or standard for a certain field or position. For instance, acquisition, development, production, liaison, attention to details, deadlines, collaboration, and quick turnaround are keywords associated with editorial jobs. Using keywords appropriately and accurately demonstrate one's knowledge of the profession and position. Furthermore, employers are looking for these words because these words define the position, as in the following example:

> Because I have worked in several editorial positions, I am fully aware of the importance of **deadlines** and how one **missed cutoff date** affects **production, marketing,** and on down the line. One of my strengths as an editor has been to **manage collaborative efforts** to ensure that each project begins with a **workable timeline,** and I continue to monitor incoming work against schedules so that there are no surprises on a deadline date.

Demonstrate Effective Writing Style. A cover letter should demonstrate clear, concise writing that is intriguing and interesting to read. It also should show effectiveness in meeting its purpose and reaching the intended audience. If a cover letter strays from what is expected by employers, then it is assumed that the applicant will be as inept at writing anything else. Understandably, for those seeking jobs in communication, spelling, grammar, and punctuation have to be perfect, and errors are usually not forgiven. It is wise to have a second or third reader to double-check one's writing for clarity, conciseness, and accuracy.

Additionally, command of the English language should be demonstrated in a cover letter. This means using proper grammar as well as words that have impact appropriate for the situation. For instance, notice the difference between the following sentences:

> I am scrupulously attentive to detail, committed to meeting deadlines, and exceptionally reliable for quick turnaround.

> I edit my work closely, meet all deadlines, and am efficient in my turnaround times.

While letters of application are not exercises in creative writing, there are some words and writing styles that are assertive, have great impact, and reach out and grab a reader, as shown in the first example. In the second example, the writing is not wrong in any way; it just is not as intriguing as the first sentence.

Ask for an Interview. In the last paragraph of a cover letter, ask for an interview. This is often forgotten or assumed on the part of the applicant, but why leave it up for interpretation? In keeping with the tone and pace of the rest of the letter, end with the same certainty expressed previously, as in the example below:

> Enclosed are my résumé, three letters of recommendation, and my portfolio on CD. I would like an opportunity to interview with you and discuss my qualifications for this position in more detail. Thank you for your consideration of my application. I look forward to hearing from you.

International Employment. For international audiences, a cover letter and résumé might have to be formatted completely different than what is mentioned above. For instance, in China, job objectives are listed after personal information (Chaney and Martin 2007). Research into the rhetorical strategy for letter writing should precede any correspondence with a foreign company or international audience because customs and expectations vary. Making an attempt to acquiesce to another country's customs can go a long way in developing a respectful and lasting relationship should one be hired.

What to Avoid. In an effort to make their résumés and cover letters stand out from the rest, some people use colored paper, print on paper with backgrounds or borders, or add graphics. These strategies are actually quite tricky. How does one measure something tasteful and appealing versus something that comes across as ostentatious or amateur? Standing out from the rest in a physical way may not always be what an employer is looking for, especially for a technical writing position. This is not to say that a visual symbol or graphic is entirely inappropriate on a résumé. It depends on the job. For instance, if applying for a writing position within a marketing department, then visual appeal is certainly appropriate. On the other hand, if applying for a technical writing position on an engineering team working on missile defense, then visual appeal may be seen as being amateur or even ridiculous. As with any piece of writing, analyze the audience and conduct research on the company. Before deciding what to include in a résumé and cover letter, determine whether the company is traditional or innovative/creative.

Letters of Recommendation

It may seem a bit elementary to include a section in this book on asking for letters of recommendation. It seems rather simple to ask someone to write a letter portraying the job applicant in a favorable light. However, often overlooked is the lack of guidance given to those writing the letter, which can affect how the letter is written and, in turn, affect the influence it has on a potential employer.

Choose carefully who to ask to write a letter of recommendation. Consider the position it puts the person in, knowing that a coworker or employee may be lost, and analyze the relationship beyond what seems obvious. Most people would not write a nasty letter just to make sure the candidate does not get the job, but it is not unheard of either. This could be the result of not reflecting on the nature of one's relationships carefully.

When asking others to write letters of recommendation, give them guidance. This means giving them the following information so that what they include in the letter is appropriate for the job, and less generic:

- **The job title and company.** With this information, the letter writer can speak to the applicant's ability to work in this position and for this particular company.

- **What the position entails.** By knowing the job requirements, the reference can comment on specific strengths and achievements of the applicant in the current position.

- **Contact information.** It is important that the letter be addressed correctly and not left open, as in "To Whom It May Concern." It can reflect poorly on the applicant when the reader assumes that the letter writers were not given any guidance, even something as basic as the name of the addressee.

- **Who they should send or give the letter to.** Some people would prefer that the applicant not see what they wrote, for several reasons, and so it is courteous to give letter writers an option to send the letter directly to the company (if that is permissible). If it is preferred that all application materials arrive at one time, however, then allow the letter writer the option to seal the letter.

The Inexperienced Letter Writer

Sometimes it may be necessary to ask a supervisor to write a letter of recommendation; however, that person's writing skills may not be up to par. In cases like this, it is best to give that person plenty of information about the job for which one is applying (the website for the position and an updated résumé) and include a sample letter of recommendation as well as some letter writing tips. The person will probably appreciate not having to compose the letter off the top of his or her head.

Especially for jobs in communications, there is an additional application requirement in many job advertisements now, and that is to submit a portfolio of writing samples. The following section discusses and describes how to portray a professional image through a portfolio, whether on paper or in electronic format.

PORTFOLIOS

A portfolio is a selection of original artifacts of an artist, writer, teacher, architect, graphic designer, or other professional who creates a product as part of his or her work. Portfolios are created for various purposes, such as in school where sometimes student portfolios are used for learning and assessment; however, the portfolios discussed in this chapter are for employment purposes only and are referred to as employment or professional portfolios. In an employment situation, a portfolio is a collection of one's best work; it is a showcase of relevant and excellent artifacts produced by the applicant for the purpose of demonstrating to a potential employer one's ability, versatility, expertise, and professionalism. These types of portfolios are also referred to as professional portfolios because the collection represents one's professional accomplishments as well.

There are two basic types of employment portfolios—paper and electronic—and it is advisable to have both. It takes a great deal of time to put together an engaging and worthwhile portfolio, and the time to begin collecting the pieces is while still in school or even brand new to a job. Every product created is a potential artifact for a professional portfolio (excluding those with certain restrictions, which are discussed below).

A paper portfolio is just that: It is a collection of published or hard-copy artifacts, such as user guides, instruction sets, policy and procedure manuals, proposals, reports, brochures, and other documents, all in paper form. The collection of artifacts should be displayed in a professional manner, such as in a three-ring binder with paper protectors or in a wire-bound document. The disadvantages of paper portfolios are that they are bulky and require a lot of copying and paper usage. If mailing a paper portfolio, especially if more than one copy is requested, this also can become a cumbersome and expensive task.

Electronic portfolios can be displayed either on CD or on a webpage. A CD is nice because it is portable and can be left with an employer after an interview or mailed easily with other application materials. A Web-based portfolio has its advantages in that it allows for more creativity. Disadvantages include access issues or other problems with technology.

When compiling a portfolio, keep in mind that the collection of artifacts is not comprehensive of one's career, but rather selective pieces of one's best work. When assembling a professional portfolio, there are several things to be aware of, such as content choices, organization, design, image, and copyright issues.

Content Choices. The content of a portfolio is dynamic because artifacts are chosen not only for their demonstration of the breadth and depth of one's work, but also for their relevance to the job for which one is applying. If applying for a graphic designer position, then including a long, technical proposal is not a good idea. What employers in a graphic design company want to see is what the applicant can do with graphics or page design. Unless the technical proposal was unique in design or included original graphics created by the applicant, then it would not be a relevant piece. Only those original images would be relevant, but certainly not the entire technical proposal. If, on the other hand, the application is for a technical writer position with a government contractor, then including a full-length technical proposal would be perfectly appropriate because that is more in line with the type of work one would do in that position. A sample list of relevant artifacts in relation to just a few job titles is shown in table 20.1.

The contents of a portfolio also say something about the applicant's personality. This is where Web-based portfolios have an advantage over paper or CD portfolios. In a Web-based portfolio, each piece can be introduced in creative ways that expresses one's personality. This can be achieved through design of the Web page, graphics, fonts, and other electronic resources. However, not all is lost if this is not an option. Some employers may not want this excess information, and instead may be interested only in seeing actual documents, in which case, a paper or CD portfolio is perfect. What is so interesting and fun about compiling the contents of a portfolio is the versatility of the pieces and what they express about the applicant.

No matter what contents are chosen, portfolio documents should be revised so that any mistakes in the original are corrected. One way to show an employer what one has learned is to have a before/after document that shows revision markup and then the revised piece. If revised documents are not included, then in the absence of the applicant, employers may see an uncorrected copy and mistakenly assume the writer did not catch the errors. There are all kinds of explanations for why certain errors may be in a document, but when the applicant is not present to enlighten employers about the situation, then the worst is usually assumed.

Organization. Organization of a portfolio begins with an effective cover letter. This cover letter is an introduction to the portfolio itself, not a repeat of the cover letter for the job. Tell readers what the portfolio contains, how it is arranged, and what skills it demonstrates. The cover letter is a substitute for what the applicant would say about the portfolio if he or she were there to present the artifacts.

The way the pieces are sequenced in a paper portfolio or arranged and presented in an electronic portfolio should have logical reasoning behind it. A

TABLE 20.1 *Samples of Relevant Portfolio Artifacts Based on Position Title*

Technical Writer	Graphic Designer	Communications Expert for Marketing
• Proposals • Reports • User guides • Instruction sets • Policy and procedure manual • Process documentation • Charts, graphs, tables created in various software programs • Relevant business correspondence	• Original graphics, drawings, photographs • Web pages • Brochures • Page design projects • Newsletters	• Brochures • Web pages • Posters • Presentations • Relevant business correspondence • Annual reports

"collection" does not mean a random sampling. Each piece may be viewed as a separate entity, but the parts also make up the whole in that the sequence, arrangement, or structure of a portfolio, whether in paper or electronic format, should convey a clear message. The organization of portfolio artifacts can show progression in ability or it can demonstrate versatility, as two examples.

Organization is first conceived when readers look at the table of contents. For a paper portfolio, the artifacts follow the table of contents. For a Web-based portfolio, the table of contents is displayed by a series of links. The most difficult format to structure might be the CD because generally a CD contains a series of folders or file names. It is important that the folders do not go more than two levels deep because readers may become impatient clicking and clicking until they finally see a file name. And, when displaying files in a folder, it is important to know for sure how those files will display from computer to computer. One option might be to use a Word document with hyperlinks to the portfolio artifacts contained on the CD. The work a reader has to go through to get to those files is minimized by having to only open one file and click on links in there. For the more technically savvy, well, the options are endless; however, always consider the work involved to get to artifacts and time constraints of the reader.

Design. Technical documents do not have to be bland and boring, especially when being displayed in a portfolio. Certainly, employers are not looking for every piece to entertain them or for any exaggerated hype; however, there are design choices that can make a portfolio look professional and creative.

Design begins with physical appearance. In paper portfolios, what is the most efficient and effective way to display one's work? As mentioned previously, a three-ring binder or wire-bound document is a good start. If using a wire-bound document, a stiff card stock used for the cover and back page gives the document a more professional look and feel. If using a three-ring binder, then a cover page should be slipped into the plastic covering on the front of the binder, and a title slipped into the spine.

In either case, the cover page conveys a message about the applicant right away. A white page with just one's name printed in the middle of the page can tell an employer a few things: this person is practical, there is nothing excessive about this person, or this person is a minimalist. It is also important to go to the extreme and know that a blank white page with just a name printed on it might also be interpreted by an employer as this person is boring or does just the minimal amount to get by. At the other extreme is the Web-based portfolio, which can go any distance with graphics or design on the home page. No matter the format, going overboard is usually not a good idea. It is advisable to have several people in different age groups visit a Web-based portfolio site to provide feedback. If the home page is busy and overwhelming, or conversely, bland or monotonous, then an employer may never get past the first page.

As noted earlier, a table of contents is essential for a portfolio whether paper or Web-based. Pages in a paper portfolio should be numbered and the table of contents should show page numbers for each individual document in the portfolio. A table of contents can further comment on the organization of a portfolio by grouping documents under headings, such as multimedia projects, technical writing projects, or Web-based projects. Additionally, a portfolio without a table of contents is a bad design decision because readers have no idea what the portfolio contains or how to get to certain documents they want to look at.

Each artifact should be introduced. This means writing up a short paragraph that tells readers what the document is, what it was written for, to whom, and what it demonstrates or why it is included in the portfolio. Also make the portfolio easy for readers to browse. If using a wire-bound document, it may be a good idea to print front/back so the portfolio is not so thick. If using a three-ring binder, then do not put a whole document into one paper protector, but instead, create a front/back effect with the paper protectors so that all readers have to do is flip through pages and not stop and pull a document out of a sleeve. If using a Web-based format, then make the table of contents and links easy to see and navigate with no more than two levels (one level may be the artifact introduction page that contains a link directly to the document).

Image. In the absence of an actual face-to-face meeting, a portfolio acts as an applicant's substitute. Content, organization, and design all portray an image. Be aware of what that image is. An applicant can come across as a moderate who is well organized, versatile, and talented, or as an eccentric who is scattered, excessive, and has no clue as to appropriateness or relevance. Once again, have several people from all age groups review the portfolio to get feedback about the image the collection portrays.

Copyright, Proprietary, and Confidentiality Issues. Most technical communicators will develop or contribute to projects that are sensitive in some way. This can mean that company proprietary information is included in the document, such as in a technical or grant proposal, and that means the document is not up for public consumption. In other situations, such as when working for a government contractor, there may be confidential or secret information in documents, which means those documents are most certainly not for public perusal. Just because someone has contributed or even has written an entire document, does not mean a person owns it. If one is using company documents as part of a portfolio, it is advisable to get written permission to use them. Do not include this permission in the actual portfolio, but keep it in a safe place in case there are ever any questions.

When it comes to graphics, drawings, or photographs, if those works are part of a document in a portfolio but they were not created by the applicant, then permission from the artist may be needed to include them. This includes any clipart or photographs used from the Internet or Microsoft applications. A thorough check of all portfolio documents regarding copyright or permissions issues should be conducted before sending out a copy or activating a website.

Once a résumé, cover letter, letters of recommendation (if applicable), and portfolio are perfected, then it is time to submit application materials. After submitting the materials, it is not necessary to wait endlessly to hear back from employers. A good time frame to wait, though, is about two weeks after the deadline for submitting application materials. After that time, it is understandable for a job applicant to follow up with an employer. This can feel like a rather uncomfortable situation, but most employers expect these calls after a certain time. The key to coming across as someone who is extremely interested in the job and not someone who is bothersome is to monitor the tone and have a good script ready. Consider the following possible dialog:

> "Hello, Human Resources."
>
> "Hi, my name is Megan Hendrix. Who am I speaking with?"
>
> "Jeanette."
>
> "Hi Jeanette, how are you?""
>
> "Fine."
>
> "Great! I am calling to follow up on the editor position advertised on monster.com a few weeks back. I submitted my application materials, because I am very interested in this position, and I would really appreciate an opportunity to interview. I was wondering if a selection has been made yet for those the company would like to interview for this job?"
>
> "No, we're still working on that job. I don't know exactly when that's going to happen."
>
> "I understand. Is Human Resources leading up this effort or has the stack of applications gone over to another department that maybe I can follow up with?"
>
> "No, application reviews are organized through this office; it's just that we're backed up with some executive positions that are in the works."
>
> "I see. Well, thank you for the information. As I mentioned, I would very much like to be considered for an interview for the

editorial position, so would you mind if I called or emailed you in another week or two to see where things are at?"

"No, that's fine."

"Thank you, Jeanette. Can I get your email address?"

"Yeah, it's jwayne@mgh.com."

"Thank you. I appreciate your time. Have a good day. Bye."

"Bye."

In this exchange, the applicant learns that the worst has not happened—there is still hope that she may be called for an interview. She also has another contact with the company. She now knows Jeanette's full name and email, which she can use to contact her in a couple of weeks. Sometimes Human Resources personnel are involved in screening applications, so if Jeanette is part of the screening process, then she now has a name that may make her look at Megan's résumé twice when she runs across the name. The point is that it does not hurt to follow up on a job application as long as it does not become bothersome to the employer. It is also a good idea to keep in mind the time that it takes for a company to process applications, because that could be an indicator of how fast everything moves at the company.

INTERVIEWING

An interview for a job begins with the very first phone call from an employer. To make a good impression, be fully prepared to speak with an employer at any time after an application has been submitted. One thing to keep in mind is how to answer the phone. Employers taken off guard by an annoyed "Yeah" take that into account when gauging the applicant's personality. Another suggestion is to be aware of with whom one is speaking. Sometimes during a job search, an applicant may put out five or more applications at one time. Keep a record or folder of the job descriptions handy so that when an employer does call, a quick reference into the folder will help identify the company and position. Asking an employer, "What job is this for? I put out so many résumés this past month I can't remember what the position is at McGraw-Hill" would not be a good start either.

When an employer calls for an interview, sometimes applicants can become so excited or flustered that they forget to ask for vital information.

Having a checklist by the telephone, such as the one shown below, is a good way to stay calm and obtain important information.

- **Be flexible on the day and time of the interview.** Employers generally have only a set block of days and times available for interviews. While it is understandable that a previously scheduled event may interfere with the suggested day and time for an interview, be flexible as to what events can be rescheduled around the interview. Certainly a lunch date can be rescheduled, but one may have to ask for an alternate day and time if there is a conflict with an important doctor's appointment. Repeat the agreed on day and time so that there is clear understanding on both ends as to the set time for the interview.

- **Ask who will be conducting the interview.** Will this be a one-on-one interview and with whom? Or will the interview be conducted by a panel? It is important to know the situation in order to be prepared, such as bringing in additional copies of a résumé if there is a panel of interviewers. It is also nice to know the name of the person conducting the interview in order to do additional research on that person's role and reputation in the company.

- **Ask where the interview will be held.** Ask the caller for specific location information, not just a room number. Ask where to park/ enter, and ask about access, such as having to stop by a security desk once inside the building. These small details actually can take up quite a bit of time and not knowing this information could result in being late for the interview. It is better to get all of this information squared away during the initial telephone call rather than winging it once on location.

Additional Research

Between the time that an interview is set and when it actually takes place is a busy time for serious applicants. Additional research about the job, company, and personnel is necessary. Return to the company's website to gain additional information about the job that might have been overlooked the first time. Revisiting the job description also helps familiarize the applicant with the responsibilities, and it should be used as a checklist for possible questions asked during the interview. Visit the rest of the site to gain more information about the company, such as what products they put out, review the history of the company again, and then review the list of employees if that information is included on the site. Other places where company information can be found are at university career centers and libraries (ask a reference librarian for suggestions), and on the Internet (besides the company site).

Preparing for the Interview

Research is only part of the preparation necessary to go into an interview well prepared and ready to get the job. Nervousness cannot be played down and neither can the importance of being prepared with answers to potential questions. There are several Internet sites that have lists of potential job interview questions aside from those that are pointed directly toward the responsibilities of the job. One such site is *http://career-advice.monster.com/job-interview-practice/100-Potential-Interview-Questions/home.aspx.* While no interview is going to cover all of these questions, they are good to review and be prepared to answer to some degree because employers are looking to learn how well applicants know themselves and how quickly they can think when asked these questions. There are other Internet sites that have lists of questions according to profession, such as jobs in the pharmacy or legal industry.

Aside from these general questions, take the responsibilities in the job description and turn them into mock questions. For example, if one of the responsibilities reads "Manage the work of freelance writers, copyeditors, proofreaders, indexers, illustrators, and designers as required to ensure the overall quality and that deadlines are met," a potential question could be: In what capacity have you managed freelancers?

In addition to preparing for the questions an interviewer might ask, compose a list of questions for the interviewer. Interview situations are often seen as being one-sided, but they are really an exchange of information. Employers are looking to see if the applicant is the right person for the job, but an applicant should also be evaluating whether the company and position are right for him or her. When applicants ask meaningful questions, it tells the employer that they are prepared, engaged, and interested in every aspect of the job.

Even if the application materials did not ask for writing samples or a portfolio, prepare these materials in a stylish and professional manner that can be left with the employer at the end of the interview.

Wardrobe

Planning what to wear to an interview is not a vanity issue, but an important consideration. Employers take note of what interviewees are wearing. That does not mean they are checking for brand-name tags or fashion statements, unless applying to a position in the fashion industry; what they are looking for is how interviewees present themselves through physical appearance. Does the person know what is appropriate attire for that particular workplace, and how will he or she appear to clients or coworkers?

For technical communicators, most interviews will be in corporate or other professional settings and so one's dress should be consistent with that image. It is, however, important to be at ease in the clothes chosen for the interview because new suits can be uncomfortable at first. It sounds funny, but practice wearing the interview clothes before going to the interview, because twitches caused by a stiff shirt collar or ill-fitted pants or skirt may be interpreted by interviewers as something else. If, however, the interview is being held in a casual setting, it is still a good idea to dress one notch up from the casual attire worn in the office.

Asking a friend to do a mock interview is a good idea, and taping the interview is even better. It is enlightening to see how one answers questions or the body movements one makes and is unaware of, especially when it comes to clothes.

In the Interview

There is no way to capture all interview scenarios in this chapter, but some general guidelines for conduct during an interview can be applied to most situations. The following are suggestions for having a successful interview:

- **Arrive on time.** Late arrivals are noted and may raise a red flag as to one's reliability and track record for being at work or at off-site meetings on time.

- **Be and stay positive.** In the introduction, when asked if it was easy to find the place, stay positive and do not complain about the traffic or the parking situation. Anything said at this point in the interview is going to be taken into account more than when the heat is on during the middle of the interview. First impressions are important and should not be underestimated.

- **Be aware of body language.** Find a comfortable sitting position that needs to be changed only periodically. Nervous twitching or adjusting clothes during an interview is distracting to the employer. Be aware of eye contact, body movements, such as crossing the arms when asked certain questions, tapping pens, pencils, or fingers, voice level, how fast one talks, and any other habits.

- **Be personable.** Be genuinely friendly and sociable during the interview. Come across as knowledgeable about the job being applied for, but also be personable and someone who other coworkers want to work with.

- **Be direct but explanatory when answering questions.** Employers have only a limited amount of time to get the information they need to make a decision about whether the applicant is right for the position. In an effort to help them through this process, be precise and concise when answering questions, all while also offering pertinent explanations. What this means is to mix directness with appropriate details, and deliver answers in a conversational tone.

- **Avoid salary negotiations in the first interview.** Unless salary is brought up by the employer, talking money during a first interview is seen as premature or tacky. Usually first interviews are a way to narrow down the pool of possibilities to one, two, or three candidates; employers are not yet ready to negotiate on salary. Some will, however, speed things up and discuss it during the interview, in which case, go with the flow of the conversation and answer accordingly. Be aware of the boundaries around which the employer is talking salary and do not go beyond those boundaries.

Telephone Interviews

On occasion, it may be necessary to conduct an interview over the telephone instead of in person. This is actually an awkward situation for both the interviewer and interviewee. The absence of being able to see a person, his or her body language and facial expressions, is seen as a real disadvantage to both parties. All is not lost, however, if one has to conduct an interview over the telephone. There are just a few things to keep in mind:

- Be personable as one would want to be in person.

- Hold the interview in a quiet place where no one will disrupt or interrupt the interview.

- Listen carefully and allow a short silence between the question being asked and giving a response. Without the advantage of seeing a person and knowing, through body language, that he or she still has more to say, this extra short silence allows the interviewer to add any remarks before the applicant responds and possibly interrupts the interviewer.

- Do not be afraid of silence. If time is needed to think, again, there are no non-verbal clues on either end, so be sure to tell the interviewer that a few moments are needed to collect your thoughts. This should not result in long waiting periods, as this would make everyone uncomfortable, but a reasonable amount of time to think through a response is acceptable, just as it is in person-to-person interviews.

- All of the other guidelines for conducting an interview apply to telephone interviews, such as thanking the person at the end of the interview, offering to send in a portfolio, and following up with a letter afterward.

- **Be prepared with a list of questions for the employer.** As mentioned earlier, it is important for the applicant to have a list of questions to ask the employer, such as additional information about the position or the company or other expectations on the job. A "list" does not imply a long list; generally two to three questions are expected.

- **Offer resources to the employer not asked for in the application.** If the job application did not ask for writing samples or a portfolio, offer to leave these with the employer. This kind of foresight shows the seriousness and preparedness of the applicant. Sometimes, employers may not have asked for these resources initially, but they may ask for

Group Interviews

Sometimes a committee is appointed to interview potential job candidates, which again, can be more uncomfortable than one-on-one interviews. There are, however, some advantages to group interviews, because while one person may not like a particular candidate, three others on the committee might like the person, thus giving the candidate a possible second chance to return for another interview. When interviewing with groups or committees, keep in mind a few things:

- Greet all individuals present with a handshake or nod and an introduction.

- Maintain eye contact with every individual on the committee. When one committee member asks a question, focus attention primarily on that person, but also look at and speak to other members of the committee. This behavior shows one's comfort level with speaking in public and in front of groups of people. Confident mannerisms in a group interview will carry an applicant a long way. Be cognizant of that fine line between showing confidence and being cocky.

- Either before or after the interview, find out who the committee chairperson is so that a follow up letter can be sent to the committee on behalf of the chairperson.

them at the end of an interview, and an applicant who can readily say, "Yes, I have a portfolio on CD right here to leave with you," will be viewed much differently than one who says, "Oh, I didn't know you wanted those. I can mail them to you later."

Follow Up

The follow up to an interview should not be dismissed. Sometimes, in corporate settings, employers are waiting for the follow up from interviewees because they want to know the person is still interested in the job after the interview. To follow up after an interview means to write a short thank you letter to the employer and express continued interest in the position. The follow-up letter is also a time to either reiterate important skills or experience the applicant wants the employer to take note of, or to give details or information that was not covered in the interview but is still pertinent for the employer to know. Mail this letter within one day of the interview. Email is seen as a less formal way of following up, so it is best to stay in the formal realm while decisions are still pending.

REFERENCES

Chaney, Lillian H., and Jeanette Martin. 2007. *Intercultural business communication,* Upper Saddle River, NJ: Pearson/Prentice Hall.

EXAMPLE 1 *Hard-copy Résumé*

MEGAN E. HENDRIX

5555 Indian Echo Terrace, Peyton, CO 80831
(555) 555-5555, *emailaddress@ngms.com*

EMPLOYMENT OBJECTIVE

To work full-time as a developmental or substantive editor in a science or engineering textbook division of a major publishing company.

EDUCATION

Master of Arts, English
New Mexico State University, 1993

Bachelor of Science, Science
New Mexico State University, 1991

PROFESSIONAL WORK HISTORY

Technical Writer, Northrop Grumman Mission Systems,
July 2001 to present

Managed all project documentation. Responsibilities included: technical editing, managing online collaborative writing projects, synthesizing information into one comprehensive document, reviewing all documentation for correctness in language, format, and standards. Aided in the design and implementation of an electronic document management system, and managed the collection and indexing of all project documentation; transferred information onto various media, and distributed to customers. Other duties included member of Change Control Board, a committee designed to track and document changes to computer laboratory baseline; composed process documentation to achieve CMMI Level III. Contributed to Northrop Grumman's Missile Defense Division Newsletter *Expressions.*

Media Specialist, New Mexico State University College of Engineering,
June 1998 to July 2001

Responsible for writing and designing promotional literature for the College, such as brochures, magazines, newsletters, legislative materials, fact sheets, and advertisements. Created and maintained the NMSU College of Engineering website (*www.nmsu.edu/~coe*). Other responsibilities included collaborating on research proposals and scholarly papers, contributing to a weekly research column in the local newspaper, and writing general college news releases.

EXAMPLE 1 *Hard-copy Résumé (continued)*

English Teacher, Gadsden High School,
1993 to 1998

Taught developmental English course for English as a Second Language and academically at-risk freshmen and sophomores. To facilitate reading, writing, and grammar skills, developed activities for the classroom and computer laboratory.

Instructor of Technical Writing, University of Texas at El Paso,
1993 to 1998

Designed a series of assignments for practicing basic technical communication skills and preparing full-length proposals. Students were encouraged to choose community topics for a service-learning experience in this course.

PUBLICATIONS

Hendrix, M. 2006. Beyond e-Learning: Approaches and technologies to enhance organizational knowledge, learning, and performance. [Review of the book *Beyond e-Learning: Approaches and Technologies to Enhance Organizational Knowledge, Learning, and Performance*]. *Technical Communication* 53(4), 486–87.

Hendrix, M. 2006. Successful writing at work [Review of the book *Successful Writing at Work*]. *Technical Communication* 42(1), 122–23.

Hendrix, M. 2005. Interviewing practices for technical writers. [Review of the book *Interviewing Practices for Technical Writers*]. *Technical Communication* 39(4), 657–58.

PROFESSIONAL MEMBERSHIP

Society for Technical Communication (STC), Member, 2001 to present

Book Review Contributor, 2005 to present. See Publications for list of book reviews.

EXAMPLE 2 *Unformatted Résumé for Online Submittal*

MEGAN E. HENDRIX
5555 Indian Echo Terrace, Peyton, CO 80831
(555) 555-5555, emailaddress@ngms.com

EMPLOYMENT OBJECTIVE

To work full-time as a developmental or substantive editor in a science or engineering textbook division of a major publishing company.

EDUCATION

Master of Arts, English
New Mexico State University, 1993

Bachelor of Science, Science
New Mexico State University, 1991

PROFESSIONAL WORK HISTORY

* Technical Writer, Northrop Grumman Mission Systems, July 2001 to present
Managed all project documentation. Responsibilities included: technical editing, managing online collaborative writing projects, synthesizing information into one comprehensive document, reviewing all documentation for correctness in language, format, and standards. Aided in the design and implementation of an electronic document management system, and managed the collection and indexing of all project documentation; transferred information onto various media, and distributed to customers. Other duties included member of Change Control Board, a committee designed to track and document changes to computer laboratory baseline; composed process documentation to achieve CMMI Level III. Contributed to Northrop Grumman's Missile Defense Division Newsletter Expressions.

* Media Specialist, New Mexico State University College of Engineering, June 1998 to July 2001
Responsible for writing and designing promotional literature for the College, such as brochures, magazines, newsletters, legislative materials, fact sheets, and advertisements. Created and maintained the NMSU College of Engineering web site (*www.nmsu.edu/~coe*). Other responsibilities included collaborating on research proposals and scholarly papers, contributing to a weekly research column in the local newspaper, and writing general college news releases.

EXAMPLE 2 *Unformatted Résumé for Online Submittal (continued)*

* English Teacher, Gadsden High School, 1993 to 1998
Taught developmental English course for English as a Second Language and academically at-risk freshmen and sophomores. To facilitate reading, writing, and grammar skills, developed activities for the classroom and computer laboratory.

* Instructor of Technical Writing, University of Texas at El Paso, 1993 to 1998
Designed a series of assignments for practicing basic technical communication skills and preparing full-length proposals. Students were encouraged to choose community topics for a service-learning experience in this course.

PUBLICATIONS

* Hendrix, M. 2006. Beyond e-Learning: Approaches and technologies to enhance organizational knowledge, learning, and performance [Review of the book Beyond e-Learning: Approaches and Technologies to Enhance Organizational Knowledge, Learning, and Performance]. Technical Communication 53(4), 486–87.

* Hendrix, M. 2006. Successful writing at work [Review of the book Successful Writing at Work]. Technical Communication 42(1), 122–23.

* Hendrix, M. 2005. Interviewing practices for technical writers. [Review of the book Interviewing Practices for Technical Writers]. Technical Communication 39(4), 657–58.

PROFESSIONAL MEMBERSHIP

Society for Technical Communication (STC), Member, 2001 to present

Book Review Contributor, 2005 to present. See Publications for list of book reviews.

EXAMPLE 3 *Cover Letter*

Megan E. Hendrix
5555 Indian Echo Terrace
Peyton, CO 80831

November 27, 2007

Mr. Alberto Suarez
Red Herring Publications
6363 Washington Ave.
Worcester, MA 01609

Dear Mr. Suarez:

I am applying for the science/math editor (educational) position as advertised
on monster.com. I am relocating to Worcester, MA, next month, and I am
looking for an editorial position in math or science. My work experience
encompasses teaching at the post-secondary and college level and technical
editing in science and engineering environments. This practical experience
provides me with the insight and background needed for the science/math
editor (educational) position at Red Herring Publications.

For the past six years, I have been working as a technical editor and writer
in an engineering environment. I have extensive experience managing and
working in teams and synthesizing information from various authors and
sources into comprehensive professional documents. A recent project involved
working with 7 writers on-site, as well as 3 engineers located around the
country. I was responsible for compiling information from all 10 engineers,
editing the final document for accuracy and consistency, and then overseeing
the production of the document for distribution to clients. In order to complete
this project, I created a project plan, timeline, and managed deadlines with
all of the engineers. The project was successful in that the document was
delivered to customers three days prior to the deadline and was received as
one of the best documents put out by our company.

My editorial experience thus far involves working in cutting-edge science
and engineering environments, so I am knowledgeable and comfortable
reading and editing technical material. Furthermore, my teaching experience
adds to my qualifications for this position because I know what science and
math teachers want and need in the classroom. I am able to relate to both
educators and scientists and understand the technical material in science
and math textbooks.

EXAMPLE 3 *Cover Letter (continued)*

I would like the opportunity to interview with you to further discuss my qualifications and interest in the science/math editorial position at Red Herring Publications. Enclosed are my résumé, CD portfolio, and three references as required. I look forward to hearing from you.

Sincerely,

Megan E. Hendrix

Megan E. Hendrix

CHAPTER 21

Professional Development in Technical Communication

*P*rofessional development is when one engages in activities that encourage original thought and research in a particular field. It also entails developing and organizing forums for people to present their work. Professional development can take on many forms, such as attending and presenting at conferences, publishing, consulting or freelancing, taking continuing education classes, and participating in professional organizations. Many people think that professional development is only for those who have many years of experience, but that is completely untrue. The time to get involved is as early as possible. Everyone has something to contribute.

While the last chapter discussed ways to find employment in the field of technical communication, this chapter covers how one can sustain his or her level of interest in a chosen profession.

PROFESSIONAL ORGANIZATIONS

Belonging to a professional organization allows for networking opportunities and provides a way to keep current on trends in the technical communication field. There are numerous degrees of involvement; however, even at the most basic level, members have access to website information and resources and usually receive a subscription to a professional journal associated with the organization. There are several ways to get involved in professional organizations, such as the following suggestions:

- Run for officer positions
- Contribute to the professional journal as either an editor or as a writer
- Be a book reviewer
- Join a local chapter of a national organization

The networking aspect of belonging to professional organizations is powerful. One can meet people through all levels of involvement, which is advantageous at both the professional and personal level (such as during employment searches).

Resources available through these organizations also have professional and personal gain, such as attending workshops, online seminars, lectures, conferences, or other events associated with the organization. If relevant to one's job, employers may pay the fees associated with those activities. Likewise, employers may also pay annual dues if the organization has direct relation to one's job. Additionally, students often receive significant discounts in dues and fees.

Like any profession, technical communication has areas of specialty, and there are also organizations devoted to such expertise. Listed below are several professional communication organizations and resources that will assist technical communicators in learning more about the field, connecting with other professionals, and learning about professional development, continuing education, and employment opportunities:

- **American Advertising Association** acts as the "Unifying Voice for Advertising" and is the oldest national advertising trade association, representing 50,000 professionals. *www.aaf.org/*

- **The American Communication Association** was founded in 1993 for the purposes of (a) fostering scholarship in all areas of human communication behavior, (b) promoting excellence in the pedagogy of communication, (c) providing a voice in communication law and policy, and (d) providing evaluation and certification services for academic programs in communication study. *www.americancomm.org*

- **American Medical Writers Association** promotes excellence in medical communication and provides educational resources in support of that goal. *www.amwa.org*

- **American Society of Indexers** is devoted solely to the advancement of indexing, abstracting, and database building. *www.asindexing.org/site/index.html*

- **American Society of Journalists and Authors** helps professional freelance writers advance their writing careers. *www.asja.org/index.php*

- **Association for Education in Journalism and Mass Communication** is a nonprofit, educational association of journalism and mass communication faculty, administrators, students, and media professionals. *www.aejmc.org*

- **Association of Teachers of Technical Writing (ATTW).** The goal of ATTW is to provide teachers of technical writing with information about the association, resources for teaching technical communication, and information of interest to those in the field. *http://cms.english.ttu.edu/attw*

- **Association for Women in Communications** is a professional organization that champions the advancement of women across all communication disciplines by recognizing excellence, promoting leadership, and positioning its members at the forefront of the evolving communications era. *www.womcom.org*

- **Communications Roundtable**'s goals include furthering professionalism, cooperation between member organizations, career and employment support, employer assistance, and membership services and benefits. *www.roundtable.org*

- **CSCA–Central States Communication Association**'s mission is to unite and educate people with both an affinity to the central region of the United States and a scholarly interest in all areas of communication for promotion of their mutual goals and advancement of their field. *www.csca-net.org*

- **ECA–Eastern Communication Association** is a distinguished service-oriented organization with a history of achievement in research, criticism, communication theory, and excellence in teaching. *www.ecasite.org*

- **HTML Writers Guild** offers a program for individuals interested in Internet design and development. *www.hwg.org*

- **National Communication Association** promotes effective and ethical communication. *www.natcom.org/nca/Template2.asp?sid = 9*

- **Public Relations Society of America** is a professional organization designed to cultivate a favorable and mutually advantageous relationship between students and professional public relations practitioners. *www.prsa.org*

- **SSCA–Southern States Communication Association**'s purpose is to promote the study, criticism, research, teaching, and application of the artistic, humanistic, and scientific principles of communication. *www.ssca.net*

- **Technical Communicators' Forum (TC-Forum)** is a service offered by technical communicators for their colleagues worldwide. *www.tc-forum.org*

- **The Society for Technical Communication** is an individual membership organization dedicated to advancing the arts and sciences of technical communication. *www.stc.org*

- **Western States Communication Association** is a professional organization of scholars, teachers, and students of communication studies. *www.westcomm.org*

CONFERENCES

A conference is a gathering of professionals from a region, across the nation, or even an international assembly. Attending and presenting at conferences increases one's professional network, invites original and creative thought, and expands the scope of the field, both individually and collectively.

Attending or presenting at conferences is an excellent opportunity for technical communicators to meet other professionals who work in all avenues of the field. These contacts can be useful in order to have someone to call on when faced with challenges on a project or to have a personal contact for employment purposes.

If interested in presenting at conferences, the following information can be used to help find appropriate events, write a conference abstract, and prepare an engaging research paper or presentation.

Conference Search

Conferences are hosted by professional organizations, universities, and special interest groups within a field. For example, the *Society for Technical Communication* (*www.stc.org*) hosts a national conference every year. The topics range across the spectrum of technical communication and can be of a practical or theoretical nature. Some professional organization websites will give links to all sorts of conferences in technical communication throughout the country, even internationally. Likewise, professional journals often advertise or list specialized forums. Other Web resources for finding technical communication conferences include the following:

- TECHWR-L at *www.techwr-l.com*

- Writers Write at *www.writerswrite.com*

- A co-op library for technical communicators at *http://tc.eserver.org*

- University of Pennsylvania, which hosts a site of conference listings for many disciplines, at *http://cfp.english.upenn.edu*

Conference listings will generally give a brief explanation of the overall theme of the symposium, suggested topics for presenters, dates, deadlines for submitting abstracts, and email and website information. It is best to visit the

Web address given in conference descriptions in order to get full details and other pertinent information. When selecting a conference at which to present, it is not just a matter of locating the right conference; the list of topics should generate original ideas or a desire to research a subject so that new or creative perspectives or activities can be presented at the conference.

Writing the Proposal Abstract

To present at a conference requires first submitting a conference abstract or proposal. (For the sake of clarity, conference abstract is used in this section.) A conference abstract is a short description that outlines a relevant idea for a presentation. Just like proposals in the workplace are preceded by a request for proposal (RFP), conferences are advertised through a call for proposals/ papers (CFP). A CFP serves two purposes: 1) it advertises the conference for those who want to attend; and 2) it tells potential presenters what the focus or theme of the conference is and asks for abstracts.

The CFP provides guidelines for submitting an abstract, such as a list of possible topics, word count, how to submit the abstract, and to whom. The abstract functions independently from the research paper or presentation. Its primary audience is the conference selection committee, who will read each abstract submitted and determine if it fits with the theme of the conference. The abstract is also a writing sample, and shows one's ability to demonstrate coherence and clarity. A secondary audience for the abstract is the conference attendees because sometimes abstracts are published in conference programs to advertise presentations.

Abstracts are read quickly because conference organizers may end up with hundreds of submissions. There are key items to include in an abstract to ensure the primary audience clearly understands a proposed idea and how it relates to the conference theme. As with any writing assignment, writing the abstract is a process, which should begin with getting ideas out first and then editing for word count later. The following are suggestions for writing a conference abstract:

- Define the problem clearly and concisely using keywords or phrases from the CFP.

- Describe the scope of the research.

- Explain what the presentation will cover:
  - Narrow the scope of research or presentation so that it correlates with the theme of the conference or topics listed in the CFP.
  - Captivate the reader with questions or concepts, but do not answer research questions in the abstract unless it is controversial enough to make readers interested in learning how one can prove that point.

- Stay within the word count (usually 100–500 words); work this out once the ideas are in place.

- Provide any additional information the CFP asks for, such as equipment requirements, length of presentation, and contact information (this information is not usually part of the word count).

- Add a title, which should be descriptive, intriguing, and use keywords from the CFP if possible.

An example abstract is shown below.

Meeting Writing Demands of the Workplace

What it means to teach the basics of writing depends on whom one asks. For employers, college graduates should enter the workplace with the skills to write intelligently and competently. In response to preparing students for the workplace, a subsequent writing course to freshman composition was added to many degree programs, most in the form of introductory technical or business writing. In the hopes of giving students one more chance at learning basic writing skills, the technical or business writing course has a tall order to fill. But this course is only one requirement in a needed sequence of writing classes that will adequately prepare students for workplace writing. The goal of an introductory technical or business writing course should be to introduce students to various types of writing in the workplace, and have them practice these forms, but master them—probably not. Advanced writing courses geared toward career-specific writing are needed beyond freshman composition and technical or business writing courses. The objective is not to simply increase the number of writing courses, but to sequence classes so they build on the writing demands of a particular career. This 20-minute presentation will show a suggested sequence of courses that progress toward meeting career-specific writing demands.

Additional Information

1. Name: Diane Hendrix, Kaplan University

2. Address: P.O. Box 1234, Colorado Springs, CO 89999, (555) 555-5555 emailaddress@kaplan.edu

3. Presentation will be delivered as a PowerPoint presentation.

Presenting at the Conference

Once an abstract has been submitted, there is usually a short waiting period to hear back from the selection committee. If an abstract is accepted, it is appropriate to send the selection committee a thank-you email confirming the approval email was received and that one still intends to present.

Deciding on the correct format for a presentation can be tricky. Should the presentation be in PowerPoint and delivered as a speech, or should it be a research paper, which will be read at the conference? This varies from conference to conference. One way to clear the air is to review the CFP again to see if there is mention about expected format. If not, it would not hurt to contact conference organizers and pose the question. If it is left up to the presenter, then there are a couple of things to think about:

- **Consider the audience when choosing delivery options.** How many days is the conference? How long are the days? How many presenters are scheduled in one day? All of these questions help formulate a picture of what the audience will endure during the run of the conference. A tightly packed schedule and long days usually result in tired attendees who are overwhelmed with information overload. In cases like this, reading a paper versus delivering a more conversational presentation may be taxing on the audience. Furthermore, depending on the complexity of the subject matter, reading a detailed and technical paper may be torturous, especially if the paper is presented after lunch or near the end of the day. This in no way is meant to sway readers from reading research papers at conferences, because there are plenty of instances when this is completely appropriate. It is good, however, to plan for the best method of delivering the information so that the audience is interested and engaged.

- **Be aware of, prepare for, and adhere to time constraints.** Many CFPs will state how long presentations can be, and the approval email often reemphasizes this important consideration. No matter how important one's research is or how detailed and technical it can be, it is rude and unacceptable to run over the specified time constraints. Besides being inconsiderate of the audience and fellow presenters, a presentation that takes liberty and runs past its scheduled time frame can throw off an entire conference schedule.

  If reading a research paper, then a good rule of thumb is that a 10-page double-spaced paper can be read in 20 minutes—as long as the presenter does not stop to comment on certain points while reading. This is only a general rule and several practice runs should be made prior to the conference to ensure adherence to time constraints.

  If presenting either with or without PowerPoint, again, practice is important to make sure all information can be covered in the time given. There is nothing worse for presenters and audiences than to have someone be cut off abruptly due to timing issues, which can thwart all objectives of presenting in the first place.

A presenter should make sure that while writing a paper or developing a presentation the information stays true to the original abstract, because this is what the presenter was accepted on in the first place. A paper or presentation that goes off on a tangent can make audience members feel like they have wasted their time coming to a presentation that does not fulfill the promise of the abstract, which, as mentioned earlier, may appear in the conference program.

Overall, conferences can be a rewarding experience for both presenters and attendees; however, much of how that experience is determined, to some degree, on the way presenters deliver their information and whether or not they consider their audience.

PUBLISHING

The benefits of being published are to get ideas out to others, provide feedback, and demonstrate one's professionalism. Publishing for the sake of professional development can mean submitting to scholarly journals or commercial publications. It is not always easy to get works published; it takes research, work, revision, and sometimes multiple submissions. When one is published, however, it has many rewards, such as showing employers and potential employers one's critical and creative thinking skills, writing ability, and motivation. This may translate into promotions, selection for high-profile projects, or even salary raises. As with any type of professional development, there is really no downside.

A good way to get a foot in the door to publishing articles or other types of documents is to use conference resources, such as the following:

- **Contact people from the conference.** Contact conference organizers, fellow presenters, or attendees to share ideas and ask for suggestions of publications that might be relevant for a certain topic. This also can result in collaborative projects, which can be rewarding as well as open up additional opportunities.

- **Check out journals associated with the conference organization.** Organizations that sponsor an event usually have a professional publication as part of their repertoire of resources. Especially if one presented at a conference, then the the research presented is mostly like relevant to a publication associated with that conference. Check out the journal for guidelines and past articles to get a solid idea of what that publication puts out for their readers.

- **Reworking presentation material.** While it is perfectly acceptable to start from scratch, revising a conference research paper or reworking a presentation into a full-blown professional article is a good way to use what has already been written and then integrate feedback from the audience at the conference.

Before submitting, make sure the article follows publication guidelines and that several reviewers have seen the paper. Publications are supposed to be representations of selected professional work, so it is well worth the extra time it takes to revise as necessary and ensure the final piece adheres to journal guidelines.

Peer-reviewed Journals

A peer-reviewed journal is a publication that has a panel of experts who determine whether an article is accepted for publication in that periodical. This means it is not just a single editor's decision. There is some amount of credibility that goes with acceptance by a peer-reviewed journal because that means that one's research has passed the scrutiny of several experts in the field. These may also be some of the more difficult journals to be accepted by because of this process.

Whether reworking conference material or starting from scratch, not all publications allow writers to submit full-length manuscripts. Sometimes they will, and if it is stated, then feel free to send in a complete manuscript of an article or other document, as long as it adheres to all of the other guidelines. Include a cover letter with the submission. A cover letter can be short and direct, but it gives editors a context for the piece that they now have in their hands. An example cover letter is shown below:

Dear (name of editor):

Attached is an article for your consideration for publication in *TETYC* regarding how electronic text is changing literacy in the 21st century. A version of this paper was presented at the TYCA–West conference in Utah this past October, and the audience response was that the issues presented in this paper touch every classroom, no matter the subject, and they are issues educators must address now before reading, as we know it today, becomes obsolete.

This article has not been published or submitted elsewhere.

Thank you for your consideration. I look forward to your response.

Writer's name
Title and/or affiliation (if relevant)

Query Letters

If, on the other hand, a journal or other publication requests a query first, then that should be respected and followed. *Query letters* are used to pitch an idea for a story, article, or book. They serve several purposes for editors: 1) they propose an idea for a publication; and 2) they serve as a writing sample. It is much easier and less time consuming for editors to go through a stack of letters in one day than a desk full of manuscripts. From the query letter, editors should be able to ascertain the main idea of the proposed article, its significance, relevance, and timeliness. Additionally, if the writer is engaging and creates intrigue through a query letter, then that is a good indication that the rest of his or her writing will follow the same pattern.

The format and writing of a query letter is most important to getting an editor's attention. Email queries are not yet commonplace in the publishing world, although that is changing. Publications will state whether email queries are accepted. If it does not state so, then most likely they are not accepting queries in that format and a regular hard-copy letter should be used instead. The following are guidelines for writing query letters:

- **Name of editor/address.** The publishing world is quite dynamic in that personnel move from one position to another or from one publishing house to another regularly. Given that print publications take weeks or sometimes months to go to market, the editor that is listed in the most recent issue of a professional journal may have already moved on by the time that journal is available to the public. A quick call to the publisher to verify the name, spelling, and address of the appropriate editor will pay off tremendously and lessen the chance of a query letter being misplaced or thrown out because it was addressed to the wrong person or the editor's name was misspelled. Wrong names and misspellings also indicate one's inattention to detail.

- **One page.** As mentioned earlier, editors may read through a stack of query letters as only part of their responsibilities in one day, which means they do not have time to read a short novel query. Query letters should be contained to only one page, with no less than 1-inch margins and 12-point type. Do not try to fit more on the page by using 10-point Times New Roman. The editor will not appreciate that and may end up glossing over or setting the letter aside.

- **Strong opening.** The opening paragraph is the most critical part of the query letter because, in the first one to two sentences, the editor has to be intrigued enough to read on. There are several ways this can be achieved, such as writing the first paragraph as one intends to write the opening in the proposed article. Or the query opening can include other attention-getting techniques, such as using shocking statistics or other timely information to arouse interest in a subject.

- **Content of the article.** The body of a query letter will tell editors more about the subject and how the writer plans to develop the story or idea. A brief outline or a general discussion on the structure of the article is necessary for editors to gauge whether the idea fits with the publication in which it will appear. This can be done by showing a high-level outline or using headings and subheadings as a way to cover the intended content and perspective of the piece. Some editors even want to know how much of the article is already written, what supplemental materials the writer has, such as drawings or photographs, and even how long the writer expects it would take to complete the project.

- **Writer's expertise.** Editors also expect to read about a writer's expertise or experience with the subject and/or writing. Why should they trust the writer to produce this piece for them? What level of expertise can they expect from the writer?

- **Request to write the article.** Just like an employment cover letter ends with a direct request to interview, a query letter should end with the obvious: a writer's request to write the article.

An example query letter for a freelance piece to a commercial magazine is found in figure 21.1.

Book proposals are much more involved and each publisher has specific guidelines, which can range from a simple one-page query letter to a query plus a detailed outline and sample chapters. It is best to read publishers' guidelines and call the main office to double-check if the information is current and correct. Many publishers do not accept manuscripts directly from writers; instead, they deal only with literary agents. This information is generally noted on the publisher's website or in books such as *The Writer's Market*.

Simultaneous Submissions

Usually in guidelines, publishers will tell how long it takes to receive word back on a query. This can range anywhere from two weeks to several months. Writers grow impatient due to the timeliness of their work, and sometimes can be tempting to send out several queries at one time to see who responds first. While this seems like a logical approach, it can be rather disastrous, and in fact, it could prevent a writer from getting published in certain journals and magazines for quite a while. Magazines and journals thrive on delivering the most interesting and up-to-date information to their readers. They usually do not like their copy to be duplicated somewhere else. Some publications do not mind this and they will state in their guidelines something to the effect of "Simultaneous submissions accepted as long as they are noted." What this means is that writers can submit their query to that publication and another place where the same comment is made in the guidelines as long as in the query letter it states that the idea is being pitched to someone else too. On the other hand, some publications do not want queries that have been sent elsewhere, because if publisher A accepts the query before publisher B, then publisher A will most likely run the story before publisher B, in which case, publisher B is rerunning another publication's article. Playing a game with publishers is not advisable because one never knows who will pick up the idea, and if two publishers accept the same query and they do not accept

FIGURE 21.1 *Query Letter*

Penelope Grass
55 Rider Lane
Las Cruces, NM 88001

October 31, 2007

Editor's name
Publication name
Publication address

Dear Mr./Ms. Editor:

Salsa is giving all other condiments a run for their money, and what better way to introduce readers to the benefits and taste of this chopped spicy delight than to show them how to plant their own salsa garden?

Green chiles, onions, tomatoes, and cilantro—these are the makings of a beginner's vegetable or herb garden as well the very ingredients for a heart-healthy relish that compliments any meal. Readers will learn how to plant salsa veggies for pest control, as well as learn about the numerous varieties of green chiles, as some really do like it hot! They will enjoy reading about the versatility and health benefits of the green chili—and determine for themselves whether it is a fruit or vegetable, a long-standing debate among the most avid southwest gardeners. And, while not every part of the country has the benefit of 363 days of sunshine each year like the southwest region of the United States, there also will be tips on how to grow their salsa garden indoors.

As a regular contributor to other gardening publications, such as *Gardens Gone Wild* and *The Botanist,* I am familiar with gearing content for a particular readership. "Growing your own salsa garden" is written specifically for the gardener who eagerly awaits the arrival of your magazine each month.

The complete article is available to you upon request. A self-addressed, stamped envelope is enclosed for your convenience. Thank you for your consideration. I look forward to hearing from you.

Sincerely,

Penelope Grass
Penelope Grass

simultaneous submissions, then the writer may end up in a compromising spot where both publishers may drop the writer completely.

Resubmit

The number of queries an editor receives in one day is daunting and so the competition in the publishing market is high. Rejections, however, easily can be turned around and resubmitted somewhere else. Sometimes, editors will even give writers feedback on their manuscripts about how the idea or the writing might be reworked to better fit what they are looking for. It is advisable to use this information and evaluate the comments against one's goal and intended purpose of the piece. If the comments may compromise the intention of the writer, then it is best to simply submit a query to someone else. If the comments are reasonable, then it is usually worth the time to revise the query and/or manuscript and resubmit. Timing is important in doing this because, if the new query gets to the same editor, then there is more of a chance the editor will remember the writer and idea, and will be able to see how well the idea or writing was reworked according to the editor's suggestions. This can increase one's chances at being accepted for publication.

It is easy to get discouraged when submitting for publication. Take rejection lightly, but be critical about the feedback received. Sometimes this means broadening the perspective of the subject, whereas other times it means more research has to be done in order to find the right publisher. Either way, publishing for professional development is an excellent way to sharpen one's writing skills and increase network possibilities as well.

CONSULTING AND FREELANCING

Consulting is when a professional is hired by a company or individual to offer his or her expertise, and it usually is a result of active networking. For example, a technical communicator who writes user guides for a software company may be hired by an advertising corporation to offer advice to employees about how to write office process documentation. This can result in training sessions or just an overall assessment and list of suggestions to the company by the technical communicator. Consulting is usually done in addition to one's regular job, and often is considered a side business. That small business can, however, certainly grow into a full consulting firm one day. Before accepting a position as a professional consultant, there are few things to consider:

- **Conflict of interest.** Conflict of interest means that there are competing or unethical considerations between two or more parties. In other words, if two companies are in competition with one another because they both sell a similar product, then a technical communicator who works for company A should not offer consultation services to company B. Neither company would feel comfortable having an employee offer another company advice about how to improve its products or services when the two companies are in competition. Because of the nature of the business, an employee who engages in such behavior may be terminated with just cause.

  Additionally, a person who does consulting on the side should not use his or her work time or resources to do any work on the consulting job. For example, if a technical communicator is consulting for another firm where she is putting together a training plan, it would be unethical or in conflict with her regular job if she used the computer at work to write up or develop any materials associated with the consulting job; it would be even more unethical if she were using company time to do that. A consulting job should be kept completely separate from one's regular occupation.

- **Legal ramifications.** A consultation has to be defined as simply advice and not a prescription for guaranteed success. Careful wording of contracts and subsequent documentation as part of the consult is necessary because 1) the consultant has no control over how his or her suggestions will be carried out, and 2) guaranteeing results is not usually in anyone's best interest because of multiple factors. One does gain a certain reputation, however, when suggestions are carried out and result positively for a company, but it should be made clear from the start that there is no guarantee.

- **Scope of work.** Another issue to make clear from the start of a consulting job is that the consultant will perform only certain duties associated with providing feedback to the company, and not the actual work (unless that is part of the agreement). It should also be made clear when the consultant will be on-site, how often, what information he or she needs access to, and what cooperation will be needed from employees.

- **Payment.** As with any nontraditional job, payment can be an issue for consultants, which is why having a contract before any actual work is completed is so important. Generally, consultant work is paid by the hour or on a project basis; the amount is determined by the two parties involved. Most times, the consultant is responsible for his or her own tax deductions, which should be figured into the amount charged. Depending on the scope and length of the job, it is not unheard of to require a certain percentage of payment at the beginning of the project, at some point during the project lifecycle, and then a final payment upon completion and delivery of all contracted work. Every

Online Freelance Resources

- **Freelance Writing** includes articles, discussion, jobs, resources, contests, and events. *www.freelancewriting.com*
- **Absolute Write** offers discussion forums, articles, interviews with freelance writers, information on markets, and resources. *www.absolutewrite.com*
- **Worldwide Freelance Writer** offers information on markets worldwide, setting up a home office, and help to getting published. *www.worldwidefreelance.com*
- **Sunoasis Jobs** lists jobs for freelance writers. *www.sunoasis.com/ freelance.html*
- **Freelance Writing Jobs** offers job listings and discussions. *www.freelancewritinggigs.com*
- **Writers Write** offers multiple links and resources for all types of writers. *www.writerswrite.com*

situation is different, and so it is up to the consultant to carefully review his or her commitments and financial situation and then word the contract accordingly.

Freelancing is similar to consulting in that one is working on his or her own without the umbrella of a company to pay a salary or offer benefits. Freelancing in technical communication can be in writing, photography, or art work. Generally, freelance writers provide individual stories or articles to a magazine or individual pieces of photography or art work. As with consulting, a freelancer must consider conflict of interest, scope of work, and payment issues. Additionally, publication rights and/or copyright should be a part of every freelance contract.

LEVERAGING SKILLS INTO OTHER PROFESSIONS

Bad times roll around in every profession, and technical communicators are not immune to the volatile economy. A downturn in the profession, however, does not have to mean one will end up unemployed. Technical communicators have a variety of skills that can be leveraged from one type of job to another. For instance, the ability to write complex or technical information for varied audiences can be applied to several situations. The fact that one can write audience-specific material is a skill that can be carried over from technical communication to a public relations or marketing position, for instance. The key is to read job advertisements carefully, as discussed in chapter 20, and then rework skills according to the new set of responsibilities.

Technological skills also can be a way to move across disciplines. Companies are always interested in individuals who can communicate with others using older as well as the most recent technology. It is sometimes difficult for companies to introduce new technology to long-term employees who are comfortable with the technology they currently use. New employees give companies a chance to introduce cutting-edge technology into current work practices.

Knowledge of other cultures and the ability to communicate effectively with diverse audiences is another plus and a skill that can be leveraged when moving from one position to another. While there are general stereotypes about other cultures that make their way into office conversations, having an employee on board who knows how to research the rhetorical strategies of another culture and then effectively execute such documents is a tremendous asset.

CONTINUING EDUCATION

Continuing one's education beyond a college degree is advisable for any professional. This does not mean signing up for another round of courses or a degree program at a university; instead, continuing education can take on many different scenarios and may be achieved through professional development activities, such as attending conferences, presenting papers, or even submitting for publication. All of these activities require a person to research, think critically and creatively, and produce a product in the end. Other continuing education activities include attending workshops, training, or lectures. The Society for Technical Communication hosts live Web seminars several times a year, so attending such events does not always involve money for travel and lodging. Because continuing education is often associated with one's job, some employers will even pay for these activities or provide a pay increase due to participation in these events.

WRITING A PROFESSIONAL DEVELOPMENT PLAN

A professional development plan is a useful tool to map out one's career goals and steps toward achieving those goals. Working on a professional development plan requires reflection on one's current situation as well as future goals. It also requires critical thinking to decide the best plan of action. A professional development plan should be revisited at least once every year in order to add or modify responses.

An example plan, shown in figure 21.2, is provided to help readers reflect and plan ways to achieve their professional aspirations.

FIGURE 21.2 *Professional Development Plan*

PROFESSIONAL DEVELOPMENT PLAN

Reflection

What areas of technical communication are most interesting to you whether or not you have education and/or experience within that part of the field?

_____

_____

_____

Your Future

What are your short-term professional development goals? Short-term usually implies 1–3 years.

_____

_____

_____

What are your long-term professional development goals? Long-term usually implies 3–5 years or more.

_____

_____

_____

Continuing Education

What continuing education do you want to take?

_____

_____

_____

The Profession

What are some new developments in technical communication that you have limited or no experience with? What developments pertain to your current position? What developments pertain to your future goals?

_____

_____

_____

FIGURE 21.2 *Professional Development Plan (continued)*

Where can you get more information on these topics?

_____

_____

_____

Your Employment

What are absolutes you must have in a job?

_____

_____

_____

What areas are you flexible about in a job?

_____

_____

_____

What is your dream job? List position, responsibilities, company, location, and any other aspects about your career that are important to you.

_____

_____

_____

Plan of Action

What courses or other activities do you need in order to achieve your short-term goals?

_____

_____

_____

What courses or other activities do you need in order to achieve your long-term goals?

_____

_____

_____

FIGURE 21.2 *Professional Development Plan (continued)*

How can you get experience with current technology or other trends in technical communication that currently are not part of your job description?

_____

_____

_____

Affiliation

What professional organizations are associated with your career or interests in technical communication?

_____

_____

_____

Will your employer pay for membership? If not, how can you budget for annual membership?

_____

_____

_____

List of Contacts

Name of Contact	Where you Met	Who He or She Work For	That Person's Position Title	Address, Phone, Email Information

Grammar and Usage

There are set rules for grammar and usage in the English language that define how the language should be used. For example, the words *affect* and *effect* have distinct meanings and must be used in a particular way in order to make sense. Technical communicators must be able to use proper grammar and punctuation in all of their work. Below is a brief account of the most commonly used concepts, terms, and rules. Please note that a company's style guide will always take precedence over the rules below, so that should always be consulted first.

Parts of Speech

Nouns

- People, places, things, and ideas are all nouns.

- Proper nouns are specific people, places, things, or ideas and are capitalized (see section on capitalization rules later in this appendix).
  Example: Doctor Smith

- Common nouns are general people, places, things, or ideas and do not need to be capitalized.
  Example: doctor

Verbs

- Express action
  Example: run, jump, speak

- Express a state of being: am, is, are, was, were, be, being, been
  Example: Janice *is* 11 years old today.

- Help action verbs: have, has, had, do, does, did, shall, will, should, would, may, might, must, can, could
  Example: She *will run* the race on Saturday.

Pronouns

- Used in place of nouns

- Personal pronouns: you, he, she, we, it, I, me, they, them, us

- Possessive pronouns: mine, yours, ours, hers, his, its, their

- Relative pronouns: who, whose, whom, that, which

- Indefinite pronouns: everyone, anyone, both, each, either, neither, no one, someone

Adjectives

- Modify nouns and can precede or proceed the word they describe
  Example: The *red* balloon was Jackie's favorite.

Adverbs

- Modify verbs
  Example: Please run to the bathroom *quickly;* we need to get started.

- Modify adjectives or other adverbs
  Example: The china must be handled *very gently.*

Conjunctions

- Link words, independent clauses, and phrases

- Coordinating conjunctions join equal components such as two independent clauses: for, and, nor, but, or, yet, so.
  Example: We are going to the movies this evening, *so* I arranged to get off of work early.

Clauses

As the name implies, an independent clause can stand on its own; it is a complete sentence. A dependent clause, on the other hand, is directly tied to another part of the sentence and does not make sense without it. A dependent clause may have a subject and a verb, but it does not express a complete thought; therefore, it cannot stand by itself. For example, "Although the sun was shining brightly" contains both a subject (sun) and a verb phrase (was shining), but it does not express a complete thought—it does not tell the reader anything conclusive. It must be linked with an independent clause in order to be a complete sentence: "Although the sun was shining brightly, the wind was still quite chilly."

- Subordinating conjunctions join different components such as an independent and dependent clause: because, before, although, as, even though, since, than, that, though, unless, when, where, why, how, while, after.
  Example: *After* the movie, we will be going to dinner.

- Conjunctive adverbs are used with independent clauses. They indicate to the reader how the two clauses are connected: moreover, indeed, thus, therefore, or, furthermore, consequently, however, incidentally, nonetheless, also.
  Example: We were going to go to the movies; *however,* the car broke down on the way there.

Prepositions

- Indicate location, time, orientation, direction, or other relationships between nouns and/or pronouns

- Preposition + Object = Prepositional Phrase

- Common Prepositions:

aboard	behind	despite	near
about	below	down	next
above	beneath	during	of
across	beside	except	off
after	between	for	on
against	beyond	from	onto
along	by	in	over
among	concerning	inside	though
before	considering	into	

Subject–Verb Agreement

- A plural subject requires a plural verb.
  Example: The greatest *gifts* <u>are</u> those that come from the heart.

- A singular subject requires a singular verb.
  Example: *Janet* <u>is</u> the best player on the team.

- Compound subjects occur when one verb has two or more subjects. Those joined with "and" should be treated as plural and paired with a plural verb. The exception to this is in the event that the two parts refer to the same object or person, or if the two parts form a single unit.
  Example: *Sandra* and *Lou* <u>are going</u> to the mall to finish their shopping.
  My one and only love is the sea.

- Compound subjects joined with "or" or "nor" should agree with the subject that is closer to the verb. So, if the noun closer to the verb is singular, the verb should be singular and vice versa.
  Example: Neither *Sam* nor *Jenny* <u>owns</u> a blue convertible.
  Either an *apple* or *grapes* <u>are</u> my favorite fruit.

- Collective nouns are nouns that represent groups made up of members. Because they are generally viewed as a unit, collective nouns should be paired with singular verbs unless individual members of the unit are singled out.

  Example: The *jury* <u>is going</u> into deliberations now.

  The *members* of the jury <u>are moving</u> back into the courtroom to reveal the verdict.

- Indefinite pronouns like everyone and each should be paired with singular verbs. The exceptions to this rule are the pronouns *all, any, none,* and *some.* They vary in number according to the noun they refer to.

  Example: Each girl is responsible for her own uniform.

  All of the girls need to make sure they are ready to go by 9 AM.

Indefinite Pronouns

Indefinite pronouns are those that do not refer to a specific noun. Instead, they refer to an undefined group, individual, location, amount, etc. Indefinite pronouns include the following: everyone, everything, anyone, someone, anybody, somebody, anything, nothing, no one, each, all, any, most, none, both, few, and several.

Pronoun Agreement

- Singular nouns require singular pronouns.

  Example: *Alan* has been looking for *his* dog all morning.

- Plural nouns require plural pronouns.

  Example: The *Millers* just brought *their* new baby home from the hospital.

- Compound subjects joined with "and" should be treated as plural and paired with a plural pronoun.

  Example: *Jeff* and *Kate* are heading up to *their* cabin this weekend.

- Compound subjects joined with "or" and "nor" should be paired with a pronoun that agrees with the noun closest to it. So, if the noun closer to the pronoun is singular, the pronoun should be singular and vice versa.
  Example: Either *Sally* or *Jane* should lend you *her* jacket for the party.
  Neither *Alice* nor her *parents* could retrieve *their* prizes.

- Collective nouns should be paired with singular pronouns unless individual members of the unit are singled out.
  Example: The *congregation* planned *its* picnic for late July.
  The *jury* agreed it was time to cast *their* votes.

Run-on Sentences and Comma Splices

- Run-on sentence: Two complete sentences joined together with no punctuation
  Example: I went to the store I bought eggs and milk.

- Comma splice: Two complete sentences joined together with only a comma
  Example: I went to the store, I bought eggs and milk.

- There are three ways to punctuate a compound sentence to avoid creating a run-on or a comma splice.

  1. independent clause , coordinator independent clause
     Example: I went to the store, and I bought eggs and milk.

  2. independent clause ; independent clause
     Example: I went to the store; I bought eggs and milk.

  3. independent clause; conjunctive adverb, independent clause
     Example: I went to the store; then, I bought eggs and milk.

Fragments

- Fragment: Incomplete sentence; does not contain a subject or a verb, or does not express a complete thought.
  Example: In the front of the room.

Who, Whom, Whose

In speech, using "who" exclusively is accepted. "Whom" is generally required only if the writing is extremely formal or a style sheet demands it.

- Use "who" for the subject form.
  Example: Who said that?

- Use "whom" for the object form.
  Example: The registrar is the person whom you should contact if you have questions about your transcript.

- "Whose" shows possession.
  Example: Whose shoes are these?

PUNCTUATION

English also has a set of rules that govern the usage of punctuation marks such as the comma, semicolon, colon, and period. A brief explanation of the most commonly used marks is included below.

Comma

- After introductory words
  Example: Mrs. Smith, have you seen my keys?

- After introductory phrases
  Example: For the record, I did not lose her cat.

- Surrounding interrupting words and phrases
  Example: Jessica Jones, our senior account manager, is on vacation this week.

- In between items in a series
  Examples: I went to the store and bought bread, milk, and eggs.
  I live at 46 Guadiana Street, Seattle, Washington.
  The retreat will take place on May 15, 2008, in Hollywood.

Commas and Lists

Formal writing dictates the need for a comma before the end (or at the end) of a series. Typically, journalists and the British exclude this comma.

- To indicate parenthetical information of equal emphasis
  Example: The parallel port, located on the text monitor adapter card, enables the computer to be connected to the largest number of text and graphics printers.

Semicolon

- To separate independent, related clauses
  Example: I went to the store; I bought milk, eggs, and bread.

- Before a conjunctive adverb joining two independent clauses
  Example: The movie was entertaining; however, the ending was disappointing.

- To separate items in a list containing internal punctuation
  Example: The meeting was attended by Julie, my composition instructor; Ann, my math teacher; and Tom, my history professor.

Colon

- To introduce a list
  Example: Please bring all of the following: tent, sleeping bag, pillow, towel, and flashlight.

- To introduce a quotation
  Example: John F. Kennedy said it best: "Ask not what your country can do for you, but what you can do for your country."

- To introduce a clause that summarizes or explains the first word group
  Example: Many software developers are taking the scrum approach: a term borrowed from rugby, which means to make a formation and move the ball using the mass of players instead of individually.

- With salutations, time, and subtitles
  Example: Dear Ms. Smith:

Em Dashes

- To introduce a list or a restatement
  Example: We brought all of the necessary ingredients—milk, eggs, sugar, and flour.

- To identify nonessential information that warrants additional emphasis
  Example: The events of September 11—from the fall of the towers to the dramatic aftermath—changed the American people forever.

En Dashes

- To show a range of time or numerical value
  Example: The store is open Monday - Friday from 9:00 AM–6:00 PM.

Hyphens

- To form compound nouns that clarify meaning
  Example: light-year

- To form compound adjectives
  Example: The well-to-do couple bought a huge new home right on the water.

Parentheses

- To surround and identify nonessential information
  Example: The cat (who was 35 pounds) jumped on top of the tiny table.

- To surround abbreviations included after the full term
  Example: The Federal Bureau of Investigation (FBI) has formed a new task force to deal with the growing smuggling problem.

Apostrophes

- To show possession
  - Sally Mae's book is on the counter.
  - Goldilocks is accused of eating the three bears' porridge.

- Note: Personal pronouns are possessive in their very nature and so do not require an apostrophe as with hers, its, and his.

Problems with Possessives

Many people get confused when dealing with possessives ending in s. When a singular noun ends in s, an 's should be added. Example: The *boss's* daughter visited him on his birthday. However, it is also acceptable to simply include an ' to avoid confusion. Example: The *boss'* daughter visited him on his birthday. When the noun is plural and ends in an s, only an apostrophe should be added. Example: The *parrots'* cages were dirty.

- To show omission
  - I'm = I am
  - it's = it is
  - he's = he is

- To prevent confusion
  - Fifteen students received 0's on the final project for plagiarism.

Quotation Marks

- Around direct quotes
  Example: John F. Kennedy said it best: "Ask not what your country can do for you, but what you can do for your country."

- For titles of articles, poems, short stories, songs, or chapters in books
  Example: My favorite song is "Let It Be" by The Beatles.

- To identify words used as words
  Example: The word "clutch" means to hold tightly.

End Punctuation

There are several marks that occur at the end of the sentence. They vary depending on the intent of the sentence. For example, when asking a question, the sentence should close with a question mark. When showing strong emotion, however, an exclamation point is used. Each mark and a brief explanation of its usage are included below.

- **Period.** A period expresses a full stop. It is used at the end of most complete, declarative sentences. It is also used after some abbreviations.

- **Question mark.** The question mark is used at the end of a complete sentence that makes an inquiry. It should be used even when asking a hypothetical question. No question mark is needed, however, when referring to a question. For example, the sentence "She asked when the paycheck would arrive." does not require a question mark because it is not actually asking a question.

- **Exclamation point.** An exclamation point is used in lieu of a period when very strong emotion or emphasis is being indicated. It should be used sparingly to avoid overemphasizing things that do not require additional attention. For example, "I won!" is an excited utterance that is appropriate with an exclamation point. On the other hand, "She crossed the street!" does not require such emphasis.

SPELLING

Using correct spelling ensures accuracy and clarity of meaning in a document. American English spelling rules are different than the rules for British or Australian English, and it is important that the author identify what set of rules is appropriate for the audience.

Homophones

The English language features a number of words that sound very similar but have different spellings and meanings. These words often cause great confusion and can drastically alter the meaning of a document if used incorrectly. A list of some of the most commonly confused words follows:

A lot/Alot

- A lot is two words, not one—"alot" is not a word.

Affect/Effect

- Affect is a verb that means "to influence."
  Example: The injury affected her performance in the games.

- Effect is a noun. It means "results."
  Example: The effects of the hurricane were felt throughout the state.

Its/It's

- Its shows possession.
  Example: They returned the lost dog to its owner.

- It's is a contraction that can stand only for "it is."
  Example: It's getting late.

Loose/Lose

- Loose is an adverb meaning "not rigidly fashioned" (Woolf 1974).
  Example: That bolt is loose.

- Lose is a verb that means "to destroy or suffer deprivation of" (Woolf 1974).
  Example: Did you lose something?

Principle/Principal

- Principle is a noun that describes an established truth or belief.
  Example: I will not abandon my principles, no matter the cost.

- Principal can function as both a noun and an adjective. As a noun, a principal is the individual who heads up a school or institution. It also has special meaning in the fields of law, music, and finances.
  Example: If you misbehave, you'll be sent to the principal's office.

- As an adjective, principal means "most important" (Woolf 1974).
  Example: The principal character in the novel did not translate well in the film version.

Than/Then

- Than is used for comparing things.
  Example: Jane is prettier than Joe.

- Then is used to express time.
  Example: We went to the store, and then we went to the movies.

They're/Their/There

- They're is a contraction that can only mean "they are."

- Their is a pronoun that shows possession. It is used only to show possession in reference to people or objects.
  Example: Their car broke down on the way to the party.

- There is an adverb that specifies place, location.
  Example: Please pick up that piece of trash over there.

Two/To/Too

- Two only refers to the number 2.

- To is a preposition. It indicates direction (We were walking to school) or delivery (Please give this to Sally).

- Too is an adverb that most commonly means "in addition to" or excessively (There is too much sugar in this).

Who's/Whose

- Who's is a conjunction that means "who is."
  Example: Who's going to take the movies back?

- Whose shows possession.
  Example: Whose shoes are these?

Your/You're

- Your is the possessive form of the pronoun, you.
  Example: Your coat is in the closet.

- You're is a conjunction that can only mean "you are."
  Example: You're going to be late for school.

CAPITALIZATION

The first word of every sentence and proper nouns are capitalized in English. A writer should carefully observe other rules of capitalization to ensure that respect is given to people and places. The general rule of thumb is that all proper nouns, the names of specific people, places, things, or ideas, should be capitalized. As examples, languages, races, religions, deities, sacred texts, government organizations, political parties, and company names should all be capitalized. However, there are also additional, more specific rules that should be followed.

Titles of Works

The titles and subtitles of books, magazines, newspapers, articles, songs, and poems should be capitalized. First, last, and all major words in between should be capitalized. Insignificant words such as articles and conjunctions are not generally capitalized unless they are the first or last word of the title.

> **Example:** *The Wall Street Journal; Gorillas in the Mist*

Titles of People

Titles such as Doctor, Professor, and Reverend should be capitalized when used in conjunction with a person's name as in Doctor Smith or Reverend

Mitchell. However, when they are used generically, as in "He went to see the doctor," they do not need to be capitalized. The exception to this rule in the United States is the office of the President; that is always capitalized.

Locations

The names of places should be capitalized. This includes city and state names, as well as other locations, such as Wrigley Field.

> **Example:** Sacramento, California; Museum of Tolerance

Agencies/Companies

The names of agencies, companies, and departments should be capitalized because they are proper nouns. However, when words such as company or agency are used in a generic sense, they should not be capitalized.

> **Example:** Human Resources Department; Federal Bureau of Investigation; General Mills

Trade Names

Many times, trade names become synonymous with the product they represent. For example, Q-tip is a brand name, but many people call all cotton swabs Q-tips regardless of the brand. In a technical document, trade names should only be used when referring to the actual product, and they should be capitalized. A brief list of commonly misused trade names is included below:

Astroturf®	Jell-O®	Q-tip®	Vaseline®
Band-Aid®	Kleenex®	Rolodex™	Velcro®
Frisbee®	Plexiglas®	Scotch Tape®	Xerox®

ABBREVIATIONS AND ACRONYMS

Sometimes an author may wish to abbreviate lengthy words that are repeated throughout a document. There are specific rules for abbreviating which must be observed so that what the abbreviation stands for is clear to the reader. A list of the most commonly used abbreviations and the rules that apply appear in the following tables.

Rules

- Within a document, write out the word(s) being abbreviated before using the abbreviation unless it would be common knowledge to all audience members or it is noted in a dictionary as a word rather than *abbr.* Include the abbreviation in parentheses for clarity.

  Example: The Occupational Safety and Health Administration (OSHA) reported that the majority of employers are maintaining safe work environments.

- If a document contains a large number of unknown abbreviations, it is a good idea to include a glossary of abbreviations within the text.

- Abbreviations comprised of all capital letters can be used without spacing or periods as with FBI or EPA. Academic degrees are an exception to this rule. They require periods in between, as with Ph.D. or M.A.

Locations

Generally, abbreviations for locations should only be used for addresses. Included below are the accepted abbreviations for states within the United States.

Alabama: AL	Iowa: IA	New Hampshire: NH
Alaska: AK	Kansas: KS	New Jersey: NJ
Arizona: AZ	Kentucky: KY	New Mexico: NM
Arkansas: AR	Louisiana: LA	New York: NY
California: CA	Maine: ME	North Carolina: NC
Colorado: CO	Maryland: MD	North Dakota: ND
Connecticut: CT	Massachusetts: MA	Ohio: OH
Delaware: DE	Michigan: MI	Oklahoma: OK
Florida: FL	Minnesota: MN	Oregon: OR
Georgia: GA	Mississippi: MS	Pennsylvania, PA
Hawaii: HI	Missouri: MO	Rhode Island: RI
Idaho: ID	Montana: MT	South Carolina: SC
Illinois: IL	Nebraska: NE	South Dakota: SD
Indiana: IN	Nevada: NV	Tennessee: TN

Texas: TX	Virginia: VA	Wisconsin: WI
Utah: UT	Washington: WA	Wyoming: WY
Vermont: VT	West Virginia: WV	

Titles

Titles can go before or after a person's name to indicate his or her position or level of expertise. A few of the most commonly used abbreviations for titles are included below.

Attorney: Atty.	Honorable: Hon.
Bachelor of Arts: B.A.	Junior: Jr.
Bachelor of Science: B.S.	Master of Arts: M.A.
Doctor of Divinity: D.D.	Master of Science: M.S.
Doctor of Laws: L.L.D.	Miss: Ms.
Doctor of Medicine: M.D.	Missus: Mrs.
Doctor of Philosophy: Ph.D.	Mister: Mr.
Doctor of Veterinary Medicine: D.V.M.	Professor: Prof.
Doctor: Dr.	Reverend: Rev.
Esquire: Esq.	Senior: Sr.

Units of Measurement

Units of measurement should be abbreviated in technical documents. Abbreviations for measurements are generally not capitalized, and they should only be followed by a period if they can be mistaken for another word, as with the abbreviation for inch *in.* Some of these abbreviations are found below.

Celsius: C	hour: hr	ounce: oz
centimeter: cm	inch: in.	pint: pt
Fahrenheit: F	kilogram: kg	pound: lb
fluid ounce: fl oz	liter: L	quart: qt
foot: ft.	meter: m	yard: yd
gallon: gal.	millimeter: mm	year: yr
gram: g	minute: min	

NUMBERS AND MEASUREMENTS

Numbers and measurements can appear out of place amongst lines of text, but it is often necessary to include them in technical and scientific documents. To ensure consistency and understanding, there is a set of rules that govern how these should be written. Following are some of the most commonly used rules that a technical communicator should be familiar with.

Numbers

- Numbers less than 10 should be written out, and numerical figures should be used for numbers 10 and over.
  Example: The average American family owns three cars.

- In the event that a sentence contains numbers both above and below ten, numerical figures should be used for all of them to ensure consistency.
  Example: They have 14 fish and 3 cats living in the same house.

- If a sentence begins with a number, it should always be written out.
  Example: Thirty-five percent of all dogs have fleas.

- When labeling figures or illustrations, numerical figures should be used rather than written out.
  Example: Figure 3.8

- Numerical figures should be used to express time, money, distance, or other units of measurement.
  Example: $35.00, 4:30

- Commas should be used for numerical figures of more than four decimal places.
  Example: 3,000

REFERENCES

Woolf H. B. (ed.). 1974. *The Merriam-Webster dictionary.* New York, NY: Pocket Books.

Citation Guidelines for APA, Chicago Manual of Style, and MLA

itations are shorthand for readers to be able to look up a source used in a document. *Style guides* are manuals used by writers so that all citations are written in consistent and proper format. There are several formal style guides, as well as corporate style guides. Which one a writer uses can depend on what field he or she is working in and whether a company has developed its own guide. Although there are many different styles, in the United States, the sciences generally use the American Psychological Association (APA) style guide; news or popular culture publications use the *Chicago Manual of Style* (although some news publications will use the Associated Press style guide), and the humanities, mainly English programs, use the Modern Language Association (MLA) style guide. For complete details about each style and how to properly cite sources, one should consult those official publications (titles provided at the end of the appendix). This appendix is meant to provide a general overview of all three style guide formats with examples for most documents that are referred to in this book.

There are two basic types of citations. One is called a *full citation,* which appears on the references page, in the bibliography section, or a works cited page. The other is an *in-text citation,* which appears in the actual text. A full citation is just that—it provides complete information about a source so that a reader can look up the publication. The in-text citation is a shortened version of the full citation and it appears in the body of a document. It is shortened so that the citation information does not interfere with the reading and yet signals that the information is borrowed. In-text citations are required for both direct quotes and paraphrased material.

The information for a full citation depends on the source type, such as whether the publication is a book, newspaper, website, or legal document. A citation has to follow or use the unique information for how a source is published in order to provide that information to the reader. For instance, a book and a newspaper have completely different formats, and so their publication information also differs. Books are published by year, whereas a newspaper has a day and issue usually attached to it. Likewise, a website and a corporate document are completely diverse mediums and so their source information also will differ. Therefore, citation formats are derived from these different means of publication in order to present the comprehensive information needed in order to look up a source.

Citation is taken seriously in both academic and professional settings, and adhering to a formal style guide is sometimes paramount to having a paper accepted. Proper citation shows attention to detail and that a writer follows the standard conventions of the field in which he or she is working.

AMERICAN PSYCHOLOGICAL ASSOCIATION (APA)

The following explanations and examples refer to APA guidelines. Placement of punctuation, proper capitalization, syntax, and order are all important details in each citation and should be followed precisely. There are times, however, when a source will not have all of the components of a citation as noted in a style guide. In such cases, the citation should be followed as closely as possible.

Reference List

A reference page lists only those works cited in a document. The following are basic guidelines for creating a reference page in APA format:

- Double space reference pages and include the title, "References," centered at the top of the page.

- Invert authors' names on a reference page so that the last name comes first followed by a comma and the initial of the author's first name. Sometimes a middle initial will be included and that will follow the first name initial. For example, an author's name of Tom L. Smith becomes Smith, T. L. on a reference page.

- Alphabetize according to the author's last name. If there is no author, use the organization's name in place of the author; if there is no organization, use the title in place of the author's name. Alphabetize according to whichever is used in place of the author's name; however, do not include articles such as *the, a, an* in the alphabetization; use the word next to the article. For example, if there was no author for a book titled *The Way to Happiness,* it would be alphabetized according to the word "Way" and not "The."

- Use a hanging indent. This is where the first line of the citation is flush with the left margin and the second and subsequent lines of the citation are indented five spaces from the margin. This helps readers to be able to scan a list quickly to find an author's name or the title of a publication as it was cited in the text.

- Do not number entries.

In-text Citation

There are three ways to cite in the text of a document.

1. **Parenthetical citation.** This is where the citation information appears at the end of the sentence and in parenthesis. The standard format is to use the author's last name only and the year of publication, as in the following example:

   Only a handful of students were reported as skipping school on the day in question (Smith, 2003).

   Note the period goes after the citation.

2. **Insert the author's name directly into the sentence,** which is immediately followed by the year of publication. This often helps with the readability of the piece, as shown in the following example:

Smith (2003) reported that only a handful of students skipped school on the day in question.

3. **Insert the author's name and year into the sentence directly,** as in:

Tom Smith, in his 2003 study of public schools, states....

Dates

Generally, all that is needed is the year of publication as will be shown in the examples in the following sections. Instances when dates other than the year are needed are only for daily publications, such as newspapers and sometimes corporate or government documents. If no date is noted in the original, then "n.d." is substituted, as in (Rodriguez, n.d.) or Rodriquez (n.d.) states....

Quotations and Paraphrases

When a quotation precedes the parenthetical citation, the page number where the quote appears in the original is shown like this: (Parrish, 2002, p. 3). When the author's name is inserted directly into the sentence, then the page number where the quote appears in the original is shown like this: Parrish (2002) states "insert quote" (p. 3). Note the period goes after the citation and not at the end of the quotation. In APA style, paraphrases do not include the page number in the citation.

Anonymous

The use of the word "anonymous" in a citation should be used only when the work is designated as such. This means that just because a publication may not have an author cited in the original does not make it anonymous. In works that are designated as such, "anonymous" takes the place of the author's name, as in (Anonymous, 2003) and on the reference list too.

Books with One Author

Author's last name, first name initial. (year of publication). *Title of the book*. City where published: Publisher.

Reference page citation

Parrish, T. (2002). *The Grouchy Grammarian*. Hoboken: John Wiley & Sons, Inc.

In-text citation

(Parrish, 2002) or Parrish (2002) states....

Books with Two Authors

First author's last name, first name initial., & second author's last name, first name initial. (year of publication). *Title of the book*. City where published: Publisher.

Reference page citation

Lederer, R., & Shore, J. (2005). *Comma Sense*. New York: St. Martin's Press.

In-text citation

Use the ampersand (&) between the authors' names in a parenthetical citation, and include the word "and" between authors' names when inserted directly into the sentence.

(Lederer & Shore, 2005) or Lederer and Shore (2005) state....

Books with Three or More Authors (Up to Six)

Author's last name, first name initial., second author's last name, first name initial., & third author's last name, first name initial. (year of publication). *Title of the book*. City where published: Publisher.

Reference page citation

Oliu, W.E., Brusaw, C.T., & Alred, G.J. (2007). *Writing that Works*. Boston: Bedford/St. Martin's.

In-text citation

In the first citation instance, list all of the authors' last names; in subsequent citations use only the last name of the first author followed by "et al." (note the period after "al.") as shown in the following examples:

First use: (Oliu, Brusaw, & Alred, 2007) or Oliu, Brusaw, and Alred (2007) state....

Subsequent use: (Oliu et al., 2007) or Oliu et al. (2007) contend....

Books with an Editor

The abbreviation (Ed.) follows the first name initial of the author. All other citation information for a book stays the same.

Beaudoin, M.F. (Ed.). (2007). *Perspectives on Higher Education in the Digital Age.* New York: Nova Science Publishers, Inc.

Conference Papers

If a paper is presented at a conference, but is not published, the way to cite that source would be as follows:

Author's last name, first name initial. (year, month of the conference). *Title of paper.* Paper presented at title of the conference, city, state.

Martinez, D.L., & Peterson, T.J. (2007, September). *Cultural shifts and identity crisis in the wake of online education.* Paper presented at the First Global Multiculturalism, Conflict, and Belonging Conference, Oxford, United Kingdom.

Corporate Author/Brochure

A corporate author citation format is shown below:

Company Name. (year of publication). *Title of document.* City, State: Author (if applicable).

Brochures are cited the same way as books, but identify the publication as a brochure in brackets:

> Company Name. (year of publication). *Title of document.* [Brochure].
> City, State: Author if applicable.

Some variation of this format may be needed depending on the source and retrieval information, as shown below:

> Ciba Specialty Chemicals. (n.d.) *Effects to Improve the Quality of Life.*
> [Brochure]. Basel, Switzerland.

Corporate Documents

Printed corporate documents follow the general citation guideline as shown below; however, this may not fit all types of corporate publications and a more detailed search using the official guide to APA should be referenced:

> Name of company. (year, month). Title of document (document
> number). City: Author (if applicable).

Online publications, such as a corporate newsletter is cited as follows:

> Author's last name, first name initial. (year, month). Title of newsletter
> article. *Title of the newsletter.* Retrieved month day, year from main
> web address.

> Righter, K. (2007, August). Program News. *Antarctic Meteorite
> Newsletter.* Retrieved December 17, 2007 from *http://curator.jsc.
> nasa.gov/antmet/amn/anu.cfm.*

Email, Interviews, Letters, and Memos

Personal communications, email, interviews, letters, and even memos, are not part of a reference page, but they do get an in-text citation. These types of communication can be cited in one of two ways:

> As part of the sentence: T.J. Peterson (personal communication, May
> 27, 2003) gives her views on....

> As a parenthetical citation: (T.J. Peterson, personal communication,
> May 27, 2003)

Legal Material

When referring to legal materials in documents, those sources should be cited according to *The Bluebook: A Uniform System of Citation.* If this guide is not readily available, the following website provides some of the rules for citing legal material in APA format: *www.lib.wsc.ma.edu/legalapa.htm.*

Newsgroup Message

Author's last name, first name initial. (year, month day of the post). Subject line of the message [include any specific information about the message]. Message posted to newsgroup URL.

Oakley, A. (2003, September). Re: News from Germany. Message posted to *www.newsforyoutouse.com.*

Periodicals

Periodicals are serial publications that contain a collection of articles in each issue or volume, and they are published on a regular basis, such as monthly or quarterly. Examples of periodicals include magazines, journals, and newspapers. Depending on the type of periodical, the citation information and format for those sources will vary. A few common periodical citations are shown below:

Journal or magazine (print)

Author's last name, first name initial. (year of publication). Title of article. *Title of the Periodical, Volume number(issue number),* page numbers.

Johnson, T. (2007). Podcasting: A New Layer of Communication. *Intercom, 54(1),* 20–24.

Online periodical

Author's last name, first name initial. (year of publication). Title of article. *Title of the Periodical,* Volume number(issue number), page numbers. Retrieved month day, and year from source.

The source for an online periodical can vary from a Web address for an online journal, for instance, to an online database. In the case of an online database, only the name of the database is used and not the entire Web address, as shown in the following example:

Hansen, T., (2006). Landfill gas provides solution to rising natural gas prices. *Power Engineering,* 110(1), 50. Retrieved November 5, 2007 from Academic Search Elite.

Online newspaper

Author's last name, first name initial. (year, month day). Title of story. *Title of the Newspaper.* Retrieved month day, year from main Web address.

Weiss, R. (2007, December 17). Synthetic DNA yields advances. *The Washington Post.* Retrieved December 17, 2007 from *www. washingtonpost.com.*

Government report retrieved from the Government Printing Office (GPO) database

Agency. (year, month). Title of document (publication number). Retrieved month day, year from Agency or Office via GPO Access Web address.

U.S. Department of Agriculture. (2007, May). *Accomplishing and applying national fire plan research and development from 2001–2005* (General Technical Report RMRS-GTR-187). Retrieved December 17, 2007 from U.S. Department of Agriculture via GPO Access *www.fs.fed.us/rm/pubs/rmrs_gtr187.pdf.*

Technical and Research Abstracts and Reports

Abstract and report citation information will vary depending on where the information was retrieved. Usually, such reports are retrieved from university, government, or private organization websites. The general format for such citations is shown below; however, variations of this format are necessary depending on where the information originates (as shown in the example):

Name of university, government agency, or private organization. (year, month day). *Title of the Report.* Retrieved month day, year from the source.

Parker, J.S., & Lo, M.W. (2004, August 16). *Unstable Resonant Orbits near Earth and Their Applications in Planetary Missions.* Retrieved from NASA Technical Reports Server December 17, 2007 at *http:// ntrs.nasa.gov/search.jsp?R = 329346&id = 2&qs = Ntt%3Djupiter %26Ntk%3DKeywords%26Ntx%3Dmode%2520matchall%26N%3 D0%26Ns%3DHarvestDate%257c1.*

Websites

Websites are formatted the same way as print publications; however, they include retrieval dates and Web addresses.

Author's last name, first name initial. (year). Title of web page. Retrieved month day, year from main web address.

Jane Goodall Institute. (n.d.). Chimpanzee Central. Retrieved December 17, 2007 from *www.janegoodall.org/chimp_central/chimpanzees/ behavior/default.asp.*

CHICAGO MANUAL OF STYLE

The following explanations and examples refer to the Chicago Manual of Style guidelines. When using this style, documentary, footnotes, or endnotes can be used; however, the shortened author-date in-text citation is also allowed. In some cases, notes are reserved for cumbersome information that would interfere with the reading if included in the text.

Bibliography and Reference List

When using the Chicago Manual of Style, the list of sources is sometimes referred to as a bibliography, select bibliography, works cited, or reference list. A full bibliography or select bibliography refers to all of the sources that an author referred to while composing a document, whether or not all are cited in the text. A works cited or reference list are generally the same; it is where the list of publications refers only to those sources cited in the document.

For the sake of clarity in this section, the term reference list is used to show examples of full citations.

Bibliographies and reference lists are placed at the end of a document before the index, but after notes, appendixes, or endnotes. There are several differences in format between bibliographies and reference lists and the official guide should be consulted for details.

In-text Citations

The basic format for an in-text citation when using this style guide is the author's last name and year of publication with no comma between, as in (Fuller 1999). When citing more than three authors, use "et al." after the last name of the first author, as in (Conners et al. 1999). If a page or figure has to be referred to in the citation, then it follows the year and is preceded by a comma, as in (Fuller 1999, fig. 3) or (Fuller 1999, 23).

Anonymous

Begin with the title of a work when the author's name is unknown. The word "anonymous" should not take the author's place. Alphabetizing for the reference list begins with the first word of the title minus articles, such as *the, a,* or *an.*

Books with One Author

Author's last name, first name. Year of publication. *Title of the book.* City where published: Publisher.

Reference list

Parrish, Thomas. 2002. *The grouchy grammarian.* Hoboken: John Wiley & Sons, Inc.

In-text citation

(Parrish 2002, 6)

Books with Two Authors

Begin these citations with the first author's name inverted, but the second author's name is written in natural form: first name last name.

Author's last name, first name, and second authors first and last name. Year of publication. *Title of the book.* City where published: Publisher.

Reference list

Lederer, Richard, and John Shore. 2005. *Comma sense.* New York: St. Martin's Press.

In-text citation

(Lederer and Shore 2005, 13)

Books with Three Authors

Sometimes authors will include their middle initial in addition to their first and last names or they will use only initials for their first and middle names. In cases with three or more authors who use initials, use a comma or semicolon to separate names, just be sure that whichever one is used is consistently used throughout the the references list.

First author's last name, first name, second author's first and last name, and third author's first and last name. Year of publication. *Title of the book.* City where published: Publisher.

Reference list

Oliu, W. E., C. T. Brusaw, and G. J. Alred. 2007. *Writing that works.* Boston: Bedford/St. Martin's.

In-text citation

(Oliu, Brusaw, and Alred 2007, 23)

Books with More Than Three Authors

The term "et al." is instituted after the first author's name when there are more than three authors. This goes for both the reference list and in-text citation. In the reference list, there is an option to list all authors (as shown above) or just the first author and "et al." after that name.

Books with an Editor

The abbreviation ed. follows the first name or middle initial of the author. All other citation information for a book stays the same.

> Beaudoin, Michael F., ed. 2007. *Perspectives on higher education in the digital age.* New York: Nova Science Publishers, Inc.

Conference Papers

If a paper is presented at a conference, but is not published, the way to cite that source would be as follows:

> Author's last name, first name. "Title of paper." Paper presented at title of the conference, city, state, and date.

> Martinez, D. L., and Peterson, T. J. "Cultural shifts and identity crisis in the wake of online education." Paper presented at the First Global Multiculturalism, Conflict, and Belonging Conference, Oxford, United Kingdom, September 3–6, 2007.

Corporate Author

When no personal author is credited with composing a document, and instead an organization or corporation is given, then the name of the organization takes the place of the author's name:

> Company Name. Year of publication. *Title of document.* City, State: Organization or Company.

Some variation of this format may be needed depending on the source and retrieval information, as shown below:

> Ciba Specialty Chemicals. n.d. *Effects to improve the quality of life.* Basel, Switzerland.

Corporate Documents

Corporate documents, such as pamphlets, brochures, proceedings from meetings, and reports, are cited as a book would be cited. The author may be a corporate author, and the publication information may vary. What is important is that enough identifying information is included in the citation.

Email, Interviews, Letters, and Memos

Interviews conducted by an author are usually noted in the text; however, if they appear on the reference list, then the following information is included: the interviewee's name, who the person was interviewed by, and the place and date of the interview. For example:

> Peterson, T.J. Interview by author. Valencia, Calif., 17 December 2007.

Other personal communications, such as letters, phone conversations, emails, or memos, generally are referred to right in the text and not called out as a specific note or as a source in the reference list.

Legal Material

When referring to legal material in documents, those sources should be cited according to either *The University of Chicago Manual of Legal Citation* or *The Bluebook: A Uniform System of Citation.*

Newsgroup Message

Web logs or other informal communication via the Internet, such as through a newsgroup, can be cited in the actual text and not as a formal entry in the references list. If it is cited in a bibliography, then the name of the list, date or posting, URL, and access date are needed.

Periodicals

Periodicals are serial publications that contain a collection of articles in each issue or volume, and they are published on a regular basis, such as monthly or quarterly. Examples of periodicals include magazines, journals, and newspapers. Depending on the type of periodical, the citation information and format for those sources will vary. A few common periodical citations are shown below:

Journal or magazine

> Author's last name, first name. Year of publication. "Title of article,"
> *Title of the periodical* Volume number, issue number preceded by
> "no.": page numbers.

Johnson, Tom. 2007. "Podcasting: A new layer of communication," *Intercom* 54, no. 1: 20–24.

Online periodical

Author's last name, first name. Year of publication. "Title of article," *Title of the periodical* Volume number, no. issue number, Web address.

The source for an online periodical can vary from a Web address for an online journal, for instance, to an online database. In the case of an online database, provide the name of the library where the item was accessed:

Hansen, Teresa. 2006. "Landfill gas provides solution to rising natural gas prices," *Power Engineering* 110, no. 1. Kaplan Higher Education Online Library. *http://libsys.uah.edu:3245/kaplan/*.

Newspaper from an electronic source

Newspaper articles are commonly cited in the text of a document, such as providing the author's name or title of the article and the title of the newspaper, and not included in the bibliography.

Government documents retrieved online

Agency. Year of publication. "Title," document numbers or other identifying information, year, URL.

U.S. Department of Agriculture. 2007. "Accomplishing and applying national fire plan research and development from 2001–2005," General Technical Report RMRS-GTR-187, *www.fs.fed.us/rm/pubs/rmrs_gtr187.pdf*.

Technical and Research Abstracts and Reports

Technical reports are corporate documents and should be cited as a book. Varying author and publication information for such documents may differ from the normal book citation. Abstracts are cited as a journal would be except that the word "abstract" precedes the journal title.

Websites

Websites are commonly integrated into the text of a document and generally omitted from bibliographies as well. A writer may instead simply state "According to its website, National Geographic states...." If, however, a Web address is needed and listed in the bibliography, then it can be cited as follows:

> Author's last name, first name or name of organization. "Title of Web page." Web address (accessed date).

MODERN LANGUAGE ASSOCIATION (MLA)

The following explanations and examples refer to the MLA guidelines. These examples are general guidelines, and depending on the source, the formats may have to be modified. For details about these citations and for more specialized citations in MLA, the official guide should be consulted.

Works Cited

When compiling a works cited page in MLA style, the same rules as for a reference page in APA apply; however, the order of the citation elements differ. One example is that the date comes last in an MLA full citation instead of immediately following the author's name in APA. For example:

> Parrish, Thomas. The Grouchy Grammarian. Hoboken: John Wiley & Sons, Inc., 2002.

In-text Citations

One important distinction between in-text citations and full citations in MLA is that the publication date is left out of the in-text citation, but always included on the works cited page.

When using MLA, there are several ways to cite in the text of a document, two of the more common forms are explained and shown below:

1. **Parenthetical citation.** This is where the citation information appears at the end of the sentence and in parenthesis. The standard format is to use the author's last name only and the page number from where the information was borrowed (whether quoting or paraphrasing), as in the following example:

Only a handful of students were reported as skipping school on the day in question (Smith 13).

Note the period goes after the citation.

2. **Insert the author's name directly into the sentence** and include the page number(s) in parenthesis. This often helps with the readability of the piece, as shown in the following example:

Smith reported that only a handful of students skipped school on the day in question (13).

Quotations and Paraphrases

Whether quoting or paraphrasing, page numbers from where the information was borrowed are included in MLA in-text citations. If there are no page numbers available, then it is preferred that the citation take the form of inserting the author or other identifying information, such as the title, directly in the text.

Anonymous

Begin with the title of a work when the author's name is unknown. The word "anonymous" should not take the author's place. Alphabetizing for the works cited page begins with the first word of the title minus articles, such as *the, a,* or *an.*

Books with One Author

Author's last name, first name. <u>Title of the book</u>. City where published: Publisher, year of publication.

Works Cited

Parrish, Thomas. <u>The Grouchy Grammarian</u>. Hoboken: John Wiley & Sons, Inc., 2002.

In-text citation

(Parrish 6) or Parrish argues ... (6).

Books with Two or More Authors

Author's last name, first name, and second authors first and last name. Title of the book. City where published: Publisher, year of publication.

Works Cited

Lederer, Richard, and John Shore. Comma Sense. New York: St. Martin's Press, 2005.

In-text citation

(Lederer and Shore 13)

If a book has more than three authors, then only the first author's name can be used with "et al." for both the in-text and works cited citations.

Books with an Editor

The abbreviation Ed. precedes the name of the editor, which follows the title of the book. All other citation information for a book stays the same.

Perspectives on Higher Education in the Digital Age. Ed. Michael F. Beaudoin. New York: Nova Science Publishers, Inc., 2007.

Conference Papers

A citation for a single presentation from the published proceedings of a conference are cited like a work in a collection:

Author's name. "Title of paper." Title of published collection of presentations from the conference. Date. Page numbers.

Unpublished conference papers fall under the category of a speech and are formatted as follows:

Authors name. "Title of paper." Title of conference. Location, date.

Corporate Author

When citing a corporate author, the corporation or organization can be cited in the text or in a parenthetical citation as shown above. The readability of the document should determine how one cites. A general format for a corporate author is as follows, even when the author and publisher are the same entity:

> Company Name. <u>Title of document</u>. City: Publisher, date.

> Ciba Specialty Chemicals. <u>Effects to Improve the Quality of Life</u>. Basel, Switzerland, n.d.

Corporate Documents

Corporate documents, such as brochures, pamphlets, and reports, are cited the same as a book, even when the author may be a company and not an individual.

Email, Interviews, Letters, and Memos

Email

> Author of the email. "Title taken from the subject line." Email to recipient's name. day month year.

> Carson, John F. "Re: Waste management." Email to Karen Jones. 17 December 2007.

Interviews

> Name of interviewee. Personal Interview. Date.

Memos

> Author's name. Memo to recipient, even if it is a department or organization. Company, Location. Day month year.

Unpublished letters

> Author's name. Letter to recipient. Day month year.

Legal Material

When referring to legal material in documents, those sources should be cited according to *The Bluebook: A Uniform System of Citation.*

Newsgroup Message

> Author's name. "Title from subject line." Online posting, date, discussion group name, date of access <URL>.

Periodicals

Periodicals are serial publications that contain a collection of articles in each issue or volume, and they are published on a regular basis, such as monthly or quarterly. Examples of periodicals include magazines, journals, and newspapers. Depending on the type of periodical, the citation information and format for those sources will vary. A few common periodical citations are shown below:

Print journal

> Author's last name, first name. "Title of article." Title of periodical volume.issue (date): page numbers.

> Johnson, Tom. "Podcasting: A New Layer of Communication." Intercom 54.1 (2007): 20–24.

Online journal

> Author's last name, first name. "Title of article." Title of the periodical Volume.issue (year of publication): page numbers. Access date <URL>.

To cite a source that originated from an online database, the name of the database and library system are added to the citation, as well as the date of access:

> Author's last name, first name. "Title of article." Journal date: volume. issue. Name of database. Library information. Access date <library URL>.

Hansen, Teresa. "Landfill gas provides solution to rising natural gas prices." Power Engineering 110.1. Academic Search Elite. Kaplan Higher Education Online Library. 17 December 2007 < http:// libsys.uah.edu:3245/kaplan/ > .

Newspaper from an electronic source

Author's last name, first name. "Title of story." Title of the newspaper. day month year of the article. day month year of retrieval < URL > .

Schneider, Howard. "Feds Unveil Mortgage Rules." The Washington Post. 18 December 2007. 18 December 2007 < www.washingtonpost. com > .

Government publication from GPO

Agency. Title of document. Document number. Washington: GPO, year.

To show that the government document came from an online source, then add the URL at the end of the citation.

U.S. Department of Agriculture. Accomplishing and applying national fire plan research and development from 2001–2005 General Technical Report RMRS-GTR-187. Washington: GPO, 2007 < www. fs.fed.us/rm/pubs/rmrs_gtr187.pdf > .

Websites

Citations will vary depending on where one retrieves information from the web. Generally, a website citation will follow the format as shown below.

Author's name. "Title of the document." Date. Publication information. Access date < URL > .

"Chimpanzee Central." n.d. Jane Goodall Institute. 17 December 2007 < www.janegoodall.org/chimp_central/chimpanzees/behavior/ default.asp > .

The official style guides for the three styles as noted in this appendix are:

Chicago Manual of Style (15th ed.). 2003. Chicago: University of Chicago Press.

Gibaldi, Joseph (2003). *MLA handbook for writers of research papers* (6th ed.). New York: Modern Language Association of America.

Publication manual of the American Psychological Association (5th ed.). 2001. Washington, DC: American Psychological Association.

Below are official websites for each style guide:

Chicago Manual of Style, *www.chicagomanualofstyle.org/home.html*

Modern Language Association (MLA), *www.mla.org*

American Psychological Association (APA), *www.apa.org*

INDEX